Simulation for Supply Chain Management

Simulation for Supply Chain Management

Edited by
Caroline Thierry
André Thomas
Gérard Bel

Series Editor
Jean-Paul Bourrières

ISTE Ltd
6 Fitzroy Square
London W1T 5DX
UK

www.iste.co.uk

John Wiley & Sons, Inc.
111 River Street
Hoboken, NJ 07030
USA

www.wiley.com

Library of Congress Cataloging-in-Publication Data

Simulation for supply chain management / edited by Caroline Thierry, André Thomas, Gérard Bel.
    p. cm.
 Includes bibliographical references and index.
 ISBN 978-1-84821-090-5
 1. Business logistics. 2. Production management. 3. Production management--Computer simulation. 4. Business logistics--Computer simulation. I. Thierry, Caroline. II. Thomas, André, 1956- III. Bel, Gérard.
 HD38.5.S563 2008
 658.701'1--dc22
                                                                        2008015206

British Library Cataloguing-in-Publication Data
A CIP record for this book is available from the British Library
ISBN: 978-1-84821-090-5

Printed and bound in Great Britain by CPI Antony Rowe, Chippenham, Wiltshire.

Table of Contents

Chapter 3. Discrete-event Simulation for Supply Chain Management 69
Valérie BOTTA-GENOULAZ, Jacques LAMOTHE, Florence PICARD, Fouad RIANE
and Anthony VALLA

Chapter 4. Simulation Games 103
Thierry MOYAUX, Éric BALLOT, Michel GREIF and Bertrand SIMON

Chapter 8. Simulation for Product-driven Systems 221
André THOMAS, Pierre CASTAGNA, Rémi PANNEQUIN, Thomas KLEIN,
Hind EL HAOUZI, Pascal BLANC and Olivier CARDIN

Chapter 9. HLA Distributed Simulation Approaches for Supply Chains . . 257
Fouzia OUNNAR, Bernard ARCHIMEDE, Philippe CHARBONNAUD
and Patrick PUJO

Chapter 1

Supply Chain Management Simulation: An Overview

1.1. Supply chain management

In this book we are concerned with the simulation of supply chain management (SCM). We focus on simulation approaches which are used to study SCM practices [VOL 05].

The existence of several interpretations of SCM is a source of confusion both for those studying the concept and those implementing it. In fact, this term can express two concepts, depending on how it is used: supply chain orientation (SCO) is defined ([MEN 01]) as "the recognition by an organization of the systemic, strategic implications of the tactical activities involved in managing the various flows in a supply chain". SCM is the "implementation of this orientation in the different member companies of the supply chain".

1.1.1. *Supply chain viewpoints*

As already mentioned, the main topic of this book is related to the use of simulations for supply chain management and control. However, in order to understand what simulations can be useful for this objective, it is important to highlight the different issues of SCM, and to understand what a supply chain is or how many types of SC can be considered. Thus, two viewpoints can be considered:

Chapter written by Caroline THIERRY, Gérard BEL and André THOMAS.

– the system under study is the SC of a given business, and we can consider:

- the internal SC of a business which focuses on functional activities and processes and on material and information flows within the business. In this case SCM may be viewed as the integration of previously separate operations within a business,

- the external SC of the business which includes the business, suppliers to the company and the suppliers' suppliers, customers of the company and the customers' customers (SCOR). In this case SCM mainly focuses on integration and cooperation between the enterprise and the other actors of the supply chain;

– the supply chain under study is a network of businesses (without focusing on one particular business of the supply chain): a supply chain is a "network of organizations that are involved, through upstream and downstream linkages, in the different processes and activities that produce value in the form of products and services in the hands of the ultimate consumer" ([CHR 92]). In this viewpoint, the focus is on the virtual and global nature of business relationships between companies. In this case, supply chain management mainly focuses on cooperation between the supply chain actors.

1.1.2. *Supply chain management*

1.1.2.1. *Supply chain processes: the integrated supply chain point of view*

To describe supply chains from a process point of view, we refer to the supply chain operations reference (SCOR) model. SCOR is a cross-industry standard for supply chain management and has been developed and endorsed by the supply-chain council (SCC). SCOR focuses on a given company and is based on five distinct management processes: plan, source, make, deliver and return.

SCOR Process	Definitions
Plan	Processes that balance aggregate demand and supply to develop a course of action which best meets sourcing, production and delivery requirements
Source	Processes that procure goods and services to meet planned or actual demand
Make	Processes that transform product to a finished state to meet planned or actual demand
Deliver	Processes that provide finished goods and services to meet planned or actual demand, typically including order management, transportation management, and distribution management
Return	Processes associated with returning or receiving returned products for any reason. These processes extend into post-delivery customer support

Figure 1.1. *The SCOR processes ([SCO 05])*

SCM addresses different types of problems according to the decision horizon concerned. Long range (strategic) decisions are concerned with the supply chain configuration: number and location of suppliers, production facilities, distribution centers, warehouses and customers, etc. Medium and short range (tactical and operational) decisions are concerned with material management decisions: inventory management, planning processes, forecasting processes, etc.

On the other hand, information management is also a key parameter of supply chain management: integrating systems and processes using the supply chain to share valuable information, including demand notices, forecasts, inventory and transportation, etc.

Figure 1.2 which is adapted from the SSCP-Matrix [STA 00] summarizes the different supply chain decision processes.

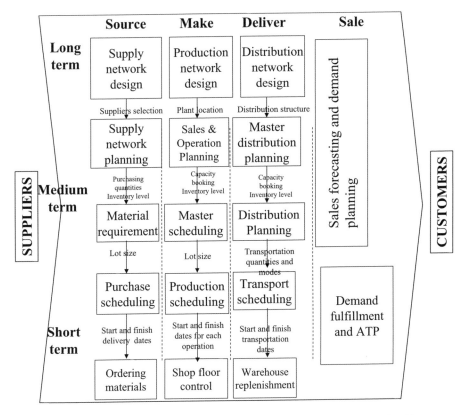

Figure 1.2. *Different supply chain decision processes (1 organizational unit)*

SCM deals with the integration of organizational units. Thus the different supply chain processes will be more or less distributed according to the level of integration of the different processes.

1.1.2.2. *Dynamic behavior of supply chain management system*

There is a process which organizes the decisions at different levels in the supply chain management system. This system (virtual world) is connected to the production system (real world) in order to compose a "closed loop" dynamic system.

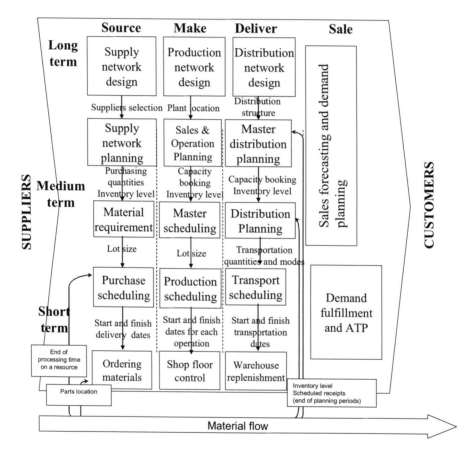

Figure 1.3. *Dynamic behavior of SCM system*

1.1.2.3. *Supply chain processes: the collaborative supply chain point of view*

Let us now consider (Figure 1.4) at least two independent organizational units (legal entities).

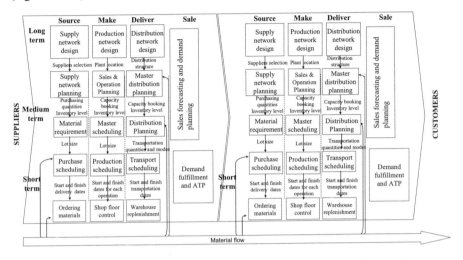

Figure 1.4. *Different supply chain decision processes (2 independent units)*

In this collaborative supply chain, as far as a supplier-buyer partnership is established, several problems arise:

– how can we exchange/share information?

– is it possible to perform mutual problem solving?

– how can we set up global supply chain indicators?

– etc.

Thus, the problem of the centralization or distribution of the information and decision processes within the supply chain becomes a main challenge for the supply chain managers.

1.2. Supply chain management simulation

1.2.1. *Why use simulation for SCM?*

As far as simulation is concerned the objective is to evaluate the supply chain performances. We distinguish three ways of carrying out SC performance measurement:

– analytical methods, such as queueing theory;

– Monte Carlo methods, such as simulation or emulation;

– physical experimentations, such as lab platforms or industrial pilot implementations.

In this SC context, analytical methods are impractical because the mathematical model corresponding to a realistic case is often too complex to be solved. Obviously, physical experimentations suffer from technical- and cost-related limitations. Simulation seems the only recourse to model and analyze performances for such large-scale cases. Simulation enables, on the one hand, the design of the supply chain and on the other hand, the evaluation of supply chain management prior to implementation of the system to perform what-if analysis leading to the "best" decision. This simulation includes supply chain flow simulation and decision process dynamics. In the field of SCM, simulation can be used to support supply chain design decisions or evaluation of supply chain policies. As far as supply chain design decisions are concerned, the following decisions can be considered:

– localization:
  - location of facilities,
  - supply and distribution channel configuration,
  - location of stocks;

– selection:
  - suppliers,
  - partner;

– size:
  - capacity booking,
  - stock level,
  - etc.

As far as the evaluation of supply chain control policies is concerned, the following decisions can be considered:

– control policies:
  - inventory management, control policies,
  - planning processes;

– collaboration policies:
  - cooperation/collaboration/coordination, etc.,
  - information sharing, etc.

1.2.2. *How can we use SCM simulation?*

To attempt to specify the different ways to use SCM simulation it is important to differentiate, on the one hand, the real system (the "real world") and on the other, its simulation model.

In fact, the simulation model must be built according to its usage and/or the SCM function that we want to model or to evaluate. Different classes of models can be highlighted to understand the variety of SC simulation models according to:

– the systemic decomposition of the SCM system:

- decision system,

- information system,

- physical system;

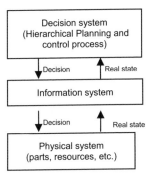

Figure 1.5. *Systemic decomposition of the SCM system*

– the level of distribution of the system:

- simulation model for centralized SCM system evaluation. A centralized SCM system consists of a single information and decision system for the different entities of the supply chain under study;

- simulation model for distributed SCM system evaluation. A distributed SCM system consists of a distribution of the decision system over different entities of the supply chain under study.

As a matter of fact, the execution of the simulation can be performed:

– in a centralized way on a single computer;

– in a decentralized way:

- on multiprocessor computing platforms: parallel simulation,

- or on geographically distributed computers interconnected via a network, local or wide: distributed simulation.

Decentralization of the simulation is "the execution of a single main simulation model, made up by several sub-simulation models, which are executed, in a distributed manner, over multiple computing stations" [TER 04].

The need for a distributed execution of a simulation across multiple computers derives from several main reasons [TER 04]:

– to reduce execution simulation time;

– to reproduce a system geographic distribution;

– to integrate different simulation models that already exist and to integrate different simulation tools and languages;

– to increase tolerance to simulation failures;

– to test different control models independently;

– to progressively deploy a control system;

– to prepare protocol modifications at supply chain control.

Furthermore, it is important to stress that simulation mostly focuses on the dynamics of the supply chain processes concerning both physical and decision systems (i.e. production management systems, see section 1.3.1).

1.3. Supply chain management simulation types

This section is dedicated to the presentation of the different types of models and approaches mainly used for supply chain management simulation.

As seen before, an important part of the model is the decision system model (hierarchical planning and control processes). Thus, section 1.3.1. presents the main production management models which are used in SCM.

Then, the different types of well known simulation models will be quickly presented. For each of them we will highlight how the different production management models can be linked with the simulation model.

1.3.1. *Production management models focus*

The objective of this section is to focus on and present a very synthetic and simplified description of production management models in order to introduce, in a following section, how they can be integrated in a supply chain simulation model. Here we focus only on production processes. The approach could be extended to supply and distribution processes.

There are two main categories of production management models.

1.3.1.1. *Time bucket models*

In production planning and control, and mainly for the long and medium term, we are concerned with the determination of quantities to be produced per time period for a given horizon in order to satisfy demand or/and forecast. In order to perform these decision processes, time bucket models are needed. They are characterized by:

– decision variables: produced, stocked or transported quantities;

– data: resource capacities (in number of parts per period, for example);

– constraints: conservation of flow, cost of materials, limited capacities, demand satisfaction, etc.

EXAMPLE.– for a production line composed of two production resources (see Figure 1.6).

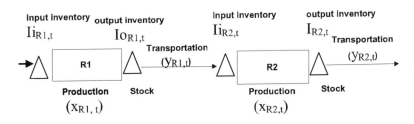

Figure 1.6. *Time bucket model (example)*

The demand is d_t and the production resource capacities are $C_{R1,t}$, $C_{R2,t}$. Each item is produced from one single component.

The planning model variables are:

– $x_{Ri,t}$ = quantity of items to be produced with resource Ri during time period t;

– $y_{Ri,t}$ = quantity of items to be transported from resource Ri during time period t;

– $Ii_{Ri,t}$ = input inventory level of resource Ri at the beginning of time period t;

– $Io_{Ri,t}$ = output inventory level of resource Ri at the beginning of time period t.

The planning model constraints are:

$- Ii_{R1,t+1} = Ii_{R1,t} - x_{R1,t};$

$- Io_{R1,t+1} = Io_{R1,t} + x_{R1,t} - y_{R1,t};$

$- Ii_{R2,t+1} = Ii_{R2,t} - x_{R2,t} + y_{R1,t};$

$- Io_{R2,t+1} = Io_{R2,t} + x_{R2,t} - y_{R2,t};$

$- y_{R2,t} = d_t;$

$- x_{R1,t} \leq C_{R1,t};$

$- x_{R2,t} \leq C_{R2,t};$

$- Ii_{R1,t0} = \infty;$

$- Ii_{R,t} \geq O \ \forall R \in \{R1, R2\}, \forall t;$

$- Io_{R,t} \geq O \ \forall R \in \{R1, R2\}, \forall t;$

$- x_{R,t} \geq 0 \ \forall R \in \{R1, R2\}, \forall t;$

$- y_{R,t} \geq 0 \ \forall R \in \{R1, R2\}, \forall t.$

Associated with these models, the following methods are used to perform the plan: MRP-like methods, mathematical programming, constraint programming, metaheuristics.

1.3.1.2. *Starting time models*

In production planning and control, and mainly in the short-term, we are also concerned with the determination of the starting time of tasks on different resources. For that we use starting time models (sequence of timed events). These models are characterized by:

– decision variables: starting time of tasks (t_i);

– data: ready dates (r_i,) due dates (d_i);

– constraints: precedence, resource sharing, due dates.

Example:

$- t_i \geq r_i;$

$- t_i \geq t_j + p_j \ \text{OR} \ t_j \geq t_i + p_i;$

$- t_i + p_i \leq d_i.$

Associated with these models, the following methods are used to perform the schedule: mathematical programming, constraint programming, metaheuristics, etc.

1.3.2. *Simulation types*

Due to the special characteristics of supply chains, building the supply chain simulation model is difficult. The two main difficulties are highlighted, and then the different types of models for SCM simulation are quickly presented.

1.3.2.1. *Size of the system*

One characteristic of supply chain simulation is the huge number of "objects" to be modeled. A supply chain is composed of a set of companies, a set of factories and warehouses, a set of production resources and stocks. Between all these production resources circulate a set of components, parts, assembled parts, sub-assemblies and final products. Thus, the number of "objects" of the model can be very large.

1.3.2.2. *Complexity of the production management system*

To simulate a system it is necessary to simulate the behavior of the "physical" system and the behavior of the "control" system. For a supply chain this implicates that it is necessary to model the behavior of the supply chain management system of each company and the relationship between these production management systems (cooperation).

As this SCM system is very complex, it can be difficult to model it in detail. However, it is absolutely necessary to model it, as it is this system which controls the product flow in the supply chain. Thus, according to the objective of the simulation study and the type of model chosen, various aggregated or simplified models of the production management system must be designed. The following sections present different examples of these models.

1.3.2.3. *Different types of models for SCM simulation*

1.3.2.3.1. Simulation model

A simulation model is composed of a set of "objects" and relationships between these objects; for example, in a supply chain the main objects are items (or sets of items) and resources (or sets of resources).

Each object is characterized by a set of "attributes". Some attributes have a fixed value (for example, name), while others have a value which varies over time (for example, position of an item in a factory).

The state of an object at a given time is the value of all its attributes. The state of a system at a given time is the set of the attributes of the objects included in the system.

The purpose of a simulation model is to represent the dynamic behavior of the system.

There are various modeling approaches according to how state variations are considered:

– states vary continuously: continuous approach;

– states vary at a specific time (event): discrete-event approach.

The following parts of this section will introduce Chapters 2 to 4 which will go into detail on the viewpoint and present related works (state of the art and recent works).

1.3.3. *SCM simulation using continuous simulation approach*

In this section we will introduce system dynamics, a continuous simulation approach where states vary continuously. Chapter 2 will go into detail and present recent works related to SCM simulation from this point of view.

1.3.3.1. *System dynamics*

This new paradigm was first proposed by Forester for studying "industrial dynamics".

Companies are seen as complex systems with [KLE 05]:

– different types of flows: manpower, technology, money and market flows;

– stocks or levels which are integrated into time according to the flow variations.

System dynamics are centered on the dynamics behavior. This is a flow model where it is not possible to differentiate between individual entities (such as transport resources).

Management control is performed by making variations on rates (production rates, sale rates, etc.). Control of rates can be viewed as a strong abstraction of common production management rules.

The model takes into account the "closed loop effect": the manager is supposed to compare the value of a performance indicator to a target value continuously. In case of deviation he implements corrective action.

Example:

$- I_{t2} = I_{t1} + p(xr_{t1,t2} - dr_{t1,t2});$

$- xr_{t1,t2}$ = production rate between two dates t1 and t2;

$- dr_{t1,t2}$ = sale rate between two dates t1 and t2;

$- p$ = time duration between t1 and t2.

1.3.3.2. *Production management models/simulation models*

The two models do not consider the same objects states:

– in system dynamics, objects are continuous flows. The behavior of these flows is represented by a differential equation (with derivative) which is integrated using a time sampling approach;

– in planning models, the objects are resources and their activities. It is considered that the attributes of these activities change only at a special periodic date. There is no notion of a derivative.

This type of model seems well adapted to supply chain simulation as it was designed by Forester for "industrial dynamics" studies which used the same concepts as those recently used in supply chain studies.

1.3.4. *SCM simulation using discrete-event approach*

In this section we will detail the discrete-event approach. We will distinguish between the time bucket-driven approach and event-driven approach. This differentiation is based on the time advance procedures which characterize these two approaches. Chapter 3 will go into detail and present recent works related to SCM simulation from this point of view.

For the "discrete-event approach" they are:

– different ways of "looking at the world": event, activity and process,

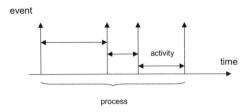

Figure 1.7. *Events, activities, processes*

– different procedures to make the time advance in the simulation:
- event-driven,

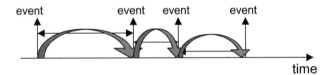

Figure 1.8. *Event-driven discrete-event simulation*

- time bucket-driven.

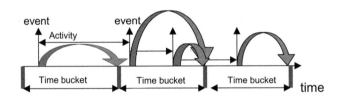

Figure 1.9. *Time bucket-driven discrete-event simulation*

The main practices for "mixing" various types of models and time advance procedures are listed below.

	continuous	activities	events	process
Time bucket driven	**X**	**X**	x	x
Event driven	Not possible with the approach	x	**X**	**X**

Figure 1.10. *Discrete-event simulation*

1.3.4.1. *Time bucket-driven approach*

Discrete-event simulation using the time bucket-driven approach is rarely used for job shop simulation but it fits well for simulation of supply chain management (see the specific characteristics of this simulation in sections 1.3.2.1 and 1.3.2.2).

1.3.4.1.1. Time bucket-driven discrete-event models

In such a model:

– time is divided into periods of a given length: time bucket;

– time is incremented step-by-step with a given time bucket. At the end of each step a new state is calculated using the model equations. Thus, in this approach it can be considered that events (corresponding to a change of state) occur at each beginning of a period;

– the lead time for an item on a production resource is considered small compared to the size of the time bucket;

– the main states are the states of resources (or set of resources) during a given period: they describe the activities in which resources are implicated in a given time period. They are characterized by the quantities of items processed in this activity in a given time period: for example, the number of items of a given type manufactured, stocked or transported by a given resource in a given period;

– the simulation has to determine all the states of all the resources at each period of a simulation run.

This type of model is also called a "spreadsheet simulation" [KLE 05]. We do not use this designation because a spreadsheet is a tool which it is possible to use with all the modeling approaches.

1.3.4.1.2. Simulation models

It must be noted that the planning models presented in section 1.3.1 are also time bucket models which are well known and used in the production management domain. We will see hereafter that they are very similar to time bucket-driven discrete-event simulation models but that they are used in a different way in simulation.

In order to illustrate this, we consider a very simple example of a production line composed of two production resources with no specific production management. Shop floor control is a first-in first-out strategy; k is the number of parts from M1 to be used to produce one part on M2.

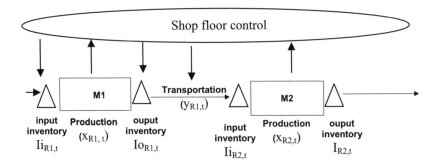

Figure 1.11. *Production management models/simulation models (example)*

The simulation model uses the following state variables:

– $Ii_{Ri,t}$ is the input inventory level of resource Ri at the beginning of time period t;

– $Io_{Ri,t}$ is the output inventory level of resource Ri at the beginning of time period t;

– $x_{Ri,t}$ is the quantity of parts produced by resource Ri during the time bucket t (available at the end of t);

– $y_{Ri,t}$ is the quantity of parts transported from Ri during time bucket t (available at the end of t).

The model of the dynamic behavior of the system is the following:

– $Ii_{R1,t+1} = Ii_{R1,t} - x_{R1,t}$;

– $Io_{R1,t+1} = Io_{R1,t} + x_{R1,t} - y_{R1,t}$;

– $Ii_{R2,t+1} = Ii_{R2,t} - x_{R2,t} + y_{R1,t}$;

– $Io_{R2,t+1} = I_{oR2,t} + x_{R2,t} - y_{R2,t}$;

– $x_{R1,t} \leq C_{R1,t}$;

– $x_{R2,t} \leq C_{R2,t}$.

It can be noted immediately that this model is very similar to the production management model presented in section 1.3.1.1.

In order to illustrate this, let us consider a simulation with this model corresponding to the following hypothesis: resource R1 sends parts to resource R2 according to a production and transportation plan determined outside of the system. Thus, $Ii_{R1,t0}$, $Ii_{R2,t0}$, $x_{R1,t}$, $x_{R2,t}$, $y_{R1,t}$, $y_{R2,t}$ are known at the beginning of the simulation.

In this case, the true state variables of the model are $Ii_{R1,t}$, $Ii_{R2,t}$, $Io_{R1,t}$ and $Io_{R2,t}$.

The simulation must determine the variation over time of these variables taking into account the values of the exogenous variables ($x_{R1,t}$, $x_{R2,t}$, $y_{R1,t}$, $y_{R2,t}$). Thus, simulation allows the evaluation of the proposed production and transportation plan. It is also possible to introduce hazard into the behavior of the model.

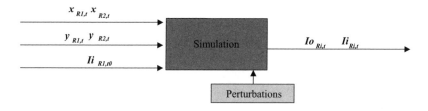

Figure 1.12. *Simulation process*

This shows that the same model can be used in a:

– simulation decision process: taking into account $x_{R1,t}$ $x_{M2,t}$, $y_{R1,t}$ and $y_{R2,t}$. The problem is to determine $Ii_{R1,t}$, $Ii_{R2,t}$, $Io_{R1,t}$ and $Io_{R2,t}$;

– production planning decision process: in a centralized planning (APS or SCM like) the problem is to determine $x_{Ri,t}$ and $y_{Ri,t}$ which satisfy the constraints of the planning model (stock capacity, supplier demand).

NOTE.– it is possible to use a "what if" approach with the planning model testing different demands or different production management policies. In this "what if" approach, the problem is solved several times, each time with this different data. Then it is possible to see the influence of these data on the generated plan. This approach is not considered in this book; we refer to simulation only when the dynamics of the system are considered.

1.3.4.1.3. Production management models/simulation models

Now the question is: how can the different production management models be linked to a discrete-event simulation model with the time bucket approach?

The time bucket production planning model can be easily linked to the global simulation model as the modeling approach is the same. In this case the two models will be joined up: the simulation model focuses on the circulation of the flow of parts, the planning model determines the quantities to be produced. Chapter 3 provides a study of both discrete-event and time bucket simulation used for supply chain management and proposes case studies to illustrate the pivotal role that simulation can play as a technique to aid decisions.

If we now consider the other category of production management models that we call in section 1.3.1.2 "starting time models" (scheduling, etc.) we can state that:

– "time bucket-driven discrete-event simulation models" do not use the same "object states" as "starting time production management models" (which use the "start time of an activity");

– between two periods the bucket-driven activity simulation model does not represent the state of the system. Thus, the start time of an activity is not known and cannot be used as data in a "starting time" scheduling model. The only way to obtain a good approximation of this date is to use a very small time period. However, this is often not possible because this will contradict the fundamental hypothesis for this kind of model: the production duration for an item on a production resource is much less than the time bucket of the model.

1.3.4.2. *Event-driven approach*

In this section the main characteristics of the discrete-event models for an SCM simulation using an event-driven approach are presented. Remember that this approach is intensively used for job shop simulation. Thus, it can be considered as convenient to use this type of model for supply chain simulation.

However, using the specific characteristics of supply chain management simulation (see sections 1.3.2.1 and 1.3.2.2) can lead to some difficulties for this type of simulation. The main difficulty comes from the size of the model induced by this context. It can be inefficient to model the circulation of each individual part in each production resource of the different companies of the supply chain: the number of events can become prohibitive and considerably slow down the simulation which can become unworkable. This is why it is often necessary to use model reduction techniques introduced here in section 1.5.2. We recall hereafter the main characteristics of this approach.

1.3.4.2.1. Event-driven approach for discrete-event simulation

In an event-driven discrete-event model:

– the main states are the states of items (or set of items);

– the simulation must determine the dates of all the events (state variation) which occur during a simulation run;

– each state is characterized by the resource used by a given item at a given time and correlatively the "occupation state" of the resources; for example, the position of a given item ("on a given production resource", "in a given stock", or "being transported by a given cart");

– each state variation is represented by a "state variation logic";

– time advance event to event. A "simulation engine" using a "timetable" determines the date of the "next event" (for example, the delivery date of a job).

1.3.4.2.2. Production management models/simulation models

Consider again the question of how the different planning models can be connected in an event-driven discrete-event simulation.

The time bucket planning models cannot be directly connected to an event-driven discrete-event simulation because the modeling approach is not the same. We will see in Chapter 3 how different adaptations can be produced in order to allow connections.

The "starting time models" presented in section 1.3.1.2 (scheduling level) can be directly connected to an event-driven discrete-event simulation because they use the same modeling approach.

In summary for this event-driven approach:

– simulation models and planning models do not use the same "object states";

– simulation models and scheduling or shop floor control models use the same "object states".

1.3.5. *Simulation of supply chain management using games*

In this section we will introduce business games, then Chapter 4 will go into more detail and present recent works related to SCM simulation from this point of view.

1.3.5.1. *Games and simulation*

Different games can be used to perform simulation. Games make it possible to simulate real conditions offline, and explore new ideas or strategies in a safe, interactive and also fun environment. Basically, the complexity of their model allows us to split games into two classes:

– board games have a model simple enough to be played with tokens or pieces that are placed on, removed from or moved across a "board" (a premarked surface, usually specific to that game);

– sophisticated games have a more realistic model which may need, for example, to be run on computerized devices.

1.3.5.2. *Production management models/simulation models*

In this type of simulation model (board games), the simulation of time can be performed using either a clock which synchronizes the players, or the time of the simulation is the real time (each player evolves independently). [KLE 05] distinguishes:

– strategic games: in these games every player represents a company competing or collaborating through other companies by interacting with the simulation model during several rounds. The well-known Beer Game belongs to this category;

– operational games: in these games every player represents an actor (for example, a worker in a workshop) interacting with the simulation model either during several rounds or in real time. Examples include games for training in production scheduling.

1.4. Decision systems and simulation models (systems)

The preceding sections have presented the main concepts which are used in supply chain management simulation and introduce the first part of the book (Chapters 2 to 4).

The second part of the book is dedicated to the problem of distribution of the supply chain management simulation. This concept of simulation distribution is extremely important in the case of supply chain simulation because of the naturally distributed aspect of the supply chain itself. This section introduces this part of the book (Chapters 5 to 10).

1.4.1. *Models and system distribution*

There is a consensus on the architecture of simulation environments putting the emphasis on modularity between the control system *CS* and the shop-floor system *SF*.

This separation principle enables us to introduce the concept of emulation. Emulation is not new: it is used in automation to test computer-aided manufacturing software, for example [COR 89].

Fusaoka proposed a theoretical formulation and an experimental run consisting of verifying the assertion $SF \wedge CS \supset G$ [FUS 83], where G is the required performance level of the shop floor. The real shop-floor system (SFr) may be replaced by a model (SFm), that we call an *emulated* shop floor. Likewise, a model of the control system (CSm) can be used instead of the real one (CSr). Therefore, four experimental situations can be defined, using either models or real systems [PFE 03]:

1. (SFr, CSr): experimentation consists of deployment of the real control system at the shop floor. This is the more traditional case;

2. (SFr, CSm): a control system model is applied for the real shop floor. This configuration could be used to test a new control system;

3. (SFm, CSr): the real control system is used with a shop floor model (emulation with the real control system);

4. (SFm, CSm): both shop floor and control system are modeled.

Let us first focus on a single company of the supply chain or on a centralized SCM system. The real system is made up of the physical system, the information system and the control (or decision) system (cases 1 and 4 in Figure 1.13). These three systems make up the SCM system. Basically, building a simulation model leads to the design of a virtual model representation of these (or at least one of these) three preceding systems implemented on a computer S1, as seen in section 1.3.

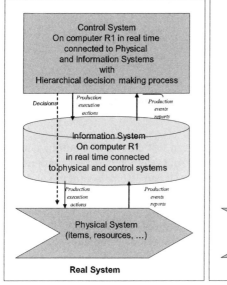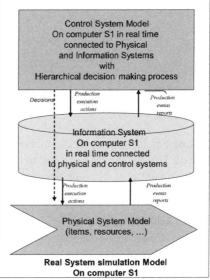

Figure 1.13. *Real-time simulation model*

Let us now consider different cases where this model can be distributed.

If we want to evaluate the effect of different control rules, on a specific physical system, it could be interesting for example to build an emulation system corresponding to this physical system. This emulation model is controlled by the real decision system (case 3 in Figure 1.14) connected to the actual information system. Actually, emulation aims to mimic the behavior of the physical system only. It can be seen as a virtual shop floor which can be connected to an external control system. Like simulation, emulation can be used to model complex cases, but emulation removes the additional task of modeling decision processes (this task is often one of most difficult as stated by [VAN 06] and presented here in section 1.3.2.2).

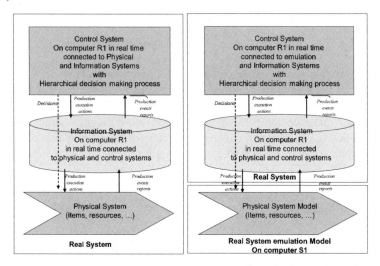

Figure 1.14. *Emulation system connected to real control system*

Using emulation provides modularity between test cases and control systems to be tested. This modularity is useful to try a control system in various situations, or to try various control systems on the same test case. It can also be useful to validate the real control system before actually deploying it.

Obviously, the same concept can be used for a supply chain system (Figures 1.15 and 1.16). However, as with supply chains of networks of companies that are often independent (i.e. section 1.1.1), simulation models can be built in a centralized way (Figure 1.15) or in a distributed way (Figure 1.16). In a distributed context, different simulation models can be implemented on different computers, each one representing company behavior.

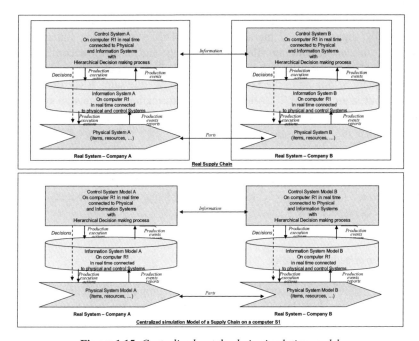

Figure 1.15. *Centralized supply chain simulation model*

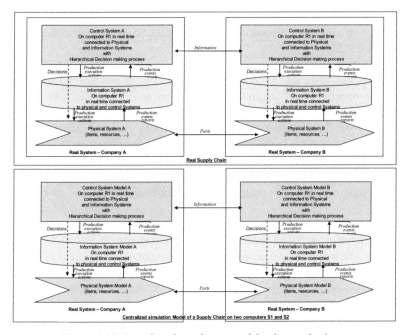

Figure 1.16. *Distributed simulation models of a supply chain*

As underlined in the preceding sections, SC management systems are traditionally organized in a hierarchical way. Different decision functions exist: planning, master scheduling, detail scheduling and control according to the traditional MRP² system described by [VOL 05]. This type of architecture exists in each company belonging to the SC. In an internal SC, the same ERP software could be used, but in an external SC, often different information and decision system ERP must be connected, leading to interoperability problems and/or synchronization problems.

The following parts of this section will introduce Chapters 5 to 10. These different chapters will describe simulation problems relating to centralized architectures, simulation synchronization problems and distributed simulation architectures respectively.

1.4.2. *Centralized simulation*

The decisions that are usually taken before planning the implementation of any supply chain can be classified into two categories: structural (for long-term objectives) and operational (for short-term goals). Simulation can be used as a tool for carrying out the decision-making process for both structural and operational decisions thanks to dynamic simulation of material flow and taking into account all random phenomena. The opposite of distributed simulation, in a centralized approach, one single simulation model reproduces all the supply chain structures (entities and links).

Chapter 5 is dedicated to this type of approach. It presents a brief literature review on supply chain centralized simulation and discusses two developed centralized simulation approaches. Effectively, for most simulation evaluation approaches, supply chain processes are modeled to perform "what-if" analysis. Firstly, a discrete-event simulation-based optimization is used to estimate the operational performances of the solutions suggested by the optimizer. The optimizer was developed based on the NSGA-II, which is considered to be one of the best multi-objective optimizations using a genetic algorithm [DEB 02].

Furthermore, Chapter 5 illustrates the applicability and efficiency of the two preceding approaches using three industrial applications. In the first one, a case study from the automotive industry will be presented. The objective is to improve the profitability and responsiveness of the company's supply chain by redesigning its production-distribution network. A centralized simulation-based optimization approach is used for the optimization of facility open/close decisions, production order assignment and inventory control policies. In the second case, the authors applied the centralized simulation-based multi-objective genetic algorithm approach to a real-life case study of a multi-national textile supply chain, which consists of several suppliers, a single distribution center and all customers seen as a whole. The modeling and simulation details are discussed and numerical results are presented and analyzed. In the third case, another automotive industry case, a generic model is proposed, which can be used by different automotive industries. The developed model is limited only to the interactions between the assembly line and its direct suppliers. Taking into account that the model is generic, it is able to help supply chain decision makers in their choices.

1.4.3. *Multi-agent system decision simulation*

New forms of organizations have emerged from the supply chain concept in which partners have to collaborate and have strong collaboration. Production businesses operate as nodes in a partner network and share activities to produce and deliver their goods. In such a context, the integration of planning of all the nodes is needed, i.e. partners have to be able to distribute and synchronize their activities.

To obtain the optimal performance level in such a dynamic environment, multi-agent systems (MAS) can be used. Effectively, MAS are composed (as a supply chain network is) of a group of agents that can take specific roles within the organizational structure. Different agents may represent different objects belonging to the studied network. This idea is not new; Parunak used agents for manufacturing control or collaborative design ([PAR 96] or [PAR 98]) but these approaches are particularly well adapted when studying SCM.

Chapters 6 and 7 are dedicated to MAS usage for SCM. Chapter 6 highlights the interest of using MAS for supply chain simulation and Chapter 7 considers MAS decision system simulation for a business network.

Just as in a supply chain in which distributed activities and decisions are carried out in order to obtain a global optimal performance, MAS simulation leads to a distributed system, within which there is generally no centralized control, to have a global point of view; where agents act in an autonomous way and do not locally have global knowledge, but obtain a global optimum. Effectively, several analogies between supply chains and MAS can be highlighted:

– the multiplicity of acting entities;

– the entities' properties, abilities or decision-making capabilities, etc.;

– information sharing and task distribution, etc.

A review of research works on agent-based supply chain modeling and simulation is also carried out in Chapter 6. On the other hand, Chapter 7 presents specific contributions in agent-based supply chain modeling and simulation for decision system development. The first part of this chapter will concern the supply chain control, and the second one, is related to the design of a decision system based on simulation.

1.4.4. *Simulation for product-driven systems*

As mentioned before, in the distributed supply chain and manufacturing control context, MAS are often used according to the fact that each company could act, in some circumstances, in an autonomous way. Consequently, it is possible to implement agents to describe their behavior. Thus, the SCM system could be composed by planning and scheduling agents and by agents representing physical elements as products, for example.

Moreover, it is also possible to build emulation models for distributed supply chains. This type of model can be produced in a centralized or distributed way (using several models and computers for physical, control and decision systems). This last possibility is interesting for all contexts where products and/or physical entities are able to take some autonomous decisions. The main idea is to focus the decision-making processes as near as possible to the shop-floor or physical system, where events (disturbing or not) actually occur. Current research focusing on autonomy includes, for example, holonic manufacturing systems (HMS), multi-agent-based control or more generally intelligent manufacturing. These take their roots both in fundamental research such as distributed artificial intelligence, artificial life or cooperative control, and also in practical experiences such as Kanban-controlled systems or powered operators.

Centralized control systems showed their limits to efficiently respond to frequent changes, which put researchers on the path of distributed manufacturing systems [DIL 91]. However, advances in this domain show limitations with system stability and global optimization.

The qualities and complementarities of both centralized and distributed approaches (hybrid architectures) make it possible to see considerable benefits of coupling them together, adding the global optimization abilities from centralized control systems to the reactivity and possible robustness of decentralized systems. Both hierarchical and heterarchical approaches share benefits and drawbacks. As a consequence the idea of coupling both systems has emerged, with the aim of ensuring global optima while keeping the heterarchical system reactivity. This concept would be realistic by using technologies such as RFID. This technology enabled us to postulate that embedding intelligence into the product could lead to some types of product-driven systems ([WON 02; MOR 03]).

This concept needs to use simulation in a different way; in particular, the simulation tool must reproduce the "communicant product" behavior. Consequently, the simulation tool is built in two parts: the first is an "emulation model" where the entities represent items and do not have any attributes (no information or decisions are implemented in the model), and the second is a "control model" where the entities represent an information flow activated by events occurring in the emulation model.

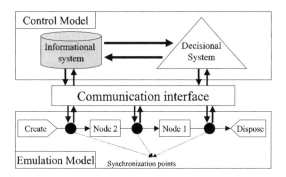

Figure 1.17. *Product-driven system simulation*

As shown previously, in order to assess the impact of synchronizing physical and informational flows we need to model them as distinct flows (Figure 1.17). In that way, it could be interesting to represent them in two distinct models that work simultaneously and have to be synchronized. Moreover, the interface standardization enables us to exchange different control models with the same physical emulation model. To represent the implementation of RFID technologies, with fixed readers, the notion of synchronization points is implemented in the model, which are points where the physical system emits events to update the information system. This event update could launch a decision process that will react by acting on the emulation model. Chapter 8 will be dedicated to this concept.

1.4.5. *Model synchronization = HLA distributed simulation approaches*

To face flexibility and reactivity SC problems, recent research consists of developing adapted simulation environments, allowing the analysis and the evaluation before considering an operational deployment. In a supply chain context, we can imagine that building a unique SC model could be a very difficult task, that could lead to simplifying, to strong hypotheses and finally to unrealistic results. Furthermore, running such a model could lead to data problems. As a result, there is a real need for distributed simulation (DS) in SCM, i.e. a unique control system could manage several physical system simulation models (Figure 1.18) or such an implementation needs a communication protocol allowing the exchange of information between the various components.

The appearance of distributed simulation specification standards allows us to facilitate the implementation of such simulations. A treatment in distributed simulation must be ensured to respect the existing causality relations. Moreover, it is important to take into account all events arising as time goes on, i.e., it is important to manage the time. In fact, the problems of message coordination between the partners of the supply chains and of synchronization of these partners must be managed. Chapter 9 will present various techniques of existing distributed modeling and simulation (DEVS (discrete-event system specification), SIMBA (simulation-based applications), HLA (high level architectures)) by exposing the characteristics.

To have an unambiguous description of the system and a definition of discrete-event simulation algorithms whose validity is founded and verifiable, DEVS and SIMBA formalisms can be useful to obtain a model formal specification. The American defense has developed the HLA (high level architecture) protocol in order to synchronize within a large simulation, simulators being carried out on different computers.

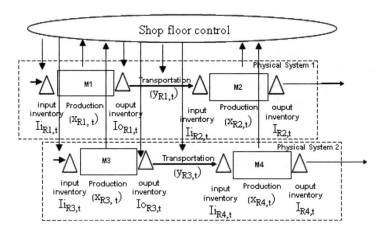

Figure 1.18. *Multi-line synchronization problems*

Chapter 9 relates to the study of the multi-line synchronization problems in internal logistics. Emulation and control models will be presented. This study is illustrated by an industrial case. This application takes into account two production sites containing several lines of assembly. HLA ensures interoperability between these various models.

1.5. Simulation software

To evaluate decision impact or to choose a management production or SC organizations, today it is natural to use simulation. Law and Kelton [LAW 91] summarize several reasons for the spectacular increase in the use of simulation in the field of manufacturing and SC systems. Consequently, today we can find a lot of relevant simulation software, increasingly used according to the complexity inherent in SC problems.

The main goal of Chapter 10 is to highlight simulation software functionalities. Firstly, a software typology will be proposed. This typology is established for discrete-event simulation, according to some literature criteria as event, activity or process approaches, etc. Secondly, supply chain test games will be presented. They are described by a knowledge model and particular formalism that will be explained. These test games are useful to choose or to analyze different simulation software. Finally, a special methodology will be proposed to help the modeler to specify his needs and choose his simulation tool.

1.6. Simulation methodology

1.6.1. *Evaluation of simulation models*

The simulation model quality evaluation is a hard problem. It is not possible to carry it out in a formal way (especially for discrete-event simulation). At least, we want to have a model behavior leading us to obtain simulation measure indicator values, as close as possible, as the same indicator measures on the real system. As we said previously, the model always contains approximations due to necessary simplifications. Thus, to evaluate this quality, we have to focus on the simulation system architecture, on the one hand, and on its proposed results (indicators), on the other.

Two criteria concern the study of reference architecture quality:

– the first concerns the architecture structural proprieties (nature of information, easiness of use and implementation, reusability, etc.);

– the other concerns the operational performances of the simulation model.

It is possible to study the structural aspects using a theoretical approach, without any application. However, on the other hand, operational performances must be evaluated by simulation runs.

1.6.2. *Reduction of simulation models*

In the simulation model, the number of "objects" of the model and the number of event occurrences can be very large. As a consequence, the simulation duration on a computer can be unacceptable for an operational use as stressed previously in section 1.3.4.2. Thus, it is necessary to reduce the model size of a supply chain.

To reduce the model of a supply chain, various approaches exist:

– abstraction, which is a "method for reducing the complexity of a simulation model while maintaining the validity of the simulation results with respect to the question that the simulation is being used to address" ([FRA 95] – Figure 1.19). Its objective is to reduce the calculus combinatory;

– aggregation, which is a "form of abstraction by which a set of data or variables with common characteristics can replaced by an aggregated piece of data or variable" [MER 87];

– number of events reduction which consists of replacing "part of a discrete-event model by a variable or formula" ([ZEI 76]).

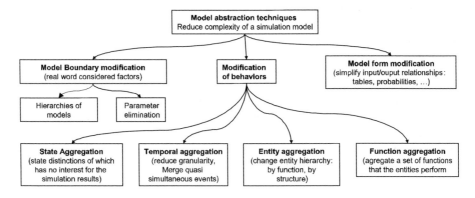

Figure 1.19. *A taxonomy of a model: abstraction techniques [FRA 95]*

1.6.2.1. *Reducing model literature review*

Even though most research concerning model reduction relates to manufacturing flows, it could be useful to analyze their results, especially concerning reduction problems, in order to highlight similarities between manufacturing process simulation models and SC simulation models.

Amongst various authors, Zeigler was the first to deal with the reduction simulation model problem [ZEI 76]. In his view, the complexity of a model relates to the number of elements, connections and model calculations. He distinguished four ways of simplifying a discrete simulation model by replacing part of the model by a random variable, coarsening the range of values taken by a variable and grouping parts of a model together.

Innis *et al.* [INN 99] first listed 17 simplification techniques for general modeling. Their approach was comprised of four steps: hypotheses (identifying the important parts of the system), formulation (specifying the model), coding (building the model) and experiments.

Brooks and Tobias [BRO 00] suggest a "simplification of models" approach for those cases where the indicators to be followed are the average throughput rates. They suggest an eight stage procedure. The reduced model can be very simple and then an analytical solution becomes feasible and the dynamic simulation redundant. Their work is valid in cases where the required results are averages and where the aim is to measure throughput.

Hung and Leachman [HUN 99] propose a technique for model reduction applied to large wafer fabrication facilities. They use "total cycle time" and "equipment utilization" as decision-making indicators to do away with the work center (WC). In their case, these WC have a low utilization rate and a fixed service level (they use standard deviation of the batch waiting time as a decision-making criterion).

Tseng [TSE 99] compares the regression techniques applied to an "aggregate model" (macro) by using the "flow time" indicator. In fact, he suggests reducing the model by mixing "macro" and "micro" approaches so as to minimize errors in the case of complex models. Here again, for the "macro" view, he only deals with the estimation of flow time as a whole. For the "micro" approach, he constructs an individual regression model for each stage of the operation to estimate its individual flow time. The cumulative order of flow time estimates is then the sum of the individual operation flow time estimates. He then tries to mix the macro and micro approaches.

1.6.2.2. *The reducing model problem*

Within the framework of control decision-making scenario evaluation, such model reductions could be useful. Moreover, concerning SC planning, the more interesting decision-making level is the master planning. At this level of planning, load/capacity equilibrium is obtained via the "management of critical capacity" function or rough-cut capacity planning. Consequently, it could be interesting to put forward a reduced model (Figure 1.20 explains its principle) in which we find the bottlenecks and the "blocks" which are "aggregates" of the work centers required by released manufacturing orders (MO) [THO 05].

The WC remaining in the model are either conjectural and structural bottlenecks or WCs which are vital to the synchronization of the MO. All other WCs are "aggregated blocks" upstream or downstream of the bottlenecks.

By "conjunctural bottleneck" we mean a WC which, for the MPS and predictive scheduling in question, is saturated, i.e. it uses all available capacity. By "structural bottleneck" we mean a WC which (in the past) has often been in such a condition. Effectively, for one specific portfolio (one specific MPS) there is only one bottleneck – the most loaded WC – but this WC can be a different WC from the traditional bottlenecks.

We call a "synchronization work center" one or several resources enabling the planning of MO with bottlenecks and those without to be synchronized. To minimize the number of these "synchronization work centers", we need to find WC having the most in common amongst all this MO portfolio not using bottlenecks and which figure in the routing of at least one MO using them.

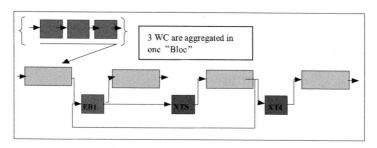

Figure 1.20. *Reduced model – principle*

A reduction algorithm highlights these so-called "synchronization" WC. In fact, the MO using structural or conjunctural bottlenecks may be synchronized and scheduled in comparison with one another thanks to the scheduling of these bottlenecks. However, for certain MO that do not use them, the synchronization WC will need to be used.

1.6.2.3. *Another state reduction using the bottleneck notion*

In this section we show examples of model reduction using the bottleneck notion.

With this modeling approach, the "physical part" of the factory is modeled as a network of interconnected flow shops with the following hypothesis:

– in each flow shop, items cannot overtake each others;

– in a given flow shop, there can be an identical machine in parallel;

– an item is launched in a given flow shop only when all its components are available (assembly);

– these hypotheses are consistent with the tendency to use the "product line" organization of a business:

- detailed model,

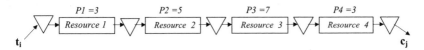

- reduced model (state reduction using the bottleneck notion),

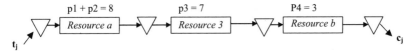

- industrial application: this reduction method has been applied (i.e. [TEL 03]) to a factory included in an aeronautic supply chain. The model of the factory is shown on the right side of the following figure. The reduced model using this type of method is presented on the left side of the figure. There is a strong reduction of the number of resources nevertheless modeled in a validation phase; the results of the simulation with the reduced model have been compared successfully with the real case.

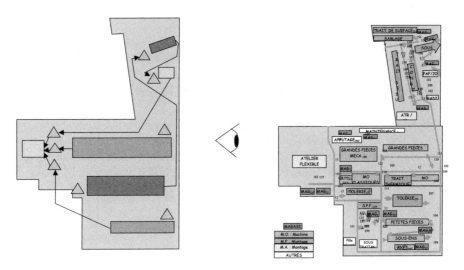

Figure 1.21. *Model reduction – a case study*

1.7. Conclusion

In this introductory chapter we have presented the main concepts which are used in supply chain management simulation. The specificities of this type of simulation and the modeling problem difficulties in this context have been highlighted. Different types of approaches and models have been presented to solve this problem. Finally, the links between the distribution level of both the system and the model have been characterized.

The remainder of the book includes three mains parts.

The first part takes the viewpoint of the simulation model types:

– continuous simulation (Chapter 2);

– discrete-event system – event-driven or time bucket-driven (Chapter 3);

– simulation games (Chapter 4).

The second part takes the viewpoint of the distribution level of the system and the model:

– centralized approaches (Chapter 5);

– interest of agents for supply chain simulation (Chapter 6);

– decisional system simulation of a business network with MAS (Chapter 7);

– simulation for product-driven systems (Chapter 8);

– HLA distributed simulation approaches for supply chain (Chapter 9).

The third and final part is dedicated to the simulation products (Chapter 10).

Even if we are convinced of the importance of the simulation methodology, no part of this book is explicitly dedicated to this aspect. However, the simulation methodologies (reduction simulation models, simulation model validation and simulation analysis) will be mentioned throughout the different chapters:

– a presentation of such simulation concepts and techniques highlighted in Chapter 1;

– applications of these concepts and techniques in case studies that illustrate the pivotal role of simulation in the decision-making process.

1.8. Bibliography

[BRO 00] BROOKS R.J. and TOBIAS A.M., "Simplification in the simulation of manufacturing systems", *IJPR*, Vol. 38, pp. 1009-1027, 2000.

[CHR 92] CHRISTOPHER M.L., *Logistics and Supply Chain Management*, Pitman Publishing, London, 1992.

[COR 89] CORBIER F., Modelisation et emulation de la partie opérative pour recette en plateforme d'équipement automatisés, PhD Thesis, University of Nancy I, 1989.

[DEB 02] DEB K., PRATAP A., AGARWAL S. and MEYARIVAN T., "A fast and elitist multi-objective genetic algorithm: NSGA-II", *IEEE Transactions on Evolutionary Computation*, Vol. 6, pp. 182-197, 2002.

[DIL 91] DILTS D.M., BOYD N.P., WHORMS H.H., "The evolution of control architectures for automated manufacturing systems", *Journal of Manufacturing Systems*, 1(10), 79-93, 1991.

[FRA 95] FRANTZ F.K., "A taxonomy of model. Abstraction techniques", *Proceedings of the 1995 Winter Simulation Conference*, Washington DC, December 1995.

[FUS 83] FUSAOKA A., SEKI H., TAKAHASHI K., "A description and reasoning of plant controllers in temporal logic", in *International Joint Conference on Artificial Intelligence.* pp. 405-408, 1983.

[HUN 99] HUNG Y.F. and LEACHMAN R.C., "Reduced simulation models of wafer fabrication facilities", *IJPR*, Vol. 37, pp. 2685-2701, 1999.

[INN 83] INNIS G.S. and REXSTAD E., "Simulation model simplification techniques", *Simulation*, no. 41, pp. 7-15, 1983.

[KLE 05] KLEIJNEN J.P.C., "Supply chain simulation tools and techniques: a survey", *International Journal of Simulation and Process Modelling*, 1(1/2), pp. 82-89, 2005.

[LAW 91] LAW A.M. and KELTON W.D., *Simulation Modeling and Analysis*, McGraw-Hill, 2nd edition, 1991.

[MEN 01] MENTZER J.T., DEWITT W., KEEBLER J.S., MIN S., NIX N.W., SMITH C.D., ZACHARIA Z.G., "Defining supply chain management", *Journal of Business Logistics Management*, Vol. 22, no. 2, 2001.

[MER 87] MERCE C., Cohérence des décisions en planification hiérarchisée, PhD Thesis, Paul Sabatier University, Toulouse, 1987.

[MOR 03] MOREL G., PANETTO H., ZAREMBA M., MAYER F., "Manufacturing Enterprise control and management system engineering: paradigms and open issues", *Annual Reviews in Control 27*, 2003.

[PAR 96] PARUNAK H.V.D. "Applications of distributed artificial intelligence in industry", in O'Hare G. and Jennings N. (eds.), *Foundations of Distributed Artificial Intelligence*, John Wiley & Sons, 1996.

[PAR 98] PARUNAK H.V.D. "What can agents do in industry, and why? An overview of industrially-oriented R&D at CEC", *Proceedings of the Second International Workshop on Cooperative Information Agents II, Learning, Mobility and Electronic Commerce for Information Discovery on the Internet*, 1998.

[PFE 03] PFEIFFER, A., KÁDÁR, B., MONOSTORI, L., "Evaluating and improving production control systems by using emulation", *Proc. of the 12 IASTED Int. Conf. on Applied Simulation and Modelling, ASM 2003*, p. 261-267, 3-5 September, Marbella, Spain, 2003.

[SCO 05] SCOR version 7, Supply Chain Council, 2005.

[STA 00] STADTLER H. and KILGER C. (eds.), *Supply Chain Management and Advanced Planning*, Springer, Berlin, 2000.

[TEL 03] TELLE O., THIERRY C., BEL G., "Modélisation macroscopique des systèmes de production pour la simulation de la relation donneur d'ordres/fournisseur dans les chaînes logistiques", *5e Congrès International de Génie Industriel : le génie industriel et les défis mondiaux*, Quebec, Canada, 2003.

[TER 04] TERZI S., CAVALIERI S., "Simulation in the supply chain context: a survey", *Computers in Industry*, Vol. 53, pp. 3-16, 2004.

[THO 05] THOMAS A. and CHARPENTIER P., "Reducing simulation models for scheduling manufacturing facilities", *European Journal of Operation Research*, Vol. 161, pp. 111-125, February 2005.

[TSE 99] TSENG T.Y., HO T.F. and LI R.K., "Mixing macro and micro flowtime estimation model: wafer fabrication", *IJPR*, Vol. 37, pp. 2447-2461, 1999.

[VOL 05] VOLLMANN T.E., BERRY W.L., WHYBARK D.C., JACOBS F.R., *Manufacturing Planning and Control Systems for Supply Chain Management*, 5th edition, McGraw-Hill, New York, 2005.

[WON 02] WONG C.Y., MCFARLANE D., AHMAD ZAHARUDIN A., AGARWAL V., "The intelligent product driven supply chain", *IEEE International Conference on Systems, Man and Cybernetics*, 2002.

[ZEI 76] ZEIGLER B.P., *Theory of Modeling and Simulation*, John Wiley, New York, 1976.

Chapter 2

Continuous Simulation for SCM

2.1. System dynamics models for SCM

2.1.1. *Complexity in supply chain logistics*

The current understanding of the mechanisms of supply chain management (SCM) is often based on empirical research. For example, in order to control a daily-based supplying activity, we observe that companies often use certain simple rules to solve common problems. They also usually reduce the complexity of these problems to ensure a suitable reactivity. On the other hand and from a wider point of view, to date, the highly complex and unsolved problems always exist. For example, how can we explain such a large (but probably necessary!) number of inventories along the supply chain? There are many causes of such dysfunction and the consultants, who advise companies on personal polyvalence, production and distribution flexibility, delivery time reduction, total quality control, new investments, etc., have today reached the limit of their efficiency. Many successive and partially political choices do not lead to the expected results. These consultants often base themselves on their past experiences, which lead unfortunately to failure. Even though Trotter and Connel [TRO 80] noticed that previous experience had an important place in problem solving and that people have a tendency to look for solutions which were successful in the past, Senge [SEN 90] describes the limit of this learning-based experience. According to him, there are some situations where the observation of consequences of each of our actions is not visible: "when the effects of an action are beyond our field of view, it is not possible to learn by experience".

Chapter written by Daniel THIEL and Vo Thi Le HOA.

In fact, many decisions are "easy" to make[1] and are essential to the real time control of the supply chain activities. In the short term, we observed the companies whose objective is to increase their reactivity capacity that helps rapidly overcome the simple problems or even, simplified problems by reducing the level of complexity. Meanwhile, globally, very complex problems are not solvable. Other field observations show that usual practices in supply chain management are often empirical. This can be described as what we call a procedural decision-making process which is based on a formal reasoning and deterministic basis. Another point of view consists of what we call an expert mode of decision-making based on normal job rules acquired by "organizational learning".

Facing this complexity, we will present in the next section how a cybernetic view can approach SCM by using first and foremost the essential feedback mechanisms.

2.1.2. *Cybernetics and feedback concept*

In his first patent in 1914, Armstrong used the term cybernetics to specify the signal regeneration circuit in a radio set. For a long time, the notions of energy and information have not been clearly dissociated: information was essentially conceived as the support of an action which enables the user of the feedback to maintain his influence on the system [ESC 76]. In 1943, Rosenblueth, Wiener and Bigelow introduced the feedback concept as an energy return from the output to the input. Wiener [WIE 48] considers the concept of feedback as an instrument at the origin of all trials of rational explanation of intentional behaviors. His work also contributed to system thinking and to the foundations of the general systems theory proposed by Von Bertalanffy [BER 51].

At the beginning of the cybernetics movement and servomechanism technology, the idea of negative feedback really started to be taken into consideration thanks to the work on the concept of homeostasis[2] proposed by two physiologists Bernard [BER 78] and Cannon [CAN 32]. The term "cybernetics" was also used along with David's expression [DAV 65] and was also due to the work by Maxwell who chose the term *governor* in the sense of *pilot* (*kubernetes* in Greek) to represent the principle of devices such as flyball regulators. From these last works stemmed the first cybernetic applications in firm control which were limited to the theoretical

---

1 Programmable decisions according to Simon [SIM 60].
2 The term homeostat itself stems from Ashby [ASH 52] and corresponds to the devices which aim at an automatic re-establishment of a previous forecasted equilibrium between many interconnected elements.

representation of homeostatic mechanisms and "ultrastability" proposed by Ashby[3]. The mathematics for supporting this problem formalization was limited with some theories: probabilities, combinatory logic, information theory and Boolean algebra. At that point, there had never been any differential equations applications that modeled the feedback system dynamics.

During this developing period, the applications of cybernetic loops by Deutsch [DEU 48]; [DEU 63], Beer [BEE 59] or others had been restricted to circular communication chains. Positive or negative causal circular processes were not taken into consideration. Only these communication circuits were perceived and conceived as being able to explain social phenomena. Later, thanks to Ashby [ASH 56], the "information feedback" concept was then introduced but only for a verbal or behavioral reaction which corresponds to a correct understanding (positive feedback) or incorrect understanding (negative feedback) of an emitted message by the receptor(s).

In opposition to this first interpretation considering the feedback concept applied only in informational terms, the theoretical work by Hebb [HEB 49] leant more towards the dynamical dimension, taking into account the learning phenomena. The term feedback was then used to describe the stimuli-responses behavior sequences with a first approximation of the cause-effect closed loop notion. From these works completed with a causal perspective not only limited to communication issues, Forrester proposed his "industrial dynamics" theory. We will now present the essential foundations of this theory.

2.1.3. *Basic principles of system dynamics*

2.1.3.1. *Forrester's theory*

Between 1950 and 1960, Forrester's working field at the *Massachusetts Institute of Technology* was oriented towards the dynamic analysis of multi-echelon supply systems [FOR 58]; [LYN 88]; [ROB 84]. Following his seminal book *Industrial Dynamics* [FOR 61], his methodology for studying and managing complex feedback systems was applied to many other research domains. For this reason his theory is now called "system dynamics".

---

3 An ultrastable system is defined by Ashby as follows: "two systems of continuous variables (that we called 'environment' and 'reacting part') interact, so that a primary feedback (through complex sensory and motor channels) exists between them. Another feedback, working intermittently and at a much slower speed, goes from the environment to certain continuous variables which in turn affect some step-mechanisms, the effect being that the step-mechanisms change value when and only when these variables pass outside given limits. The step-mechanisms affect the reacting part; by acting as parameters to it, they determine how it shall react to the environment" [ASH 45]; [ASH 52].

The fundamental principle of Forrester's work was the idea that organizations can be more closely described if we focus more on the regulation flows rather than the component entities. His theory is based on the existing closed loop rule where a control variable works on an action variable which returns a feedback to this control variable via other possible variables. This mechanism proves the mutual interaction between different variables of a complex system where the driving notion evolves in every spatiotemporal transition.

In practical terms, Forrester initially suggested that the feedback structure can be described by a causal diagram based on signal flow graphs which can represent the organizational networks [FOR 61]; [ROB 84]. Richardson [RIC 81] proposed a top-down approach for model conceptualization that at first describes the physical structure of the systems, then the information flow and finally the consequences of the actions which are at the origin of the changes which occur in the real systems.

Secondly, from this first qualitative representation, the system dynamics model would be built using stock (or level) variables and flow (or rate) variables [FOR 68]. The level or stock variables completely explain the states of the systems by continuous integration of the results of the actions inside these systems. The flow variables express the action with input and output flows which influence the level. The levels always exist even when all activities stop and the flow disappears. This form of representation can subsequently convert the variations of these states by differential equations.

Figure 2.1 shows an example of a system dynamics model describing one situation where the evolution of a level is in accordance with the variation of the input and output rates. A negative feedback loop regulates the level according to the gap between the desired level and the current level (correction action). This gap is re-injected into the input flows which correspond to the decision variable. This example illustrates the Forrester decision paradigm [FOR 84] showing that all decisions are taken inside a *feedback* loop.

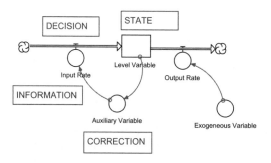

Figure 2.1. *An example of a stock-and-flow model*

Forrester considered that the decisions are not taken immediately but progressively showing a spatiotemporal "decision-action" *continuum*. The time delays in the systems present one of the essential factors of their dynamics.

There is a difference between conservative time delays and smoothing delays. The conservative time delays are integrated inside a flow pipeline, which transfers a quantity from one point to another. What "enters" in this type of time delay necessarily goes out without quantitative loss. In permanent regime, the time delay can be the average time for a flow element to move through the pipeline. This time delay is also called a discrete time delay and can correspond, for example, to a constant duration of a continuous bakery oven.

On the other hand, smoothed time delays or information delays set inside the information pipeline consist of smoothing the information history; the time delay constants (or smoothing coefficients) correspond to the weighted average age of the output information.

Forrester empirically observed that human reactions often follow a third order exponential time delay (see Figure 2.2) after two common types of stimulations: *pulses and steps* (see [FOR 61]; [POP 73]).

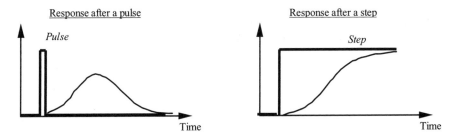

Figure 2.2. *Third order exponential response*

This type of third order exponential smoothing can be represented by a succession of first order exponential smoothings, as shown in Figure 2.3.

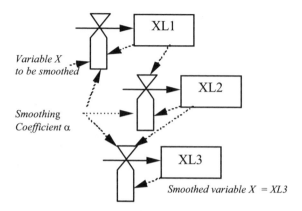

Figure 2.3. *Principle of a third order exponential smoothing*

Mathematically, this model can be built as follows:

– given a time interval dt between t and $(t + dt)$ and a smoothing coefficient α, the third order smoothing of a variable X written $XL3$, is calculated by the following equations:

$$XL1_{t+dt} = XL1_t + (dt/\alpha) . (X_t - XL1_t),$$
$$XL2_{t+dt} = XL2_t + (dt/\alpha) . (XL1_t - XL2_t),$$
$$XL3_{t+dt} = XL3_t + (dt/\alpha) . (XL2_t - XL3_t) = \text{variable } X_{smoothed.}$$

2.1.3.2. *Simulation techniques*

From the previous stock-and-flow representation, the level differential equations will be transformed into finite difference equations and can be simulated by using numerical techniques such as *Euler, Runge-Kutta* or others. The calculation will be performed gradually depending on the existing causal relationships. After choosing a time step dt^4, the equations corresponding to the level variables calculations are:

$$LEVEL(t) = LEVEL(t-1) + (RATE_{input} - RATE_{output}) . \text{dt}$$

The corresponding integrodifferential equation is:

$$LEVEL(K) = LEVEL(t=0) + \int_{t=0}^{K} (RATE_{input} - RATE_{output}) . \text{dt}$$

---

4 The value of dt must be lower than or equal to half of the smallest time delay of the model (see Shannon's theorem). If the lowest delay is a third order exponential time delay, then dt must be lower or equal to a sixth of this smallest delay.

The step-by-step calculation procedure is demonstrated in the next Figure 2.4. The rate variable values T depend on the level variable values N or other variables called auxiliary variables A which are identified at the beginning of the calculation period[5].

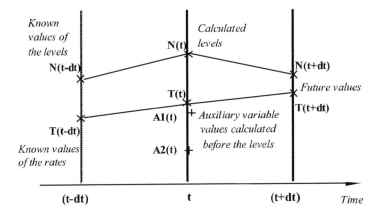

Figure 2.4. *Step-by-step calculation procedure*

The calculation is performed gradually following the existing causal relationships and then, indirectly, according to the initial conditions of the level variables. In supply chain simulation, system behavior is usually simulated based on the demand variations. Statistical time series analysis of the sales history is useful to examine the validity of such models. However, the correspondence between the past behavior and the model simulation results is not good enough to ensure the validity of the model and its future behavior. In accordance with the suggestions of Forrester [FOR 61] and Lyneis [LYN 88], we recommend studying first of all the model with order variations consisting of a combination of four types of entries i.e. *steps, pulses, noises*[6] and *seasonal components*. This stage consists of defining the type of perturbations that can occur in the studied supply chain. These perturbations can be simulated by a "test input generator" (see the following equation) or by a specific forecasting model[7]:

---

5 According to Alj and Faure, the system dynamics "method" can be assimilated to the fluency graph theory because the arrows which link the vertices representing the levels and the variation rates of these levels, show how the rates or gains interact to modify the initial levels when the system develops over time [ALJ 90].

6 For example, simulated by a normal distribution.

7 "More complicated input patterns, such as actual historical data, make it difficult to isolate the behavior generated by the model's structure from the input pattern. Once the dynamics of the structure are understood, it is usually possible to grasp how the structure will behave with more complicated inputs such as the actual historical input data" [STE 00].

$$D\ (t) = D_m * (1 + normal(M_b, S_b) + step(H_s,D_s) + pulse(H_p,D_p, F_p)$$
$$+ A_m * cos(2\pi\ t\ /\ P)\ ) \tag{2.1}$$

given:

$D\ (t)$ = *demand at time t*
D_m = *average demand*
M_b = *average of normally distributed noise*
S_b = *standard deviation of noise*
H_s = *step height*
D_s = *pulse start time*
H_p = *pulse height*
D_p = *first pulse start time*
F_p = *pulse frequency*
A_m = *amplitude of a sinusoidal component*
P = *period of a sinusoidal component*

The model can now be simulated based on the previous description of their cybernetic mechanisms. In the following section, we will present the current system dynamics software.

2.1.4. *How can we represent the supply chain decision system?*

In the following figures, we propose different methods of representing the knowledge of complex supply chain decision systems. The first approach (Figure 2.5) develops qualitative aspects that are somewhat objective and formalized. The second approach (Figure 2.6) presents the classical method according to Forrester's theory [FOR 68]; [FOR 84].

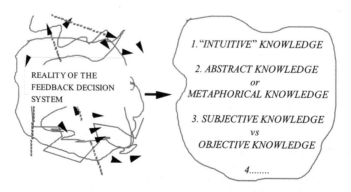

Figure 2.5. *Qualitative approach for representing SCM knowledge*

We will not put into opposition these two representation schemes of the knowledge since they are complementary. The first approach that we advise to use consists of discovering the reality with the immersion in the company by trying objectively to emerge the relationships between various variables under a systemic view. This is what is meant by "systemic audit" consisting of understanding complex reality. The second approach enriched by the first, consists of transforming this subjective, abstract or intuitive[8] knowledge in a model gradually worked out from the causal relations (non-linear in the majority of cases).

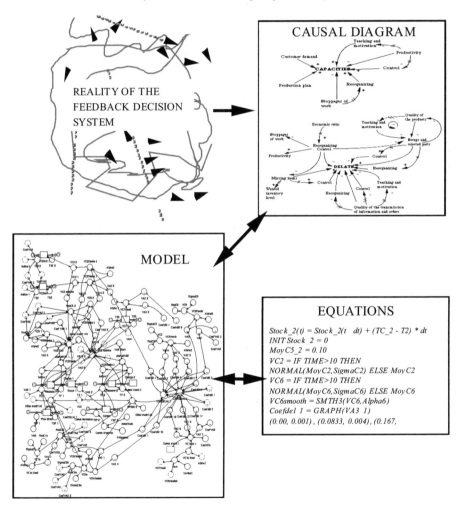

Figure 2.6. *System dynamics approach for representing SCM knowledge*

---

8 Simon asserts that intuition is a recognition phenomenon [SIM 69].

2.1.5. *Literature review*

In recent research on SCM, simulation models offer an interesting basis for studying the representation of complex interdependences between the supply chain members as well as the possibility of analyzing the global performance resulting from different inter-organizational decisions [SWA 94]. Among different simulation models, there are a considerable number of applications of system dynamics (objective of this chapter) discrete models [HO 89], [JAF 02] also significantly developed in other chapters of this book.

The first production-distribution system [FOR 58] identifies six types of flow in the systems: material, information, order, capital, work force, capital equipment all along the four supply chain echelons. At each echelon, it takes into account the order and shipment delays and explains that the success of industrial businesses depends on the interaction of these six flows and the ability to understand and control the system.

The current applications of SC system dynamics particularly focus on studying: *i.* the subsequent behaviors according to supply and demand fluctuations and amplifications, *ii.* the supply chain integration and *iii.* the global control of the SCM. By completing a state of art proposed by Angerhofer and Angelides [ANG 00], we show in Table 2.1 many recent system dynamics works on supply chain analysis, inventory management, planning and decision-making in SCM.

Application domains	Research references
Supply chain behavior and performance	[STE 89], [THI 93], [THI 96], [TOW 96], [AND 97], [BAR 97], [AKK 99], [STE 00], [GON 03], [PIE 04], [DAW 06], [PIE 07], [DEG 07]
Corporative planning and policy conception	[FOR 61], [LYN 80]
Economic behavior of the actors	[STE 83]
Dynamic decision-making	[STE 89]
Complex non-linear dynamics	[MOS 91]

Table 2.1. *The applications of system dynamics modeling*

We will now briefly describe some of this research.

Inventory management modeling

Sterman [STE 89] develops a generic model of inventory management, building a basic structure of the supply chain in order to simulate the decision-making processes based on raw material order policy, production control and capital at the macroeconomic level as well. Barlas and Aksogan [BAR 97] build a simulation model of inventory management policies regarding market demand modification.

Investment choice modeling

Anderson *et al.* [AND 97] propose a system dynamics model to explain the demand amplification of a capital equipment supply chain and to test different strategies that can improve the functioning of the industry.

Performance modeling

Towill [TOW 96] proposes that the paradigm of delay reduction is effective for reacting quickly to the market changes and his model also allows forecasting the progression of global performance. His work makes it possible to propose new strategies of *supply chain* re-engineering by reducing product shipment delays, decision-making delays and by providing available information for all SC upstream deciders.

Lu *et al.* [LU 06] study the impact of structural changes on the economic performance of the entire supply chain. Pierreval *et al.* [PIE 07] shows that dynamic analysis of the behavior of automotive industry supply chains using simulation can provide important information to improve their performance.

Instability modeling

Thiel [THI 96] applies Forrester's system dynamics paradigm based on non-linear feedback systems to improve the understanding of the regulations of industrial firms in the event of dysfunctions in their production systems. On the other hand, Goncalves [GON 06] uses system dynamics and the simulation approach to study the impact of endogenous customer demand on supply chain instability. His analysis suggests that the endogenous customer demand influences the shifts in modes of operation modes using the *lost sales* and *production push loops*, leading to higher supply chain instability than when customer demand is modeled as exogenous. Moreover, in their work [DEG 07], Degres *et al.* favorably demonstrated the impact of *pulse-type* perturbations on the behavioral dynamics of the studied systems.

2.2. Application: recent research into the bullwhip effect

2.2.1. Bullwhip effect in supply chains

2.2.1.1. *Bullwhip effect definition*

The bullwhip effect (BE), one of the main causes of the production-distribution supply chain inefficiency, is a phenomenon of order amplification resulting from the demand variability at each supply chain echelon [LEE 97]. This phenomenon is particularly produced by the inherent uncertainty in the system's operational environment such as the future demand uncertainty or the real lead-time. This means that a small perturbation of the demand can bring about a "waterfall" exaggerated reaction at the local level of lower links and spread out the entire supply chain.

It is worth analyzing this effect because it causes the following problems:

– in order to make up for the unpredictability of sale variation, the managers usually maintain amplified inventory levels;

– even if the inventory levels are globally considerable in the entire supply chain, the problems of synchronization between supply and demand at different stages sometimes give rise to delivery issues;

– the BE amplifies not only the inventory levels but also logistics operating costs.

Moreover, an information shortage or incorrect information can involve an inventory excess, worse service quality, an increase in transportation costs, loss of turnover, and planning and production management problems.

2.2.1.2. *Supply chain perturbations*

It is initially necessary to distinguish the supply chain stability that reacts to some perturbation and the roots of this reaction leading to disequilibrium of the chain. These disturbing roots, that can be endogenous or exogenous, are the origin of the BE. First, the endogenous perturbations rise up from the system itself. For example, the managers who estimate that their clients or suppliers make inaccurate decisions can decide to deviate their balance searching strategy by forming one inventory regulator against the risk of "non-optimal" behavior. This type of behavior will cause one perturbation in their own suppliers. Then, the exogenous perturbations result from an unforeseeable variation of the consumption.

2.2.1.3. *Bullwhip effect causes*

In general, there are two principal BE causes: operational and behavioral causes.

The operational causes can come from the structural characteristics of the supply chain that lead the rational agents to amplify the demand variability. For example, Lee *et al.* [LEE 97] divide these causes into four categories arising from different problems: demand forecasting updating, order batching, price fluctuations and rationing, and shortage gaming.

Chen *et al.* [CHE 00], Simchi-Levi *et al.* [SIM 00] and Shen [SHE 01] also note that independent local optimization choices of each manager without global vision are one BE cause. Taylor [TAY 99] proposes in his work on demand amplification two other causes of the BE: the variability in machine reliability and output and variability in process capability and subsequent product quality [MOY 06].

The second category of behavioral causes introduced initially by Forrester [FOR 58] [FOR 61] and then detailed by Sterman [STE 89] focuses on behavioral causes resulting in the instability of the supply chain. These causes principally come from the rationality limits of the managers, in particular their blurred justification in feedback effects and their reaction delay. Additionally, there is other research showing these cognitive restrictions [CRO 02].

2.2.1.4. *Bullwhip effect reduction solutions*

The following table, taking inspiration from the research of Moyaux *et al.* [MOY 06], shows some so-called BE operational causes and proposed solutions to different authors.

BE causes	Proposed BE reduction solutions	References
Inaccurate demand forecasting updating	- Information sharing (e.g., Vendor-Managed Inventory (VMI) or Continuous Replenishment Program (CRP)…) - Echelon-based inventory - Lead-time reduction	[LEE 97a] [LEE 97b]
Order batching mistakes	- Electronic data interchange (EDI) - Internet technologies	[LEE 97a] [LEE 97b] [TAY 99]
Price fluctuations	- Every day low pricing (EDLP)	[LEE 97a] [LEE 97b]
Misperception of feedback	- Giving a better understanding of the supply chain dynamics to managers	[FOR 58] [FOR 61] [STE 89] [DEJ 02] [DAG 03]

Table 2.2. *Operational causes and proposed solutions for reducing the BE* [MOY 06]

Concerning the so-called behavioral causes, Forrester [FOR 61] considers as one consequence of the lack of communication and information, looping between the managers in the whole supply chain. The proposed solution is bringing to these managers a better understanding of the global supply chain. The research on this field is exhibited in experiment studies into decision-making as well as supply delay. This research shows that the managers are short of good perception in delays, feedbacks and nonlinearity of the system. The managers tend to make an order basing on actual and desired inventory gaps and estimate wrongly the order backlog usually underestimated that generally are one cause of observed perturbations [STE 99] [STE 00].

2.2.2. Bullwhip effect modeling

2.2.2.1. *Example of a BE diffusion model*

In this section, we will describe one of the several interesting research studies by Helbing [HEL 04] which points out how the exogenous perturbations resulting from transportation problems could perturb the stability of a particular supply chain.

The Helbing model is described as a model of serial multi-echelon supply chain (see Figure 2.7) where:

– N_b for b = (1 to u) represents the available product inventory of each supplier b;

– N_o is the stock level of producers in the first upstream stage of the supply chain and N_{u+1} the last stage of the final consumer;

– λ_b represents product delivery flow from supplier $(b-1)$ to its client (supplier) b.

Figure 2.7. *The supply chain structure proposed by Helbing [HEL 04]*

N_b (t) is the weighted mean value of the own stock level of supplier b and those of n upstream and n downstream suppliers (with $2n + 1 \leq u$). In addition, c represents n upstream and n downstream suppliers. The weights ω_c are normalized to one:

$$\sum_{c=-n}^{n} \omega_c = 1 \tag{2.2}$$

Δt is the forecasting time horizon, if $\Delta t = 0$, the delivery rate λ_b of the supplier is based on his actual stock level; if $\Delta t > 0$, the delivery rate λ_b is based on the anticipated weighted stock level.

So, N_b (t) is defined in the following equation:

$$N_b(t) = \sum_{c=-n}^{n} \omega_c (N_{b+c} + \Delta t \frac{dN_{b+c}}{dt}) \tag{2.3}$$

The inventory variations dN_b are calculated according to the gap between the product reception rate with one supplier or the final consumer b ($b \in \{1, u+1\}$ as income rate) and delivery rate to his client $b+1$ (($b \in \{0, u\}$ as outcome rate) during one interval of time dt.

$$\frac{dN_b}{dt} = \lambda_b(t) - \lambda_{b+1}(t) \tag{2.4}$$

Moreover, the temporal variation of the delivery rate λ_b is proportional to the difference of the actual delivery rate and the (desired) order rate W_b as well as its adaptation takes on average a time interval τ.

$$\frac{d\lambda_b}{dt} = \frac{1}{\tau} [W_b(t) - \lambda_b(t)] \tag{2.5}$$

W_b will usually be reduced with increasing stock levels N_a (actual stock levels of other suppliers a, with $a = (b+c)$) and W_b will also be influenced by the temporal changes of $N'_a = dN_a/dt$.

We can write down:

$$W_b = f(N_a(t), dN_a(t)/dt) \tag{2.6}$$

In particular, Helbing paid attention to this variable with its delay τ as strategic factors for each supplier. According to Helbing, function f reflects here the management strategy, i.e. the order policy regarding the desired delivery rate as a function of the actual stock levels $N_a(t)$ or anticipated stock levels:

$$(N_a(t) + \Delta t dN_a(t)/dt) \approx N_a(t + \Delta t) \tag{2.7}$$

On the other hand, he also defined a stability condition of the order rate W_b as follows:

$$\tau \prec \Delta t + \frac{1}{\left| W'(N_0) \right|} (\frac{1}{2} + \sum_{c=-n}^{n} c\omega_c) \tag{2.8}$$

where W' is the derivative of management function W.

One of the interesting results of this model of non-linear interaction dynamics makes it possible to underline that the supply chain has stable behavior if:

– the adaptation time τ is small;

– Δt is large; or

– the change of management function W and stock level N_b are small.

However, if these conditions are not respected, perturbation will grow and generate oscillations in the inventories $N_b(t)$ and this phenomenon is called the *bullwhip effect*.

2.2.2.2. BE system dynamics models

Further to Forrester research works [FOR 58] [FOR 61] introducing the concept of BE, numerous recent publications are appeared; we propose a summary of these publications in Table 2.3.

Authors	Cause analysis	Recommended BE reduction solutions	Basic model references
Sterman *et al.* [STE 89]	The managers' insufficient understanding of the supply chain dynamics and their "non-optimal" order decisions.	Improving the understanding of supply chain dynamics: feedback loops, delays and order policy.	[FOR 61]
Lee *et al.* [LEE 97]	The distortion of upstream and downstream demand information of the supply chain and the amplification of distortion variance.	Supply chain member's coordination by information flow of the production plan, stock control and delivery planning.	[FOR 61]
Anderson *et al.* [AND 00]	The amplification of demand volatility and its consequences on production, productivity, inventory and delivery delay.	Demand forecasting, delivery delay reduction, order and employment policies.	[LEE 97]
Chen *et al.* [CHE 00]	The problems of delivery delay, demand satisfaction, and demand forecasting mistakes.	Demand centralized information can reduce the BE and better demand forecasting can restrict the upstream amplification of the supply chain.	[KAH 87] [LEE 97a] [LEE 97b]
Daganzo [DAG 05]	The amplification of demand.	Use of advance demand (ADI) and decentralized negotiation schemes can reduce the BE.	[COO 93] [LEE 97a] [LEE 97b]
Villegas-Moran *et al.* [VIL 06]	The management policies and information flows can distort and amplify the demand signals.	Establishing a relationship among information flow structures, decision rules and policies of the supply chain.	[DOY 98] [LAN 01] [STE 02]
Oliva Gonçalves [OLI 06]	The excessive reaction to order backlog.	Using of all available information of stock level and order backlog in order to obtain a global vision that allows a coherent estimation in decision-making processes.	[TOB 58] [GRE 97] [CHE 99]

Table 2.3. *References of BE solutions using system dynamics*

We will now present an example of a simulation game developed in MIT [STE 84] used by numerous authors: the *Beer Distribution Game (BG)*. In this game, the player acts as the head of department of one supermarket where he has to define a beer ordering policy in accordance with consumption variations. As usual, the players induce the BE.

In fact, the BG is an exercise that simulates the material and information flows of a production-distribution supply chain. The players are divided into four groups representing the roles of retailer, wholesaler, distributor and factory. At each playing round, the player can make one and only one decision: defining the number of beer cases to order to the upstream supplier. The retailer receives the client orders and places an order to the wholesaler, the wholesaler then places an order with the distributor and finally the distributor sends his order to the factory. The factory will decide how many beer cases to produce rather than place an order with one supplier. Furthermore, it is important to take into account the production delay of the factory and the product transportation delay. At each level of the supply chain, the player suffers the inventory cost and order backlog cost. The game objective is to minimize the total costs resulting from the inventory and order backlog.

We will now show one BG model of the three-echelon supply chain inventories and flows realized in *Ithink®* software [3]: Producer (S_0), Supplier 1 (S_1) and Supplier 2 (S_2). In Figure 2.8, the influence diagram represents the causal relations between different variables at each echelon of the supply chain.

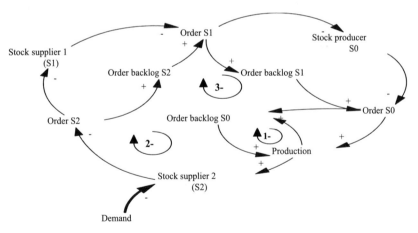

Figure 2.8. *Stock-flow Beer Game diagram*

In this diagram, the polarity of each arrow indicates the direction of change that a change in the cause induces in the effect[9]. It demonstrates that the orders and the order backlog at each supply chain level increase when the demand increases because of production and delivery delays. This means that the final orders placed with producer S_0 are significantly higher than those with supplier S_2. In the diagram, there are three control loops of the homeostatic type.

Following this representation, we build a simulation model that allows us to understand the supply chain dynamics (see equations in Appendix 1, section 2.5). Figure 2.9 represents the model structure of the supply chain.

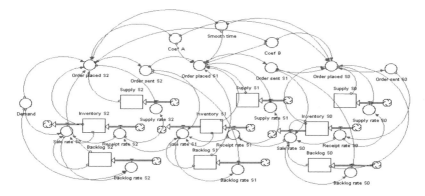

Figure 2.9. *The BG one echelon supply chain structure*

The simulation starts at time $t = 0$. Each group of players makes one decision about how many cases of beer to order and then deliver to the client each week. At each supply chain level, the inventory level at time t is presented by:

*Inventory(t) = Inventory (t - dt) + (Receipt_rate - Sale_rate) * dt*
INIT Inventory = 100

and the order backlog level at time t is:

*Backlog(t) = Backlog(t - dt) + (Backlog_rate) * dt*
INIT *Backlog* = 0

In general, the order placed in the upstream supplier is:

O(t) = max(0, $D_O(t)$)

---

9 A positive sign indicates change in the same direction while a negative sign indicates change in the opposite direction.

where $D_O(t)$ is the decided order rate based on three factors:

– the forecasting level: FL,

– the gap between actual and desired inventory: AI,

– the gap between actual and desired supply level: AS.

$D_O(t) = LI(t) + AI(t) + AD(t)$

This means that:

$D_O(t) = Forecasting + Actual\ inventory\ gap + Actual\ shipment\ level\ gap$

or

Order_placed_S0 =
MAX(0,SMTH1(Order_sent_S1,Smooth_time)+Coef_A*(100-(Inventory_S0-
Backlog_S0)-Coef_B*Supply_S0))

$D_O(t) = Forecasting + Coef\,A*(100-(Inventory\text{-}backlog)(t))\text{-}Coef\,B*S(t)$

where $S(t)$ is the actual shipment level gap: $S(t = S(t\text{-}1) + O(t) -i(t)$; the desired inventory: $I^* = 100$; $Coef\,A$, B: weighted factors.

We have realized the simulation in *Ithink®* software [3] with one period of time of 100 weeks. The demand is constant with 10 cases of beer for the first 14 weeks, 20 cases for the 15th week and remains constant until the end of the simulation.

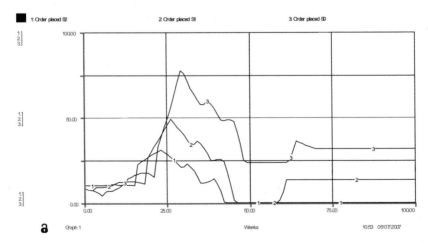

Figure 2.10. *Order rate evolutions at each level of the supply chain*

The results of the simulation model presented in Figure 2.10 show that the order rate increases from 10 cases to 31 cases for Supplier S_2, from 10 cases to 49 cases for Supplier S_1; from 10 cases to 78 for Producer S_0 (see Figure 2.10). This is a phenomenon of demand amplification along the supply chain. This result reflects one phenomenon of the so-called *bullwhip effect*.

Moreover, Chen *et al.* [CHE 00] propose a modification of BG in *Stationary Beer Game* by changing certain parameters: periodic order, periodic revision-based inventory, benchmark theory for the supply chain. They model the material and information flows of a production-distribution supply chain that supplies to one stationary market, i.e. the orders at different periods are independent and identically satisfied.

On the other hand, Haartveit *et al.* [HAA 02] use this game in order to analyze the relationship between supply and demand in the northern European forest industry.

2.2.2.3. *BE multi-agent models*

Dodd *et al.* [DOD 01] and Fox *et al.* [FOX 93] introduce the idea of a supply chain as an intelligent agent network carrying out one or more functions (logistics, transportation management, SCM control, resource management and planning, etc.). These agents interact with each other and favor the supply chain coordination at both a tactical and operational level. Other authors propose a decomposition of the supply chain into subsystems of heterogenous production gathered in the virtual coalition and dynamics [MOY 06]. These authors already use the multi-agent system (MAS) in order to build a model of decentralized coordination in the supply chain to reduce the BE resulting from the demand fluctuations placed on the suppliers by each of their clients [MOY 03]. In addition, they enrich their model by developing an information sharing system between the agents [MOY 07].

The following table presents other research in this field of BE multi-agent modeling.

Authors	Studied problems	Approach and solutions	Basic model references
Yung *et al.* [YUN 00]	The different perspectives and behavior of the managers in different geographical regions. The issues of scalability and adaptability to the quickly increasing of the product variety. The problem of the transmission of real-time information to support decision-making at each facility.	Using one system that integrates the constraint network model and multi-agent model in order to support coordination and management of supply chain.	[BEC 94] [SWA 98]
Carlsson *et al.*, [CAR 00]	The retailer's orders do not coincide with the actual retail sales and the wholesaler's orders to the producer do not coincide with the actual demand of the retailers.	Using a multi-agent system to show that if the members of the supply chain share information and agree on better and better fuzzy estimates on future sales for the upcoming period then the BE can be significantly reduced.	[LEE 97]
Yan, 2001 [YAN 01]	The impact of different lead-time distributions on the BE and supply chain performance under centralized and decentralized information sharing strategies.	Simulation of an extendable multi-agent linear supply chain in order to show that different lead-time distributions will lead to different supply chain performance and BE remains unchanged.	[TAN 99] [LI 00] [CHE 00]
Gamoura-Chehbi *et al.*, [GAM 06]	The demand amplification and the problem of collaborative decision-making.	One model based on the mechanisms of decentralized coordination carried out by the agents having the ability to communicate and reason that enables them to make collective decisions.	[ROT 98] [SIM 00] [HON 03]

Table 2.4. *Some bullwhip effect multi-agent models*

2.3. Conclusion

This chapter shows that continuous simulation can be an effective tool for the design and re-engineering of the SCM driving mechanisms at the tactical and strategic levels. Forrester's system dynamics go well beyond a "simple" simulation technique while being initially focused on the model design through a systemic representation of the cybernetic mechanisms. Once the model is built according to a well defined methodology, SD can then extract "qualitative knowledge" from the simulation results to improve the system driving behaviors. SD is currently well used by consultants and firm executives often as a decision support system whereas researchers are more interested in studying the stability of SCM faced with endogenous and exogenous disturbances. SD continuous simulation software has gradually evolved at the ergonomic level by facilitating for example the feedback loop representations. In addition, they make it possible, directly after simulations, to carry out an interactive causality research which is interesting for the researcher and decision maker. In certain cases, the simulation model is used as a teaching tool and thanks to the interactivity and multimedia resources, it can facilitate the understanding of the SCM complex mechanisms. SD could see its evolution in hybrid solutions coupling discrete-event models at the SCM operational level, with continuous models simulating the decisions at the tactical or strategic level. The interfacing of a continuous logistical model with a multi-agent model of the customer demand evolution by agent interactions could improve the whole SCM dynamic representation.

2.4. Bibliography

[AKK 99] AKKERMANS H.A., BOGERD P. and VOS B., "Virtuous and vicious cycles on the road towards international supply chain management", *International Journal of Operations and Production Management*, vol. 15, no. 11, pp. 565-581, 1999.

[ALJ 90] ALJ A. and FAURE R., *Guide de la recherche opérationnelle*, Masson, vol. 2, pp. 275-280, 1990.

[AND 00] ANDERSON E.G., FINE C.H. and PARKER G.G., "Upstream volatility in the supply chain: the machine tool industry as a case study", *POMS Series in Technology and Operations Management, Teaching Supply Chain Management*, USA, vol. 9, pp. 239-261, 2000.

[AND 97] ANDERSON E.G., FINE C.H. and PARKER G.G., *Upstream Volatility in the Supply Chain: The Machine Tool Industry as a Case Study*, Department of Management, University of Texas, 1997.

[ANG 00] ANGERHOFER B.J. and ANGELIDES M.C., "System dynamics modelling in supply chain management: Research review", *Proceedings of the 2000 Winter Simulation Conference*, 2000.

[ASB 45] ASHBY R., "The effect of controls of stabilities", *Nature*, no. 155, pp. 242-243, USA, 1945.

[ASB 52] ASHBY R., *Design for a Brain*, London, Chapman & Hall, 1952.

[ASB 56] ASHBY R., *An Introduction to Cybernetics*, London, Chapman & Hall, 1956.

[BAR 99] BARLAS Y. and AKSOGAN A., *Product Diversification and Quick Response Order Strategies in Supply Chain Management* [website], Bogazici University 1997 (cited in 1999), available at: http://ieiris.cc.boun.edu.fr/faculty/barlas/.

[BEC 94] BECK J.C. and FOX M.S., "Supply Chain Coordination via Mediated Constraint Relaxation", *Proceedings of the First Canadian Workshop on Distributed Artificial Intelligence*, 1994.

[BEE 59] BEER S., *Cybernetics and Management*, London, English University Press, 1959.

[BER 73] Von BERTALANFFY L. (translated by G. Braziller), *Théorie générale des systèmes*, Paris, Dunod, 1973.

[BER 78] BERNARD C., *Leçons sur les phénomènes de la vie commune aux animaux et aux végétaux*, Paris, Baillière, 1878.

[CAN 32] CANNON W.A., *The Wisdom of the Body*, New York, Norton & Co, 1932.

[CAR 00] CARLSSON C. and FULLÉR R., "Soft computing and the bullwhip effect", *Economics and Complexity*, vol. 2, no. 3, 2000.

[CHE 00] CHEN F. and SAMROENGRAJA R., "The Stationary Beer Game", *Production and Operations Management*, vol. 9, no. 1, pp.19-30, 2000.

[CHE 00] CHEN F., DREZNER Z., RYAN J.K. and SIMCHI-LEVI D., "Quantifying the bullwhip effect in a simple supply chain: The impact of forecasting, lead times, and information", *Management Science*, vol. 46, no. 3, pp. 436-443, 2000.

[CHE 99] CHEN F., "Decentralized Supply Chains Subject to Information Delays", *Management Science*, vol. 45, no. 8, pp. 1076-1090, 1999.

[COO 93] COOKE J.A., "The $30 billion promise", *Traffic Management*, vol. 32, pp. 57-59, 1993.

[CRO 02] CROSON R. and DONOHUE K., "Experimental economics and supply-chain management", *Interfaces*, vol. 32, no. 5, pp. 74-82, 2002.

[DAG 03] DAGANZO C., *A Theory of Supply Chains*, Springer, 2003.

[DAG 05] DAGANZO C. and OUYANG Y., Counteracting the Bullwhip Effect with decentralized negotiations and advance demand information, Research Reports, Institute of Transportation Studies, University of California, Berkeley, 2005.

[DAV 65] DAVID A., *La cybernétique et l'humain*, Paris, Gallimard, 1965.

[DEG 07] DEGRES L., PIERREVAL H. and CAUX C., "Analyzing the Impact of Market Variations for Steel Industries: a Simulation Approach", *Production Planning and Control*, 2007, forthcoming.

[DEJ 02] DEJONCKHEERE J., DISNEY S.M., LAMBRECHT M.R. and TOWILL D.R., "Transfer function analysis of forecasting induced bullwhip in supply chains", *International Journal of Production Economics*, vol. 78, pp.133-144, 2002.

[DEU 48] DEUTSCH K.W., "Towards a cybernetic model of man and society, Notes on research on the role of models in the natural and social sciences", *Synthese*, no. 7, pp. 506-533, 1948.

[DEU 63] DEUTSCH K.W., *The Nerves of the Government*, London, Collier MacMillan, 1963.

[DOD 01] DODD C. and KUMARA S.R.T., "A distributed multi-agent model for value nets", *IEA/AIE*, pp. 718–727, 2001.

[DOY 98] DOYLE J.K. and FORD D.N., "Mental models concepts for system dynamics research", *System Dynamics Review*, vol. 14, no. 1, pp. 3-29, 1998.

[ELH 05a] ELHAMDI M., Modélisation et simulation de chaînes de valeurs en entreprise - Une approche dynamique des systèmes et aide à la décision: SimulValor, Doctoral thesis, Ecole Centrale Paris, Laboratoire Génie Industriel, 2005.

[ELH 05b] ELHAMDI M. and YANNOU B., "Évaluation des flux de valeurs d'une entreprise: une approche de dynamique des systèmes multicritère", *Proc. CIGI'05: 6ème Congrès International de Génie Industriel*, Besançon, 7-10 June, 2005.

[ESC 76] ESCARPIT R., *Théorie générale de l'information et de la communication*, Paris, Hachette, 1976.

[FOR 58] FORRESTER J.W., "Industrial dynamics: a major breackthrough fo decision makers", *Harvard Business Review*, 36, no. 4, pp. 37-66, July-August 1958.

[FOR 61] FORRESTER J.W., *Industrial Dynamics*, MIT Press, Massachusetts Institute of Technology - Cambridge, Massachusetts, 1961.

[FOR 68] FORRESTER J.W., "Industrial Dynamics after the first decade", *Management Science*, vol. 14 no. 7, pp. 398-415, March 1968.

[FOR 84] FORRESTER J.W., *Principes des systèmes*, Presses Universitaires de Lyon, 1984.

[FOX 93] FOX M.S., CHIONGLO J.F. and BARBUCEANU M., The integrated supply chain management, Internal report of the Enterprise Integration Laboratory, Department of Industrial Engineering, University of Toronto, Ontario, Canada, 1993.

[GAM 06] GAMOURA-CHEHBI S., OUZROUT Y. and BOURAS A., "Simulation de prise de décision dans la supply chain: Une approche multi agents", *Modélisation, Optimisation et Simulation des Systèmes : Défis et Opportunités, 6ᵉ Conférence Francophone de Modélisation et Simulation – MOSIM'06*, Rabat, Morocco, 2006.

[GRE 97] GREENE W.H., *Econometric Analysis*, 3rd edition, Prentice Hall, Upper Saddle River, NJ, 1997.

[HAA 02] HAARTVEIT E.Y. and FJELD D.E., "Experimenting with industrial dynamics in the forest sector – a Beer Game application", in *Symp. on Systems and Models in Forestry*, Chile, 2002.

[HEB 49] HEBB D., *The Organization of Behavior*, Wiley, 1949.

[HEL 04] Helbing D., "Modelling and optimisation of production processes: Lessons from traffic dynamics", in G. Radons and R. Neugebauer (eds.), *Non-linear Dynamics of Production Systems*, Wiley-VCH, Weinheim, pp. 85-105, 2004.

[HO 89] HO Y.-C., "Introduction to special issue on dynamics of discrete event systems", *Proceedings of the IEEE*, vol. 77, no. 1, pp. 3-6, 1989.

[HON 03] HONG Y., ZHENXIN Y. and EDWIN T.C., "A strategic model for supply chain design with logical constraints: Formulation and solution", *Computer and Operations Research*, vol. 30, pp. 2135-2155, 2003.

[JAF 02] JAFARI et al., "A distributed discrete event dynamic model for supply chain of business enterprises", *Discrete Event Systems, 2002, Proceedings, Sixth International Workshop October 2-4*, 2002, pp. 279-285.

[KAH 87] KAHN J.A., "Inventories and the volatility of production", *The American Economic Review*, vol. 77, no. 4, pp. 667–679, 1987.

[KIR 01] KIRKWOOD *Chapter 4: The Beer Game*, Business Process Analysis Workshops: System Dynamics Models, 2001, http://www.public.asu.edu/~kirkwood/sysdyn/SDWork /SDWork.htm.

[LAN 01] LANE D.C., "Rerum Cognoscere Causas: How do the ideas of system dynamics relate to traditional social theories and the voluntarism determinism debate?", *System Dynamics Review*, vol. 17, no. 2, pp. 97-118, 2001.

[LEE 97a] LEE H.L., PADMANABHAN V. and WHANG S., "The bullwhip effect in supply chain", *Sloan Management Review*, vol. 38, no. 3, pp. 93-102, 1997.

[LEE 97b] LEE H.L., PADMANABHAN V. and WHANG S., "Information distortion in the supply chain: The bullwhip effect", *Management Science*, vol. 43, pp. 546-558, 1997.

[LEF 02] LEFÈVRE J., "Kinetic Process Graphs: Building Intuitive, Suggestive and Parsimonious Material Stock-Flow Diagrams with Modified Bond Graph Notations", *Proc. International Conference of the System Dynamics Society*, Palermo, Italy, July 28-August 1, 2002.

[LI 00] Li J., SHAW M.J. and TAN G.W., "Evaluating information sharing strategies in supply chain", in *8th ECIS*, Vienna, vol. 1, pp. 437-444, 2000.

[LU 06] LU D., TENNANT C., and CURTIS A., "A case study of dynamic supply chain development", *Paper ID 174*, http://www.ht2.org/conference/pdf/174.pdf.

[LYN 80] LYNEIS J.M., *Corporate Planning and Policy Design: A System Dynamics Approach*, Pugh-Roberts Associates, Cambridge, Massachusetts, 1980.

[LYN 88] LYNEIS J.M., *Corporate Planning and Policy Design: A System Dynamics Approach*, Pugh-Roberts Associates, Cambridge, Massachusetts, 3rd edition, 1988, pp. 83-114.

[MOS 91] MOSEKILDE E., LARSEN E.R. and STERMAN J.D., "Coping with complexity: Deterministic chaos in human decision-making behaviour", in *Beyond Belief: Randomness, Prediction, and Explanation in Science*, CASTI J.L. and KARLQVIST A. (eds.), CRC Press, Boston, Massachusetts, 1991.

[MOY 03] MOYAUX T., CHAIB-DRAA B. and D'AMOURS S., "Agent-based simulation of the amplification of demand variability in a supply chain", in *Proc. 4th Workshop Agent-Based Simulation (ABS4)*, CIRAD, Montpellier, France, 2003.

[MOY 06] MOYAUX T. CHAIB-DRAA B. and D'AMOURS S., "Supply Chain Management and Multiagent Systems: An Overview", in *MultiAgent-Based Supply Chain Management*, B. Chaib-draa and J.P. Müller (eds.), Springer, 2006.

[MOY 07] MOYAUX T., CHAIB-DRAA B. and D'AMOURS S., "Information Sharing as a Coordination Mechanism for Reducing the Bullwhip Effect in a Supply Chain", *IEEE Transactions on Systems, Man, and Cybernetics*, vol. 37, no. 3, pp. 396-409, 2007.

[OLI 06] OLIVA R. and GONÇALVES P., "Evaluating overreaction to backlog as a behavioural cause of the Bullwhip Effect", *Behavioral Research in Operations and Supply Chain Management Conference*, Penn State University, Smeal College of Business, 2006.

[PIE 07] PIERREVAL H., BRUNIAUX R. and CAUX C., "A continuous simulation approach for supply chains in the automotive industry", *Simulation Modelling Practice and Theory*, vol. 15, no. 2, pp. 185-198, 2007.

[POP 73] POPPER J., *La dynamique des systèmes, principes et applications*, Paris, Les Editions Organisation, pp. 25-90, 1973.

[RIC 81] RICHARDSON G.P. and PUGH A.L., *Introduction to System Dynamics Modeling with Dynamo*, MIT Press, Cambridge, Massachussets, 1981.

[ROB 84] ROBERTS E.B., *Managerial Applications of System Dynamics*, MIT Press, Cambridge, Massachussets, 1984.

[ROS 43] ROSENBLUETH A., WIENER N., BIGELOW J., "Behavior, Purpose and Teleology", *Philosophy of Science*, no. 10, 18-24, 1943.

[ROT 98] ROTA K., Coordination Temporelle de Centres Gérant de Façon Autonome des Ressources. Application aux Chaînes Logistiques Intégrées en Aéronautique, Doctoral thesis, University of Toulouse, 1998.

[SEN 90] SENGE P., *The Fifth Discipline: The Art and Practice of the Learning Organization*, Doubleday, New York, 1990.

[SHE 01] SHEN Y., "Impact of asymmetric information on inventory policy", *Term paper to Dr. Miller for the partial fulfilment of "Production Control"*, 2001.

[SIM 00] SIMCHI-LEVI D., KAMINSKY P. and SIMCHI-LEVI E., *Designing and Managing the Supply Chain*, McGraw-Hill Higher Education, 2000.

[SIM 69] SIMON H.A., *The Sciences of the Artificial*, p. 91, MIT Press, Cambridge, 1969.

[STE 83] STERMAN, J., *A Simple Model of Energy Dynamics* D-3484, MIT System Dynamics Group, 1983.

[STE 84] STERMAN J.D., "The MIT Beer Game", *The MIT Forum for Supply Chain Innovation*, 1984.

[STE 89] STERMAN J.D., "Modelling managerial behaviour: Misperceptions of feedback in a dynamic decision making experiment", *Management Science*, vol. 35, no. 3, pp. 321-339, 1989.

[STE 00] STERMAN J., *Business Dynamics*, McGraw-Hill, USA, 2000.

[STE 02] STERMAN J., "All models are wrong, reflection on becoming a systems scientist", *Systems Dynamics Review*, vol. 18, no 4, pp. 501-531, 2002.

[SWA 98] SWAMINATHAN J.M., SMITH S.F. and SADEH N.M., "Modelling Supply Chain Dynamics: A Multiagent Approach," *Decision Sciences*, vol. 29, no. 3, 1998.

[TAN 99] TAN G.W., The Impact of Demand Information Sharing on Supply Chain Network, PHD thesis in Business Administration in the Graduate College of the University of Illinois at Urbana-Champaign, 1999.

[TAY 99] TAYLOR D., "Measurement and analysis of demand amplification across the supply chain", *The International Journal of Logistics Management*, vol. 10, no. 2, pp. 55-70, 1999.

[THI 93] THIEL D., "Modèles génériques de comportement des systèmes de production", *Revue Internationale de Systémique*, AFCET, Dunod, vol. 7, no. 2, pp. 117-142, 1993.

[THI 96] THIEL D., "Analysis of the behaviour of production systems using continuous simulation", *International Journal of Production Research*, vol. 34, pp. 3227-3251, 1996.

[TOB 58] TOBIN J., "Estimation of Relationships for Limited Dependent Variables", *Econometrica 26*, pp. 24-36, 1958.

[TOW 96] TOWILL D.R., "Time compression and supply chain management- a guided tour", *Supply Chain Management*, vol. 1, no.1, pp. 15-27, 1996.

[TRO 80] TROTTER R.J. and MCCONNEL J., *Psychologie, science de l'homme* Montréal, Les Editions HRW Ltée, 1980, pp. 185-221, (translation of *Psychology, The Human Science*, Holt, Rinehart and Wintson, 1978).

[VIL 06] VILLEGAS-MORAN F., CARRANZA O. and ANTUN J.P., "Supply chain dynamics, a case study on the structural causes of the Bullwhip Effect", *INGENIERIA Investigacion y Tecnologia*, vol. 7, no. 1, pp. 29-44, 2006.

[WIE 48] WIENER N., *Cybernetics. Or Control and Communication in the Animal and the Machine*, MIT Press, Cambridge, 1948.

[YAN 01] YAN L., "Impact of lead-time distribution on the bullwhip effect and supply chain performance", in *Proc. Americas Conference on Information Systems*, 2001.

[YUN 00] YUNG S.K., YANG C.C., LAU A.S.M. and YEN J., "Applying multi-agent technology to supply chain management", *Journal of Electronic Commerce Research*, vol. 1, no. 4, pp. 119-132, 2000.

2.5. Appendix 1

Description of the essential variables of the model

1) Level variables:

– Inventory_S0, S1 and S2:   *Current inventory at producer S0, suppliers S1 and S2.*

– Backlog_S0, S1 and S2:   *Unfilled orders at producer S0, suppliers S1 and S2.*

– Supply_S0, S1 and S2:   *Shipment sent by producer S0, suppliers S1 and S2.*

2) Rate variables:

– Receipt_rate_S0, S1 and S2:   *Rate of products received by S0, S1, S2.*

– Sale_rate_S0, S1 and S2:   *Rate of products sold by S0, S1, S2.*

– Backlog_rate_S0, S1 and S2:   *Rate of unfilled orders at S0, S1, S2.*

– Supply_rate_S0, S1 and S2:   *Rate of products shipment at S0, S1, S2.*

3) Auxiliary variables:

– Demand: *Customer demand.*

– Order_placed_S0, S1, S2:   *Number of orders placed by S0, S1, S2.*

– Order_sent_S0, S1, S2:   *Number of orders sent by S0, S1, S2.*

4) Constants:

– Coef_A: *Weighted factor for the gap between inventory and backlog.*

– Coef_B: *Weighted factor for the shipment level.*

– Smooth_time: *Time of correction.*

5) Glossary of functions:

– DELAY: *Delayed value of the input.*

– STEP: *One-time step change of specified height.*

– MIN: *Minimum value.*

– MAX: *Maximum value.*

– SMOOTH 1:   *First order exponential smoothing.*

Equations of the continuous simulation model

Level of inventory at S0, S1, S2:
Inventory_S0(t) = Inventory_S0(t - dt) + (Receipt_rate_S0 - Sale_rate_S0) * dt
INIT Inventory_S0 = 100
Receipt_rate_S0 = DELAY(Order_sent_S0,5,10)
Sale_rate_S0 = MIN(Inventory_S0+Receipt_rate_S0,Order_sent_S1+Backlog_S0)

Inventory_S1(t) = Inventory_S1(t - dt) + (Receipt_rate_S1 - Sale_rate_S1) * dt
INIT Inventory_S1 = 100
Receipt_rate_S1 = DELAY(Sale_rate_S0,5,10)
Sale_rate_S1 = MIN(Inventory_S1+Receipt_rate_S1,Order_sent_S2+Backlog_S1)

Inventory_S2(t) = Inventory_S2(t - dt) + (Receipt_rate_S2 - Sale_rate_S2) * dt
INIT Inventory_S2 = 100
Receipt_rate_S2 = DELAY(Sale_rate_S1,5,10)
Sale_rate_S2 = MIN(Inventory_S2+Receipt_rate_S2,Demand+Backlog_S2)

Level of unfilled orders at S0, S1 and S2
Backlog_S0(t) = Backlog_S0(t - dt) + (Backlog_rate_S0) * dt
INIT Backlog_S0 = 0
Backlog_rate_S0 = Order_sent_S1-Sale_rate_S0

Backlog_S1(t) = Backlog_S1(t - dt) + (Backlog_rate_S1) * dt
INIT Backlog_S1 = 0
Backlog_rate_S1 = Order_sent_S2-Sale_rate_S1

Backlog_S2(t) = Backlog_S2(t - dt) + (Backlog_rate_S2) * dt
INIT Backlog_S2 = 0
Backlog_rate_S2 = Demand-Sale_rate_S2

Shipment line at S0, S1, S2:
Supply_S0(t) = Supply_S0(t - dt) + (Supply_rate_S0) * dt
INIT Supply_S0 = 0
Supply_rate_S0 = Order_placed_S0-Receipt_rate_S0

Supply_S1(t) = Supply_S1(t - dt) + (Supply_rate_S1) * dt
INIT Supply_S1 = 0
Supply_rate_S1 = Order_placed_S1-Receipt_rate_S1

Supply_S2(t) = Supply_S2(t - dt) + (Supply_rate_S2) * dt
INIT Supply_S2 = 0
Supply_rate_S2 = Order_placed_S2-Receipt_rate_S2

Customer demand:
Demand = 10+STEP(10,15)

Number of orders placed by S0, S1, S2:
Order_placed_S0 = MAX(0,SMTH1(Order_sent_S1,Smooth_time)+Coef_A*(100-(Inventory_S0-Backlog_S0)-Coef_B*Supply_S0))
Order_placed_S1 = MAX(0,SMTH1(Order_sent_S2,Smooth_time)+Coef_A*(100-(Inventory_S1-Backlog_S1)-Coef_B*Supply_S1))
Order_placed_S2   =   MAX(0,SMTH1(Demand,Smooth_time)+Coef_A*(100-(Inventory_S2-Backlog_S2)-Coef_B*Supply_S2))

Number of orders sent by S0, S1, S2:
Order_sent_S0 = DELAY(Order_placed_S0,2,8)
Order_sent_S1 = DELAY(Order_placed_S1,2,8)
Order_sent_S2 = DELAY(Order_placed_S2,2,8)

Other parameters:
Coef_A = 0.25
Coef_B = 0.30
Smooth_time = 1
INITIAL TIME = 0
FINAL TIME = 100
TIME STEP = 1

Chapter 3

Discrete-event Simulation for Supply Chain Management

3.1. Discrete-event simulation and supply chain

3.1.1. *Introduction*

Numerous authors have identified discrete-event simulation as an effective tool for evaluating the performances of control policies of complex systems prior to their implementation. Simulation enables decision makers to perform powerful what-if analyses allowing them to correctly understand the system, to build appropriate decisions and to compare various operational alternatives. The ability to assess the possible impact of a decision on a given system and reconsider the decision when necessary are key elements that define a firm's competitiveness.

The exacerbated globalization of the economy is nowadays pushing managers to strive for further optimization of their limited resources and processes. This can be achieved if all the decision levels within a company cooperate and interact efficiently and if managers develop and pursue collaborations with their logistics partners. These new forms of doing business enhance the structural complexity of the system to be controlled and augment the difficulty of managing the conflicts resulting from local objectives versus global strategies.

For supply chain management purposes, there is no doubt that actual business efficiency depends on the extent of integration within each actor company and on

Chapter written by Valérie BOTTA-GENOULAZ, Jacques LAMOTHE, Florence PICARD, Fouad RIANE and Anthony VALLA.

the collaboration and coordination with suppliers and customers with a supply network.

Simulation is, in this context, a useful technique for evaluating potential designs, or potential changes in decisional or physical processes of a supply network according to several metrics.

It can be used for a local optimization based on local and single models representing the system. It can also be used to model complex systems, implementing different models, integrating optimization techniques and executed in parallel. Whichever way it is applied, the simulation technique makes it possible to take into account the complexity and the dynamic behavior of a supply chain and to consider the uncertainty related to its environment (e.g. customer demand, lead-time, bullwhip effect).

The ultimate success of supply chain simulation is determined by the modeler skills, the involvement of decision makers, the modeling capabilities of the simulation tool and the ability to qualify realistic and coherent inputs for the system. Numerous replications of the simulation model corresponding to possible situations can then be carried out in order to evaluate the robustness of the considered supply chain. Simulation does not guarantee an optimal solution and does not aim to. However, this technique offers the manager real help in establishing and evaluating the consequences of their choices.

This chapter provides a study of both discrete-event and time bucket simulation used for supply chain management and proposes case studies to illustrate the pivotal role that simulation can play as a technique to aid decisions. Several decision support problems dealing with supply chain management are associated with the design of a supply network, with the collaboration of decision makers in order to meet the required performance levels or with planning and risk management in uncertain environments.

3.1.2. Event-driven and time bucket-driven simulation for supply chains

Discrete event simulation aims at evaluating the evolution along the time of a system. It is based on some principles:

– a model of the system is created. This model expresses the usage or transformation of objects in order to make activities;

– objects are:

- either entities that are transformed by the activities: orders, products, customer demand, etc.,

- or resources used to make this transformation;

– state attributes are associated with the objects. The state of the system at a given instant is the set of the state attribute values of all the objects. These attributes can be:

- static: they do not evaluate along the time (customer order size, operation duration, etc.),

- variable: their value is modified during the simulation (number of products in an inventory, forecasted demand, etc.);

– an event characterizes the start of an activity at a given instant in time. It depicts how the state of the objects associated with the activity changes when it happens. It also expresses how other events are generated during or at the end of the activity;

– the principle of the simulation algorithm is:

1. initialize the system with objects, objects' initial attribute value, and a list of events,

2. select in the list the next event in time. Here, rules must be defined to distinguish events that happen at the same date,

3. update the system state (generate new objects, change objects' attributes) considering the consequences of the selected event,

4. post into the list, the events generated by the selected event. Go to 2 until the simulation final date is achieved.

Two approaches exist for managing the advance of time during a simulation:

– event-driven approach: in this approach it is assumed that the system changes are instantly generated by an event. Thus, the system state does not change between two events. The management of the list of events (point 2 in the algorithm above) guarantees the simulation of all the changes in the system state. In principle, this approach requires all the events that generate a state change to be modeled. Sometimes, this can limit the ability to make a simple model using time aggregation. Nevertheless, commercial discrete event simulation softwares are dedicated to this approach (ARENA, WITNESS, etc.). They "hide", from the user, the diversity of events to be managed, throughout the definition of macro-object models (of complex configurable machines with inventories, transfer systems, etc.);

– time bucket-driven approach: in this approach, the time is divided into periods of a given length, the time bucket. All the simulated events occur at the beginning of a time period. Here, the system state can change between two time periods. Thus, knowing the system state once all the events that occur at a given time period have been simulated, a simulation "period synthesizing" model must explain how the system state is obtained at the beginning of the next time period. All the activities that are carried out during the time bucket must be considered in this last model: physical flow transformations, but also some decisional or informational activities that are periodically launched with a shorter period than the time bucket. In this approach, state attributes represent either punctual quantities associated with resources (quantity in an inventory at the beginning of a time period), or flows expressed as quantities during a time bucket (available capacity, production, demand, orders, in process, in transport). In principle, this approach enables us to make models using long time buckets and thus an effective aggregation of time, while still having an effective simulation of periodical processes. On the other hand, it cannot model precisely short-term activities because they are rarely periodically launched.

Making a simulation model, especially for a system as large as a supply chain, necessitates making some assumptions that drive the model reduction. One of the major skills of the modeler is to be able to make such assumptions. Here systemic and enterprise modeling principles give key orientations.

In a systemic approach, the physical, the informational and the decisional sub-systems are distinguished from the environment. Usually, the simulation study mainly focuses on one of these sub-systems which is detailed, while the other sub-systems are only depicted with macro-activities and macro-objects or even considered in the environment. Characterizing this environment and its dynamics is a key problem of the modeler. In a supply chain context, such an environment describes: the market (how demand is generated; the market predictability or ability to be forecasted and the evolution of this predictability during the simulation; competition or not of actors on this market); results of upper decision levels (the whole decision sub-system is rarely simulated; thus, it is usually assumed that upper tactical or strategic decisions do not change during the simulation); raw material disposal at the last stage of the supply chain.

Enterprise modeling distinguishes two more points of view for modeling a system. The functional point of view enables us to select the functions of the system to be modeled (does sales management need to be modeled?) and the level of detail when describing these functions into processes and activities and when identifying entities. The organizational point of view underlines the organizational decomposition of the system. This is of primary interest in a supply chain simulation context. It drives the modeling question: which view of the system state does each organizational unit have?

The three examples depicted in the following underline these modeling issues. Section 3.2 focuses on the simulation of the physical subsystem in order to precisely evaluate physical flows that result from a supply chain strategic design optimization procedure. Section 3.3 is dedicated to the coordination of production management decisions in a supply chain with independent organizations. Section 3.4 focuses on the sales function and integrates various points of view.

3.2. Discrete-event simulation for supply chain redesign

3.2.1. *Problem definition*

The major problems encountered in supply chain redesign are the location problem (which consists for a multi-site business of determining the geographical position of its production and distribution facilities), the allocation problem (which concerns the determination of the activities to take place in and between the different facilities), the capacity problem (which seeks to determine the resources necessary to carry out the activities of the business within each facility) and finally the control problem (which makes it possible to specify the way the supply network must operate). All these problems are to be handled in an integrated way.

To solve the decision-aid problems relating to the redesign of a supply chain, several analytical approaches based mainly on mixed-integer programs are proposed in the literature (e.g. [GEO 74], [ARN 95], [JAY 01], [VID 01], [FAN 04], [JOL 04], [MEL 05], [MAR 05], [AMI 06]). These approaches require many simplifications in the modeling of the problem to be solved in a reasonable computational time. Several relevant factors for the redesign such as the multi-period aspect, the initial state of the supply network, the management policies, the lead-times, tactical elements or elements related to uncertain characters of the environment in which the company evolves are not taken into account. Moreover, concerning the solution approaches of these programs, most of those developed in the literature are only validated on fictitious problems of small size. This does not guarantee that these methods could find the optimal solution, or even a feasible solution of a good quality, for real problems in a reasonable computational time. To cope with the complexity inherent to supply chain systems, some simulation approaches (e.g. [VAN 01], [REI 04], [LAL 04]) and hybrid approaches combining optimization and simulation techniques ([KAR 00], [LEE 02], [DIN 04]) are developed. The majority of these approaches are either specific to a given subproblem or developed to optimize a part of the supply network.

3.2.2. Problem statement

The case study we consider in this part is based on two real life applications encountered in the pharmaceutical industry and the paper industry. The supply network of these two multi-site businesses is deeply developed in [PIR 05]. The two networks are quite similar in terms of their structure (number of sites, number of customers, etc.). For illustrative purposes, we created a fictitious network similar to the two real ones, depicted in Figure 3.1. The multi-site business consists of 16 facilities spread over different geographical areas in Europe. Among these sites, 6 are manufacturing plants and 10 are distribution centers. These latter sites deliver the finished products to 20 customer zones. Each zone places orders. The multi-site enterprise produces a wide range of finished products. We aggregate these products into 20 product groups. These product groups are manufactured from 25 groups of components and require different kinds of production resources, which are present in various proportions in the production sites. To prepare the customers' orders, the company uses one type of preparation resource, which is present in various proportions in the distribution sites. Components and finished products are kept in stock at the sites. These stocks are replenished according to a given inventory policy. The multi-site business is supplied upstream by 10 suppliers.

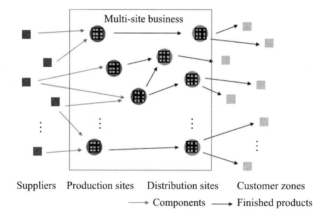

Suppliers   Production sites   Distribution sites   Customer zones
⟶ Components ⟶ Finished products

Figure 3.1. *Supply network structure*

We have observed for different real life applications that multi-site businesses re-structure their supply network in such a way that they improve their efficiency and develop competitive advantages. The structure of the supply network is characterized by the number, the location, the size, the mission and the operating mode of the different entities which constitute it. The redesign of a supply network implies changing one or several of these characteristics.

3.2.3. *Decision aid approach*

We developed a decision aid approach for supply networks of multi-site enterprise redesign and planning. As for a certain number of problems (e.g. scheduling, production planning [KIM 01], [RIA 01]), the effectiveness of the combination of discrete-event simulation and analytical methods have been proven, we opted for a decision aid approach integrating these two techniques. We adopted an iterative and integrated approach because on the one hand, a mathematical model does not enable us to take into account all the characteristics of the problem (e.g. control policies) and on the other hand, the simulation technique does not enable us to guarantee the optimality of the considered design. The principle of the decision aid approach is illustrated in Figure 3.2.

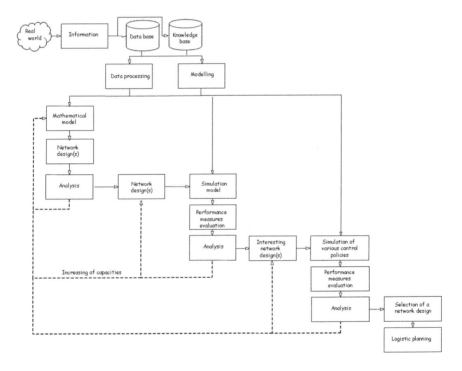

Figure 3.2. *Principle of the developed decision aid approach*

From a certain amount of data extracted from the real system, and based on the experience of the managers, an analysis study of the current state of the system is conducted and a linear mixed-integer program can be instantiated and solved. An analysis of the results provided by this program is carried out by the manager in order to identify a set of profitable supply network designs. Next, the obtained designs enable the instantiation of a discrete-event simulation model which reproduces the dynamic behavior of the studied supply network. This reproduction is produced in a detailed way. New elements such as control policies, lead-times or some random factors affecting the supply network are taken into account. The simulation model is run for several replications of the stochastic parameters of the model. At the end of each simulation run, several performance measures are evaluated. These measures notably inform the manager about the profit and the provided service level of his business. One of these designs can be selected for a deep and elaborate analysis (adjustment of the different parameters of the considered control policies). If the evaluated designs are not satisfactory for the manager, new supply network designs can be generated using the same mathematical model with a different instantiation and the re-examining or re-adjusting of some parameters such as the capacity of the production or distribution resources. We can then run new simulations for detailed evaluation.

3.2.4. *Models of the decision aid approach*

The mixed-integer programming model and the simulation model constituting the decision aid approach are complementary and concern different decisional levels: the mathematical model is a strategic/tactical model and the simulation model is a tactical/operational model. These two models are based on the same modeling framework of the supply network.

The mathematical program is a multi-commodity, multi-echelon and multi-period program. This model is generic. The solution of the mathematical program enables the decision maker to determine, simultaneously and for each considered period of time, the state of the total system as manifested in the openings and closings of facilities, the available capacity of the resources in each site, the investments and disinvestments in capacity in each site, the material flows between the suppliers and the production sites, the material flows between sites, and between the sites and the customers, as well as production plans. All these decisions are made in order to maximize the after-tax profit of the multi-site business. The interested reader can find a detailed description of the mathematical model and the approaches used in [PIR 05].

The simulation model reproduces the dynamics of the supply network and the circulation of its information and material flows in and between the sites. We developed this model in order to evaluate in-depth the effectiveness of a certain number of network designs and to evaluate various control policies. In addition to the set of production and distribution sites, a network design is characterized by an allocation of the components and the finished products to the sites, by the list of the resources available in each site, by the capacity of the resources for each given time period and by the parameters of the considered control policies.

3.2.5. *Discrete-event simulation model*

The simulation model is developed to be as generic as possible so that it can be used to simulate supply networks with various structures. It is supported by the discrete-event RAO (Resource – Action – Operation) simulator which is based on the RAO method for presenting knowledge about complex discrete systems and processes [ART 98]. In RAO, the studied system is represented as a set of resources. Each resource is characterized by a set of parameters. The resources interact in order to process a set of operations which are described by modified production rules (If (conditions) Then (action 1) Wait (time interval) Then (action 2)). In the following, we describe in detail the resources of the model, the logic of the simulated process and the performance measures calculated during each simulation run.

3.2.5.1. *Resources*

Among the resources used to simulate the supply network, we can distinguish those which describe the structure of the network and those which represent the information and material that flow in the network. The first are permanent resources i.e. they exist during the entire duration of simulation. The second are temporary resources because they have a limited life span and are destroyed during simulation.

The simulation model requires the definition of five permanent resources. The first one, called "*supply network*" is associated with the supply chain. The four others are attached to each type of node of the network. They are called "*supplier*", "*production site*", "*distribution site*" and "*customer*". Each of these permanent resources has its own mission and is characterized by a set of variable parameters (e.g. identification number, working state, capacity, available quantity in stock) whose values can be modified during a simulation run. These resources share common information (e.g. distance between nodes, lead-times, bill of materials, consumption of resources, costs).

To model exchanged information and material flows in the supply network, we define three types of temporary resources: "*demand*", "*replenishment order*" and "*production order*". These resources are characterized by a set of variable parameters (e.g. state, required quantity, arrival date, allocated production site).

3.2.5.2. *Simulated processes*

The general logic of the simulation model is illustrated in Figure 3.3, which represents the circulation of the information and the material flows in and between the entities of the supply network. This representation starts from the customers to the suppliers and focuses on the information flows. We take an interest in these flows because they trigger the production, distribution and transportation activities.

At the beginning of each period, the customers express their demands concerning a given finished product. These demands are then allocated to a distribution site and treated depending on the availability of the requested quantity in stock, on the availability of the resources necessary for the preparation, on the internal orders and inventory control policies. The execution of the treatment operation can take several periods of time. At the beginning of each period, the concerned inventory and the available capacity of the specified resources are updated. As soon as an order is prepared, it is shipped to the customer concerned. The transportation lead-time depends on the distance between distribution sites and customer locations.

Inventories in the distribution sites mainly concern finished products. The level of these stocks decreases according to the demands allocated to the sites. At certain time periods, these inventories must be replenished. Consequently, a replenishment order is placed by the relevant distribution site. This order notably stipulates the finished product and the desired quantity. Next, the order is allocated to a production site that manufactures the requested product. Finally, this allocation generates a production order for the selected production site.

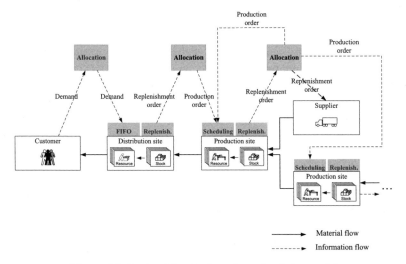

Figure 3.3. *Logic of functioning of our simulation model*

When a production site receives a production order, this site begins by setting aside the components necessary to manufacture the required quantity of the desired finished product. According to the availability of these components, the availability of the necessary manufacturing resources and the internal control policies, the production is launched. This operation can take several periods of time. At the beginning of each period, the concerned component inventories and the available capacity of the necessary resources are updated. When the desired quantity of the production order is fulfilled, the products are transported to the appropriate distribution site. The duration of the transport operation depends on the distance involved. At the end of this operation, the stock of the distribution site is updated.

The production sites have stocks of components. The consumption of these components is related to the production activities which take place at the sites. At certain time periods, these inventories must be replenished according to a local replenishment policy. A replenishment order is then created. This order specifies the required components and the desired quantities. The order is transmitted to the multi-site business. Based on which component is required, this order is either allocated to a production site which manufactures the component or sent on to a supplier which provides the component. In the first case, the multi-site business generates a production order and transmits it to the concerned production site. The arrival of this production order triggers a series of operations of the same type as those carried out when it is a production order related to a finished product. In the second case, i.e. the allocation of the replenishment order to a supplier, the replenishment order is transmitted to the selected supplier. The required quantity of the component is delivered to the production site after a lead-time related to the transport activity. This lead-time depends on the distance to travel. At the end of this operation, the inventory of the involved production site is updated.

3.2.5.3. *Simulation and decision-making*

The operational decision-making plays an important role in the simulation model. In fact, following the working logic of the system described above, we need, at certain moments during the simulation, to make choices in order to develop the system. These choices are made according to the current state of the system and respecting the minimization or maximization of one or several criteria. These decisions points are indicated in gray rectangles in Figure 3.3. The different decisions mentioned are expressed as rules that make it possible: to allocate the customer demands to the distribution sites, to replenish distribution orders to the appropriate production sites, to allocate the replenishment orders to the production sites or to the suppliers, to determine the order in which the customer's orders are treated in each distribution site, to determine when and how much a distribution site must replenish its inventories, to determine the scheduling of the production orders in each production site and to determine when and how much a production site must reload its inventories. Some of these decision rules are quite simple (e.g. handling of the customer orders in the order of their arrival at the distribution site). Others are more complex and require the evaluation of parameters such as the probable tardiness of a demand delivery or the probable moment when there is a stock outage.

3.2.5.4. *Performance indicators*

Various performance measures are evaluated during the simulation. These measures make it possible to estimate the effectiveness of the supply network design being evaluated. Among the observed measures, we can distinguish financial measures on the one hand and non-financial measures on the other hand. The first relate to the costs and revenues. These measures are used in order to evaluate the profit of the multi-site business. The observed non-financial measures refer to the service level, the use rate of production or preparation resources and the lead-times.

3.2.6. *Illustrative application*

We applied the decision aid approach to the case described in the introduction. Table 3.1 contains the characteristics of the mathematical and simulation approaches. The spatiotemporal granularity of the two approaches is different. We know all the data necessary for the execution of the model, except for those used for the simulation model since they result from the design obtained after the mathematical program has been solved (i.e. the state of the sites, the available capacity of the resources and a parameter of the inventory management rules).

	Mathematical approach	Simulation approach
Suppliers	10	10
Sites	16	16
Demand zones	20	20
Finished products	20	20
Components	25	25
Periods of time	5 (years)	365 (days)
Production site resources	1	5
Distribution site resources	1	1
Demand	Deterministic	Stochastic
Material flows	Optimization of the flows	Dynamic allocation
Control policies	No	Yes

Table 3.1. *Characteristic of the mathematical and simulation approaches*

The multi-site business seeks to maximize its profit under the constraint of satisfying customer demands. In the simulation model, we check that this constraint is satisfied by examining the performance measure called "order fill rate" which indicates the percentage of demands that are satisfied the same day or the day after their arrival.

We started by simulating the existing design of the supply network of the multi-site business (i.e. all the sites are open and the capacity of the resources is the initial capacity). The parameters of the management rules used by the company are as follows. For the inventory management rules, we should specify that inventories are replenished when the available quantity of the product is lower than a minimum level and that the ordered quantity is the quantity necessary to refill the stock. Therefore, two parameters are necessary: the minimum level and the capacity of the considered stock. In our application, the minimum level of stock is equal to 11 times the daily average demand for this stock and its capacity is equal to double the minimum level (i.e. 22 days of consumption). To determine the order of treatment of the production orders in the production sites, the business uses the earliest due date (EDD) rule. Table 3.2 contains the observed performance measures for the existing design. For this design, the order fill rate is about 94% and the profit of the multi-site business is about €865 million. Let us note that for this design, we studied the variability of the performance measures. We carried out 30 simulation runs. In Table 3.2, we indicated the mean values of the observed performance measures and the standard deviation of the means expressed as a percentage. This table shows that the observed measures vary little from one simulation run to another.

The integrated use of the mathematical program and the simulation model enabled us to identify, for the studied supply network design problem, a design that, compared to the existing network, improves the performances of the multi-site enterprise. Table 3.2 contains the observed performance measures for this best found design. This design leads to an increase of about 5% to the profit of the business and to an increase of about 0.5% for the order fill rate. This new design involves closing one production site and four distribution sites and modifying the capacities of the existing sites. The set of experiments to find this design was carried out on a Pentium IV, 3.4GHz, 1Gob. This cost us approximately 5 days of computation and allowed us to gain about €45 million.

In order to determine whether the observed performance measures for the existing design and the best design found are significantly different, we carried out an equality test of the means[1] [DAN 98]. For each performance measure shown in

---

1 The used test is valid only when the number of observations for each design is equal to or higher than 30. In our case, we carried out for each design 30 simulation runs being characterized by the base of the random number generator.

Table 3.2, we tested the H0 assumption = the performance measure for the existing design has the same value as those obtained by the best design found. The sixth column of Table 3.2 contains the values of the observed statistics Z. Under H0, the statistics Z follows a distribution N(0,1). For a significant level of 0.05, we reject H0 if |Z| > 1.96. After analyzing the values of the statistics Z, we concluded that the existing design and the best design found are significantly different.

	Existing design		Best design found		
	Means	Standard deviation means (%)	Means	Standard deviation means (%)	Statistic Z
Costs and receipts					
Profit of the multi-site business (M€)	865	0.025	910	0.033	-206.85
Service					
Order fill rate (%)	93.8	0.016	94.4	0.215	-3.25
Utilization of the resources					
Utilization rate of the production resources (%)	76.7	0	86,6	0	-272.65
Utilization rate of the preparation resources (%)	84.8	0	87,6	0	-102.36
Other measures					
Amount of stock out	2092	0.236	678	1.276	144.44
Average duration of stock out (time period)	3.04	0.296	64,2	0.996	-97.27

Table 3.2. *Comparison of the performance measures obtained for the existing supply network design and the best design found by the proposed decision aid approach*

The proposed approach being a decision aid approach, it is the best design found that we would suggest to the manager of the multi-site business. It is up to the manager to analyze if the modifications of the layout of the supply network related to this new design are really worthwhile by taking into account other factors which are not considered in our models (i.e. social factors, ecology, etc.) and which cannot be valued easily.

3.3. Discrete-event simulation for cooperation process risk analysis

3.3.1. *Context of the study*

In a recent review of "supply chain risk management" [TAN 06], Tang defines the "supply chain risks" as the consequences of some unpredicted events. He distinguishes the operational risks, which are due to the inherent uncertainties of demand, supply, production or costs, from major disruption caused by natural and man-made disasters such as earthquakes or economic crises.

The telecom market is subject to such unpredictable fluctuations (political, financial crises). Rapid changes in the sector can occur that result in the disappearance, splitting or emergence of actors. A huge competition among actors exists in product development, marketing and logistic efficiency. Products have a lifecycle of a few months while the market demand has a marked seasonal peak in December. Even technologies have short lifecycles which forces businesses to strictly control their investment in capacity. Consequently, actors are resistant to contractual structures binding their responsibility and cooperation.

Even if there are forecasts, managers involved in a telecom supply chain cannot be really confident in these forecasts and are therefore forced to adopt specific behaviors to control operational and disruption risks. Such behaviors will undoubtedly have consequences on their performance but also all along the connected supply chains: studies on the bullwhip effect [GEA 06] have shown how decision behaviors can increase or reduce the phenomenon. Supply chain risk management [TAN 06] supposes the establishment of cooperative processes in the chain, through the exchange/sharing of reliable information between the actors so as to ensure profitability and continuity. Recently, some supply chain leader actors or sector related organizations have encouraged initiatives such as RosettaNet (www.rosettanet.org), Voluntary Inter-industry Commerce Standards Association (www.vics.org) and ODETTE (www.odette.org), and scientific literature has provided papers [KUK 04], [DAN 06] dedicated to cooperation study and analysis.

In this context, a risk evaluation approach is proposed that embeds a "supply chain management simulator" so that a manager (or a set of managers) can evaluate cooperation policies on a supply chain. This approach consists of:

1. defining the supply chain under study and its environment;

2. defining admissible cooperation policies;

3. defining possible market scenarios;

4. simulating the supply chain managements that result from the combination of cooperative processes, actors' own behavior when considering the various market scenarios;

5. synthesizing and analyzing risks.

A key point of this approach is the notion of "cooperation policy". It includes a cooperative process but also how managers react to it. It is thus defined as:

– the cooperative process that links the planning processes of the actors of a supply chain (exchange, sharing of forecasts, demand, supply, etc.);

– but also the individual behavior of managers that are involved in planning processes, that assume the various risks and decisions, and that make an actor's planning processes so specific.

The current study was carried out in association with a semiconductor supplier's manager who was concerned with the capacity adjustment decision in a telecom supply chain. He mainly focuses on the capacity adjustment strategies concerning the level of workforce and equipment. This corresponds to the decision taken in a sales and operations planning (SOP).

At this level of decision, a very aggregated point of view of the supply chain is considered: decisions are modeled using time bucket plans. Therefore a time bucket simulation is chosen to measure the consequences of the successive plans. The resulting simulation tool, called LogiRisk [MAH 06], was developed in the Perl Language (www.perl.org). In the following, the simulation tool is first described, then, its application on a risk evaluation example is explained.

3.3.2. The simulator's principles

The choice of the simulator's structure comes from various aspects:

– an objective of the simulation is to analyze the consequences of decision behavior of managers involved in planning processes. Consequently, when describing a planning process, some of the activities refer to traditional operation management calculation, while others model the way a manager interprets conflicting results of these calculations;

– the simulator is centered on the capacity decisions that take place in supply chain management. Therefore, the SOP process is focused on. All the entities of the simulation model are aggregated like in a SOP process: each actor is modeled with one bottleneck resource, raw material and finished product inventories; flows are modeled as quantity per time bucket; and product references are product family references. The most important output of a SOP is a capacity plan (see Figure 3.5).

It includes the manager behavior when comparing the desired-capacity plan (which is calculated to meet the customer demand forecasts calculated at the beginning of the process) with the previous capacity plan (validated by the manager in the previous SOP process). Here, the behavior model (Figure 3.8) translates the manager's lack of confidence in the forecast process through a percentage of reluctance to change a capacity plan;

– the simulator also considers the quicker dynamics of management control loops (as defined in MRP II or APS systems) that take place between the strategic to the operational decision level. Therefore, mid-term (MPS) and short-term (STP and R&IM) decision planning processes are also modeled but in an aggregated way: products and resources are aggregated at the same level as in the SOP process (product families and bottleneck resource);

– for the mid-term planning process (MTP), the principle is to model the decision process realised at the beginning of a time period and that results in demand-forecast plans, production plans, supply plans and inventory plans. These plans are expressed in horizon and time bucket granularities that are different from those generated in an SOP process. Nevertheless, it is the same process as the SOP but without capacity decision and a greater precision;

– short-term planning processes (STP and R&IM) are nearly continuous. In a time bucket simulation, their models synthesize the result of all the decisions taken during a time bucket. Consequently, the models of short-term processes translate the result of a management philosophy and not a decision process. Here two processes have been distinguished. The STP process (Figure 3.6) models the production an actor tries to launch during a time bucket and the resulting supply orders when considering its push (priority to the MPS production and supply plans) or pull (priority to customer demand and planned inventories) philosophy. The R&IM process (Figure 3.7) models an actor's behavior when facing stock-outs of raw materials (RM) or of finished products (FP). Finally, the material flow simulation model sums up the flows during a simulation time bucket that results from the R&IM decisions;

– concerning the cooperation protocol, we focus on the customer supply plans that can be sent or not to suppliers. This is represented in Figure 3.4 as the Customer Forecast Plan that enters the SOP and MPS planning processes and the supply plans that are output. In order to make the demand forecasts, Figure 3.5 underlines that SOP and MPS processes use the customer plans if sent by customers, and otherwise demand histories with endogenous forecasting methodology.

Finally, the behavior of an actor in the supply chain is modeled with one physical process and four planning processes as shown in Figure 3.4. The detailed model equations for the various processes can be found in [MAH 06]. Each process has its own decision horizon, time bucket decision period and start-up frequency. Short-term planning and physical processes have a one simulation time bucket horizon, decision period and frequency.

Consequently all the events managed in the simulator are process start-up events. These events are put into a "stack of events". A rule is defined to sequence this stack. It fixes not only the precedence between the five processes of each actor but also the precedence of the same process for different actors. For the SOP, MPS and STP processes, this last precedence corresponds to the exchanges of supply plans and the sending of demand orders: customer SOP, MPS or STP processes have higher priority than suppliers processes. On the other hand, from the R&IM and physical process point of view, this precedence translates the fact that no decision, thus no production and no delivering, can be made before the effective deliveries from suppliers are known. The priority is given to R&IM and physical processes of the suppliers.

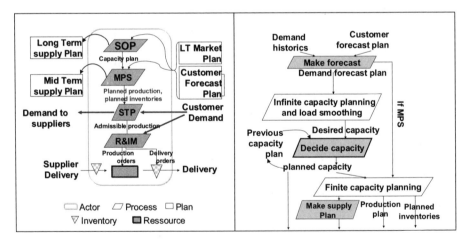

Figure 3.4. *Processes of an actor*   **Figure 3.5.** *SOP or MPS processes*

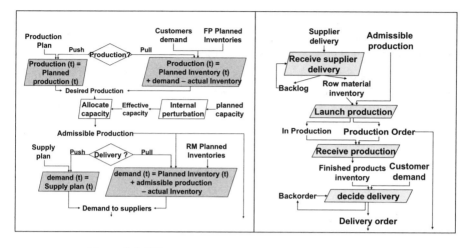

Figure 3.6. *STP process*   **Figure 3.7.** *R&IM process*

If (t< L) then

   planned_capacity(t) = previous_capacity_plan(t)

else

   planned_capacity(t) = (1-p).previous_capacity_plan(t) + p.desired_capacity(t)

L = delay before any change in capacity

p = percentage of reluctance to change a capacity plan

Figure 3.8. *SOP manager behavior model*

3.3.3. *Example of application*

This example is a simple case study which the semiconductor supplier's manager asked for when he started to use the simulation tool and the risk evaluation methodology.

Step 1: supply chain definition

The system under study is a single product, three stage supply chain in which capacity decisions must be taken dynamically (see Figure 3.9). It models a traditional telecom supply chain that includes 3 categories of actors:

– the Global Operator (GO) is responsible for his network coverage and the associated phones provided to the customers: he manages an inventory;

– the Original Equipment Manufacturer (OEM) assembles the different items of equipment (e.g. hard-drive, printers, monitors, portable phones, etc.): he can quickly adapt his capacity and process is rapid (1 week);

– the semiconductor supplier (SCS) manufactures the basic electronic components (chips) used by the OEM; the process is long and complex (10 weeks). The transport (4 weeks) between the SCS and the OEM includes a final assembly which is not managed in this study.

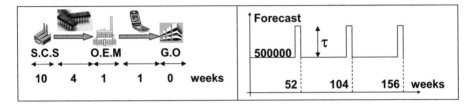

Figure 3.9. *Telecom supply chain structure*   **Figure 3.10.** *Market forecasts profile*

Step 2: cooperation policy definition

Concerning the cooperation protocol, we were interested in evaluating the added value of exchanging supply forecasts. Therefore, two cooperation protocols have been tested: exchange/no-exchange of all the supply plans between the actors.

Concerning the SCS manager's behavior, we wanted to measure the consequences of a manager's reluctance to change the capacity as defined in the SOP manager behavior model (in Figure 3.8) with $p_{SCS} \in [0.5; 0.75; 1.0]$.

Concerning the OEM and GO behavior, the objective was to evaluate the interest of a pull versus a push philosophy for production and supply. No particular behavior was analyzed for the SOP and MPS processes.

Step 3: market scenario definition

The average demand is 500,000 products per week over the first 11 months of the year. There is a more or less significant peak of the market demand in December (see Figure 3.10). This peak is expressed via a percentage of increase τ with regard to the demand of the other weeks. τ could be: weak: 10%, average: 50%, significant: 100%.

We also take into account the reliability of the demand with regard to the forecasts. This demand is calculated with a normal law $Demand\,(t) = N(Forecast\,(t), \sigma)$, where $\sigma \in \{0; 10,000; 50,000; 100,000; 250,000\}$.

Step 4: simulations run

The 180 (= 2 protocols*3 p_{SCS}*2 philosophies*3 τ *5σ) simulations were run on a 600 week horizon ($\approx$ 12 years). The first 4 years were necessary to balance the simulation; the performance assessment horizon was [208, 415] (4 years); the last 4 years were omitted in order to avoid side effects.

For each actor and each simulation, a total cost is calculated as the sum of production costs, capacity acquisition costs, stock holding costs and stock-out costs with the weights defined in Table 3.3.

Step 5: risk analysis

The definition of the cooperation policies defines a game (in the sense of game theory) in which:

– the cooperation protocol is a decision that all the actors take together and in a first time;

– then, each actor can choose his own behavior, p_{SCS} for the SCS and the push/pull philosophy for the other actors.

This can be formalized in a decision tree. The difficulty is to define the utility function that aggregates the risks for one cooperation policy. It aggregates the measures and costs relative to the various market scenarios that have been simulated for that cooperation policy. Figure 3.11 shows the resulting decision tree if each actor associates its risk evaluation with a mean cost. In this case, for each cooperation protocol (shared/not-shared forecasts), the behavior of each actor's managers depends on the choice of the others. So that the resulting cooperation policy can be defined by an equilibrium in which each manager optimizes his interest given the decision of the others, this is a Nash equilibrium which is represented in gray for both cooperation protocols in Figure 3.11. The table at the root of the tree shows that actors have to choose together one of the two resulting cooperation policies (in gray) which are not the global optimal policy.

Costs parameters	SCS	OEM	GO
Stock holding (*cs*)	1	3	4
Stock out (*cso*)	2	6	8
Capacity acquisition (*cc*)	4	1	0
Production (cp)	3	1	0

Table 3.3. *Cost structure for the total cost*

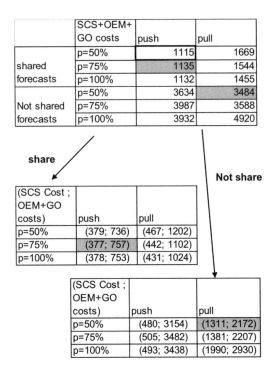

SCS+OEM+ GO costs		push	pull
shared forecasts	p=50%	1115	1669
	p=75%	1135	1544
	p=100%	1132	1455
Not shared forecasts	p=50%	3634	3484
	p=75%	3987	3588
	p=100%	3932	4920

share

Not share

(SCS Cost ; OEM+GO costs)	push	pull
p=50%	(379; 736)	(467; 1202)
p=75%	(377; 757)	(442; 1102)
p=100%	(378; 753)	(431; 1024)

(SCS Cost ; OEM+GO costs)	push	pull
p=50%	(480; 3154)	(1311; 2172)
p=75%	(505; 3482)	(1381; 2207)
p=100%	(493; 3438)	(1990; 2930)

Figure 3.11. *The final decision tree*

This small example underlines the interests and limits of the simulation model adopted in this approach:

– actors can experiment with a cooperation protocol and the consequences in terms of changes in the managers' behavior. This can be evaluated from various points of view depending on the way risks are built and aggregated: decision theory proposes various criteria that can help the risk quantification;

– actors can evaluate different types of risks (market evolution, adopting a cooperation protocol, a manager's choice of a behavior), organize them in a decision tree and analyze them from different points of view: the supply chain interest, an actor's own interest;

– limits appear in the definition of a cooperation protocol: by now, the tool does not consider any data shared among all the actors of a supply chain; nor does it model return information flows from suppliers to customers for the validation of forecasts;

– this simulation approach shows that manager behavior hardly impacts a supply chain. Modeling this behavior when the information flows are numerous becomes difficult. This is a major point for future investigations;

– results also depend on the model of the environment of the supply chain: the market behavior, the behavior of competitors on the market.

Finally, a key point which interests the simulation has not been developed here. This is all the analysis of the dynamics of inventories, stock-outs, production orders, capacities and plans that a manager can make in order to verify that results make sense so that he can consider the simulation model as realistic. As various control loops are modeled, he can track particular phenomena and verify that they have been taken into account.

3.4. Discrete-event simulation for business process reengineering

The purpose of this section is to present a methodology for business process reengineering (BPR) based on a simulation approach in order to establish an efficient diagnosis of a given business process in a supply chain context.

In section 3.4.1, we introduce the methodology that defines a former simulation model, then constructs a diagnosis and identifies possible other malfunctioning and finally evaluates the relevance of different solutions. In section 3.4.2, we present an application of the method to the order-fulfillment business process of a case study in the food industry. We conclude in section 3.4.3 with a discussion on the contribution of discrete-event simulation in such problems and propose some perspectives about the use of event-driven simulation for business processes.

3.4.1. *Methodology*

The objective of the proposed methodology is to establish a diagnosis of a business process in a supply chain context. It is made up of five steps, which can be gathered into three main stages: modeling, simulation and diagnosis, and evaluation, as proposed in Figure 3.12 [VAL 05].

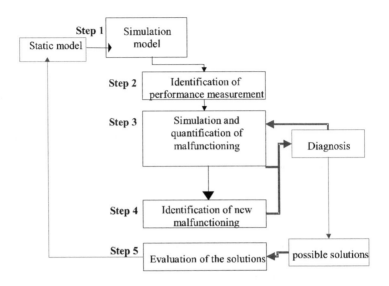

Figure 3.12. *Methodology for business process optimization*

3.4.1.1. *Modeling*

The objective of this stage is the translation of a business process into a model ready to be simulated. This major stage could be carried through to a successful conclusion using the following linking of actions:

– precise definition of the business process: tasks, resources, events and simulation entities;

– validation of the dynamic information required: task delay (using a stochastic distribution if necessary), properties of the simulation entities (initial values, costs, etc.), statistical distribution of appearance of the simulation entity, definition of the simulation parameters;

– definition of the performance measurement. The objective is to define the key indicators that will measure the performance. Considering a business process, they could be defined at two levels. They could evaluate the performance of either a single task at a local level (a productivity indicator, for example) or the whole business (a global lead-time for example). Those indicators will also be used for the validation of the simulation model. They must correspond to existing indicators in the company or be clearly understandable by the experts of the business process;

– validation of the model. A specific simulation is launched, ideally corresponding to a well-known situation in the past. The business experts must validate the behavior of the business process according to the indicators defined previously or a specific measurement specifically calculated. This is sometimes difficult because of a lack of data, mainly concerning the variability of task delay.

3.4.1.2. *Simulation and diagnosis*

This stage refers to the execution of the simulation model and the diagnosis of the business process. The objective consists of the identification and quantification of the malfunctioning of the business process studied. The four major actions to be carried out are the following:

– launching of a simulation run of the business process;

– analysis of the results. The dynamic information describing the behavior of the business process is extracted and analyzed. The business process is followed from the beginning to the end. At each step, specific elements are checked: waiting time, queue size, resource availability;

– evaluation of potential malfunction. Other potential malfunctions of the business process could have been previously detected. It could come from the static business process analysis or brought by a member of the analysis team. If the malfunction has not been found by the analysis or the results of the simulation, a specific analysis is carried out;

– quantification of a malfunction. Each malfunction identified by the analysis is precisely described. The objective is to measure the impact on the business process performance (helped by the indicators). For this, simulation data are used and specific runs with a modified model could be launched. This information will be helpful in order to give priority to their resolution.

3.4.1.3. *Evaluation of different solutions*

The objective is the evaluation of the relevance of different solutions for the business process improvement. The possible solutions are considered as entry data. Firstly, it is necessary to build a reference of the initial situation. For this, a simulation run is launched on the initial model and the results of the indicators recorded.

Then, a simulation model corresponding to a possible solution is defined, the simulation is launched and the results are recorded. This action must be repeated for each possible solution.

Finally, performances of the different solutions are compared with the reference. The decision could be difficult because solutions could have consequences on each other.

3.4.2. *Application*

This section demonstrates and evaluates the pertinence of the proposed methodology by applying it to a specific case study, a firm in the food industry. This medium-sized company is faced with a growing activity, uncertainty and seasonal aspect of demand since it delivers to more than 15,000 clients on the five continents. An internal supply chain business process-oriented analysis [VAL 04] has been launched in order to increase customer satisfaction and identify clear possible actions with the malfunction noticed.

3.4.2.1. *Description of the business process*

This business process starts when the order arrives and ends when the order is finally accepted in the information system of the company. In this case, we do not consider the availability of the products, the picking and delivery delay. This business process deals with more than 60,000 orders and 15,000 clients in two different ways:

– unconnected: orders are integrated via a CRM (customer relationship management) software. The orders are captured by a sales and marketing person (named here the VRP) using a computer. Then, the computer logs at regular intervals, the orders integrated in the central system ready to be prepared;

– connected: a sales assistant takes orders in a central customer service. They are integrated immediately and ready to be prepared.

It is important to note that some erroneous orders can be captured by the CRM system. In this case, the order is rejected by the central system and an assistant must carry out an order resumption in the central system.

A global view of the business process studied is presented in Figure 3.13.

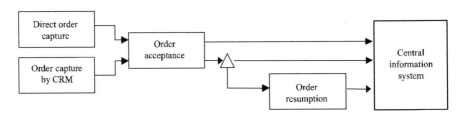

Figure 3.13. *Global view of the business process studied*

3.4.2.2. *Application of the modeling stage*

The internal supply chain of the company had been previously described using business processes [VAL 04]. The software used was ARIS Toolset, an event-driven object-oriented modeling tool specialized on the business process modeling [SCH 98].

All the work dealing with simulation has been performed using Arena software. It is a discrete-event simulation tool produced by Rockwell Software and widely used in industry [KEL 98]. Therefore, the first action was to set up a translation table from ARIS objects to Arena objects. This also allowed us to define a clear modeling framework.

The simulation of this specific business process needed to complete the simulation model with dynamic data. This was carried out with the modeling group previously formed [VAL 04].

The performance indicators chosen were the following:

– lead-time of realization: we record the time at each modification of the order, from the arrival to its final acceptance. The indicator chosen is the average realization lead-time, which corresponds to the difference between arriving time and final acceptance time;

– resource workload: we identify the different resources and record their occupation rate. We have chosen to record the workload rate of each resource corresponding to the rate of occupation time / total time.

The simulation model was validated using the company's historical data as reference. A set of data representing one week of activity has been defined. Then, managers validated the simulation results according to the indicators (mainly the resource workload), which corresponded to their experience.

3.4.2.3. *Application of the simulation and diagnosis stage*

The analysis stage began with a static analysis. According to a BPR-based methodology developed in [VAL 04], the analysis group studied the business process. Four malfunctions were identified:

– numerous resumptions of orders taken by CRM;

– CRM order integration delay;

– no delivery information given to the client;

– no visibility of order remainder.

Then, runs were launched in order to simulate the business process. The analysis of indicators allowed us to identify an additional malfunction. Considering the resource workload more precisely, and launching further simulation, we identified a waiting time on one specific resource: the "assistant". Its average workload was 41%, which is not problematic. However, just after the CRM order integration, there is a period of resource saturation. Therefore, these orders can wait for the availability of the resource, slow down the business process and have a significant impact on its performance.

Once the malfunction is defined, the next step consists of its quantification. For that, the model is used and several simulation runs are launched. The difference of results is significant considering the different malfunctions:

– resumption of orders taken by CRM. In the simulation, the resumption of orders corresponds to a basic stage of the process. Working on this malfunction means designing a new business process without this stage or decreasing the resumption of the orders. Therefore, we have modeled two versions of the process: the former (Model 1) representing the business process without resumption of orders, and the latter (Model 2) with a decrease of the resumption of the orders;

– the delay in CRM order integration. In the business process, the CRM orders are queueing for the time of the integration, and when it is over, all the orders can go on to the next step. For the quantification of this malfunction, we have designed two versions of the business process: the former (Model 3) where there is no delay (the orders have no waiting time for integration), the latter (Model 4) where there is one hour of time between integration instead of two (quicker integration of the orders).

Unfortunately, we were not able to quantify the other malfunctions: "no delivery information given to the client" and "no visibility of order remainder". The required simulation data were not available (client information). The benefits of the resolution of these malfunctions are in the relationship of the company with its clients. It might improve the customer's satisfaction and may increase the demand. This information concerning the behavior of clients could hardly be modeled in a business process simulation. The definition of the information given to the client and the order remainder visibility are "structural" problems depending on strategic decisions. It seems that there is no real advantage to using simulation in such cases. The solution of these malfunctions comes within the competence of the top management of the company.

In each case, we simulate the model for a period of 2 weeks (10 days). Table 3.4 gives the experimental results of the simulation of the four models.

Model			Average lead-time (hours/order)	Use of resources (%)		
				Total	Assistant	VRP
Reference	Standard model		0.951	69.755	41.85	27.905
Test 1 (resumption of CRM orders)	model 1	no resumption	0.934	55.892	28.851	27.041
	model 2	50% off on resumption	0.937	65.186	36.411	28.775
Test 2 (waiting integration of CRM orders)	model 3	no wait	0.154	71.467	42.897	28.57
	model 4	more integration	0.684	68.368	40.645	27.723

Table 3.4. *Results of quantification of malfunctioning*

For Test 1, we can observe a substantial reduction in the total workload of resources due to the decrease of order resumption. The assistant resource is less used (from 41 to 28.8%) whereas the VPR resource is constant. We can also see that the average lead-time decreases a little. For Test 2, we can see a significant decrease in the average lead-time (starting at 0.951 hour/order and ending at 0.154 hour/order) with a constant workload of resources.

We can translate this result quite easily into economic effects for the company and launch actions aiming at the business process optimization.

3.4.2.4. *Evaluation of different solutions in the third stage*

From the diagnosis of the business process, we have identified one solution that could increase the supply chain performance. This solution consists of giving up orders taken by CRM.

To evaluate this solution, we have to modify the simulation model: there is no change in the characteristics of the demand but we delete all the parts concerning CRM orders. We make the hypothesis that the VRP resource now spends half the time for the "order capture" stage (compared to the CRM order capture). The results are presented in Table 3.5.

Model			Average lead-time (hours/order)	Use of resources (%)		
				Total	Assistant	VRP
Reference	standard model		0.951	69.755	41.85	27.905
Test 3 (validation of a solution)	model 6	no CRM orders	0.133	46.830	31.220	15.610

Table 3.5. *Results of evaluation of the solution*

This simulation shows that the global cost is lower but we can observe the transfer of workload on one resource (Assistant). The data are interesting but we must not forget that the CRM tool provides other facilities such as detailed product information and client information. The result is also penalized by the lack of data about the stochastic distribution in the company. It does not make possible a precise sizing of a call center. Nevertheless, we obtain relevant data for decision-making about the business process performance.

3.4.3. *Discussion*

The simulation of the order-fulfillment business process led to interesting aspects. From a static business process model, four malfunctions and one solution have been evaluated. The simulation enabled two of the malfunctions with the business process simulation indicators to be characterized, i.e. the time delay and the resource workload. It also enabled us to identify one new malfunction, which has a significant impact on the business process performance (resumption of CRM orders, waiting time of integration of CRM orders).

The simulation sounds like a useful complementary approach to supply chain business process analysis and reengineering. The dynamic aspect mixed with stochastic data gives a different vision of the business process and more precisely on the following points:

– intervention of uncertainty, which is important in a supply chain context;

– quantification of dynamic workload;

– queueing effects.

We must note that there are also some points such as the different methods of information transmission, or the problem of responsibilities, which are not clearly perceptible with simulation. That is why the best method for supply chain process analysis seems to be combining business process reengineering and discrete-event simulation. This combination is efficient because the simulation model is built after a first diagnosis of the business process and assures a true representation of the real functioning; in the example presented, it was important to model the resumption of CRM orders.

According to Chang and Makatsoris [CHA 01] discrete-event simulation "allows the comparison of various operational alternatives without interrupting the real system and it allows time compression so that timely policy can be made". This quotation is an accurate explanation of the results obtained in this application.

3.5. Conclusion

This chapter tries to demonstrate the utility of the use of simulation techniques as an effective tool for evaluating the performances of different supply chain and business processes. The success of supply chain simulation is definitely determined by the involvement of decision makers, the availability of data and the ability to qualify realistic and coherent inputs for the system.

Three different applications of the use of simulation for supply chains have been addressed. This technique enables decision makers to perform powerful what-if analyses allowing them to correctly understand the way their system operates, to conduct pertinent diagnosis, to build appropriate decisions and to compare various operational alternatives. The ability to assess the possible impacts of a decision on a given system prior to its implementation is certainly the most appreciated help provide by simulation.

3.6. Bibliography

[AMI 06] AMIRI A., "Designing distribution network in a supply chain system: Formulation and efficient solution procedure", *European Journal of Operational Research*, 171:567-576, 2006.

[ARN 95] ARNTZEN B.C., BROWN G.G., HARRISON T. P. and TRAFTON L.L., "Global supply chain management at Digital Equipment Corporation", *Interfaces*, 25(1):69-93, 1995.

[ART 98] ARTIBA A., EMELYANOV V. and IASSINOVSKI S.I., *Introduction to Intelligent Simulation: the RAO Language*, Kluwer Academic Publishers, 1998.

[CHA 01] CHANG Y. and MAKATSORIS H., "Supply Chain modeling using simulation", *International Journal of Simulation*, 2(1):24-30, 2001.

[DAN 98] DAGNELIE P., *Statistique théorique et appliqué – Tome 2 : inférence statistique à une et deux dimensions*, De Boeck University, 1998.

[DAN 06] DANESE P., "Collaboration forms, information and communication technologies, and coordination mechanisms in CPFR", *International Journal of Production Research*, 44(16):3207-3226, 2006.

[DIN 04] DING H., BENYOUCEF L. and XIE X., "A simulation-based optimization method for production-distribution network design", *Proceedings of International Conference on Systems, Man & Cybernetics*, The Hague, 2004.

[FAN 04] FANDEL G. and STAMMEN M., "A general model for extended strategic supply chain management with emphasis on product life cycles including development and recycling", *International Journal of Production Economics*, 89:293-308, 2004.

[GEA 06] GEARY S., DISNEY S.M. and TOWILL D.R., "On bullwhip in supply chains – historical review, present practice and expected future impact", *International Journal of Production Economics*, 101:2-18, 2006.

[GEO 74] GEOFFRION M. and GRAVES G.W., "Multi-commodity distribution system design by Benders decomposition", *Management Science*, 20(5):822-844, 1974.

[JAY 01] JAYARAMAN V. and PIRKUL H., "Planning and coordination of production and distribution facilities for multiple commodities", *European Journal of Operational Research*, 133:394-408, 2001.

[JOL 04] JOLAYEMI J.K. and OLORUNNIWO F.O., "A deterministic model for planning production quantities in a multi-plant, multi-warehouse environment with extensible capacities", *International Journal of Production Economics*, 87:99-113, 2004.

[KAR 00] KARABAKAL N., GÜNAL A. and RITCHIE W., "Supply-chain analysis at volkswagen of America", *Interfaces*, 30(4):46-55, 2000.

[KEL 98] KELTON D., SADOWSKI R. and SADOWSKI D., *Simulation with Arena*, McGraw-Hill, New York, 1998.

[KIM 01] KIM B. and KIM S., "Extended model of a hybrid production planning approach", *International Journal of Production Economics*, 73:165-173, 2001.

[KUK 04] KUK G., "Effectiveness of vendor-managed inventory in the electronics industry: determinants and outcomes", *Information & Management*, 41:645-654, 2004.

[LAL 04] LALLEMENT P., "Simulation des systèmes logistiques : exemple d'une chaîne logistique textile", *Procédé de 5ᵉ conférence francophone de Modélisation et Simulation*, 1123-1130, 2004.

[LEE 02] LEE Y.H. and KIM S.H., "Production-distribution planning in supply chain considering capacity constraints", *Computer & Industrial Engineering*, 43:169-190, 2002.

[MAH 06] MAHMOUDI J., Simulation et gestion des risques en planification distribuée de chaînes logistiques: application au secteur de l'électronique et des télécommunications, Doctoral thesis, Ecole National Supérieure de l'aéronautique et de l'espace, 2006.

[MAR 05] MARTEL A., "The design of production-distribution networks: a mathematical programming approach", in GEUNES J., PARDALOS P. (Eds.), *Supply Chain Optimization*, Springer, 265-306, 2005.

[MEL 05] MELO M.T., NICKEL S. and SALDANHA DA GAMA F., "Dynamic multi-commodity capacitated facility location: a mathematical modelling framework for strategic supply chain planning", *Computers & Operations Research*, 33:181-208, 2005.

[PIR 05] PIRARD F., Une démarche hybride d'aide à la décision pour la reconfiguration et la planification stratégique des réseaux logistiques des entreprises multi-sites, Doctoral thesis, Facultés Universitaires Catholiques de Mons, 2005.

[REI 04] REINER G. and TRCKA M., "Customized supply chain design: Problems and alternatives for a production company in the food industry. A simulation based analysis", *International Journal of Production Economics*, 89:217-229, 2004.

[RIA 01] RIANE F., ARTIBA A. and IASSINOVSKI S., "An integrated production planning and scheduling system for hybrid flowshop organizations", *International Journal of Production Economics*, 74:33-48, 2001.

[SCH 98] SCHEER A.W., *ARIS –Business Process Frameworks*, Springer-Verlag, 1998.

[TAN 06] TANG C. S., "Perspective in supply chain risk management", *International Journal of Production Economics*, 103:451-488, 2006.

[VAL 04] VALLA A., BOTTA-GENOULAZ V. and GUINET A. "Supply chain Business process oriented analysis", *Proceedings of IEEE International Conference on Systems, Man and Cybernetics*, 4527-4534, 2004.

[VAL 05] VALLA A., BOTTA-GENOULAZ V., GUINET A. and RIANE F., "Business Process Improvement using Simulation: An industrial application", *Proceedings of International Conference on Industrial Engineering and Systems Management*, 884-893, 2005.

[VAN 01] VAN DER VORST J., BEULENS A. and VAN BEEK P., "Modelling and simulating multi-echelon food systems", *European Journal of Operational Research*, 122:354-366, 2001.

[VID 01] VIDAL J. and GOETSCHALCKX M., "A global supply chain model with transfer pricing and transportation cost allocation", *European Journal of Operational Research*, 129:134-158, 2001.

Chapter 4

Simulation Games

4.1. Introduction

Supply chains are systems of many parties interacting in complex ways. The first consequence of this complexity is that modeling then simulating a supply chain is a challenge, which is the reason for this book. The second consequence of this complexity deals with how to teach the management of such chains. In fact, describing the components and their interactions does not provide people with the know how to make decisions. As well as this educational purpose, simulation games are also used in research in order to study how managers make decisions in supply chains. Concerning both educational and research aims of simulation games, Töyli et al. ([TOY 06], p. 585-6) state that "simulation" should not be understood as a "computational simulation model to predict the future" and "game" as "entertainment", which explains why some authors may prefer to use expressions such as "learning environment" or "business game". In addition, note that supply chain games have no relationship at all to game theory applied to supply chains.

As a consequence, the goal of supply chain games is to complete the theoretical teaching of supply chain management by providing insight into supply chain dynamics. This is important because action-based learning methods are designed to provoke some changes in manager behavior, in order to take into account the many aspects necessary to make decisions in complex systems ([LIE 06], p. 597). Concerning behaviors, Kleijnen ([KLE 05], p.84) notes the difficulty in modeling human behavior in comparison with technological and economic processes, which explains why it is interesting to let managers play their own role in an interactive

---

Chapter written by Thierry MOYAUX, Éric BALLOT, Michel GREIF and Bertrand SIMON.

simulation. Furthermore, Töyli *et al.* ([TOY 06], p. 585) remind us that it is sometimes argued that knowledge taught to young professionals is abstract, and they thus need the skills necessary to translate this knowledge into efficient practice, such as (i) "the ability to penetrate problems, and then solve them (analysis and synthesis), (ii) imagination and creativity, (iii) the ability to act in ways which differ significantly from expectations formed by the competition, (iv) open-mindedness, and (v) continuous hunger for profit". Töyli *et al.* ([TOY 06], p. 593-4) summarize this by stating that "it is difficult to teach practical skills with traditional teaching methods", because learners have to "convert abstract knowledge to more practical knowledge, convey the holistic understanding of business and synthesize the fragmented knowledge learned earlier". In a similar way, Hofstede *et al.* ([HOF 03], p. 112) support simulation games by claiming that such a game "is ideally suited to abstracting a situation to keep only the most relevant aspects from whichever discipline", i.e., it "brings together the various disciplines that study the same phenomenon".

For this reason, several games were proposed: the Beer Game is the most famous of them, but it is not the only one. In order to illustrate the diversity of supply chain simulation games, several literature reviews about games with educational objectives have been written [RII 95], [RII 00], [JOH 00], [HOF 06], and Kleijnen wrote about games used in research [KLE 80]. This chapter aims at completing this literature review.

For that purpose, this review is organized as follows. Section 4.2 proposes a typology of business games used to teach supply chain management, and then describes several of these games along this typology. Next, section 4.3 describes the theories suggested about the usage of such games. Finally, section 4.4 illustrates this chapter with the insights gained by CIPE (Centre International de la Pédagogie d'Entreprise, http://www.cipe.fr/) into the actual use of many simulation games.

4.2. Literature review

Hofstede *et al.* ([HOF 03], p. 114) claim that "in the area of supply chain management, one game has acquired the status of a classic: Sterman's Beer Game" [STE 89]. As a consequence, a large part of this section is devoted to this game and its offspring. However, several other business games were designed in order to teach supply chain management, as outlined in Table 4.1. This table presents games along two dimensions, i.e., the (educational or research) goal of these games, and their complexity (i.e., a board game or a model too sophisticated to be represented with a board).

Game		Reference	Goal		Complexity		
			Educational	Research	Board game — Physical version	Board game — Electronic version	Sophisticated game (electronic version)
Beer Game derivatives	Beer Game	[STE 89]	X	X	X		
		[SIM 00]	X			X	
		[JAC 00]	X			X	
		[NIE 06]		X		X	
		[KAW 05a, b]		X		X	
		[KIM 02], [ODO 06]		X X		X X	
	Stationary Beer Game	[CHE 99] [CHE 00]	X	X		X	
	Supplying Hoop Dreams	[KAZ 98]	X		X		
	Wood Supply Game	[FJE 01] [HAA 02]					
	Quebec Wood Supply Game	[FOR 07] [MOY 04, 06, 07, 08]	X	X	X	X X	
Trust and Tracing Game		[MEI 06]	X		X		
Mortgage Service Game		[AND 00]					
Legostics Management		[TEN 00]	X		X		
Risk Pooling		[SIM 00]	X			X	
TAC-SCM		[TRA 07]		X			X
Chain Game for Distributed Trading and Negotiation		[HOF 03]	X				X
Business Network Lab		[LIE 06]	X	X			X
SIMBU		[TOY 06]	X				X

Table 4.1. *The simulation games reviewed in this section*

We use *goal* as a dimension following Kleijnen's proposal to split games depending on whether they were designed for education or research [KLE 05]. In addition to these two classes, we propose splitting games depending on the *complexity* of their model of a supply chain:

– *board games*: the games in this class have a supply chain model which is simple enough to be represented as a board game, similar to Monopoly. The Beer Game belongs to this class. Such models only emphasize one aspect of the considered supply chain. The simplicity of these models makes it possible to simulate without a computer. The players have to manually perform all the operations implementing the supply chain behavior (make decisions, simulate flows, etc.), which helps the players understand the dynamics of their supply chain in detail;

– *sophisticated games*: the second type of game is too complicated to be represented by just a board. In fact, such games can be thought of as any realistic simulation in which human players replace the algorithms of decision making, in a similar way to SimCity. The most common way to run such games is on computers.

As can be seen in Table 4.1, some games fulfil both an educational and research goal, such as the Beer Game. Whether a game has a computer implementation or not does not provide exclusive classes, because all games may be run as software, whatever their complexity. In stark contrast, the complexity of a simulation game provides exclusive classes, i.e., either a game is simple enough to be represented by a board, or it is not. In other words, "board games" and "sophisticated games" do not overlap, while the existence of an electronic version does.

Of course, Table 4.1 does not contain all extent supply chain games. Due to the length of the chapter, we did not include all the games presented in [RII 95], [RII 00], [JOH 00] and [HOF 06]. For example, we will not detail how Campbell *et al.* teach the use of supply chain management software by letting students use the products developed by CAPS Logistics [CAM 00].

Section 4.2.1 presents the class of board games, while section 4.2.2 presents the class of sophisticated games.

4.2.1. *Board games*

4.2.1.1. *The Beer Game*

The Beer (Distribution) Game was developed at MIT by Sterman [STE 89] in order to teach supply chain dynamics, and, in particular, the bullwhip effect [FOR 58], [LEE 97a, b]. In this game, four players play together as a team, each player taking the role of a company. The structure of this supply chain is outlined in Figure 4.1. Tokens (pennies, rice, etc.) represent units of beer.

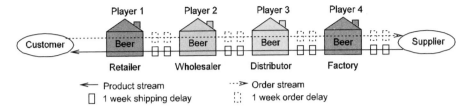

Figure 4.1. *Supply chain structure in the Beer Game*

The game is split into 35 weeks (but players are told the actual length is 50 weeks in order to avoid side effects), and each week has 5 days. In every day, the players have to perform the following operations ([STE 89], p. 327):

– *Day 1. Receive inventory and advance shipping delays.* Every player receives their inventory by moving the units of beer (sent two weeks earlier by their supplier, because there is a two-week shipping delay) from the closer "Shipping Delay" at the right-hand side of the company into the inventory of their company. Next, the products in the second "Shipping Delay" at the right-hand side of the company are moved to the "Shipping Delay" which has just been emptied.

– *Day 2. Fill orders.* Every player looks at their incoming order located in the closer "Order Delay" box at the left-hand side of the company, and tries to fulfil this order. This fulfilment is performed by moving products from the inventory into the closer "Shipping Delay" at the left of the company. The quantity to ship is the incoming order plus backorders from prior weeks (unfulfilled orders are backordered).

– *Day 3. Record inventory or backlog on the record sheet.*

– *Day 4. Advance the order slips.* Order slips in the second "Order Delay" at the left-hand side of the company are moved into the first "Order Delay" (this box was emptied in Day 2 by the supplier).

– *Day 5. Place orders.* Every player now makes their only decision in the week, when they decide what quantity to write on an order slip. This slip is placed in the closer "Order Delay" box at the right-hand side of the company (this box was emptied in Day 4). The quantity ordered is recorded on the record sheet.

Sterman used the Beer Game for research. In fact, he proposed a mathematical model to approximate how human players make their decision in this game. This allowed him to shed light on several misperceptions of the game dynamics by the players, i.e., (i) desired stocks are anchored at their initial level rather than updated accorded to the observed demand, (ii) the time lag between placing and receiving orders is underestimated, and (iii) players see game dynamics as "open-loop", i.e., these dynamics are attributed to exogenous events rather than to the policy applied by the players ([STE 89], p. 334-6).

In addition, the Beer Game has inspired other implementations and studies, for example:

– Simchi-Levi *et al.* [SIM 00] sold their book with the Beer Game on a CD-ROM;

– Jacobs [JAC 00] proposed an electronic version of the Beer Game on the Web;

– Nienhaus *et al.* [NIE 06] also put an electronic version of the Beer Game on the Web, which allowed them to collect data from a few thousand games played by people around the world. Unfortunately, they knew very little about these players. They drew two conclusions from all these games. First, two extreme strategies called "safe harbour" (overordering in order to increase safety stocks) and "panic" (underordering in order to decrease safety stocks) have a negative impact on the entire supply chain even when only one player applies them. Second, information sharing (every participant can see other participants' inventory level) reduces the bullwhip effect;

– Kawagoe and Wada [KAW 05a, b] found a counterexample of the bullwhip effect in the Beer Game. Specifically, they observed situations in which inventory levels in upstream companies are not always larger than that of downstream firms, even with many firms and long delays;

– Kimbrough *et al.* [KIM 02] used a genetic algorithm to find the best *n* for every player using an ordering rule of the form "when incoming demand is *d*, then order quantity (*d+n*)". O'Donnell *et al.* extended this work to random demand and lead-times [ODO 06].

Finally, several evolutions of the Beer Game were proposed, as will now be presented.

4.2.1.2. *Derivatives of the Beer Game*

The rows starting with "Derivatives of the Beer Games" in Table 4.1 contain the following games:

–*Stationary Beer Game*: Chen [CHE 99] and Chen and Samroengraja [CHE 00] modified some parameters in the Beer Game, such as the fact that only the retailer has backorder costs, and that inventory holding costs are higher for upstream companies than for the retailer.

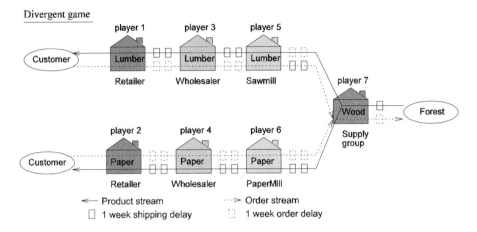

Figure 4.2. *Supply chain structure in the divergent version of the Wood Supply Game*

– *Supplying Hoop Dreams Game*: Kazaz and Moskowitz [KAZ 99] introduced several innovations to the Beer Game (price, different types of products, two clients for the distributor, two suppliers for the manufacturer, etc.) in order to model:

- the assembly of Lego or Velco pieces representing products,

- the four causes of the bullwhip effect proposed by Lee *et al.* [Lee 97a, b]. In fact, the Beer Game only implements the cause known as "information distortion" (i.e. upstream players use incoming orders as demand instead of actual sales),

- the illustration of several issues due to competition among companies. For example, this game has two suppliers selling to a single manufacturer. Due to this, in every round of the game, each supplier proposes a price to the manufacturer in a strategic way, i.e. in a way taking the other supplier into account.

– *Wood Supply Games*: Haartveit and Fjeld [HAA 02] and Fjeld [FJE 01] proposed two versions of the Wood Supply Game (WSG) as applications of the Beer Game to the North European Forest industry. The main difference between these three games (WSG and Beer Game) deals with the structure of the supply chain. Figure 4.2 presents the structure of the supply chain in the first version of the game, and Figure 4.3 in the second version.

– *Quebec Wood Supply Game*: next, FOR@C [FOR 07] modified the Wood Supply Games to create the Quebec Wood Supply Game (QWSG) in order to represent the specificities of the wood industry in Quebec (a Canadian province). Again, the main difference between the Beer Game and the QWSG is the structure of the supply chain, which is presented in Figure 4.4.

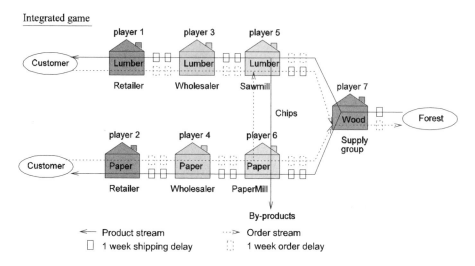

Figure 4.3. *Supply chain structure in the integrated version*
of the Wood Supply Game

Two pieces of software implement the divergent version of the QWSG, the first in a spreadsheet program by Moyaux *et al.* [MOY 04], and the second can be played online on the FOR@C website.

With their implementation of the QWSG, Moyaux *et al.* [MOY 07] studied what information should be shared and how to use this information so that the bullwhip effect is reduced. Two ordering strategies involving information sharing were proposed as illustrations. Next, these authors [MOY 06] checked whether every individual player should use one of these two illustrating ordering schemes, or whether they should instead apply a third strategy based on the (s, S) policy and which does not involve any information sharing. Finally, Moyaux *et al.* [MOY 08] explored how the choice of one of the three previous ordering strategies may change when agents take the efficiency of the overall supply chain into account to different degrees with regard to their individual efficiency.

So far, we have only presented the studies based on the Beer Game and the variants of the Beer Game which have attracted our attention. However, dozens of other papers related to the Beer Game could have been summarized here.

We now present some other board games.

4.2.1.3. *The Trust and Tracing Game*

Meijer *et al.* [MEI 06] use the structure of the Beer Game in their Trust and Tracing Game. Specifically, the players trade with the other players organized in a network, e.g. the Beer Game structure in [MEI 06], which is the only relation of this game to the Beer Game. During trade, players can either trust their trading partner about the hidden quality attribute of the product to exchange, or they may prefer to spend money on tracing in order to check whether the other party is telling the truth about quality. This way, the learners gain insight into the importance of a prior relationship in order to build trust in business.

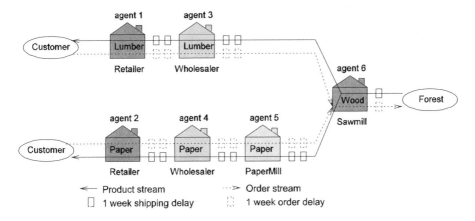

Figure 4.4. *Supply chain structure in the Quebec Wood Supply Game*

4.2.1.4. *The Mortgage Service Game*

Anderson and Morrice [AND 00] introduced a game in the same spirit as the Beer Game, i.e. both games aim at teaching supply chain dynamics, but with a service-oriented instead of product-oriented supply chain. The difference between service-oriented and product-oriented supply chains is the absence of inventories. In fact, service-oriented supply chains "can only manage backlogs through capacity adjustments".

4.2.1.5. *Legostics Management*

Ten Wolde [TEN 00] outlined a simulation game used to introduce the new students of Hogeschool Drenthe University (the Netherlands) to management. Students play in teams of 14 to 20 students. This game is played during three days divided into six sessions. The first three sessions are called "Part 1" and make the student gain initial experience and familiarity with terms and concepts. The next two sessions are called "Part 2", and teach the importance of information and cash flow.

Finally, "Part 3" has only one session in which we are introduced to the roles of suppliers and customers, who have to negotiate the terms of their operations. Specifically, the students gradually learn the features of Legostics in the following sessions:

– *Session 1*: players concentrate on the production and distribution of the goods. The goods consist of a four-level tower made of Lego blocks.

– *Session 2*: two other versions of the goods to be produced are introduced, so that the students have to plan production.

– *Session 3*: the nature of the organization is changed from functional to production.

– *Session 4*: the focus here is on cash flow and accounting issues.

– *Session 5*: while the product was produced to order before, demand forecasting is now introduced.

– *Session 6*: the concept of a Customer Order Decoupling Point is introduced.

4.2.1.6. *Risk pooling*

As well as an electronic version of the Beer Game, the CD-ROM sold with [SIM 00] also provides a game to help understand risk pooling. Risk pooling consists of aggregating the logistic risks of several companies into a single bigger company. This game illustrates this by letting a player simultaneously manage one system with risk pooling (also called the centralized system) and a system without risk pooling (the decentralized system). The centralized system is made up of a single big warehouse, and the decentralized system of three small retailers. The game illustrates the fact that, if each retailer of the decentralized system maintains separate inventory and safety stocks, then a higher level of inventory has to be maintained than in the single big warehouse of the centralized system. In fact, the sum of the safety stock of each of the three retailers needs to be greater than the safety stock of the single warehouse.

4.2.2. *Sophisticated games*

After board games, we now turn our attention to the second type of game, i.e. sophisticated games.

4.2.2.1. *Trading Agent Competition – Supply Chain Management*

The SCM track of the Trading Agent Competition [TRA 07], TAC-SCM, provides an agent-based simulation of a three-level supply chain producing and selling PCs (personal computers). The first (end-customers) and third (suppliers) levels of the supply chain are agents implemented by the organizers of the competition, while each of the six entrants proposes their PC assembly agent for the second level. These six agents compete for customer orders and for procurement of the four components needed to build a PC (CPU, motherboard, memory and disk drives). These components are available in different versions sold in different markets on the supply side. On the demand side, different markets are used to exchange different products (i.e. different kinds of PCs). As well as trading, every assembly agent must also schedule its production.

Since TAC-SCM is an agent-based simulation, this competition proposes a semi-decentralized (see Chapter 7) discrete-event (see Chapter 3) simulator. However, TAC-SCM can also be seen as a game, since human players have to design software agents which compete against the software agents proposed by other human players.

TAC-SCM has run annually since 2003. As a consequence, several papers are available on it. In particular, Wellman *et al.* [WEL 05] used empirical game theory to find that, in some circumstances, blocking another agent's strategy may be beneficial both for the agent who blocks and for competitors' agents.

4.2.2.2. *Chain Game for distributed trading and negotiation*

Hofstede *et al.* [HOF 03] proposed a Web-based simulation of a food supply chain. This tool is intended to be comprehensive and for both research and education. This gaming environment can represent different structures of food supply chains, and highlights several aspects from the performance, process and institutional perspectives. 1 to 30 teams with one to four participants per team can participate. Each team plays the role of a company. These companies are composed of, at least, a producer, a retail outlet and a market, but wholesalers and factories may also be added in order to represent different structures of supply networks. Since products are food, their quality mostly depends on their freshness. End customers may also pay attention to the price of this food, or to the way this food is produced (the players have to make decisions such as: is it possible to track the origin of food units? Was child labor involved in production? Do factories often launch the sale of new products?). This last sentence implies the realism of the supply chain modeled in this game.

Finally, note that Hofstede designed some other earlier simulation games of supply chains, such as the "Strawberry Chain" [HOF 98] and "Food for Thought" [HOF 00], as well as games of related fields, such as the "Takeover Trio" [BOT 04].

4.2.2.3. *Business Network Lab*

The Business Network Lab. (http://bnl.fbk.eur.nl/) is the computer-running simulation of a supply chain in the Dutch insurance field [LIE 06]. This simulation involves 15 teams of two players, each team taking one of five roles (insurance advice, sales, customer acceptation, service center and customer care). The goal of this simulation is to "teach the impact of quick connect capability and increased transparency in a business network, and how a modular approach may be a key enabler" ([LIE 06], p. 597). In other words, the players learn how IT technologies can be used to connect firms quickly in order to organize the supply chain so that the customer demand is met.

4.2.2.4. *SIMBU*

SIMBU is "a generic business management simulation for graduate students and managerial training", which is the title of the PhD thesis of the first author of [TOY 06]. This simulation runs on PCs, and proposes three countries, four products, four components/raw materials and three currencies. This allows the players to deal with "customer-driven approach, management of the internationalization process, coping with the transformation from traditional industry to a more high-tech industry, management of growth and change, simultaneous competition and collaboration, and adaptation to constantly changing market environments". For example, the activities within a country are affected by the characteristics of this country, and investing in R&D allows us to propose new products (i.e. companies only propose one of the four products at the beginning, and need to invest in R&D in order to be able to propose the second, then the third and finally the fourth type of product).

We now present some theories about the use of games, and, in particular, how experimental economics use them in order to model human behavior.

4.3. Theories about the usage of games

As the use of supply chain simulation board games or computerized games spread rapidly through schools and business executives, this success also raised several questions about their specific inputs. This will be the first part of the following discussion about the contribution of games to the teaching of the supply chain dynamics. The second part of the review will discuss the window opened by these games in the understanding of the behavior of managers facing some stylized situations such as ordering, managing inventories, etc.

4.3.1. *Games as a booster for learners?*

4.3.1.1. *Backgrounds*

The simulation game is a radically different way of teaching from the traditional classroom even if it is not a completely new method if we look at military teaching and the success of war games since World War II and before. The main difference between traditional classrooms and game classrooms is that the underlying theory revolved around the learner instead of the teacher.

Then the following questions rose: is this approach of learning efficient? What are the models of learning and how should we compare the results? These questions are important because nowadays nearly all supply chain courses include at least one game. Keys and Wolfe carried out a very important survey on this subject in 1990 and what follows will mainly be based on this [KEY 90].

A survey of management game use established in 1987 by Faria showed that at that time, there were nearly 9,000 professors in 2,000 business schools involved in games in the US and since that time the use of simulation game has continued to develop [FAR 87].

The experiential learning theory and behavioral change theory developed between 1950 and the mid-1960s by Lewin or Schein and Bennis creates a most favorable environment for management and the supply chain games [LEW 51], [SCH 65].

This experiential method was summarized as a four-step process [GEL 79]:

– concrete experience;

– observation and reflection;

– formation of concept;

– testing implication of concepts in new situation.

According to Bowen's review this process is more efficient if it:

– is accompanied by an optimal amount of emotional arousal;

– takes place in an environment of safety;

– is accompanied by a clear map providing the understanding of the experiment.

If we look at the Beer Game or other supply chain games, all of these components are present to varying degrees.

As defined above, this type of learning is close to Argyris and Schön 1978 double-loop learning. This learning is seen as a climate that supports both free and informed choice and internal commitment [ARG 78].

4.3.1.2. *Evaluation*

Several research studies based on course evaluation with or without games show that students that played a game had better results [KAU 76], [WHE 88], [WOL 75]. Other published research indicates the same result but in a more qualitative way [AMM 99], [HAA 01].

However, in many cases authors claim the impact of the game on a student's skills or a professional's skills in a qualitative way. For example, the Global Supply Chain Game developed at Delft University [COR 06] focused on the time pressure with a real time game of a global supply chain. At the end they found that the students were much more aware of the global supply chain dynamics.

Another study based on the Beer Game [DAV 04] indicates that this game is very useful for developing quicker responses and not over reacted attitudes to the professionals. The second finding is that the bigger the group of players is, the worse the results are. This phenomenon is explained by the panic feeling that would emerge much more from a group than from a single person, as there is always someone in the group with a fear that they do not have enough product in stock.

From a study in the military field [CAR 07] one of the most important discoveries by the players is that after the game they have tested some strategies and this will be of help when in charge of real operations. Therefore, the conclusion is all executives should play a game first.

At an organizational level, K. Korhonen reported that the game approach also gives good results in a company. The workshops including a role game proved to be a good start to the supply chain improvement program. The game workshop approach creates a positive, not a problem-oriented, start for the improvement program. The game makes it easier for participants to discuss sensitive matters in abstract form and in a socially safe atmosphere. However, there is still a reservation. The playful attitude can raise doubts about how seriously the improvement propositions will be taken into account in the future [KOR 06].

However there is no finding, even in a 5 year longitudinal study [NOR 82], that the games play a statistic significant role in the career of players versus non-players of a management game!

4.3.2. *Games as a research field for managerial behavior*

As the game involves the behavior of the player and we assume that this behavior is not too far from what it would be in a real situation, games such as the Beer Game give an opportunity to researchers to understand what information is really used by managers and in which way. This approach is in fact very close to the experimental economics approach.

4.3.2.1. *The role of the "human factor" in replenishment or inventory decisions*

The Beer Game is a stylized environment in which the supply chain is highly simplified. However, the game highlights the impact of the manager's decisions on the supply chain. In fact, from different positions in the game or from different teams, the result could be slightly different.

Despite the fact that in many businesses the order decision is aided by a replenishment policy implemented in an information system, it is still under direct control of the managers, particularly for strategic supply. Therefore, the way they understand the supply chain dynamics is very important, as it will directly influence their decisions. From this point of view the Beer Game is an experiment that could give some indications on the process they are really following.

4.3.2.2. *Why choose games to conduct supply chain research?*

The game approach could be criticized, as it is too simplified a view of the dynamics of real supply chains. For example, the demand in the Beer Game comes more from a textbook in automation than from the operation field of any company. Therefore, how can this approach be used to conduct research?

These criticisms are in fact true, but in the cases that will be studied here this is not a limitation of this approach but a necessary condition for the research. In fact, real operations involve too many factors and uncontrolled events to allow researchers to carry out investigations on manager behavior and their decision schemes. This is why supply chain games, because of their limited scope and controlled environment, can play a significant role in a better understanding of the underlying rationality involved.

4.3.2.3. *Testing hypothesis on manager behavior*

In now an old but still very important publication John Sterman demonstrates with the beer distribution game that manager behavior could be a real issue for the supply chain [STE 89]. In particular, this paper is based on an experimental economic methodology in which the behavior of each participant is analyzed according to the set of decisions he made. In the Beer Game decisions are quantities ordered at each stage of the game.

These order decisions are compared to a replenishment policy with 4 parameters. The parameters are chosen in order to highlight different information sources that can be taken into account.

The decision rule is:

$$O_t = MAX\left[0, \hat{L}_t + \alpha_s(S' - S_t - \beta SL_t) + \varepsilon_t\right]$$

with

$$\hat{L}_t = \theta L_{t-1} + (1 - \theta)\hat{L}_{t-1}$$
$$S' = S^* + \beta SL^*$$

where:

– t is the stage of the game, which typically varies from 1 to 36;

– $\hat{L}_t$ is losses expected at stage t. These losses can be taken from the last losses or expectation losses when θ varies from 0 to 1. Therefore, the optimal value for parameter θ is 0;

– a_s is a constant that puts a linear feedback between the desired stock and the actual stock;

– S^* and SL^* are the optimal stock level and optimal supply line. They are assumed to be constant;

– β indicates the fact that the order decision takes into account a proportion of the supply line. Therefore, the optimal value is 1 which means that the manager is fully aware of the forthcoming goods;

– S_t and SL_t are values of the stock level and supply line at each stage.

For more information on this decision rule identification on the beer distribution game, see [STE 89].

All the practitioners of the Beer Game know the results of this study: a strong misperception of feedback. This misperception was demonstrated by statistical identification of the 4 parameters (θ, α_s, β, S') on 48 games (192 gamers).

The averages of the results were ($\theta \Pi 0.36$, $\alpha_s \Pi 0.26$, $\beta \Pi 0.34$, $S' \Pi 17$). They are not very good when compared with the optimal values for the same decision rules ($\theta \Pi 0$, $\alpha_s \Pi 1$, $\beta \Pi 1$, $S' \Pi 28$).

These results show poor perception of the feedback by the managers as β had a low value. Moreover the fact that S' is low according to the optimal value was explained by the test of the hypothesis that the managers remained anchored to the initial stock level (12 units). A linear regression was performed by the author and revealed that S^* and SL^* could be estimated by: $S^*\prod 13.9$ and $SL^*\prod 8.4$. Thus, despite the change in the average losses the vision of the desired stock level was not really updated by the managers.

This work really demonstrates the difficulties the managers face when they try to cope with the dynamics of even a very simple and stylized supply chain. This result relies on the famous work carried out by Herbert Simon on bounded rationality [SIM 82].

Croson and Donohue also worked with the Beer Game [CRO 02]. They propose minimizing the bullwhip effect by sharing information about the retailer's inventory. This result is also shown by many cases studies, among them the study carried out by Heikkila in the highly competitive and fast growing mobile telecommunications industry [HEI 02].

All these results allege a better understanding of these phenomena and for the development of games as a learning tool for students and practitioners. It makes it possible to train people and measure the impact of the training and of different strategies such as information sharing, as established by Wu [WU 06]. Consequently, a lot of attention has to be paid to implementation and gaming methodologies.

4.4. Examples of implementation methodologies and obtained results

The Centre International de la Pédagogie d'Entreprise (CIPE) is a French company that designs and sells business games used as learning tools for supply chain management.

CIPE was created in 1985, a time when Japanese production methods were starting to spread throughout the West. This is not a simple coincidence.

At this time, the Japanese invented a method called Kanban. According to this method, part of the supply chain control is under the responsibility of workers themselves.

In such a model the optimization does not result from the fair decisions of one department only, as is the case when the scheduling department uses the MRP method.

The optimization comes from a cooperation between many parties not only the scheduling department, but also workers when they decide priorities, handling workers when they decide which lot should be transported, technicians when they accelerate tool changeovers, the sales department when improving the demand smoothness and also the human resources department when taking care of ensuring the employees are multi-skilled.

This broadening of actors involved in supply chain explains the expansion of learning games.

As a matter of fact, one of the most remarkable advantages of a game is opening the mind of players beyond the field in which they usually play:

– workers understand what happens in the company behind the wall of their workshop;

– schedulers become aware of constraints and hazards that impede their plan on the field;

– other departments find out that they have a strong influence on the production flow.

Games from CIPE are board games that include a role game feature. As in a theater performance they concentrate in the same space, same action and same time on a socio-technical script where everyone has a responsibility to assume.

Many CIPE games provide an opportunity for role reversal. In the Kanban game (see below) the reversal takes place in two directions: horizontally, when the sales manager of the company is for example responsible for production; vertically, when the production manager of the company takes care of a workstation while the operator manages the production plan.

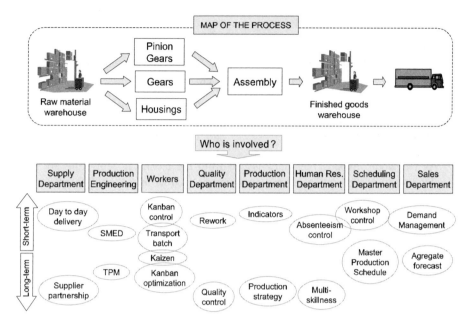

Figure 4.5. *This scheme shows the variety of decisions that contribute to supply chain management. They involve various departments and various levels of thinking (short-term and long-term)*

We understand that the purpose of the game is not only explaining how supply chains work, but above all making everyone feel to what extent positions are heterogenous inside a supply chain organization.

We will also easily admit that this type of game can only be experimented with in a company open-minded enough to allow free discussion among employees.

4.4.1. *Kanban game in academic institutions*

One specific feature of CIPE is marketing supply chain games for different audiences. Companies use games to train managers as well as technicians or workers. Academic institutions use them to train students with a strong expertise in supply chains as well as college students.

A game follows the same script whatever the audience. Differences appear when the time for debriefing comes. Debriefing is critical for the learning efficiency of a game.

Debriefing generally includes two parts:

– The first part addresses the "technical dimension" of the game. Discussion is about topics such as relations between flow profile and inventories, impact of equipment reliability on customer satisfaction, etc.

– The second part addresses what can be called the "social dimension" of the game. Discussion is about what participants have experienced when assuming their responsibility during the game.

As we would expect, messages issued from the technical debriefing are very similar whatever the audience. In a company as well as in a school, supply chain rules are the same.

On the other hand, social debriefing is very different.

In a company, as stated before, the participants express what they have discovered when assuming another role from the one they hold in the real life.

When the game is processed in a school, participants are not dedicated to a specific role in their life, so they do not react the same way.

What they feel can be summed up by saying that the world of management does not respect strict mathematical rationality.

As an example, let us quote the case of the student who went apart at the beginning of the game in order to define a mathematical model of the flow, then processed sophisticated calculation in order to obtain a formal system of equations.

The problem is that his partners were not involved in his study. Thus, when the group met to decide the production plan he was unable to prove the correctness of his calculation. His personal position was rejected by the majority.

The first lesson is that truth in action does not belong to who is right in theory, but to who is able to explain his solution to his partners. Being convincing is part of the game.

The second lesson addresses the limits of model efficiency. Most of the students have been trained to accept the paradigm which states that there is always an optimized solution to reach any goal.

However, the game demonstrates that reality inside a company is different. Chaotic interactions inside the supply chain prevent any predetermined decision pattern.

The teacher can easily conclude that spending too much effort in initial optimization is a waste of time, and that a slack of initiative must be given to field actors.

4.4.2. *A field for experimentation*

CIPE offers more than 50 different games to schools (MBA, colleges, etc.) and to companies. Since it was created, CIPE has sold 5,000 units, and trained more than 100,000 people around the world.

The training game is now part of the training curriculum inside companies as well as schools.

In companies it is used as a management tool for promoting new behavior and new rules. It creates an experimentation field where anyone can test a new role, an original position or a different state of mind without risk.

In schools it gives students the opportunity to explore an unknown world with its own logic and its own law. A good opportunity to accept that when you want to learn something new you sometimes need to forget what you have learnt before…

4.5. Conclusion

This chapter has presented the games used in supply chain management. Specifically, we first classified the existing games against two dimensions, namely their goal (educational or research) and their complexity (simple enough to be played as a board game, or so sophisticated that a computer implementation is required). We saw that the Beer Game and its offspring is the most widely used model. We then presented how practitioners and researchers use games. The first use games to improve managers' awareness of supply chain dynamics while the second use games to gain new insight on the supply chain as a system that includes the managers' behaviors. Finally, we illustrated this chapter with the insight gained by CIPE.

The next chapter starts the "decision system simulation viewpoint" part of this book by presenting the centralized simulation approaches.

4.6. Bibliography

[AMM 99] AMMAR S., WRIGHT R., "Experiential learning activities in Operations Management", *International Transaction in Operations Research*, (6), p. 183-197, 1999.

[AND 00] ANDERSON G., MORRICE D. J., "A simulation game for service-oriented supply chain management: Does information sharing help managers with service capacity decisions?", *Journal of Production and Operations Management*, 9(1), p. 40-55, 2000.

[ARG 78] ARGYRIS C., SCHON D., *Organizational Learning: A Theory Action Perspective*, Reading, MA: Addison-Wesley, 1978.

[BOT 04] BOTS P. W. G., HOFSTEDE G. J., "The Takeover Trio", *Simulation & Gaming*, 35(4), p. 505-516, 2004.

[BOT 06] BOTS P. W. G., "Experimental learning to see through strategic behaviour in large scale projects", *Production Planning & Control*, 17(6), p. 604-615, 2006.

[CAM 00] CAMPBELL A., GOENTZEL J., SAVELSBERGH M., "Experiences with the use of supply chain management software in education", *Production and Operations Management*, 9(1), p. 66-80, 2000.

[CAR 07] CARES J., MISKEL J., "Take Your Third Move First", *Harvard Business Review* (March), p. 20-21, 2007.

[CHE 99] CHEN F., "Decentralized supply chains subject to information delays" *Management Science*, 45(8), p. 1076-1090, 1999.

[CHE 00] CHEN F., SAMROENGRAJA R., "The Stationary Beer Game", *Production and Operations Management*, 9(1), p. 19-30, 2000.

[COR 06] CORSI T. M., BOYSON S., VEBRAECK A., HOUTEN S., HAN C., McDONALD J. R., "The Real-Time Global Supply Chain Game: New Educational Tool for Developing Supply Chain Management Professionals", *Transportation Journal* (Summer), p. 61-73, 2006.

[CRO 02] CROSON R., DONOHUE K., "Experimental economics and supply chain management", *Interfaces*, 32(5), p. 74-82, 2002.

[DAV 04] DAVIS C., "Game shows it's professionals who cause the bullwhip effect", *Supply Chain Europe*, 2004.

[FAR 87] FARIA A. J., "A survey of the use of business games in academia and business", *Simulation & Games*, 18(2), p. 207-224, 1987.

[FJE 01] FJELD D. E., "The Wood Supply Game as an educational application for simulating dynamics in the forest sector", in K. Sjostrom and Lars-Olaf Rask (eds.), *Supply Chain Management for Paper and Timber Industries*, p. 241-251, Växjö, Sweden, 2001.

[FOR 07] FOR@C, website http://www.forac.ulaval.ca/, visited 18 May 2007.

[FOR 58] FORRESTER J. W., "Industrial dynamics – a major breakthrough for decision-makers", *Harvard Business Review*, 36(4), p. 37-66, 1958.

[GEL 79] GELLER L., "Reliability of the learning style inventory", *Psycological Reports*, 1979 (44), p. 555-561, 1979.

[HAA 01] HAAPASALO H., HYVOKNEN J., "Simulating business and operations management a learning environment for the electronics industry", *International Journal of Production Economics*, 73, p. 261-272, 2001.

[HAA 02] HAARTVEIT E. Y., FJELD D. E., "Experimenting with industrial dynamics in the forest sector – A Beer Game application", in *Proc. Symposium on Systems and Models in Forestry*, Punta de Tralca, Chile, 2002.

[HOF 98] HOFSTEDE G. J., TRIENEKENS J. H., ZIGGERS G.W., "The Strawberry Chain", in J. H. Trienekens and P. J. P. Zuurbier (eds.), *Proc. 3rd Int. Conf. on Chain Management in Agribusiness and the Food Industry*, p. 75-85, Wageningen, Netherlands, 1998.

[HOF 00] HOFSTEDE G. J., TRIENEKENS J. H, "Food for Thought", in J. H. Trienekens and P. J. P. Zuurbier (eds.), *Proc. 4th Int. Conf. on Chain Management in Agribusiness and the Food Industry*, p. 41-45, Wageningen, Netherlands, 2000.

[HEI 02] HEIKKILA J., "From supply to demand chain management: efficiency and customer satisfaction", *Journal of Operations Management* (20), p. 747-767, 2002.

[HOF 03] HOFSTEDE G. J., KRAMER M., MEIJER S., WIJDEMANS J., "A Chain Game for Distributed Trading and Negotiation", *Production Planning & Control*, 14(2), p. 111-121, 2003.

[HOF 06] HOFSTEDE G. J., "Experimental learning in chains and networks" (guest editorial), *Production Planning & Control*, 17(6), p. 543-546, 2006.

[JAC 00] JACOBS F. R., "Playing the beer distribution game over the Internet", *Production and Operations Management*, 9(1), p. 31-39, 2000.

[JOH 00] JOHNSON M. E., PYKE D. F., "Introduction to the special issue on teaching supply chain management", *Production and Operations Management*, 9(1), p. 1, 2000.

[KAU 76] KAUFMAN F. L., "An empirical study of the usefullness of a computer-based business game", *Journal of Educational Data Processing*, 13(1), p. 13-22, 1976.

[KAW 05a] KAWAGOE T., WADA S., "A Counterexample for the Bullwhip Effect: Gaming and Multiagent Simulations", in *Proc. IEEE/WIC/ACM Int. Conf. on Intelligent Agent Technology*, p. 124-127, 2005.

[KAW 05b] KAWAGOE T., WADA S., "A Counterexample for the Bullwhip Effect in a Supply Chain", in *Proc. 1st Symposium on Artificial Economics, Lecture Notes in Economics and Mathematical Systems*, 564, p. 103-111, 2005.

[KAZ 99] KAZAZ B., MOSKOWITZ H., "An active learning excercise: Supplying hoop dreams", Working paper, Loyola University, Chicago, USA. (http://sba.luc.edu/research/wpapers/991102.pdf), 1999.

[KEY 90] KEYS B., WOLFE J., "The role of management games and simulations in education and research", *Journal of Management*, 16(2), p. 307-336, 1990.

[KIM 02] KIMBROUGH S. O., WU D. J., ZHONG F., "Computers play the Beer Game: Can artificial agents manage supply chains?", *Decision Support Systems*, 33(3), p. 323-333, 2002.

[KLE 80] KLEIJNEN J. P. C., *Computers and Profits: Quantifying Financial Benefits of Information*, Addison-Wesley, 1980.

[KLE 05] KLEIJNEN J. P. C., "Supply chain simulation tools and techniques: A survey", *International Journal of Simulation & Process Modelling*, 1(1/2), 82-89, 2005.

[KOR 06] KORHONEN K., PEKKANEN P., PIRTTILA T., "Role game as a method to increase cross-functional understanding in a supply chain", *International Journal of Production Economics*, 108, 127-134, 2006.

[LIE 06] VAN LIERE D. W., HOOGEWEEGEN M. R., VERVEST P. H. M., HAGDORN L., "To adopt or not to adopt? Experiencing the effect of quick connect capabilities on network performance", *Production Planning & Control*, 17(6), 596-603, 2006.

[LEE 97a] LEE H. L., PADMANABHAN V., WHANG S., "The bullwhip effect in supply chain", *Sloan Management Review*, 38(3), 93-102, 1997.

[LEE 97b] LEE H. L., PADMANABHAN V., WHANG S., "Information distortion in a supply chain: the bullwhip effect", *Management Science*, 43(4), 546-558, 1997.

[LEW 51] LEWIN A. Y., *Field Theory in Social Science*, New York: Harper & Row, 1951.

[MEI 06] MEIJER S., HOFSTEDE G. J., BEERS G., OMTA S. W. F., "Trust and Tracing game: Learning about transactions and embeddedness in a trade network", *Production Planning & Control*. 17(6), 569-583, 2006.

[MOY 04] MOYAUX T., CHAIB-DRAA B., D'AMOURS S., "An Agent Simulation Model for the Quebec Forest Supply Chain", in *Proc. 8th International Workshop on Cooperative Information Agents* (CIA2004), volume 3191 of Lecture Notes in Computer Science, p. 226-241, Erfurt (Germany), 2004.

[MOY 06] MOYAUX T., CHAIB-DRAA B., D'AMOURS S., "Design, implementation and test of collaborative strategies in the supply chain", in B. Chaib-draa and J. Müller (eds.), *MultiAgent-Based Supply Chain Management*, Springer, Chapter 10, 2006.

[MOY 07] MOYAUX T., CHAIB-DRAA B., D'AMOURS S., "The impact of information sharing on the efficiency of an ordering approach in reducing the bullwhip effect", *IEEE Transactions on Systems, Man, and Cybernetics, Part C*, 37(3), p. 396-409, 2007.

[MOY 08] MOYAUX T., CHAIB-DRAA B., D'AMOURS S., "Experimental study of incentives for collaboration in the Quebec wood supply game", *Production Planning & Control*, 2008 (submitted).

[NIE 06] NIENHAUS J., ZIEGENBEIN A., SCHOENSLEBEN P., "How human behaviour amplifies the bullwhip effect. A study based on the beer distribution game online", *Production Planning & Control*, 17(6), p. 547-557, 2006.

[NOR 82] NORRIS D. R., NIEBUHR R. E., "Group variables and gaming success", *Simulation & Gaming*, 11(3): p. 73-85, 1982.

[ODO 06] O'DONNELL T., MAGUIRE L., McIVOR R., HUMPHREYS P., "Minimizing the bullwhip effect in a supply chain using genetic algorithms", *International Journal of Production Research*, 44(8), p. 1523-1543, 2006.

[RII 00] RIIS J. O., SMEDS R., VAN LANDEGHEM R. (eds.), *Games in Operations Management*, Kluwer, Boston, MA, 2000.

[RII 95] RIIS J. O. (eds.), *Simulation Games and Learning in Production Management*, Chapman & Hall, 1995.

[SCH 65] SCHEIN E. H., BENNIS W. G., *Personal and Organizational Change Through Group Methods*, New York: Wiley, 1965.

[SIM 00] SIMCHI-LEVI D., KAMINSKY P., SIMCHI-LEVI E., *Designing and Managing the Supply Chain*, McGraw-Hill Higher Education, 2000.

[SIM 82] SIMON H., *Models of Bounded Rationality*, Cambridge, MA: The MIT Press, 1982.

[STE 89] STERMAN J. D., "Modeling managerial behavior: Misperceptions of feedback in a dynamic decision making experiment", *Management Science*, 35(3), p. 321-339, 1989.

[TEN 00] TEN WOLDE H., "Building blocks of education", *OR/MS Today*, http://www.lionhrtpub.com/orms/orms-8-00/education.html, 27, p. 12, 2000.

[TOY 06] TÖYLI J., HANSÉN S.-O., SMEDS R., "Plan for profit and achieve profit: Lessons learnt from a business management simulation", *Production Planning & Control*, 17(6), p. 584-595, 2006.

[TRA 07] Trading Agent Competition (2007). Website, http://www.sics.se/tac/, visited 18 May 2007.

[WEL 05] WELLMAN M. P., ESTELLE J., SINGH S., VOROBEYCHIK Y., KIEKINTVELD C., SONI V., "Strategic interactions in a supply chain game", *Computational Intelligence*, 21(1), 1-26, 2005.

[WHE 88] WHEATLEY H. J., HORNADAY R. W., HUNT T. G., "Developing strategic management goal setting skills", *Simulation & Gaming*, 19(2), 173-185, 1988.

[WOL 75] WOLFE J., "A comparative evaluation of the experiential approach as a business policy learning environment", *Academy of Management Journal*, 18(3), p. 442-452, 1975.

[WU 06] WU D. Y., KATOK E., "Learning, communication, and the bullwhip effect", *Journal of Operations Management* (24), p. 839-850, 2006.

Chapter 5

Centralized Approaches for Supply Chain Simulation: Issues and Applications

5.1. Introduction

Increasingly, supply chain simulation is very useful in the decision-making process either for implementing a new supply chain or for making changes to an existing one. The decisions that are usually taken before planning the implementation of any supply chain can be classified into two categories: structural and operational. Structural decisions affect the long-term performance of the supply chain. This could be regarding the location of a particular distributor or selection of the capacity of a particular plant. Operational decisions correspond to the short-term decisions. Examples include reorder levels for a particular item in the inventory, and rescheduling frequency. Simulation can be used as a tool for carrying out the decision-making process for both structural and operational decisions.

In addition, supply chain simulation involves the simulation of the flow of material and information through multiple stages of manufacturing, transportation and distribution. It includes the simulation of the replenishment of incoming inventory and operations at each manufacturing stage, and shipments for the products from one stage to the next. However, running a supply chain simulation requires making numerous decisions such as: raw material supply, production planning/scheduling, inventory control, distribution planning, etc. Numerous

Chapter written by Lyes BENYOUCEF, Vipul JAIN and Patrick CHARPENTIER.

random events adversely influence the performances of supply chains such as random transportation times, demand fluctuations, supply disruptions, etc.

Even if many research activities in supply chain evaluation are currently related to distributed simulation (see Chapters 6 and 7), centralized simulation is still used by researchers and practitioners. The first developed simulation approaches/tools present in the market were mostly known as centralized approaches such as (ARENA, EXTEND, FACTOR, KandanSIM, ProModel, SIMAN, SEE-WHY, SLX, WITNESS) [BAN 00] and these were dedicated to flow simulation within shopfloors. The evolution of information and communication technologies, and manufacturing systems impose changes in the design of supply chain simulation approaches. Thus, new supply chain simulation approaches are frequently developed and improved taking into account both industrial and academic needs. However, the majority of the supply chain simulation approaches currently used in the market remain centralized approaches.

It is important to state that, in a centralized approach, one single simulation model reproduces all the supply chain structures (entities and links). This means that various models, representative of several structures' behaviors, are implemented using a single controller. This practice naturally has advantages and disadvantages compared to distributed simulators, which are discussed in detail later in this chapter.

The rest of the chapter is organized as follows. Section 5.2 presents a brief literature review on centralized supply chain simulation. Section 5.3 discusses the two developed centralized simulation approaches. Section 5.4 illustrates the applicability and efficiency of the two approaches using three industrial applications. Section 5.5 concludes the chapter with some perspectives.

5.2. Supply chain centralized simulation – a literature review

Many tools have been developed to facilitate the use of simulation in designing, evaluating and optimizing supply chains, such as IBM Supply Chain Analyzer, Autofat, Supply Chain Guru, Simflex, etc. Part of these tools are internal packages developed and in use by a single company, for example, CSCAT (Compaq Supply Chain Analysis Tool) [ING 99] and LogSim (Logic Simulator) [HIE 98]. Some commercially available packages are SCS (Supply Chain Simulator) [BAG 98], Supply Solver [SCH 00], e-SCOR (Electronic Standard Operations Reference Model) [BAR 00] and SDI (*Simulation Dynamics, Inc.*) Supply Chain Builder [PHE 01]. Most of these packages are not built from scratch, but include applications of general-purpose simulation languages like e.g. ARENA [KEL 98], Micro Saint (Micro Analysis and Design, 1998), and Extend (Imagine That, 1997).

Although subtle differences exist, it is found that modeling features of these languages strongly focus on the representation of physical interactions between supply chain partners/entities, such as suppliers, producers, distributors and retailers. *Entities related to supply chain coordination are, however, often implicitly modeled.* This observation is not unique for supply chain simulation. Within the context of manufacturing, Pratt *et al.* [PAR 94] find that decision makers, control rules and their interactions are mostly hard coded and dispersed throughout the model. Consequently, not only realism but also modeling flexibility and modularity is harmed [KAR 96].

The earliest attempt to simulate supply chains dates from the birth of system dynamics called *industrial dynamics* [FOR 58]. Forrester [FOR 61] presents a continuous simulation approach, representing the use and movement of goods, orders, information, money, capital, equipment and labor for supply chains as flows, that could be described by a set of closed-form differential equations [ANG 00]. Furthermore, system dynamics take the view that the structure of the supply chain and the control of the flows determine the supply chain's performances. Later, these ideas were explored by different researchers using continuous simulation as well as discrete-event simulation methods. For example, Towill [TOW 91] and [TOW 92] used simulation to evaluate the influence on the bullwhip effect of various modifications to a three echelon supply chain.

Sterman [STE 89] contributes to system dynamics supply chain analysis with his Beer Game (a simulation in the form of a game) and with his text on business dynamics [STE 00]. The Beer Game has motivated other researchers, such as Wu and Katok [WU 06], Croson and Donahue [CRO 03] and [CRO 06] and Chatfield *et al.* [CHA 01, 03a, 03b, 04a, 04b, 06, 07]. Moreover, Sterman [STE 00] makes system dynamics easy to implement by causal loop diagrams, by material flows, by tools for modeling these flows and their inevitable delays and also by modeling human behaviors.

For many supply chain researchers and practitioners, the recent focus of supply chain simulation modeling has been traditional discrete-event simulation models that represent the supply chain as a network. Beyond one-off models, some have built supply chain specific discrete-event supply chain simulators that take a network perspective of the system. These simulation tools view the supply chain as a single organism, with numerous pieces and processes that define its structure and actions. Ganeshan [GAN 97] describes a discrete-event supply chain simulation tool that allows us to manipulate the design of a particular supply problem and analyze the performance characteristics of each new structure. Using Rockwell's Arena, Hermann *et al.* [HER 03] describe a system that follows the SCOR (Supply Chain Operating Reference) model [SUP 03] and [SU P05] as a framework for information storage.

Biswas and Narahari [BIS 04] discuss an object-oriented tool called "DESSCOM" for supporting supply chain decision-making. It is comprised of an optimization workbench, simulation solution techniques and a modeling tool featuring pre-built supply chain objects. Many of the corporate and commercial simulation modeling projects, such as IBM's Supply Chain Analyzer (SCA) [BAG 98], eSCA [CHE 99], Gensym's eSCOR [BAR 00] and LlamaSoft's Supply Chain Guru [LLA 04] take this approach as well. All are supply chain simulators built upon general-purpose simulation languages, such as SimProcess, Pro-Model and Arena.

Several comparisons between supply chain simulation approaches are often carried out in literature [FUJ 99], [MIN 02] and [TER 04]. To our knowledge, the centralized simulation approach still presents certain advantages when it is used for supply chain evaluation:

– simple to implement:

1. the architecture is not complex,

2. there are no problems of communication and synchronization between models, and

3. the validation and verification of models are much simpler than with distributed simulation approaches;

– coherence: simulation model coherence is guaranteed since the level of detail, events taken into account, etc., are ensured by the use of a single controller with (generally) a single modeling tool;

– flexibility: development of a specific and dedicated simulation tool, necessary in some situations, is simpler to implement within a centralized approach than within a distributed simulation approach;

– adaptability: coupling between a centralized simulation model and an optimization model within the framework of simulation-based optimization approaches is not complex to realize compared to distributed simulation approaches.

The centralized simulation approach is often seen with some disadvantages [TER 04] such as:

– execution time: in general longer than in a distributed simulation approach. This can be seen in some industrial applications where interactions between models (a high number of communications) is required. However, a large number of supply chain evaluations using simulation inevitably do not require an answer in real time;

– geographical distribution: does not reproduce the geographical distribution of the system. The distribution cannot be fundamentally compared to the required objectives;

– interoperability: does not make it possible to integrate various simulation models developed using different simulation tools and languages.

Some other disadvantages are also evoked when the comparison between simulation approaches are undertaken. For us, they mainly result from the same cause, i.e. the membership or not of a supply chain entity belonging to the same supply chain (company, group, industrial, etc.). *However, we believe that in the modern supply chain all the entities should be integrated partially or totally in order to increase the supply chain coordination and performances.*

Furthermore, recent development in information and communication technologies poses different problems related to risk and security issues. Complex problems related to access to information, confidentiality and security should also be addressed. The supply chain can be distributed and its controller can be centralized or distributed. Also, simulation implementation can be realized in a distributed or centralized way on the basis of the previously developed arguments.

In a supply chain partnership, companies cooperate with one company while competing with others. *The partnership is also subject to change from time to time.* Therefore, data/information should only be accessible to one company. The centralized approach involves the creation of a physical centralized data/information warehouse, where operational data/information are maintained after transformation. Each functional group, e.g. a department, refers to the data in the data/information warehouse through designated data marts when making decisions. The centralized approach has the advantage of data consistency [DU 04].

Designing a centralized data warehouse approach for supply chain partners involves issues such as global data schemas, duplication of data and homogenity of data warehouses. The centralized data warehouse designs allow companies to maintain their local databases after joining the partnership. Moreover, a centralized approach design assumes companies have their own (non-data warehouse) databases prior to entering a supply chain partnership. A common central data warehouse is built based on these local databases. With this centralized approach, data are maintained in local databases and duplicated to a central data warehouse using a global schema design. In addition, local queries are transferred to and responded to by the data warehouse center. *In this case, data security is an important issue as some information can be seen by competitors in the centralized data warehouse* [DU 04]. Centralized approach design maintains a significant amount of data for supply chain partners to improve the quality of their decision-making.

5.3. Supply chain simulation using centralized approaches

For most simulation evaluation approaches, supply chain processes are modeled to perform "what-if" analysis. Simulation plays a slightly different role in our first approach. In fact, a discrete-event simulation-based optimization is used to estimate the operational performances of *all* the solutions suggested by the optimizer. The optimizer was developed based on the NSGA-II, which is considered one of the champions in multi-objective optimization using genetic algorithms [DEB 02]. Furthermore, unlike most centralized simulation-based optimization approaches, in which decision variables are only system control quantitative parameters, our optimization targets incorporate the supply chain structure. Different combinations of candidate facilities and transportation links result in different supply chain structures. Correspondingly, information flows and material flows in the simulation model are different from one to another. The simulation model has to be regenerated each time according to the selected supply chain structure and operational rules. Thus, it should be adapted according to both supply chain structure and control parameters. Due to the numerous combinations of decision variables, it is not possible to build a simulation model manually for "what-if" analysis. A simulation model builder is indispensable to facilitate automatic simulation model creation. For more details regarding the approach, readers are advised to refer to [DIN 04].

In our second approach, simulation is used within a more traditional framework, with the objective of answering the "what-if" scenarios. The structure of the supply chain is considered as fixed. In this case, the objective is often to improve the supply chain knowledge model (partial or complete), which is used by the decision makers to control the operations in the supply chain more effectively. For important automotive groups, having geographically distributed manufacturing plants, but similar operating mode/rules, the difficulty is to perform a sufficiently generic modeling. The main objective is to reduce model development times by the instantiation of the generic model to the concerned industrial application.

In the following, we present in detail three industrial applications to illustrate the applicability and efficiency of the supply chain centralized simulation approaches developed above.

5.4. Some industrial and practical applications

5.4.1. *Production – distribution network design in automotive industry*

In the following, we present our first real-life case study from the automotive industry. The objective is to improve the profitability and responsiveness of the company's supply chain by redesigning its production-distribution network. We apply the developed centralized simulation-based optimization approach for the optimization of facility open/close decisions, production order assignment and inventory control policies.

5.4.1.1. Network description

The supply chain studied in this case is a global production-distribution network that is operated by a leading European automotive company. Products, cars in this case, are produced in one country and then exported to meet customer demands from another country. Various processes for production, transportation, stocking and final distribution are involved. The objective of the case study is to redesign the network structure and adjust its inventory policy, with consideration of both economic and customer service issues. Supply chain dynamics, such as demand fluctuation and transportation uncertainties, are important and should be taken into account in the decision-making process. The network representation of the supply chain studied is shown in Figure 5.1.

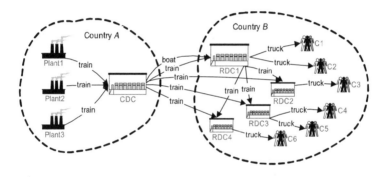

Figure 5.1. *Network representation of the studied automotive supply chain*

As a pilot case, we only study the production and distribution of a single type of car. Six customers (C1,...,C6) are introduced to represent six regions, which generate mixed demands for both MTS (Make-To-Stock), which are standard cars, and MTO (Make-To-Order), which are cars with options. These customers are served by four regional DCs (RDC1,..., RDC4), using trucks for final delivery. All the cars are produced by three plants (Plant1, Plant2 and Plant3) and then accumulated in a consolidated distribution center (CDC). From the CDC, cars are exported and transported to four RDCs via various transportation links. Note that strategic stocks of MTS cars are only held in the CDC and RDC1. The other three RDCs (RDC2, RDC3 and RDC4) act only as transit points for temporary stock holding. We suppose that there is possibly a link between each RDC and each customer. However, for each specific scenario encountered during the optimization process, each customer is served by only one RDC for economy of scale. The customer-RDC relationship is assigned with regard to the distance matrix between the customers and RDCs. The customer is always served by the closest RDC available.

The decisions to be optimized include the open/close decisions on three plants and three RDCs (RDC2, RDC3 and RDC4). The production order assignment ratios are also to be optimized, which are indispensable in case of multiple selected plants. Furthermore, both qualitative and quantitative parameters are to be optimized for inventory control at CDC and RDC1.

5.4.1.2. *Make-to-Stock and Make-to-Order strategies*

The diversity of car models leads to problems for raw material supply, production and distribution. For the automotive industry, cost is traditionally a principle factor to be considered by decision makers. Much attention has been paid to inventory issues since holding stock raises several associated costs, including interest paid on the funds, opportunity costs, warehouse rents and so on. In this context, it is not cost-efficient to store numerous components and final products to anticipate their future requirements, whereas customers often give emphasis to lead-time and after-sales service due to the considerable alternatives on the market. An optimal balance must be achieved between unnecessary inventory holding costs and lost profits due to stock-outs.

Currently, the company manages this by managing customer demands in two manners: Make-to-Order (MTO) and Make-to-Stock (MTS). The demands for best-selling and other standard cars are met directly from DCs where strategic stocks for such demands are kept in anticipation. Cars of these standard models account for the majority of the demands. They are produced using MTS strategy in order to reduce the customer demand cycle time. Of course holding stock for MTS cars incurs corresponding inventory holding costs. On the other hand, those cars that are rarely demanded are handled in an MTO manner, i.e. those cars will not be produced until corresponding customer demands are confirmed. MTO strategy has its advantage on inventory cost saving, while the demand cycle time is usually longer than that of the MTS products. Using such a mixed production and transportation strategy enables the company to balance the inventory holding cost and the response time to customer demands.

5.4.1.3. *The simulation model*

The simulation model is built based on the object-oriented simulation framework developed in [DIN 04]. Real parameter setting is not presented in this chapter due to confidentiality. More specifically, six "customer" objects are used for the generation of weekly independent demands. The demand quantity follows normal distribution, different for each customer. According to a given ratio, each customer demand is divided into two parts: MTS demand and MTO demand. The two types of demand are managed in different ways, with regard to the order assignment rule. Each MTO demand is forwarded directly to a plant that has the lowest workload. MTS demands are to be served by the RDCs regarding the on-hand inventory at RDC1. In case of stock-out at RDC1, MTS demands are backlogged and put in the waiting queue until the next replenishment. In addition, we assume that there is possibly a link between each RDC and each customer. However, for each specific scenario encountered during the optimization process, each customer is served by only one RDC for economy of scale. The customer-DC relationship is assigned with regard to the distance matrix between the customers and RDCs. The customer is always served by the closest RDC available.

The inventory control policy in CDC and RDC1, including both the type of policy and corresponding parameters, are suggested by the optimization module before each simulation run. Two candidate policies are possible in this study, (R, Q) and (s, S), for the inventory control of MTS products. The MTS replenishment orders generated by RDC1 are sent to CDC, which replenishes its stock by sending production orders to the plants. This is obviously a multi-echelon inventory system. Considering that the replenishment orders are usually of high volume, each CDC production order is split into parts according to the order assignment weight associated with each plant. Then each plant is assigned its own production order for MTS cars. Note that the order assignment weight is also an optimization variable, suggested by the optimization module before each simulation run. FIFO (first-in-first-out) production policy is used in this study to handle MTS and MTO orders, i.e. all the orders are treated sequentially according to their arrival time at the plant. Since the supply chain is managed in a "pull" manner, all cars produced in the plants already have their destination. There is no routing problem in this case. More specifically, all cars produced are firstly accumulated at CDC by train. From CDC, MTO cars are sent to corresponding RDCs by train in order to reduce the transportation time. When inventory replenishment orders arrive at CDC, MTS cars are conveyed to RDC1 by boat for transportation cost saving. MTS cars in RDC1 can be delivered directly to its serving customers or transported to other RDCs depending on the MTS demands generated by their serving customers. For all the links, the transportation time parameter is modeled as random parameters following normal distribution.

Note that we use two adaptive operational rules in the simulation model to guarantee the automatic creation of feasible models. No matter which plant is valid, MTO demands will be sent to an appropriate one since we use the workload balance policy for MTO demand assignment, and MTS orders will be sent to all valid plants since we use the order splitting policy for MTS production order assignment. Similarly, any composition of RDCs works for simulation execution, since all the customers are to be served by the closest RDC. Rules dedicated to transportation allocation are not necessary in this case, because the transportation route is unique with regard to each specific demand.

For each scenario (network configuration + parameter setting), several financial and service performance indicators are evaluated. Financial indicators include investment costs for plants and RDCs, production costs, transportation costs, ordering costs and inventory holding costs. Three indicators are evaluated representing the customer service level, respectively the average demand cycle time, the on-time delivery rate and the fill-rate for MTS demands. The demand cycle time is the time period from the moment when a customer order is placed to the moment when the corresponding product is delivered to the customer, which represents the efficiency of a supply chain. The on-time delivery rate is the percentage of orders that are delivered within a preset target. The fill-rate for MTS demands is the percentage of MTS demands that are met directly from stock without backlogging.

5.4.1.4. *Optimization variables*

Optimization variables include the "open or close" decision for each plant and three RDCs (RDC1, 2, 3). A production order assignment weight is associated with each validated plant. In addition to the strategic decisions, we also optimize qualitative variables, i.e. the inventory control policy employed at CDC and RDC1. Given the optimization variables, we code the corresponding four-segment chromosome (Figure 5.2).

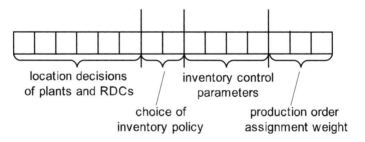

Figure 5.2. *Composition of the chromosome*

The first part contains six binary genes dedicated to open/close decisions on three plants and three RDCs, determining the supply chain structure. Two enumerative variables are used in the second segment indicating the choice of inventory policy in CDC and RDC1, which parameters are included in the third segment with four integers. At the end of the chromosome, three integers are added representing the production order assignment weight for each plant.

5.4.1.5. *Optimization specifications*

Given the optimization variables, we code the corresponding two-segment chromosome. The first part contains six binary genes for open/close decisions on three plants and three RDCs, determining the supply chain structure. The second segment includes four integers representing the control parameters for inventory policy in CDC and RDC1.

Concerning the GA parameter setting, we set the maximum generation number as 1,000 with a population size of 100. One point crossover is employed considering that the chromosome is relatively short. The probability of crossover is 0.9 and the probability of mutation is 0.1. Other genetic operations are implemented with regard to the NSGA-II, such as the Pareto dominance ranking procedure and the elitist selection.

For strategic decisions, especially in the presence of randomness, simulation should run for a long period to reflect supply chain dynamics. Thus, in this study, the simulation horizon is set as 4 years. For each set of decision variables, 5 replications are simulated using different random number streams to smooth out residual randomness. After each simulation run, two performance indicators are retrieved, respectively the average unit cost and the average demand cycle time. The average unit cost is calculated based on the total costs (the summation of investment cost, production cost, transportation cost, inventory holding cost and ordering cost) and the total customer demands. Thus, the optimization criteria are two-fold:

1. minimize f_1 the average unit cost (from the profitability point of view),

2. minimize f_2 the average demand cycle time (from the customer satisfaction point of view).

5.4.1.6. *Experimental results and analyses*

After the optimization, we obtain a set of best-so-far Pareto-optimal solutions, which are well compromised with regard to both optimization criteria. They are listed in Table 5.1. The first two columns contain the values of two optimization criteria. The remaining columns correspond to the decisions. The "configuration" column suggests open/close decisions for each facility. Obviously two types of network configurations are found with either plant 1 or plant 2. Plant 2 is selected in the case that the average demand cycle time is expected to be less than 10 days. In other cases, plant 1 is preferred which is more cost-effective. The last four columns suggest the parameters for inventory control policy in both CDC and RDC1.

Figure 5.3 shows the best-so-far Pareto front of the studied problem. We observe that the front is composed of two segments. The three points in the right part correspond to the solutions that select plant 1. The non-even distribution of points is due to the discrete solution space.

On the other hand, we observe that three RDCs are selected to be closed for all Pareto-optimal solutions. The distribution network is to be centralized according to the optimization result. Currently, distribution centralization is expected to benefit from economies of scale in comparison with a decentralized distribution solution, which aims to improve customer service by locating more distribution centers to serve customer zones. These are exactly the initiatives, which motivate the case study.

f_1 (€)	f_2 (days)	Configuration	CDC-s	CDC_S	RDC1_s	RDC_S
5,240	9.7	0 1 0 0 0 0	1,787	2,229	1,990	2,556
5,771	9.8	0 1 0 0 0 0	1,791	2,248	1,990	2,584
5,761	9.9	0 1 0 0 0 0	1,808	2,171	1,989	2,506
5,253	10	1 0 0 0 0 0	1,811	2,225	1,986	2,552
5,244	10.1	1 0 0 0 0 0	1,682	2,057	1,990	2,556
5,240	10.2	1 0 0 0 0 0	1,622	2,034	1,997	2,586
5,227	10.3	1 0 0 0 0 0	1,945	2,347	1,988	2,554
5,225	10.4	1 0 0 0 0 0	1,589	1,961	1,988	2,515
5,214	10.5	1 0 0 0 0 0	1,688	2,010	1,990	2,571
5,201	10.7	1 0 0 0 0 0	1,408	1,933	1,985	2,516
5,194	11	1 0 0 0 0 0	1,277	1,626	1,981	2,547
5,189	11.1	1 0 0 0 0 0	1,270	1,683	1,970	2,485
5,189	11.1	1 0 0 0 0 0	1,270	1,683	1,970	2,485
5,187	11.4	1 0 0 0 0 0	1,164	1,543	1,997	2,521
5,182	11.7	1 0 0 0 0 0	1,259	1,637	1,917	2,441
5,166	12.3	1 0 0 0 0 0	1,375	1,682	1,708	2,293
5,165	12.8	1 0 0 0 0 0	1,360	2,230	1,652	2,169
5,158	13.3	1 0 0 0 0 0	684	1,255	1,934	2,493
5,157	15.3	1 0 0 0 0 0	480	790	1,995	2,513
5,138	15.9	1 0 0 0 0 0	337	1,356	1,726	2,330
5,138	15.9	1 0 0 0 0 0	337	1,356	1,726	2,330
5,128	19.1	1 0 0 0 0 0	483	830	1,514	1,853

Table 5.1. *List of best-so-far Pareto-optimal solutions*

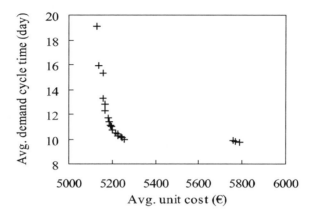

Figure 5.3. *Best-so-far Pareto front*

5.4.2. *Supplier selection problem in textile industry*

In this section, we applied the centralized simulation-based multi-objective genetic algorithm approach to a real-life case study of a multi-national textile supply chain, which consists of several suppliers, a single distribution center and an aggregated customer. The modeling and simulation details are discussed and numerical results are presented and analyzed.

5.4.2.1. *Supply chain description*

The supply chain considered in this study is a part of the supply chain for boots distributed by a textile company located in Europe. The company uses a complete outsourcing policy and focuses on the marketing facts. As a result, there is no plant in the studied supply chain. Figure 5.4 represents the network structure of the actual supply chain.

For the actual situation, a single supplier, denoted by S1 located in the Far East, provides final products to the focal company. A central warehouse is operated in Europe employing a periodic replenishment inventory policy. The replenishment order is forwarded by the company to the supplier. After a period of supply lead-time, the final products are collected into containers and then transported by boat from the Far East to a European harbor. From the harbor, they are transported to the central warehouse by trucks. Products are then distributed to the market along with other products. The motivations of the company's effort on supply portfolio optimization are two-fold. Firstly, the current order-to-delivery lead-time is relatively long because of the long distance between the Far East and Europe, using boats as the principle carrier. Secondly, the demands of the products have a high seasonality and stock-out frequently occurs. Thus, the overall objective is to redesign the supply chain, mainly by selecting new suppliers for the final products, and evaluating different solutions in term of overall costs, robustness to changes in demand and some other criteria.

In addition to the existing supplier, the company selects three other suppliers as candidates to form a new supply portfolio. One potential supplier, denoted by S2, is also located in the Far East and provides products at the lowest price. In order to reduce the lead-time, the company proposes two additional transportation links for both suppliers from Asia. One transportation link is that products are conveyed by plane from Asia to a European airport, from where they are moved to the central warehouse by truck. This is the fastest but also the most expensive way. An intermediate transportation solution is that products are transported by plane from the two suppliers to another Asian transit. Then the products are conveyed by boat to a European harbor, from where they are finally moved to the central warehouse. The third transportation solution maintains a trade-off between costs and time. Another two potential suppliers are located inside Europe, denoted by S3 and S4 respectively. These two suppliers are more responsive because they are closer to the central warehouse. Only one transportation mode, using trucks, is provided for each of them. The supply lead-time is very short, but on the other hand, the price is much higher than that of the two suppliers from the Far East.

In summary, the redesign needs the comparison of different configurations of the supply chain, by selecting one or more suppliers plus corresponding transportation modes. In addition to the network configuration, the assignment ratio should also be optimized if there is more than one supplier. Moreover, operational parameters related to inventory policy of the central warehouse are also to be optimized. Due to the various requirements of the reconfiguration, the proposed simulation optimization methodology is an appropriate means to deal with this complex problem.

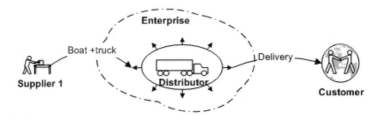

Figure 5.4. *Actual supply chain for the focal enterprise*

5.4.2.2. The simulation-optimization model

The supply chain model consists of several suppliers, a distribution center and a customer representing the whole market. Considering that the supply capacity of any of the four suppliers is much larger than the demand, we perform a simplification for network modeling. Each of the two Asian suppliers is separated into three copies, namely S1-1, S1-2, S1-3, S2-1, S2-2 and S2-3, according to the different combinations of transportation modes. The decision related to transportation modes is transferred to supplier selection. Figure 5.5 shows the complete supply chain network comprising the existing supplier and potential suppliers, plus corresponding transportation modes.

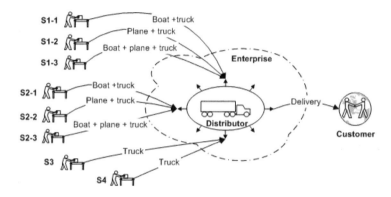

Figure 5.5. *Potential suppliers and transportation modes*

5.4.2.3. Genetic representation and operations

In the first segment of a chromosome, a binary string is used to represent the portfolio of different suppliers, where "1" means the corresponding supplier is included in the supply portfolio and "0" means the supplier is excluded from the supply portfolio. Correspondingly, eight integer variables are integrated in the second segment of the chromosome, representing the assignment weight. In this study, we set the weights in the interval [0,16]. At the end of the chromosome there is one integer variable representing the replenishment level of the central warehouse. Figure 5.6 shows the structure of the chromosome used for this case study. Other parameters related to the genetic algorithm are listed as follows:

1. the maximum number of GA generations is set as 500;

2. each population contains 20 individuals;

3. roulette wheel selection is used to select chromosomes;

4. two-point crossover operator;

5. the probability of crossover operation is set as 0.9;

6. mutation is performed immediately after the crossover with probability 0.01;

7. to balance the disruptive nature of the chosen crossover and mutation, we use the *Elitist* strategy to preserve the best individuals.

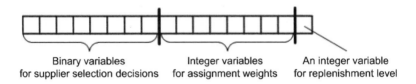

Binary variables   Integer variables   An integer variable
for supplier selection decisions   for assignment weights   for replenishment level

Figure 5.6. *Structure of the chromosome for the case study*

In order to evaluate the fitness of each individual, simulation models are generated to facilitate performance estimation. Given a candidate supply portfolio, the model generator generates a corresponding discrete-event simulation model. Then performances of each supply portfolio are available in terms of relevant KPIs after the simulation. In this study we evaluate four KPIs, including purchasing costs, transportation costs, inventory costs and total missed demands. A penalty factor α is introduced to reflect the customer service level. The penalty cost is calculated as $\alpha \times$ Missed demands and α is set as 100 in this case study. As a result the fitness is calculated as the summation of purchasing costs, transportation costs, inventory costs and penalty costs. The overall objective of the GA optimizer is set to minimize the total costs.

5.4.2.4. *Discrete-event simulation model*

"Supplier" is the most important entity in supply chain for supplier selection problems. In this study, we derive a new class of "supplier" from the basic prototype defined in the generic modeling and simulation package [DIN 04]. Supplementary attributes are added the new building block. The essential attributes are listed in the following:

1. FOB price;

2. duties;

3. supply lead-time;

4. waste ratio;

5. assignment weight.

The first four attributes are important supplier characteristics and should be given by the end-user. In order to optimize the assignment ratio in the condition that more than one supplier is selected, we introduce an attribute "assignment weight" into the building block. The assignment weight is suggested by the GA optimizer, based on which the assignment ratio is calculated by the demand planning module of the company. For example, suppliers S1-2, S2-3 and S3 are suggested by the GA optimizer to form the supply portfolio. Each of them is assigned a value for assignment weight, denoted by w_{12}, w_{23} and w_3. Then the ratio for S1-2 is concluded as $w_{12} / (w_{12} + w_{23} + w_3)$.

Concerning the simulation detail, the main processes and assumptions are briefly summarized in the following:

1. the customer generates demand periodically. The demand interval is set as one week;

2. the demand quantity follows a normal distribution (800, 100);

3. backorder is not allowed. We assume that customers are not patient, i.e. a customer order is missed if it could not be met immediately from stock;

4. the periodic replenishment level policy is employed at the central warehouse. The replenishment parameter is suggested by the GA optimizer;

5. when the order for inventory replenishment is received, the company divides it into n sub-orders according to the assignment ratio. n is the number of suppliers;

6. products will be ready for transportation after the period of supply lead-time. All the products for one order will be transported to the warehouse at one time via a specific transportation mode.

The simulation horizon is set as 2 years since supplier selection is a typical strategic decision. Since GA needs tens of thousands of simulations to search the solution space, the simulation model is implemented in an efficient way. Currently, a single simulation run takes less than one second.

5.4.2.5. *Experimental results and analyses*

After the simulation optimization process, a near-optimal solution is obtained. This best-so-far supply portfolio is composed of two suppliers from the Far East: S2-1 and S2-2. We can discover that currently just one supplier is selected using two types of transportation modes at the same time. S2-1 uses a boat plus a truck, which is the cheapest way, while S2-2 uses a plane plus a truck, which is expensive but very fast. Concerning the assignment ratio, around 73.7% of the total quantity of each order is sent to S2-1 and the rest is sent to S2-2. This means that supplier S2 separates each product batch into two parts. The bigger part is transported via sea to

Europe, while a small part is transported by plane. In addition, the best-so-far replenishment level of the central warehouse is given as 10,800.

Figure 5.7 shows the composition of the total costs in supply chain operations. Obviously the purchasing cost takes the largest share. Considering that the purchasing cost is about 80% of the total costs, it is reasonable to find that the supplier, which provides products in the lowest price, is selected in this case.

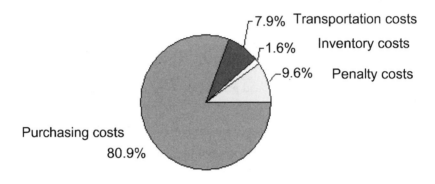

Figure 5.7. *Total costs composition*

Figure 5.8 demonstrates the development process of the proposed approach. The mean value of total costs continues to be reduced with the increasing of generations. Note that the mean value converges quickly within a relatively small number of generations.

Apart from the simulation optimization approach, we have also developed several detailed simulation models by simply extending the simulation package to verify the optimization results. These prototypes are built in collaboration with logistics managers from the company. The simulation results are considered by logistics managers as consistent both with the optimization results and the actual operational data.

The case study illustrates the applicability of the methodology developed. In addition, the case study shows the convenience offered by the object-oriented approach that evaluation of different situations and decisions can be achieved easily with the reuse of code.

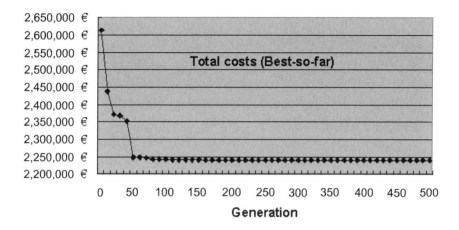

Figure 5.8. *Mean value of total costs of each generation*

5.4.3. *Another practical example from the automotive industry*

The third example presented originates from an international automotive group. For this type of production, according to the number of components and options offered to the end-customers, the diversity of feasible cars has exploded.

For economical reasons, these different models are built on the same assembly line, called "mixed model assembly line" in order to reduce the gap between small and large production volumes (concept of "mass customization" [AND 04]) and allow a Just-in-Time production deployment. Due to the high costs when modifying infrastructures and physical flows inside the assembly line, several research works have been performed in order to optimize both production resource management and the supply of components [AND 04].

In this section, we present our approach with the aim to develop a generic model, which can be used by different automotive industries. The developed model is limited to only the interactions between the assembly line and its direct suppliers. It is important to note that, the model is not built to answer a specific problem, but must be able to help supply chain decision makers in their choices.

5.4.3.1. *Supply chain description*

It is well known that at the level of the assembly lines, the main part in the added value of a car is realized. Thus, it is very important to have a perfect synchronization of cars flows and components [VIL 04]. The problem is complex and needs further research and development. This is basically due to the complex structure of automotive supply chains. Generally, a car terminal plant can have a traditional "X" structure, with 500 first level suppliers and approximately 5,000 supply flows and is managed by two Just-in-Time policies respectively (Figure 5.9):

– RECOR (REal COnsumptions Renewal)-Kanban adapted: this is ready and done factory consumption, which activates the order transmission to the supplier;

– coordinated delivery: this is firm-intended factory consumption, which activates the order transmission to the supplier.

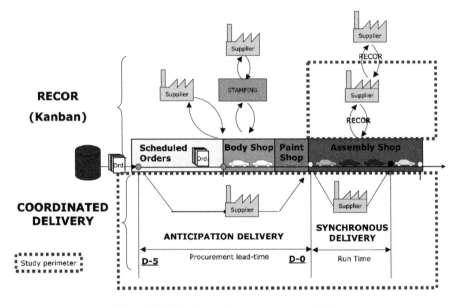

Figure 5.9. *Car flow and component supply flow*

An implementation analysis of these various kinds of relationships between automotive supply chain actors was performed. Some of the main points, which result from this analysis, are:

– very big order systems and disparity in each assembly plant due to historical and/or geographical and/or habit reasons;

– excessive reassurance and differences in between all assembly plants from the same manufacturer;

– impact measurement difficulties (sometimes impossibility) of several parameters e.g. disturbances, systems order modifications, stock security level modifications, etc.

A proposition has been made to realize a Decision-making tool for the customer-suppliers relationship analysis in the context of flows control. Several important constraints were put such as:

– model generation (or construction) must be simple and easy to realize by a non-specialist in simulation;

– detailed and realistic vision of component consumption by each car;

– possibility to model unpredictable phenomena;

– direct links between the company information system and the simulator (car name, real production sequences, etc.).

It can be noted that a large volume of supplies does not allow an exhaustive analytical study or a mathematical formalization. Therefore, in our case, we use discrete-event simulation models to study flows between the car terminal plant and suppliers.

5.4.3.2. *From the generic model of a supply flow to its simulation*

As stated in [MOI 77], one object has three elementary attributes: shape, space and time. Moreover, operators, which reproduce the real system functions and modify the three attributes of the system objects, were also discussed. Therefore, in our case, an order is the modified object and a system is one supply flow (see Figure 5.10). The order then has three basic attributes with values defined by going through the flow (see Figure 5.10). The system operators are:

– time and space attribute transformation: "Delivery", sending the empty order from customer to supplier; "Transport", transport the full order from supplier to customer;

– time and shape attribute transformation: "Consumption", transformation from full order to empty order; "Production", transformation from empty order to full order;

– time attribute transformation: "Inventory before production", "Inventory before Transport", "Inventory before consumption" and "Inventory before delivery".

To specify at the same time the static and dynamic characters of the system and to guarantee the coherence of the suggested approach, we decide to use the modeling language UML. This is reinforced by the modular character of the system. UML has become an object modeling standard and its use can be extended to manufacturing system modeling. This approach allows the representation of the various actors of the automotive supply chain and their relations, not only from the static point of view, but also their behaviors, from the dynamic point of view [CHA 02].

The generic nature of UML confers some gaps, in particular on the level of inconsistencies between the views and the lack of precise semantics. In order to complete the notation and adapt it to the application domain needs, the UML meta-model (Figure 5.11) was extended by using mechanisms specific to UML (stereotype, tag, etc.).

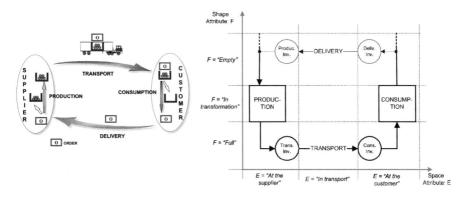

Figure 5.10. *One supply flow and systemic representation of a supply flow and order attribute values*

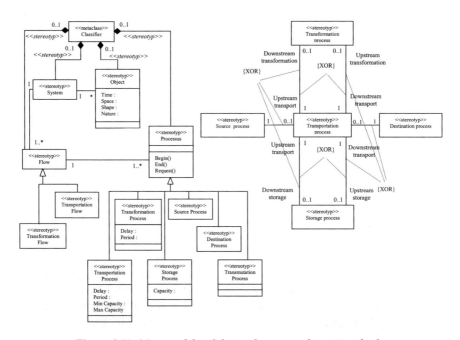

Figure 5.11. *Meta-model with basic elements and associated rules*

From this UML meta-model, several tests were conducted to obtain a version, which can then be simulated. According to the company information systems connections, simulation execution times and the complexity of the system in terms of supplier numbers, flow numbers and volumes, etc., our choice was to produce a dedicated simulator in object language (Visual C++). UML specification (Figure 5.11) makes it possible to generate the code. In addition, and even if simulation is centralized, the simulator was developed in a modular way amongst other things to allow a connection to the company information systems (interfacing). These data are then used for the automotive supply chain specific model instantiation (simulation motor) and finally, the events are traced and analyzed within a processing module.

The user interface was developed in Visual BASIC and the core (corresponding to the meta-model) is reusable for other applications as it is coded in an ActiveX form (Figure 5.12).

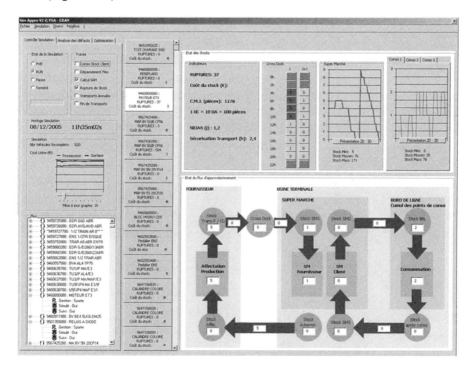

Figure 5.12. *User interface of the developed simulation platform*

This tool allows us to simulate in several minutes (between 5 and 10) approximately 3,000 different component flows over a period of one month (40,000 cars).

5.4.3.3. *Illustrative example*

The objective of our case study is to find the best possible compromise between a quality of service and ownership costs associated with each stock of components. The considered quality of service is directly related to the number of incomplete cars due to a delay of one or more of its components. To obtain a better quality of service, it is possible to increase the stock level (to avoid all delays), whereas to reduce the ownership cost, they should be reduced.

Our case is limited to the simulation of the components supplied in "coordinated by anticipation" because it is the most interesting to study (there is no level of security for the synchronous delivery and the RECOR having to be gradually abandoned). These components (approximately 1,200 different standards) "are consumed" according to the actual list of cars in production. The study is focused on the just necessary level of security making it possible to respect the production schedule subjected to risks. It does not take into account the risks related to the supply of these components.

Figure 5.13 shows a graph of the initial and real configuration of the stock levels for each component. After having controlled the parameters of the securities of each stock, with the objective to determine the best compromise between the quality of service (number of incomplete cars) and the cost of stock, it proves that these security levels strongly decrease (Figure 5.14). These costs depend naturally on the nature of the components, their storage requirements, the storage space that they use, etc.

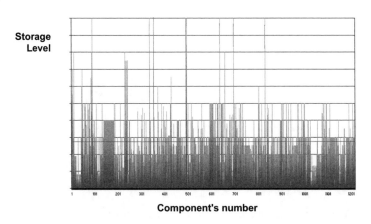

Figure 5.13. *Graph of the initial and real configuration of the stock levels given by simulation before optimization*

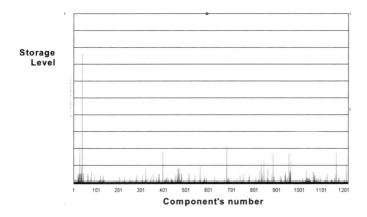

Figure 5.14. *Graph of the initial and real configuration of the stock levels given by simulation after optimization*

Finally, it is proved that it is possible to lower the costs related to the securities from approximately 30% with, at the same time, an increase of about 10% in the quality of service (the number of completely assembled cars).

The temporal performances of this dedicated simulation, developed within a centralized approach, were highlighted in several different studies. It seems that this tool is on the way to becoming the reference tool for simulation for the whole of the industrial group for which it was developed.

5.5. Conclusions and perspectives

Simulation has been identified as one of the best means to analyze and deal with stochastic facets existing in supply chains. Its ability to understand uncertainty, complex system dynamics and large-scale systems makes it well suited for supply chain studies. This can help the optimization process by evaluating the impact of alternative management policies. Therefore, this chapter was dedicated to centralized approaches for supply chain simulation where some critical issues with their industrial applications were discussed.

In two of the presented industrial applications, a centralized simulation-based multiobjective genetic algorithm approach was discussed for effective decision-making in respectively automotive and textile industries. In addition, in the third industrial application presented, a centralized simulation-based UML approach was addressed and successfully applied to a real life case study from the automotive industry.

Concerning future research, we will pay more attention to the optimization of qualitative criteria, which are considered a difficult task for traditional mathematical programming approaches. On the other hand, some benchmarking works could be performed by comparing the proposed centralized simulation approaches with some analytical approaches for simplified cases in order to emphasize their applicability in real-life challenging problems from different industries.

5.6. Bibliography

[AND 04] Anderson D.M., *Customization; The Ultimate Supply ChainManagement and lean Manufacturing Strategy for Low-Cost On-Demand Production without Forecasts*, CIM Press, USA, 2004.

[ANG 00] Angerhofer B., Angelides M., "System dynamics modeling in supply chain management", in J.A. Joines, R.B. Barton, K. Kang and P.A. Fishwick (eds.), *Proceedings of the 2000 Winter Simulation Conference, Institute of Electrical and Electronics Engineers*, Piscataway, NJ, p. 342-351, 2000.

[BAG 98] Bagchi, S., Buckley, S.J., Attl M., Lin G.Y., "Experience using the IBM supply chain simulator", *Proceedings of the 1998 Winter Simulation Conference*, D.J. Medeiros, E.F. Watson, J.S. Carson, M.S. Manivannan (eds.), Piscataway, New Jersey, pp. 1387-1394, 1998.

[BAN 00] Banks J., "Simulation in the future", *Proceedings of the 2000 Winter Simulation Conference*, J.A. Joines, R.R. Barton, K. Kang, P.A. Fishwick (eds.), Piscataway, New Jersey, USA, pp. 1568-1576, 2000.

[BAR 00] Barnett M.W., Miller C.J., "Analysis of the virtual enterprise using distributed supply chain modeling and simulation: an application of e-SCOR", *Proceedings of the 2000 Winter Simulation Conference*, J.A. Joines, R.R. Barton, K. Kang and P.A. Fishwick (eds.), Piscataway, NJ pp. 352-355, 2000.

[BIS 04] Biswas S. and Narahari Y., "Object-oriented modeling and decision support for supply chains", *European Journal of Operational Research*, 53, pp. 704-726, 2004.

[CHA 01] Chatfield D.C., Harrison T.P., Hayya J.C., "SISCO: a supply chain simulation tool utilizing SILK and XML", , *Proceedings of the 2001 Winter Simulation Conference,* B.A. Peters, J.S. Smith, D.J. Medeiros and M.W. Rohrer, (eds.), Piscataway, NJ, pp. 614-622, 2001.

[CHA 02] Changchien S.W., Shen H.-Y., "Supply chain reengineering using a core process analysis matrix and object-oriented simulation", *Information & Management*, vol. 39, no. 5, pp. 345-358, March 2002.

[CHA 03a] Chatfield D.C., Harrison T.P., Hayya J.C., The Supply Chain Modeling Language (SCML), working paper, Department of Supply Chain and Information Systems, Pennsylvania State University, 2003.

[CHA 03b] Chatfield D.C., Harrison T.P., Hayya J.C., SISCO: The Simulator for Integrated Supply Chain Operations, working paper, Department of Supply Chain and Information Systems, Pennsylvania State University, 2003.

[CHA 04a] Chatfield D.C., Harrison T.P., Hayya J.C., SCML – a generalized supply chain description language, working paper, Department of Supply Chain and Information Systems, Pennsylvania State University, 2004.

[CHA 04b] Chatfield D.C., Kim J.G., Harrison T.P. and Hayya J.C., "The bullwhip effect – impact of stochastic lead times, information quality, and information sharing: a simulation study", *Production and Operations Management*, 13(4), pp. 340-353, 2004.

[CHA 06] Chatfield D.C., Harrison T.P., Hayya J.C., "SISCO: an object-oriented supply chain simulation tool", *Decision Support Systems*, 42(1), pp. 422-434, 2006.

[CHA 07] Chatfield D.C., Hayya J.C., Harrison T.P., "A multi-formalism architecture for agent-based, order-centric supply chain simulation", *Simulation Modelling Practice and Theory*, 15, pp. 153-174, 2007.

[CHE 99] Chen H.B., Bimber O., Chatre C., Poole E. and Buckley S.J., "eSCA: a thin-client/server/web-enabled system for distributed supply chain simulation", *Proceedings of the 1999 Winter Simulation Conference*, P.A. Farrington, H.B. Nembhard, D.T. Sturrock and G.W. Evans (eds.), Piscataway, NJ, pp. 1371-1377, 1999.

[CRO 03] Croson K. and Donohue K., "Impact of point of sale (POS) data sharing on supply chain management: an experimental study", *Production and Operations Management*, 12, pp. 1-11, 2003.

[CRO 06] Croson K., Donohue K., "Behavioral causes of the bullwhip effect and the observed value of inventory information", *Management Science*, 52(3), pp. 323-336, 2006.

[DEB 02] Deb K., Pratap A., Agarwal S. and Meyarivan T., "A fast and elitist multiobjective genetic algorithm: NSGA-II", *IEEE Transactions on Evolutionary Computation*, vol. 6, pp. 182-197, 2002.

[DIN 04] Ding H., A simulation-based optimization approach for supply chain design: applications to automotive and textile industries, PhD dissertation, University of Metz, France, 2004.

[DU 04] Du T.C., Wong J., Lee M., "Designing Data Warehouses for Supply Chain Management", *Proceedings of the IEEE International Conference on E-Commerce Technology*, pp. 170-177, 2004.

[FOR 58] Forrester J.W., "Industrial dynamics – a major breakthrough for decision makers", *Harvard Business Review*, 36(4), pp. 37-66, 1958.

[FOR 61] Forrester J.W., *Industrial Dynamics*, MIT Press and John Wiley & Sons, Inc., New York, 1961.

[FUJ 99] Fujimoto R.M., *Parallel and Distributed Simulation Systems*, John Wiley and Sons, New York, 1999.

[GAN 97] Ganeshan R., Analytical essays in supply-chain management, PhD thesis, Department of Management Science and Information Systems, Pennsylvania State University, 1997.

[HER 03] Herrmann J., Lin E., Pundoor G., "Supply chain simulation modeling using the supply chain operations reference model", *Proceedings of the ASME 2003 Design Engineering Technical Conference*, September 2–6, ASME, Chicago, 2003.

[HIE 98] Hieta S., "Supply chain simulation with LOGSIM-simulator", *Proceedings of the 1998 Winter Simulation Conference*, D.J. Medeiros, E.F. Watson, J.S. Carson, M.S. Manivannan (eds.), Piscataway, New Jersey, USA, pp. 323-326, 1998.

[ING 99] Ingalls R.G., Kasales C., "CSCAT: The COMPAQ supply chain analysis tool", *Proceedings of the 1999 Winter Simulation Conference*, P.A. Farrington, H.B. Nembhard, D.T. Sturrock, G.W. Evans (eds.), Piscataway, New Jersey, USA, pp. 1201-1206, 1999.

[KAR 98] Karacal S.C., Mize J.H., "A formal structure for discrete event simulation. Part II: Object-oriented software implementation for manufacturing systems", *IIE Transactions*, 30(3), 217-226, 1998.

[KEL 98], Kelton W.D., Sadowski R.P., Sadowski D.A., *Simulation with Arena*, McGraw-Hill, 1998.

[LLA 04]   LlamaSoft   Incorporated,   Supply   Chain   Guru,   2004, http://www.llamasoft.com/Software/index.htm.

[MIN 02] Min H., Zhou G., "Supply chain modeling: past, present and future", *Computers and Industrial Engineering*, 43 (1-2): 231-249, 2002.

[MOI 77] Le Moigne J.-L., *The Theory of General Systems*, PUF editions (French version), 1977.

[PAR 99] Parunak H.V.D, Savit R., Riolo R.L., Clark S.J., DASCh: Dynamic analysis of supply chains, Final Report, Center for E-Commerce, ERIM Inc., 1999.

[PHE 01] Phelps R.A., Parsons D.J., Siprelle A.J., "SDI supply chain builder: simulation from atoms to the enterprise", *Proceedings of the 2001 Winter Simulation Conference*, B.A. Peters, J.S. Smith, D.J. Medeiros, M.W. Rohrer (eds.), Piscataway, New Jersey, USA, pp. 246-249, 2001.

[SCH 00] Schunk D., Plott B., "Using simulation to analyze supply chains", *Proceedings of the 2000 Winter Simulation Conference*, J.A. Joines, R.R. Barton, K. Kang, P.A. Fishwick (eds.), Piscataway, New Jersey, USA, pp. 1095-1100, 2000.

[STE 89] Sterman J.D., "Modeling managerial behavior: misperceptions of feedback in a dynamic decision making experiments", *Management Science*, 35, pp. 321-339, 1989.

[STE 00] Sterman J.D., *Business Dynamics: Systems Thinking and Modeling for a Complete World*, Irwin McGraw-Hill, Boston, 2000.

[SUP 03] Supply Chain Council (SCC), Supply-Chain Operations Reference (SCOR) Model V.6.0., 2003.

[SUP 05] Supply Chain Council (SCC), 2005, http://www.supply-chain.org.

[TER 04] Terzi S., Cavalieri S., "Simulation in the supply chain context: a survey", *Computer in Industry*, 53, 3-16, 2004.

[TOW 91] Towill D., "Supply chain dynamics", *International Journal of Computer Integrated Manufacturing*, 4(4), pp. 197-208, 1991.

[TOW 92] Towill D., Naim M., Wikner J., "Industrial dynamics, simulation models in the design of supply-chains", *International Journal of Physical Distribution and Logistics Management*, 22(5), pp. 3-13, 1992.

[VIL 04] Villeminot A., Modeling and simulation of supplying logistic in an automotive industry applied to an international group, PhD dissertation, Henri Poincare University, France, 2004.

[WU 06] Wu D.Y., Katok E., "Learning, Communication, and the Bullwhip Effect", *Journal of Operations Management*, 24(6), p. 839-850, 2006.

Chapter 6

The Interest of Agents for Supply Chain Simulation

6.1. Decision problems in enterprise networks

In today's increasingly global and competitive marketplace, it is imperative that companies work together to achieve the expected goals in terms of minimizing delivery delays, holding costs and transportation costs. New forms of organizations have emerged, such as the so-called extended enterprises and virtual enterprises, in which partners must demonstrate strong coordination and commitment capabilities to achieve the desired goals.

A virtual enterprise (VE) can be defined in several ways. Makatsoris *et al.* define a VE as "*a subset of units and processes within the supply chain network, consisting of a matrix of largely cooperating manufacturing, storage and transport units of mixed ownership, which behave like a single enterprise through strong co-ordination and cooperation towards mutual goals*" [MAK 96]. It should be noted that in a virtual enterprise, manufacturers no longer produce complete products in isolated facilities. They operate as nodes in a network of suppliers, customers, engineering units, producers and other specialized service functions [DAV 95].

In planning a virtual enterprise, integration of the planning of all the nodes of the enterprise is needed. This integration not only applies to the material flows from raw material suppliers to finished product delivery, but also to the financial flows and information flows from the market (i.e. the anonymous consumers) back to the

Chapter written by Thibaud MONTEIRO, Didier ANCIAUX, Bernard ESPINASSE, Alain FERRARINI, Olivier LABARTHE and Daniel ROY.

supply-chain partners. As shown in [MIN 02] and [DAM 99], the success of the integration of a supply-chain lies in the capability of the partners in distributing the information and in synchronizing their activities. Srinivasan *et al.* proved that, in a Just-in-Time environment, the exchange of information increases the execution of deliveries [SRI 94].

Companies are now facing growing global competition and continual success in the marketplace depends very much on how efficient and effective the companies are able to respond to customer demands. The formation of a virtual enterprise network is taking up momentum to meet this challenge. The idea of a virtual enterprise network is intended to establish a dynamic organization by the synergetic combination of dissimilar companies with different core competencies, thereby forming a "best of everything" consortium to perform a given business project to achieve the maximum degree of customer satisfaction. In this emerging business model of virtual enterprise network, the decision support functionality, which addresses issues such as selection of business partners, coordination in the distribution of production processes and the prediction of production problems, is an important domain to be studied.

In order to guarantee a level of optimal performance in a dynamic environment, approaches of the multi-agent system (MAS) type can be used. In fact, MAS is composed of a group of agents that can take specific roles within an organizational structure. Different types of agents may represent different objects, with a different authority and capability, and perform different functions or tasks. They can be dynamically organized based on a control or connection structure.

Supply chain management by its very nature has characteristics that make agent technology very suitable to support collaboration in supply chain management. MAS can be used to model or actually perform tasks in supply chain management due to the similarities of the nature of these two systems. For example: i) a supply chain consists of multiple parties working on multi-stage tasks; *a multi-agent system consists of different types of agents with different roles and functions*; ii) there is no single authority: knowledge is distributed among members in the supply chain, decision-making in a supply chain is through multiparty negotiation and coordination; *agents are autonomous: they are responsive to monitor changing environment, proactive to take self-initiated action, and social to interact with humans and other agents*; iii) the structure of the supply chain is flexible: it can be organized differently to implement different strategies; *the agent system is flexible: agents can be organized according to different control and connection structures*; or, iv) the supply chain is dynamic: entities may join or leave a supply chain; *agents can be created or discarded from a multi-agent system* [KAR 07].

The application of MAS in manufacturing and supply-chain management is not new. In intelligent manufacturing, agents have been used in the following functional areas: manufacturing control, collaborative design, coordination in MAS for flexible manufacturing, [BAR 96] and [PAR 98]. Montreuil *et al.* have developed a strategic network for supply chains [MON 00]. Lin and Solberg have developed a market mechanism to coordinate agents in real time in an integrated shop floor control model [LIN 92]. Sikora and Shaw have provided a multi-agent framework for the coordination and integration of information systems [SIK 98]. Shen and Norrie have provided a survey of agent-based systems for intelligent manufacturing [SHE 99]. In supply chain management, Yung and Yang have proposed the integration of multi-agent technology and constraint network for solving the supply chain management problem [YUN 99].

The topic of Chapters 6 and 7 concern the decision problems in the enterprise network. In Chapter 6, we consider the interest of agents for supply chain simulation. Initially, we will use a state of the art on the MAS, where we will tackle the problems of task allowance, planning and negotiation, using cognitive, reactive and hybrid agents. Then, we detail their behavior like their interactions. Then we will approach the simulation of the supply chain through a whole project on directed modeling and simulation agents, applied to the industrial systems. We can quote, for example, ISCM (Integrated Supply Chain Management), developed by "Enterprise Integration Laboratory – University of Toronto", or MASCOT (Multi-agent Supply Chain Tool coordination), developed by "Intelligent Coordination and Logistics Laboratory – Carnegie Mellon". Lastly, we conclude this chapter with comparisons of these various projects and approaches.

Then in Chapter 7, we consider the aspect decisional system simulation of enterprise network using MAS.

6.2. State of the art: modeling and simulation of supply chains with agents

6.2.1. *Introduction to the agent and MAS*

Artificial Intelligence (AI) strives to represent, build and understand intelligent capacities involved in individual entities. This approach appears insufficient to resolve certain types of complex problems. To fill certain limits of AI a subfield appeared advocating the passage of an "individual intelligence" to a "collective intelligence". The alternative of distributed artificial intelligence (DAI) consists of distributing the expertise on a group of autonomous entities in interactions [FER 99]. As distributed problem solving, parallel problem solving and MAS constitute an important stream of research in DAI [MOU 96]. The MAS concentrates on the study of the collective behavior which results from the organization and the interactions between agents for the resolution of problems.

6.2.1.1. *Agent definition and typology*

Through the literature, works recognized as precursors in the field of research of agents and MAS are: i) the Actor Model for the resolution of problems by sending asynchronous messages [HEW 77]; ii) the Blackboard system for sharing information between agents [ERM 80]; iii) the Contract Net protocol for task allocation [SMI 80] and iv) the Distributed Vehicle Monitoring Test bed to evaluate alternative designs of distributed networks to solve problems [LES 83]. Currently there is no consensus in the scientific literature on the definition of an agent. Disciplines in which reference is made are numerous and various authors have proposed different definitions. However, the definition proposed in [JEN 98] is commonly used within the MAS community: "*an agent is a computer system, situated in some environment that is capable of flexible autonomous action in order to meet its design objectives...*". In [WOO 95], the authors define the concept of an agent according to the following properties:

– *autonomy*: an agent operates (task selection, decision-making, etc.) without human or other direct intervention and neither the actions it realizes nor its internal state are submitted to any intervention;

– *reactivity*: an agent perceives its environment and reacts in an appropriate way to the environment changes;

– *pro-activeness*: agents are able to act by taking initiatives driven by their goals;

– *social ability*: agents are able to interact with other agents through communication language or social rules.

The importance accorded to the properties expressed above depends on what the application needs. Currently, agents constitute an active research field within which numerous applications are developed. In [NWA 96] and [WOO 02] the authors propose surveys of the agents according to various application domains (cognitive agents, software agents, mobile agents, etc.). Agents perceive the modifications of their environment and perform actions on it. Among the possible actions, agents have to determine the most suited decisions that can reach their objectives. In addition to the application domain, environment, interaction and organization influence the design of the agent. Three main traditional approaches defined as general methodology are used to build agents: deliberative or cognitive architectures, reactive architectures and hybrid architectures.

Deliberative or cognitive agents have an explicit representation of their environment and an explicit representation of other agents. According to this architecture, agents are capable of making decisions, collaborating to solve problems and taking actions to satisfy their internal goals. The decisions are made via logical reasoning and based upon their perceived environment. One particular model to build a rational agent is the Belief-Desire-Intention (BDI) model [RAO 99a and b]. Beliefs represent the informational state of the agent about itself and other agents. Desires represent the motivational states of the agent according to objectives or situations it would like to accomplish. Intentions represent the deliberative state towards which the agent chose to make a commitment. According to the information perceived from the environment, the agent revises it beliefs, defines the various options (from its desires and its current intentions) and filters the possible options and acts based on the associated intentions. Numerous implementations of architectures for building BDI agents are presented in the literature as: IRMA (Intelligent Resource-bounded Machine Architecture) [BRA 87], PRS (Procedural Reasoning System) [GEO 89], dMARS (distributed Multi-agent Reasoning System) [DIN 97], COSY [BUR 92] and RETSINA (Reusable Environment for Task-Structured Intelligent Networked Agents) [SYC 03]. In order to build deliberative or cognitive agents, Shoham proposed a new programming paradigm, Agent Oriented Programming (AOP) [SHO 93], which declines in three components: i) a formal language with a syntax and a semantic to define the mental state of agents, ii) an interpreted programming language for programming agents, and iii) an agentification process to translate agent programs into executable systems. Each agent is specified in terms of: i) a set of capabilities, ii) a set of initial beliefs, iii) a set of commitments, and iv) a set of commitment rules. Each commitment rule contains a message condition, a mental state condition and an action. If the messages received by an agent match with the commitments rules, the rule fires and the agent becomes committed to the action.

Reactive agents react on a stimulus-response basis. Their behavior is directed by a series of rules in response to the stimuli of the environment. These agents maintain no internal model of their environment. They do not have explicit goals and they use reduced communication language and protocols. The reactive agents do not possess an intelligent individual behavior, but an intelligent behavior which appears from their interactions. The first works realized according to this approach are related to the subsumption architecture presented in [BRO 86]. According to this architecture, an agent has of a set of behavior which is organized into a hierarchy according to its complexity. A behavior can inhibit any action of a behavior from a lower level. In [SAU 02], the agents represent synthetic pheromones and automated vehicles. The automated vehicles use pheromones to move during fight missions. The metaphor of insect societies is widely used to define reactive agent systems (for example: ethology). Within these societies the activities of individuals are coordinated, without exhibiting communication or complex reasoning. In [BON 99], numerous models are presented which are inspired by phenomena of group behavior exits in insect societies. Detailed reviews of this approach are proposed in [NWA 96] and [MÜL 98].

Hybrid agents combine both approaches of cognitive and reactive agents. These architectures are based on a layered decomposition of the behavior to obtain a more efficient management of the agent resources. The reactive approach is used for the realization of the reflexes activities in answer to the stimuli of the environment. These activities do not require complex reasoning. The cognitive approach is used for the realization of activities based on the planning and deliberation requiring complex reasoning. The InteRRaP architecture (Integration of Reactive Behavior and Rational Planning) [MÜL 98] is a layered architecture. The first layer, above the world interface component, is the behavior-based layer dedicated to implementing and controlling the reactive capability of the agent. The second layer, above the behavior-based layer, is the plan-based layer, which is dedicated to the generation of plans directed by the goals of the agent. The third layer, the cooperation layer, concerns cooperative planning for the modeling and management of the interactions with the other agents (for example: negotiation strategies). Among other hybrid agent architectures Ferguson developed the Touring Machine, each layer of which corresponds to a level of abstraction [FER 92], which joins as horizontal architecture according to the classification proposed in [MÜL 98]. The reaction, planning and modeling layers are situated between the perception and the action. The hybrid architectures turn out more effective for estimating the capacities of decisions and actions of the agents during the phase of conception of the multi-agent system. The following is dedicated to the definition of the compound systems of a group of interacting agents: the multi-agent system.

6.2.1.2. *MAS*

Whatever the application domain or the degree of intelligence of the agents, a multi-agent system requires the definition of different elements. In [FER 99], a MAS is a system consisting of the following elements:

– an environment E, generally a space having a measurement;

– a set of objects O. Objects are positioned and for each object it is possible to determine with a position in E. Objects can be perceived, created, destroyed and modified by agents – representing passive entities of the system;

– a set of agents A. Agents are a subset of objects ($A \subseteq O$) representing the active entities of the system;

– a set of relations R which link objects and also agents to each other;

– a set of operations Op enabling the possibility for agents to perceive, create, transform, manipulate, destroy objects of O;

– a set of operators with the task of representing the application of the operations and the reactions of the world to this attempt of modification, which are called the laws of the universe.

To develop a MAS, it is not enough to place several agents in the same environment, these agents also have to interact. The analysis and development of a MAS require the consideration of multiple dimensions. In the VOWELS multi-agent oriented framework [DEM 95] four dimensions are identified: the agent, the environment, the interactions and the organization. The agent models concern more particularly the internal description of the agents (architectures, knowledge representation, etc.). The environment models correspond to the fields in which the agents evolve (for example, spatial representation). The interaction models concern the elaboration of a set of rules in adequacy with the granularity of an agent (communication, coordination, etc.). The organization models are interested in the structures and the rules of cohabitation between the agents (hierarchies, auto-organizations, etc.). To describe an organization the agent/group/role model (AGR) considers three primitives concepts [FER 04]. An *agent* is an active and communicating entity that plays *roles* within *groups*. A *group* is composed of a set of *agents* and delimits organizational structures. The role is the abstract representation of a functional position of an *agent* in a *group*.

MAS are systems in which several entities evolve in a common environment. This cohabitation is performed according to a competitive or cooperative approach (delegation of tasks, reached a common goal, resource sharing, etc.). The relations between agents can engender diverse forms of interactions (collaboration, conflict, competition, coordination, negotiation, dependence, etc.). The interactions between agents can be directed by the goals (compatible or incompatible), the resources (conflicting or not) or the capacities of the agents (sufficient or insufficient) [FER 99]. The agents can interact either directly, from agent to agent, or indirectly by modification of their environment. The various forms of interactions are presented in detail in [BON 88]. The communication (by sending of messages) makes it possible to develop various types of interactions in conflicting contexts or not: from the coordination to the negotiation passing by the collaboration or the cooperation.

Two modes of the communication are distinguished in MAS: indirect communication via the environment and direct communication. In the indirect communication mode signals placed in the environment are detected and interpreted by the agents (example: ant pheromones as reactive agents). During this part we focus more particularly on direct communication by exchange of messages between cognitive agents. Communication allows the agents to exchange data, information and knowledge so that they can coordinate to accomplish their activities. This interaction mode forms one of the fundamental aspects in the definition of the sociability property. One of the social characteristics of an agent is its capacity to interact with the other agents. The sending, reception and interpretation of messages require communication languages. These languages make it possible to support the communication between the agents. There are two main languages of communication which both have speech act theory proposed in [SEA 69] as their basis. These languages are:

– KQML (Knowledge Query Manipulation Language) developed in 1993 by the consortium DARPA-KSE (Knowledge Sharing Effort), [FIN 94].

– ACL (Agent Communication Language) proposed in 1997 by the FIPA (Foundation for Intelligent Physical Agents) [FIP 97].

These languages are based on the definition of performatives (KQML) or communication act (ACL) which constitutes the expression of an act (fulfilment of an action). KQML and ACL distinguish at the level of semantics used; the content of the performative varies from system to system. In fact, the ACL language strongly inspired by the works of KQML, proposes a language adding the definition of interaction protocols with a semantic based on ARCOL [SAD 97]. Protocols form the skeleton of the interaction modes between the agents in the exchange of messages. The FIPA proposes numerous protocols among which is the Contract-Net protocol, presented in [SMI 80]. This protocol allows us to specify the interactions by clarifying the nature of the communication acts, the role of the agents and the sequence of messages. The communication is a key element in the implementation of a coordination process between agents.

A MAS is a distributed system in which there is generally no centralized control or global point of view. The agents act in an autonomous way but do not locally have the knowledge, the resources or the information required to ensure the coherence of the concerted actions in the MAS [JEN 96]. The distributed nature of the control, the data, the knowledge associated with the dynamic nature of the environment, generates an increased degree of uncertainty in the decision-making and the realization of actions by the agents. This uncertainty is mainly due to the partial vision of the agents on the system, the heterogenity of the individual objectives, the use of shared or rare resources and the interference of actions. Consequently, the collective behavior produced by the interactions between the agents requires the definition of an adapted coordination process. These processes enable a global coherence of the system resulting from individual actions [BON 88]. In the literature, numerous approaches are proposed to coordinate the actions or the goals of the agents. We then present the major works related to the task allocation, planning and negotiation mechanisms.

Task allocation

In the context of centralized task allocation, an agent decomposes a problem into sub-problems and assigns the tasks necessary for his resolution to various agents. For the decentralized task allocation, each agent has the capacity to decompose a problem into sub-problems and distribute the tasks associated with various agents. The Contract Net Protocol [SMI 80] allows us to make a distributed and dynamic task allocation. An agent with the role of contractor can decompose a task into subtasks, send requests for bids on each specific subtask to all the other agents and finally select the most appropriate bid and allocate the task to that subcontractor.

Planning

The coordination by multi-agent planning makes it possible to confront plans generated by the agents to detect possible conflicts. Georgeff proposes an approach in which an agent centralizes the plans of the other agents [GEO 83]. All the agents communicate their plans to an agent who manages to synchronize them. This operation consists of detecting possible conflicts in order to resolve them by sending synchronization messages. To consider the dynamics of the environment [DUR 88; 89] proposes a coordination model called PGP (Partial Global Planning). According to this approach each agent builds a representation of the actions and the interactions of a group of agents. The agents use this representation (PGP) to determine how the actions and interactions of the group of agents can affect their activities. With the aim of considering the dynamics of the environment, Jennings proposes a coordination approach by planning based on commitments and agreements [JEN 93; 96]. The commitment is generally studied in the perspective of punctual actions, which the agents undertake to carry out if circumstances remain unchanged. The agreement describes the circumstances according to which an agent has to reconsider his commitments and indicate the appropriate management of the actions to maintain, rectify or abandon his commitments.

Negotiation

The coordination concerns the organization of the agents' actions in space and in time. This organization has to facilitate a coherent behavior of the multi-agent system facilitating the synergy of the agents for the achievement of their individual objectives. However, certain situations can occur out of conflicts. To limit their effects, numerous negotiation techniques of for the coordination in the MAS are proposed in the literature [JEN 01]. These techniques to resolve conflicts arise from various research domains (decision theory, economy, etc.). Game theory is used for the research for compromise between agents for the sharing of tasks or the resolution of conflicts. A rational agent tries to maximize his individual interests represented by the utility of individual players. The negotiation, modeled in the form of a game, consists of finding a solution which is convenient for all the players without disadvantaging one player [ROS 94]. The auction offers protocols of negotiation in which an auctioneer wishes to maximize his profit and the buyers wish to minimize their costs. Several bid processes are proposed in the literature (English auction, Dutch auction, etc.). Other numerous approaches are based on the negotiation to coordinate the agents (the vote, the coalition, etc.) [SAN 99].

6.2.2. *Supply chain simulation with agents*

In the global competitive context, companies have to face numerous decisional problems related to the integration and the management of their organizations in an enterprise network. From a management and decision-making perspective, this sets the stage for increased complexity and dynamics. From an operational perspective, orchestrating the flow of more and more specific products through a supply chain implies complex decision-making in a highly stochastic fast-paced environment. The properties which characterize MAS in the agent paradigm seem particularly adapted for representation and simulation of these distributed and dynamic industrial systems. Multi-agent supply chain simulation makes it possible to represent and evaluate the behavior of the entities composing the chain, as well as the existing interactions.

6.2.2.1. *Interests of the agent approach*

The properties of the agents are well adapted for the representation and study of the behavior of the entities which constitute the supply chains. The definition of such studies allows organizations or companies to estimate the risks or profits associated with multiple decision-making processes. These organizations have objectives, constraints and different configurations (organizational, decision-making, etc.). However, these organizations are interdependent for the improvement of the global system performances. The application of the MAS as a modeling approach in an industrial context makes it possible to represent the decision centers as networks for planning and control of manufacturing systems. Agent-based modeling allows us to capture the dynamic nature of the supply chain, facilitating the study of resource coordination associated with multiple companies in interaction.

6.2.2.1.1. Analogies between supply chains and multi-agent systems

Supply chains and MAS can define themselves as networks of entities which cooperate for the achievement of common and individual objectives, resource sharing, as well as problem solving; these problems exceeding their individual capacities or knowledge. The actor denomination defines the decision-making entity or entities related to the supply chains and the agent denomination the autonomous entities of the MAS. In general, the following analogies between supply chains and the MAS can be noted [YUA 02]:

– the multiplicity of acting entities: multiple actors realize common and various production and business tasks; a MAS is composed of multiple agents with different roles and abilities;

– the entity properties: the actors have goals, means and skills needed for task execution and follow management rules. The agents have goals, abilities, roles, reasoning abilities and perform complex decisional modes;

– the entity social abilities: the actors take decisions through coordination and/or negotiation methods. The agents are autonomous, perceptive to the environment modifications, proactive, and have social capabilities;

– the decision-making capabilities of the entities: learning and reasoning are needed for the actors in order to take decisions. Agents have reasoning capacities, knowledge acquisition or modification through interactions with the environment;

– the coordination between entities: coordination between the actors is made through material, informational, monetary or decisional interaction. Coordination of the agents' activities is realized through informational interaction with other agents;

– the information sharing and their incompleteness: an actor has access to incomplete information shared within the chain. An agent has incomplete information and knowledge shared by message exchanges;

– the task distribution: the actors' tasks can be decomposed and given to other actors. The agents can delegate tasks to other agents;

– the structure flexibility: actors belong to a supply chain with flexible structure, organized by actors' strategies. Agents belong to flexible MAS which have organizational structures;

– the system evolution abilities: a supply chain is dynamic: actors can join or quit the supply chain. Agents can be added to the MAS and others can be deleted.

6.2.2.1.2. Agent-based modeling and simulation of supply chains

Individual-based models are of interest in the study of the interactions between basic entities and their organizations. These models are based on a modeling approach which is widely considered in the community of the MAS. Agent-based modeling is of interest in the representation of the behavior of the entities of the system and their interactions. The use of the MAS to model complex dynamic systems leads to more realistic models than those obtained by conventional modeling approaches. Autonomous agents are adapted for the study of decentralized, dynamic and modular systems. The agent paradigm offers the possibility of designing models close to the physical systems studied. In fact, the association agent/entity allows us to represent in a more realistic way a series of entities and decision-making processes. This mode of representation allows us to represent the system as an organization of entities in interactions, within which the knowledge and the decision-making are decentralized. This is mainly due to the modularity of the behavior representation. Furthermore, the actions adopted by the entities in response to the changes in the environment, by reactivity or proactivity, allow us to consider the dynamic nature of the system.

In [PAR 98], two modeling approaches are contrasted for the study and behavioral observation of the systems considering their dynamics: equation-based modeling and agent-based modeling. These approaches are based on the description of two types of entities: individuals and observables:

– the individuals are different entities which carry out actions through a behavior defined inside active regions. The individuals are characterized by observables which are values transformed by their actions;

– the observables are measurable characteristics of the individuals. The observables are connected by equations. They are used to predict the global behavior of the system over time.

Equation-based modeling or EBM expresses relationships between observables using a set of equations. The execution of the model consists of estimating equations including the behavior of all the individuals. This produces the evolution of the observable through time. The basic unit of the model, the equation, results from the behavior of the individuals, but does not represent it explicitly. Agent-based modeling or ABM is based on the design of models which are established by a set of agents. These agents encapsulate the behavior of each individual. The execution of the model consists of simulating its behaviour, through which the individuals interact. The tendency of the ABM is to define the behavior in terms of an observable accessible by the individuals. The behavior of an individual can depend on observables generated by other individuals. Agent-based modeling is adapted for the representation of organizations which have modular structures, distributed decision-making and strongly dynamic environments.

MAS and supply chains are composed of entities which interact according to their role and abilities inside organizational structures (companies or agents' societies). Agents and supply chain actors have the means, resources and capabilities to allow them to carry out in an individual or collective way various functions, tasks or activities. The multi-agent modeling and simulation allows us to easily take into account:

– the distributed nature of the chains, and the non-linearity of the behavior;

– the modifications to the environments: the agent autonomy allows the model to change by updating by agent addition or removal;

– the decision complexity and variety, and the MAS ability to solve problems by cooperation in a distributed way;

– a behavior of cooperation without altruism thanks to the definition of the agents' properties through interaction modes.

The analogies show that the actors of supply chains possess incomplete information and knowledge as well as limited capacities. Furthermore, control, data, information, knowledge and decision-making are decentralized and distributed within the network of companies. MAS propose a modeling framework adapted for the representation of autonomous agent networks in which heterogenous decision-making is emitted. The MAS properties facilitate the definition of behavioral simulations based on autonomous entities to understand the complex functioning of the real system modeled. This type of simulation is of interest in the description and the behavioral study of the real system by the execution of the agents in interactions in a dynamic context. The agent-based simulations are made up of a set of autonomous entities, the agents, whose behavior depends on their interactions and the environment in which they are situated. These models represent the individual actions of the agents, the interactions between the agents as well as the consequences of these interactions on the environment. The development of agent-based simulations has to supply tools to decision makers authorizing them to carry out studies on the behavior of their organization. As decision support systems, agent-based simulations are exploited for the analysis of different types of elements such as: supply chain performances, flow management and decision-making processes. These performances are defined in terms of diverse objectives which are related to qualitative and/or quantitative factors. The global performance of the system depends on the local performance of the companies. The evaluation of these performances can be obtained using simulations according to different contextual scenarios. The simulations and observation of the behavior of the entities underline the exploitation of applications based on the agent paradigm. In fact, the treatment, analysis, management and information sharing joins as a characteristic and fundamental element allowing the decision makers of supply chains to lead behavioral experiments allowing them to determine the robustness, efficiency and flexibility of the decision-making relative to the resources management.

6.2.2.2. Review of works on agent-based supply chain modeling and simulation

Many projects of agent-based modeling and simulation applied to industrial systems have begun since the beginning of the 1990s. These works grasp and represent the manufacturing systems like networks of intelligent and organized entities (production workshops, companies, supply chains, etc). In [PAR 99a], [SHE 99], [WU 00] and [CAR 04] and more recently in [SHE 06], [MON 06] and [FRA 08], states of the art are proposed that are based on multi-agent modeling for the representation of manufacturing systems.

This section proposed a non-exhaustive presentation of agent-based research works for the modeling and simulation of supply chains. The aim is to propose a comparative analysis based on four comparison criterions: i) the objectives of the research works, ii) the problem addressed, iii) the agent modeling step retained, and iv) the major characteristics of the research works.

ISCM (Integrated Supply Chain Management) EIL, University of Toronto, Canada

The ISCM project, developed at EIL at the University of Toronto is based on the study of the coordination problems in a supply chain, at a tactical and operational level. This project led to the design of the Agent Building Shell (ABS) for the development of multi-agent applications and to the formalization of a coordination language [BAR 96]. The COOL language, for COOrdination Language, is of interest in modeling conversation protocols implied in complex negotiation processes between agents. The validation of the COOL language induced the realization of an agent simulation platform. The Supply Chain Demonstrator platform, developed by Teigen, makes it possible to model the company and its integration in a supply chain using the COOL language. The platform has two types of cooperating agents (functional and informational) for the resolution of constraint-based problems [TEI 97]. Simulations performed with this platform allow us to study and analyze the degree of cooperation between agents according to the system's performance levels. The Supply Chain Demonstrator models and simulates more or less complex types of conversations which have a high degree of cooperation. The validation of COOL is reached by the development of coordination protocols between agents for conflict resolution [FOX 00]. This platform allows a rich representation of communications.

Supply Chain Modeling and Analysis ICL, Carnegie Mellon University, USA

The Supply Chain Modeling and Analysis project, developed by Sadeh, Smith and Swaminathan in the ICLL of Carnegie Mellon, proposes a modeling and simulation environment for analyzing the management strategies of supply chains. In [SWA 98], a design approach for multi-agent models is presented. Following the analysis of characteristic elements resulting from the corporate networks, the authors present a modeling approach based on a generic element library, which is composed of structural and functional elements. The structural elements represent the actors who participate in the composition of the supply chain. These elements are represented by agents ensuring the activities of production and transport (Supplier agent, Retailer agent, etc.). The functional elements describe the behavior of each agent by the specification of decisions and actions. These elements are used for the definition of the coordination modes related to the movement of material flows. These modes are based on interaction protocols using message exchanges.

MASCOT (Multi-agent Supply Chain cOordination Tool) ICL, Carnegie Mellon University, USA

The MASCOT project, developed by Hildum, Sadeh and Tseng at the ICLL of Carnegie Mellon, focuses on the coordination protocols for supply chain planning. MASCOT is a multi-agent simulation platform for planning and scheduling according to two decisional levels. At the operational level, the agents ensure the decision-making on a short-term horizon. At the strategic and tactical level, the agents are responsible for the decisions in the long and medium term. Coordination between agents is carried out in horizontal and vertical directions according to various interaction protocols. Figure 6.1 illustrates the MASCOT architecture.

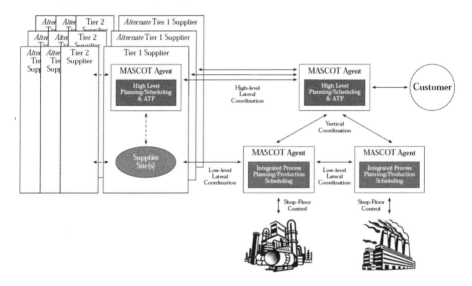

Figure 6.1. *The MASCOT architecture*

Based on this architecture, the impact of four management policies is examined in [KJE 98] to analyze the behavior of supply chain actors. This work is resumed in [SAD 03] in order to study three policies of horizontal coordination. The first policy estimates the delivery dates of the future orders on the basis of historical data (Lead-Neg/C). The second policy is based on finished capacity schedules for companies situated downstream of the one which receives the offer (FCS-Neg/C). The third policy is based on finished capacity calculations for each company (Sync-Neg/C). The average results, obtained after twenty 150 day simulations shows that the policy which has the smallest delay and the best profit is that based on lateral coordination with finished capacity (Sync-Neg/C). This policy makes it possible to anticipate commitments on the deliveries according to stock and estimated load. The

MASCOT project is of interest in the coordination of the actors according to two levels. The demand is considered as an input parameter and conceptual choices for the elements of the supply chain are led by the project objectives.

Research works at Iowa State University, National Sun Yat-Sen University and University of Illinois, USA

Strader, Flax and Shaw are interested in the simulation of three supply chain management strategies, using the multi-agent simulation SWARM platform developed at the Santa Fe Institute. Efficient information sharing is used to absorb uncertainty, while maintaining acceptable cycle times [STR 99]. The model is composed of the controller that orchestrates simulation, the statistical model for the data generation and the model to be simulated. Figure 6.2 presents the architecture of the simulation platform.

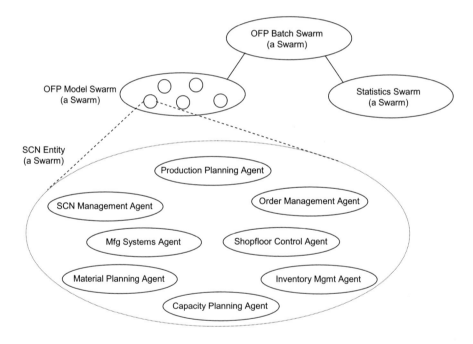

Figure 6.2. *SWARM simulation model*

The information sharing strategies are: no shared information, information shared on supply and information shared on forecasts and demand. Simulations are performed according to three client relationship policies: Make-to-Order (MTO), Assemble-to-Order (ATO) and Make-to-Stock (MTS). An ATO relationship has better performances in terms of order cycle time and inventory costs. In the case of

MTS, policy sharing forecasts and orders reduce the stock level but increase the order cycle time. The proposed modeling approach facilitates the representation of complex supply chains due to its recursive decomposition structure.

DASCh (Dynamic Analysis of Supply Chains) ERIM's Center for Electronic Commerce, Ann Arbor, USA and University of Michigan, USA

The DASCh project, developed at the Center for Electronic Commerce under Parunak, aims to simulate and analyze the dynamics of supply chains [PAR 99b]. The models are composed of the following agents: i) the company which represents sites receiving as inputs objects that they transform into outputs (semi-finished or finished product), ii) PPIC (Production Planning and Inventory Control) which models the algorithms of planning and inventory control of the MRP type, and iii) shipping which models the delays and the uncertainties generated by the movements of material and information. The shipper agents ensure the transport of the materials and the mailer agents ensure the transmission of information. This modeling approach is shown in Figure 6.3 [PAR 99b].

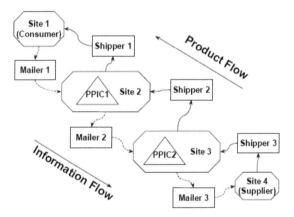

Figure 6.3. *DASCh model of supply chain*

This modeling approach was applied to the case of the DaimlerChrysler supply chain [BRU 05]. The model is composed of two component production sites, one raw materials site and the DaimlerChrysler site. The authors propose a policy of information propagation in which the forecasts are calculated by DaimlerChrysler and broadcast to all the sites. The multi-agent model does not make it possible to represent various decisional levels. Furthermore, only the MRP management policy is taken into account for the planning of manufacturing and purchasing orders.

ANTS (Agent Network for Task Scheduling) ERIM's Center for Electronic Commerce – Ann Arbor, USA

The ANTS project, developed at the Center for Electronic Commerce under Sauter, concerns the management of supply chains. The supply chain is composed of producers and customers [SAU 99]. The agents develop a task scheduling with minimal commitment (Least Commitment Scheduling), delaying scheduling until the last moment possible. The agents go over the entire time window of commitment profiles searching for opportunities to optimize the schedule. The agents transmit decisions according to probabilistic criteria, thus enabling them to adjust their activities according to the environment dynamics. The approach by minimal commitment is based on the capacities' flexibility and makes it possible for the system to quickly answer the dynamic changes of the environment. The system must be able to favorably answer the changes even after commitments are contracted. This approach shows that the agents can have workloads that are largely overcapacity. Moreover, the agents present simple behaviors (centered on reactivity) and limited conversations.

NETMAN (NETworked MANufacturing) CIRRELT, Laval University, Canada.

The NETMAN project, developed at the CENTOR laboratory of Laval University initiated by Montreuil, D'Amours and Lefrançois, proposes a heterarchic approach for the representation of the organisational structure of manufacturing networks. This modeling approach is based on the identification and the establishment of autonomous and inter-dependent business units [MON 00]. Each business unit is represented by NetMan centers which collaborate and coordinate between themselves. Each NetMan center is defined like an agent system responsible for the management of its activities and its resources within the manufacturing network. Thus, the concepts developed in this modeling approach, through the definition of NetMan centers (autonomous, reactive, pro-active and sociable) define the organizational structure of multi-agent system. Definition of the responsibilities induces developed decision-making processes as well as establishment of relations between NetMan centers. The interaction modes between the agents are specified using coordination frameworks [CLO 01]. Coordination frameworks are formalized using contracts and conventions. The contracts and conventions are based on the CAT model (Convention Agreement Transaction), (Espinasse et al., 1998) [ESP 98]. This model developed at the LSIS laboratory at Aix-Marseille University (France), supports the coordination activities between agents within the same NetMan center for capacity requirement planning and inventory management. Moreover, this model concerns coordination between different NetMan centers. The approaches developed during this project were applied in an industrial context within the Prévost Car Inc. company of the Volvo group. In this context a multi-agent simulation platform was developed with the aim to establish the adequacy between demand and production capacity of the coach assembly lines according to a broad range of customization options.

Research work at DAMAS/FORAC, Laval University, Canada.

These research works focus on the reduction of the impact of the bullwhip effect in a supply chain. The aim is to propose and test various coordination mechanisms in order to evaluate the business management strategies implied in a manufacturing network of the forest product industry [MOY 04]. The two principles defined for the coordination mechanisms are: i) to order to the suppliers the exact needs issued by the customers, and ii) the companies can react once to each change of consumption in the market. Each company is modeled by an agent that has a specific strategy for ordering. The objective is to compare distributed coordination mechanisms resulting from the ordering strategies. Simulations relate on the one hand to a homogenous supply chain (identical order strategy for every company), and on the other hand to a heterogenous supply chain (order strategy which minimizes each company's individual cost). The simulation results show that the use of proposed coordination mechanisms allow us to reduce the bullwhip effect in the two types of supply chains. The selected modeling approach, one agent per company, makes it possible to evaluate multiple strategies of placing orders along the supply chain.

Research work at the ONERA, Toulouse, France

These works focus on the evaluation of supplying activities in the aircraft industry. The objectives are to propose a tool for decision-making in a supplying network. The proposed tool facilitates the evaluation of the profits resulting from the improvements related to the control of flows between a customer and its suppliers. The purpose is to determine the relevant information to be exchanged in the aim to improve the company's individual performances and supply chain performances. Figure 6.4 presents the agent based modeling approach retained for the design of enterprise models [TEL 03].

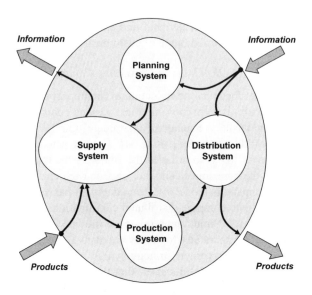

Figure 6.4. *Model of the enterprise agent*

The modeling approach suggested in [TEL 03] defines an enterprise agent itself structured into four sub-agents. The set of sub-agents represents the enterprise using a planning system and a physical system (supply, distribution and production). The experiments are concerned with the influence of the customer on the performances of its suppliers. The simulation evaluates the impact related to the share of the procurement planning and the forecasts by the customer to its suppliers. The study focuses on the frequency of sending the procurement plans and the size of the forecast horizons.

Research work at University College London and Imperial College London, UK

These research works focus on the coupling of MAS to optimization techniques [GJE 01]. Optimization, used in a local way to identify an optimal schedule, provides to the agents a set of goals to be reached in order to guide their decisions (production policy, use of resources, etc). The benchmarking concerns the supplying control system and its effect on a supply. One of the aims is to reduce its operation costs while maintaining a high degree of response to the demand. Two warehouse agents apply stock orders for the same process to two factory agents via the IntLogistics agent. Consequently, the two warehouse agents share the same procurement resources. The IntLogistics agent must determine the factory agent that will be in charge of restocking the warehouse agent according to the lowest cost. The performance of the supply chain is measured using an indicator named OTIF (on time in full), which corresponds to the sum of the orders that can be delivered by the manufacturing sites (factory) divided by the total sum of the orders delivered by the manufacturing sites and subcontractors. An optimization tool solves the problem of the scheduling of each production site, while tactical decision-making and control policies are carried out by a multi-agent system. The represented interactions only concern the inter-site level. This agent-oriented modeling approach concerns the description of the operation of the supply chain at the inter-site level.

MAMA-S, GII, ENS Mines de Saint-Étienne, France

These works propose a methodological approach for multi-agent simulation: MAMA-S [GAL 03]. This approach is based on four phases: i) specification, ii) design, iii) realization and iv) experimentation. These phases support the modeling and simulation of distributed industrial systems. The specification phase concerns the design of a conceptual model based on a formalism inspired by enterprise modeling. The design phase translates the conceptual model into a multi-agent model. Throughout the realization phase, data-processing considerations are taken into account with the choice of simulation tools and multi-agent platforms. The experimental phase is concerned with the deployment and use of the simulation model resulting from the preceding phase. The infrastructure supporting the simulation process is based on a multi-agent system and simulation tools. The multi-agent system is composed of multi-agent subsystems. Each simulation tool can be a different item of software. A multi-agent subsystem is composed of a simulation tool and a set of agents belonging to two main classes. The agents of the AgS type represent physical or abstract entities of the considered system. The agents of the AgF type are facilitators that support the interactions between the multi-agent subsystems. An example of a multi-agent system is presented Figure 6.5 [GAL 03].

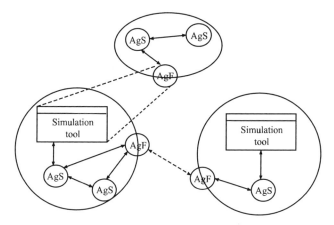

Figure 6.5. *Architecture of the distributed MAS simulation*

The proposed architecture takes place in a distributed simulation context. This methodological approach furthers the design of interacting simulation models. The exploitation of the proposed formalism for the design of the abstract model requires competences in the area of simulation.

Research works at LSIS – University of Aix-Marseille, France, and CIRRELT – Laval University, Canada

This research proposes first of all an agent-oriented methodological framework for modeling and simulation of supply chains, in particular mass customizing supply chains. This methodological framework has to enable the development of simulation-based decision support systems enabling smart management of such highly dynamic chains. This framework defines two main models, the Conceptual Agent Model (CAM) and the Operational Agent Model (OAM), which makes it possible to simulate the physical activities, the decisional processes, and the informational and material flows of the supply chain. From the OAM, a MAS is derived and integrated inside a simulation environment enabling simulated experiments on the supply chain. The *translation from conceptual to operational agent* modeling associated with this methodological framework is presented in Figure 6.6.

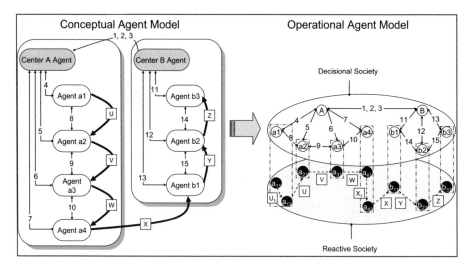

Figure 6.6. *From conceptual to operational agent modeling for supply chain simulation [LAB 05]*

The second contribution of this research is the specification of a specific hybrid agent-oriented simulation platform that has been developed to implement the AOM model and to enable experimentations. In this platform the cognitive agents are implemented in the MAJORCA platform developed at the LSIS that is written in Java, integrates the JESS rule engine and is FIPA (Foundation for Intelligent Physical Agent) compliant. The reactive agents are implemented in the Anylogic© simulation software for the development of discrete systems. This methodological framework and this simulation platform have been used to model and simulate a mass customizing supply chain in the golf industry field to study various coordination strategies between actors of the chain, according the position of a decoupling point [LAB 07].

6.3. Conclusion and summary of the projects

In the scientific literature, we can note an increasing number of publications related to agent-oriented modeling and simulation of supply chains. These research works implement the agent approach in different ways. A comparison of the research projects is proposed Table 6.1, adapted from [LAB 07].

Projects	Areas	Class of problems	Supply network modeling	Characteristics
ISCM - Supply-Chain Demonstrator [TEI 97]	Supply Chain Cooperation	Enterprise integration in a supply chain	One logistic agent One agent/enterprise One customer agent	Complex conversations for cooperation
SCMA – [SWA 98]	Supply Chain Design	Design of MAS for supply chain simulation	Four production agents One transportation agent Five control elements	Modularity, Reuse
MASCOT [SAD 03]	Supply Chain Coordination	Coordination by planning and scheduling	Three agents/enterprise: One planning agent Two Scheduling agents	Intra-level and inter-level coordination
[STR 99]	Supply Chain Management	Information sharing in a divergent supply chain	One agent/enterprise department: eight agents (inventory, planning, etc.)	Management according to the network
DASCh [PAR 99b]	Supply Chain Management	Propagation of forecasts to the network's actors	One agent/enterprise One agent/information One agent/material One agent MRP/enterprise	Study of the Bullwhip Effect, Precise forecast window size
ANTS [SAU 99]	Supply Chain Scheduling	Task allocation on resources by commitments	One agent/resource One agent/material One agent-process	Scheduling engagement on capacities
NETMAN [MON 00]	Agile and distributed networks	Distributed coordination modes	One agent/NetMan center	Organizational structure of the MAS

[MOY 04]	Supply Chain Coordination	Reducing the bullwhip effect in a supply chain	One agent/enterprise	Proposition of coordination modes
[TEL 03]	Supply Chain Relations	Performance studies of a supply network	One agent/enterprise composed of four agents	Information sharing frequencies
Opt./MAS [GJE 01]	Supply Chain Inventory	Service level versus inventory level stock	One agent spot market One agent/network site One agent/transportation	Study of replenishment policies
MAM-S [GAL 03]	Distributed Simulation	Methodological agent modeling and simulation	Simulation tools Facilitators agents Simulation agents	Proposition of a MAS architecture
[LAB 05; 07][1]	Supply Chain Coordination	Methodological approach for agent based simulation	Two classes of agents associated: Cognitive and Reactive	Three levels of modeling
[FRA 08][1]	Supply Chain Management	MAS and operations research-based tools	Source agent Make agent Deliver Agent	Distributed planning for synchronization of interactions
SPEE [MON 06][1]	Supply Chain Management	Holistic modeling, simulation and visualization	One agent/client Four agents/assembler 2 agents/logistic provider One agent/supplier Tree to n agents/dealer	Breadth and depth simulation of demand and supply chains
[ROY 04 ; MON 07][1]	Supply Chain Management	Multi-site coordination using MAS	Negotiator agent Planner agent Supply chain mediator agent	Intervention of mediator when perturbation occurs

Table 6.1. *Agent-oriented modeling and simulation projects*

All the research projects shown in Table 6.1 propose various initiatives of agent-oriented modeling and simulation. The specter covered by these projects extends from the management of an industrial unit [SAU 99] to the global management of a supply chain [BRU 05]. This difference of representation from an organizational point of view influences the modeling approaches proposed for the design of the simulation models. The domain of the study and the studied problems influence the level of abstraction considered to obtain a model as well as the design of the multi-agent organization.

The agents are used for the representation of supply chain entities. The specification of their behavior is determined by the abstraction level of the model.

---

1 For more information see Chapter 7.

Currently, the roles played by the agents and their number are different from one project to another. The agents possess skills, behavior, communication and decision-making capacities, which extend from the management of a material resource to the strategic management of a company. In the majority of projects an agent is often associated with a company or a distribution center.

Although in certain projects the classes of problems and the modeling approaches are close, models are focused on a specific part of the business. The way in which problems are formalized does not allow us to compare the simulation results obtained. This is the case for the DASCh project and the works presented in [STR 99]. In fact, these two projects concern the impact of information sharing on the performances of the supply chain. Only in the case of the works of Strader, Lin and Shaw, this study focuses on the identification of the best management policies to be adopted according to the customer relationship. The DASCh project used in [BRU 05] concentrates on the variation of the inventory levels at different places in the supply chain.

All the projects diverge on the approach held to obtain an agent-oriented model for the simulation. Within the framework of the NETMAN project the multi-agent system is obtained further to the representation of the studied system by a modeling framework of an industrial network. The consideration of concepts stemming from enterprise modeling is also ensured within the framework of the MAMA-S approach. The analysis of the various projects shows that the agents are used to model actors or decision-making processes within the supply chains.

In Chapter 7, some simulation works based on SMA, and related to the decisional system of enterprise network, are presented in more detail.

6.4. Bibliography

[BAR 96] Barbuceanu M., Fox M.S., "The Architecture of an Agent Building Shell", in M. Wooldridge *et al.* (Eds.), *Intelligent Agents II*, p. 235-250, Springer-Verlag, 1996.

[BON 99] Bonabeau E., Dorigo M., Theraulaz G., *Swarm Intelligence: From Natural to Artificial Systems*, Oxford University Press, New-York, 1999.

[BON 88] Bond A.H., Gasser L., *Readings in Distributed Artificial Intelligence*, Morgan Kaufmann, 1988.

[BRA 87] Bratman M.E., Israel D., Pollack M., "Plans and resource bounded practical reasoning", *Computational Intelligence*, vol. 4, p. 349-355, 1987.

[BRO 86] Brooks R., "A robust layered control system for a mobile robot", *IEEE J. of Robotics and Automation*, vol. 2, no. 1, p. 14-23, 1986.

[BRU 05] BRUECKNER S., BAUMGAERTEL H., PARUNAK H.V.D., VANDERBOK R., WILKE J., "Agent Models of Supply Network Dynamics: Analysis, Design, and Operation", in T.P. HARRISON *et al.* (Eds), *The Practice of Supply Chain Management: Where Theory and Application Converge*, Springer-Verlag, 2005.

[BUR 92] BURMEISTER B., SUNDERMEYER K., "Cooperative problem solving guided by intentions and perception", *Proc. of the Third European Workshop on Modelling Autonomous Agents and Multi-agent Worlds*, 1992.

[CAR 04] CARIDI M., CAVALIERI, S., "Multi-agent systems in production planning and control: an overview", *Production Planning & Control*, vol. 15, no. 2, p. 106-118, 2004.

[CLO 01] CLOUTIER L., FRAYRET J.-M., D'AMOURS S., ESPINASSE B., MONTREUIL B., "A Commitment-Oriented Framework for Networked Manufacturing Co-ordination", *Int. J. of Computer Integrated Manufacturing*, vol. 14, no. 6, p. 522-534, 2001.

[DAM 99] D'AMOURS S., MONTREUIL B., LEFRANÇOIS P., SOUMIS F., "Networked manufacturing: The impact of information sharing", *Int. J. of Production Economics*, vol. 58, p. 63-79, 1999.

[DAV 95] DAVIDOW W., MALONE M., L'entreprise à l'âge du Virtuel, MAXIMA, Collection Institut du Management d'EDF et de GDF, Paris, 1995.

[DEM 95] DEMAZEAU Y., "From Interactions to Collective Behaviour in Agent-Based Systems", *Proc. of the First European Conf. on Cognitive Science*, 1995.

[DIN 97] D'INVERNO M., KINNY D., LUCK M., WOOLDRIDGE M., "A Formal Specification of Dmars", *Proc. of the Fourth Int. Workshop on Agent Theories, Architectures and Languages*, 1997.

[DUR 88] DURFEE E.H., LESSER V.R., "Using Partial Global Plans to Coordinate Distributed Problem Solvers", in A.H. BOND *et al.* (eds.) *Readings in Distributed Artificial Intelligence*, Morgan Kaufmann, p. 285-293, 1988.

[DUR 89] DURFEE E.H., LESSER V.R., "Negotiating Task Decomposition and Allocation Using Partial Global Planning", in M. HUHNS, *Distributed Artificial Intelligence*, Morgan Kaufmann, Chapter 10, p. 229-243, 1989.

[ERM 80] ERMAN L.D., HAYES-ROTH F., LESSER V.R., REDDY D.R., "The Hearsay II speech understanding system; integrating knowledge to resolve uncertainty", *ACM Computing Survey*, vol. 12, p. 213-253, 1980.

[ESP 98] ESPINASSE B., CLOUTIER L., LEFRANÇOIS P., "A Coordination Framework for Intelligent Agents in the Distributed Enterprise", *Proc. of the Tenth International IFIP*, Kluwer Academic, p. 565-578, 1998.

[FER 99] FERBER J., *Multi-agent Systems. An Introduction to Distributed Artificial Intelligence*, Addison Wesley, London, 1999.

[FER 04] FERBER J., GUTKNECHT O., MICHEL F., "From Agents to Organizations: an Organizational View of Multi-agent Systems", *Agent-Oriented Software Engineering IV*, Lecture Notes in Computer Science, Springer, 2004.

[FER 92] FERGUSON I.A., Touring Machines: An Architecture for Dynamic, Rational, Mobile Agents, PhD Thesis, University of Cambridge, 1992.

[FIN 94] FININ T., LABROU Y., MAYFIELD J., "KQML as an agent communication language", *Proc. of the 3rd Int. Conf. on Information and Knowledge Management*, 1994.

[FIP 97] FIPA, Agent Communication Language, Foundation for Intelligent Physical Agents, www.fipa.org/specs/fipa00018/, 1997.

[FOX 00] FOX M.S., BARBUCEANU M., TEIGEN R., "Agent-Oriented Supply-Chain Management", *Int. J. of Flexible Manufacturing Systems*, vol. 12, no. 2-3, p. 165-188, 2000.

[FRA 08] FRAYRET J.-M., D'AMOURS S., ROUSSEAU A., HARVEY S., GAUDREAULT J. "Agent-based supply-chain planning in the forest products industry", *Int. J. of Flexible Manufacturing Systems*, accepted, 2008.

[GAL 03] GALLAND S., GRIMAUD F. BEAUNE P., CAMPAGNE J.P., "MAMA-S: an introduction to a methodological approach for the simulation of distributed industrial systems", *Int. J. of Production Economics*, vol. 85, no. 1, p. 11–31, 2003.

[GEO 83] GEORGEFF M.P., "Communication and interaction in multi-agent planning", *Proc. of the 3rd National Conf. on Artificial Intelligence*, 1983.

[GEO 89] GEORGEFF M.P., INGRAND F.F., "Decision-Making in an Embedded Reasoning System", *Proc. of the 12th Int. Joint Conf. on Artificial Intelligence*, 1989.

[GJE 01] GJERDRUM J., SHAH N., PAPAGEORGIOU L.G., "A combined optimization and agent-based approach to supply chain modelling and performance assessment", *Production Planning & Control*, vol. 12, no. 1, p. 81-88, 2001.

[HEW 77] HEWITT C., "Viewing Control Structures as Patterns of Message Passing", *Artificial Intelligence*, vol. 8, no. 3, p. 323-364, 1977.

[JEN 93] JENNINGS N.R., "Commitments and Conventions: The Foundation of Coordination in Multi-agent Systems", *Knowledge Engineering Review*, vol. 8, no. 3, p. 223-250, 1993.

[JEN 96] JENNINGS N.R., "Coordination Techniques for Distributed Artificial Intelligence", in G. O'HARE *et al.* (Eds), *Foundations of Distributed Artificial Intelligence*, John Wiley & Sons, 1996.

[JEN 98] JENNINGS N.R., SYCARA K., WOOLDRIDGE M., "A Roadmap of Agent Research and Development", *Autonomous Agents and Multi-agent Systems*, vol. 1, no. 1, p. 7-38, 1998.

[JEN 01] JENNINGS N.R., FARATIN P., LOMUSCIO A.R., PARSONS S., SIERRA C., WOOLDRIDGE M., "Automated Negotiation: Prospects, Methods and Challenges", *Int. J. of Group Decision and Negotiation*, vol. 10, no. 2, p. 199-215, 2001.

[KAR 07] KARIMI R., LUCAS C., MOSHIRI B., "New Multi Attributes Procurement Auction for Agent-Based Supply Chain Formation", *Int. J. of Computer Science and Network Security*, vol. 7, no. 4, p. 255-261, 2007.

[KJE 98] KJENSTAD D., Coordinated Supply Chain Scheduling, Ph.D. Thesis, Norwegian University of Science and Technology, 1998.

[LAB 05] LABARTHE O., ESPINASSE B., FERRARINI A., MONTREUIL B., "A Methodological Approach for Agent Based Simulation of Mass Customizing Supply Chains", *J. of Decision Systems*, vol. 14, no. 4, p. 397-425, 2005.

[LAB 07] LABARTHE O., ESPINASSE B., FERRARINI A., MONTREUIL B., "Toward a Methodological Framework for Agent-Based Modelling and Simulation of Supply Chains in a Mass Customization Context", *Simulation Modelling Practice and Theory*, vol. 15, no. 2, p. 113-136, 2007.

[LES 83] LESSER V.R., CORKILL, D.G., "The Distributed Vehicle Monitoring Testbed: A Tool for Investigating Distributed Problem Solving Networks", *AI Magazine*, vol. 4, no. 3, pp. 15-33, 1983.

[LIN 92] LIN G.Y.J., SOLBERG J.J., "Integrated shop floor control using autonomous agents", *IIE Transactions: Design and Manufacturing*, vol. 24, no. 3, p. 57-71, 1992.

[MAK 96] MAKATSORIS C., LEACH N.P., RICHARDS H.D., RISTIC M., BESANT C.B., Addressing the planning and control gaps in semiconductor Virtual Enterprises", *Proc. of the Conf. on Integration in Manufacturing*, p. 117-129, 1996.

[MIN 02] MIN H., ZHOU G., "Supply chain modeling: past, present and future", *Computers & Industrial Engineering*, vol. 43, p. 231-249, 2002.

[MON 06] MONOSTORI L., VÁNCZA J., KUMARA S.R.T., "Agent-Based Systems for Manufacturing", *Annals of the CIRP*, vol. 55, no. 2, p. 697-720, 2006.

[MON 07] MONTEIRO T., ROY D., ANCIAUX D., "Multi-site coordination using a multi-agent system", *Computers in Industry*, vol. 58, no. 4, p. 367-377, 2007.

[MON 00] MONTREUIL B., FRAYRET J.-M., D'AMOURS S., "A Strategic Framework for Networked Manufacturing", *Computers in Industry*, vol. 42, no. 2-3, p. 299-317, 2000.

[MON 06] MONTREUIL B., CLOUTIER C., LABARTHE O., LOUBIER J., "Holistic agent-oriented modelling of demand and supply chains", *Proc. of the Int. Conf. on Information Systems Logistics, and Supply Chain*, 2006.

[MOU 96] MOULIN B., CHAIB-DRAA B., "An Overview of Distributed Artificial Intelligence", in G. O'HARE *et al.* (Eds), *Foundations of Distributed Artificial Intelligence*, John Wiley & Sons, 1996.

[MOY 04] MOYAUX T., Design, Simulation and Analysis of Collaborative Strategies in Multi-agent Systems: The Case of Supply Chain Management, PhD Thesis, Laval University, 2004.

[MÜL 98] MÜLLER J.-P., "Architectures and applications of intelligent agents: a survey", *Knowledge Engineering Review*, vol. 13, no. 4, p. 353–380, 1998.

[NWA 96] NWANA H.S., "Software agents: an overview", *Knowledge Engineering Review*, vol. 11, no. 3, p. 205–244, 1996.

[PAR 97] PARUNAK H.V.D., BAKER A.D., CLARK S. J., "The AARIA agent architecture: an example of requirements-driven agent-based system design", *Agents-97*, 1997.

[PAR 98] PARUNAK H.V.D., SAVIT R., RIOLO R.L., Agent-Based Modeling vs. Equation-Based Modeling: A Case Study and User's Guide, Center for Electronic Commerce Report, 1998.

[PAR 99a] PARUNAK H.V.D., "Industrial and Practical Applications of DAI", in G. WEISS (Ed), *Multi-agent Systems*, MIT Press, 1999.

[PAR 99b] PARUNAK H.V.D., SAVIT R., RIOLO R.L., CLARK S. J., DASCh: Dynamic Analysis of Supply Chains, Center for Electronic Commerce Final Report, 1999.

[RAO 99a] RAO A.S., GEORGEFF M.P., "Asymmetry thesis and side-effect problems in linear time and branching time intention logics", *Proc. of the 12th Int. Joint Conf. on Artificial Intelligence*, 1991.

[RAO 99b] RAO A.S., GEORGEFF M.P., "Modeling rational agents within a BDI-architecture", *Proc. of Knowledge Representation and Reasoning*, 1991.

[ROS 94] ROSEINSCHEIN J.S., ZLOTKIN G., *Rules of Encounter: Designing Conventions for Automated Negotiation Among Computers*, MIT Press, 1994.

[ROY 04] ROY D., ANCIAUX D., MONTEIRO T., OUZIZI, L., "Multi-agent architecture for supply chain management", *J. of Manufacturing Technology Management*, vol. 15, no. 8, p. 745-755, 2004.

[SAD 03] SADEH N.M., HILDUM D.W., KJENSTAD D., "Agent-based e-Supply Chain Decision Support", *J. of Organizational Computing and Electronic Commerce*, vol. 13, no. 3-4, p. 225-241, 2003.

[SAD 97] SADEK M.D., BRETIER P., PANAGET F., "Artimis: natural dialogue meets rational agency", *Proc. of the 15th Int. Joint Conf. on Artificial Intelligence*, 1997.

[SAN 99] SANDHOLM T.W., "Distributed Rational Decision Making", in G. WEISS (Ed), *Multi-agent Systems*, MIT Press, 1999.

[SAU 99] SAUTER J.A., PARUNAK H.V.D., "ANTS in the Supply Chain", *Proc. of the Workshop on Agent based Decision Support System for Managing the Internet-Enabled Supply Chain*, 1999.

[SAU 02] SAUTER J.A., MATTHEWS R., PARUNAK H.V.D., BRUECKNER S., "Evolving adaptive pheromone path planning mechanisms", *Proc. of the 1st Int. Joint Conf. on Autonomous Agents and Multi-agent Systems*, 2002.

[SEA 69] SEARLE J.R., *Speech Acts*, Cambridge University Press, 1969.

[SHE 99] SHEN W., NORRIE D.H., "Agent-Based Systems for Intelligent Manufacturing: A State-of-the-Art Survey", *Knowledge and Information Systems*, vol. 1, no. 2, p. 129-156, 1999.

[SHE 06] SHEN W., HAO Q., YOON H. J., NORRIE D.H., "Applications of agent-based systems in intelligent manufacturing: an updated review", *Advanced Engineering Informatics*, vol. 20, p. 415-431, 2006.

[SHO 93] SHOHAM Y., "Agent oriented programming", *Artificial Intelligence*, vol. 60, no. 1, p. 51-92, 1993.

[SIK 98] SIKORA R., SHAW M., "A multi-agent framework for the coordination and integration of information systems", *Management Science*, vol. 44, no. 11, p. 65–78, 1998.

[SMI 80] SMITH R.G., "The contract net protocol: high-level communication and control in distributed problem solver", *IEEE Transactions on Computers*, vol. 29, no. 12, p. 1104–1113, 1980.

[SRI 94] SRINIVASAN K., SUNDER K., MUKHOPADHYAY T., "Impact of electronic data interchange technology on JIT shipments", *Management Science*, vol. 40, no. 10, p. 1291-1304, 1994.

[STR 99] STRADER T.J., LIN F.R., SHAW M., "The impact of information sharing on order fulfillment in divergent differentiation supply chains", *J. of Global Information Management*, vol. 7, no. 1, p. 16-25, 1999.

[SWA 98] SWAMINATHAN J.M., SMITH S.F., SADEH N.M., "Modeling Supply Chain Dynamics: A Multi-agent Approach", *Decision Sciences*, vol. 29, no. 3, p. 607-632, 1998.

[SYC 03] SYCARA K., PAOLUCCI M., VAN VELSEN M., GIAMPAPA J.A., "The RETSINA MAS Infrastructure", *Autonomous Agents and Multi-agent Systems*, vol. 7, no. 1-2, p. 29-48, 2003.

[TEI 97] TEIGEN R., Information Flow in a Supply Chain Management System, PhD Thesis, University of Toronto, 1997.

[TEL 03] TELLE O., Gestion de chaînes logistiques dans le domaine aéronautique : Aide à la coopération au sein d'une relation Donneur d'Ordres/Fournisseurs, PhD Thesis, École Nationale Supérieure de l'Aéronautique et de l'Espace, 2003.

[WOO 95] WOOLDRIDGE M., JENNINGS N., "Intelligent agent: theory and practice", *Knowledge Engineering Review*, vol. 10, no. 2, p. 115-142, 1995.

[WOO 02] WOOLDRIDGE M., *An Introduction to Multi-agent Systems*, John Wiley & Sons, 2002.

[WU 00] WU J., ULIERU M., COBZARU M., NORRIE D., "Agent-based Supply Chain Management Systems: State of the Art and Implementation Issues", *Proc. of the Int. Congress on Intelligent Systems and Applications*, 2000.

[YUA 02] YUAN Y., LIANG T.P., ZHANG J.J., *Using Agent Technology to Support Supply Chain Management: Potentials and Challenges*, McMaster University, 2002.

[YUN 99] YUNG S., YANG C., "A New Approach to Solve Supply Chain Management Problem by Integrating Multi-agent Technology and Constraint Network", *Proc. of the 32nd Annual Hawaii Int. Conf. on System Sciences*, 1999.

Chapter 7

Agent-based Simulation of Business Network Planning and Coordination Systems

7.1. Decision system in a supply chain

Chapter 6 presented some relevant analogies between supply chains and multi-agent systems (MAS) and showed the interest of using MAS to model and simulate supply chains. A brief review of various research projects on agent-based supply chain modeling and simulation was also presented. The specter covered by these projects spreads from the management of an industrial unit to the management of a global supply chain, influencing the modeling approaches proposed for the design of the simulation models.

The domain of study as well as the specific characteristics of the studied problems influence the level of abstraction a model should aim for as well as the design of the multi-agent organization.

In this chapter, a series of specific contributions addressing agent-based supply chain modeling and simulation to support the design process of planning and coordination systems are presented. The contributions focus on three complementary aspects of the decision systems: the supply chain control, the design of specific planning and coordination systems and finally supply chain simulation. Through the research contributions discussed in this chapter, these three aspects are discussed; more specifically in terms of some methodological propositions and some ongoing platforms development.

Chapter written by Thibaud MONTEIRO, Didier ANCIAUX, Sophie D'AMOURS, Bernard ESPINASSE, Alain FERRARINI, Olivier LABARTHE and Daniel ROY.

Section 7.2 concerns the supply chain control and the development of related decision support systems focusing on cooperative tactical planning. An agent architecture, a planning process and an experimental agent-based platform are presented. Specific applications are discussed.

Section 7.3 addresses the design of supply chain planning and coordination systems using agent-based simulation. This section focuses on different aspects of the planning and coordination systems.

It presents contributions in regard to the design of order promising systems, the location of the decoupling point within the supply chain and therefore the definition of the demand-supply propagation logic and the design of cooperation mechanisms. Finally, platform propositions for establishing the holistic performances of a specific design of a planning and coordinating system are presented. Some industry-based applications are described providing insights on the challenges of building such platforms.

The scientific contributions presented in this chapter were proposed by the LGIPM laboratory (INRIA and ENIM/ENSAM/Metz University – France), the CIRRELT laboratory (FORAC Research Consortium and NSERC/Bell/Cisco Research Chair, Laval University, Quebec, Canada), and the LSIS laboratory (CNRS and Aix-Marseille University, France).

7.2. Decision-making tools to supply chain control

In most business networks, each business unit or entity plans its own operation locally. Many reasons support this approach. Demand and supply information are widely spread within the business networks, they are continuously changing as the business environment is stressed by many internal and external factors, and finally the amount of information to deal with is still too large in some instances to centralize the planning process. However, this decentralization raises some interesting questions which emerge from the difficulty of synchronizing the planning and coordination decisions without an extensive share of information that would be found in a centralized approach. This section presents a distributed approach, based on the multi-agent paradigm aiming to address this issue.

The first part deals with cooperative tactical planning proposing a methodology to deal with contingency in supply chains. The second part of this section describes a solving approach. Finally, a particular illustration concerning the tactical planning in the softwood lumber industry is presented in section 7.2.3.

7.2.1. Distributed planning in supply chain

This part deals with necessary tactical decisions to establish a coherent distributed planning. The information considered here is the global volume of the product family and induced load by demands. The agents presented are used to simulate the negotiation and propagation decisions needed to find and maintain a coherent distributed planning as contingencies occur.

7.2.1.1. *Multi-agent architecture*

The enterprise network (Figure 7.1) is represented as a set of tiers (according to the product breakdown structure and to the need propagation), in which each partner, defined as a Virtual Enterprise Node (VEN), has a relationship with customers and suppliers on the adjacent tiers. It is assumed that each VEN is in relationship only with its adjacent VENs (i.e. no loop exists between the VENs). As a result, each VEN belongs to one tier. This VEN could be, as well as a manufacturer, a distribution center or a carrier.

This enterprise network is modeled as a multi-agent system, in which the agents use cooperative negotiation to establish a global consistent coordination.

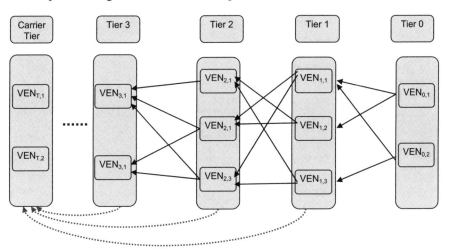

Figure 7.1. *Model of a network of enterprises*

In our approach, we model VENs using multi-agent architecture. An agent is a combination of a reactive software entity and a human decision actor, with its own environment and decision-makings tools. However, to improve its performance, it collaborates with the other entities existing in its environment; see [LUC 04]. The

VEN is a meta-agent which is composed of three types of software agents, each of which collaborate to achieve the company goals (Figure 7.2):

– the Negotiation Seller Agent manages and negotiates sales. It contacts the Negotiation Planner Agent and several external Negotiation Buyer Agents (its customers) directly;

– the Negotiation Buyer Agent manages and negotiates purchase operations. It contacts the negotiation planning agent and several external sales agents (its suppliers) directly;

– the Negotiation Planner Agent manages production planning . It also provides forecasted planning and finished product availability. It contacts the two other VEN agents directly. It uses either planning software which pre-exists in the company or imposes the design of planning rules.

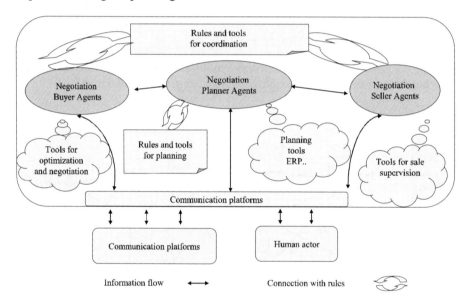

Figure 7.2. *Internal VEN structure*

7.2.1.2. *Planning the supply chain*

Each first tier VEN collects information about future sales from the customers, generally with uncertainty estimation. The forecasts are transmitted to all the VENs of the supply chain. It is assumed on the one hand that agreements are signed between first tier VENs and customers, and on the other hand between SC partners. Thus, it is assumed that information is always shared truthfully (trusted relationships) [GAV 99] and [CAC 01].

On the basis of the forecasting data and contracts established, each VEN carried out its planning. In the event of unforeseen production problems of a VEN, or of a forecasting change, it must commit to its current customer and supplier VENs, so that they try to overcome the problem collectively, which ensures the continuity of the global non-stop production and of the manufacturing chains.

Using a rolling horizon [OUZ 03], the VENs carry out the planning with new forecasting (Figure 7.3).

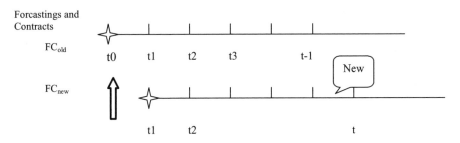

Figure 7.3. *Rolling horizon for planning*

It is assumed that (1) in the last unit of time, planning throughout the supply chain is negotiated and coherent, (2) at the first of the next period of planning, each VEN of the first tier must readjust its planning according to the variation in demands for the finished product, or possible risks that can occur during the period. Thus, the consequences are:

– to correct forecasts of finished products from periods 1 to T-1 (these forecasts are the same corresponding to periods 2 to T with corrections);

– to add a new forecast for the period T;

– to update stocks of all upstream and downstream components of the supply chain.

The problem of each VEN is to determine if it is sufficient to add one period for the planning in order to cope with variations or if it is necessary to change the previous planning to varying degrees so as to find a coherent and negotiable planning [ROY 04].

In principle, each VEN is faced with internal constraints, related to its capacity limits, and with external constraints, related to:

– on the one hand, its customer VENs which require products with, for example, minimal delays or low costs;

– on the other hand, its supplier VENs which also have lead-time cost constraints, etc.

The VEN could be in two different situations depending on its ability to carry out the request or not. Firstly, no consistency problem occurs. In this case, VEN is used only to propagate client needs to supplier requests. Secondly, local problems occur, so a negotiation process has to be initiated. To cope with these issues, the internal structure of the VEN is as discussed in the following sections [MON 07].

7.2.1.2.1. VEN internal processes

The three negotiator agents, buyer (NBA), planner (NPA) and seller (NSA), have a similar internal behavior. Statechart modeling makes it possible to understand the negotiation process within agents. The agent behavior is illustrated with a generic statechart (Figure 7.4) where only events and internal processes differ between each one.

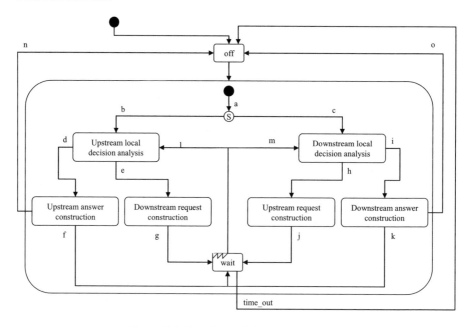

Figure 7.4. *Statechart of the generic behavior*

In Figure 7.4, different messages used by the agents are shown. They correspond to different states of negotiation with downstream or upstream agents.

Follow several events which modify the agent state:

message	NBA	NPA	NSA	comments
a – ←	R_NPA R_NSA	R_NSA R_NBA	R_NBA R_NPA	Request which makes agent to wake up
b	R_NPA	R_NSA	R_NBA	Upstream request
c	R_NSA	R_NBA	R_NPA	Downstream request
d	Local decision possible			
e	Local decision impossible			
f →	A_NBA	A_NPA	A_NSA	Proposal to upstream
g – →	R_NBA	R_NPA	R_NSA	Request propagation to downstream
h	Local decision impossible			
i	Local decision possible			
j – →	R_NBA	R_NPA	R_NSA	Request propagation to upstream
k – →	A_NBA	A_NPA	A_NSA	Proposal to downstream
l – ←	A_NSA	A_NBA	A_NPA	Downstream answer
m – ←	A_NPA	A_NSA	A_NBA	Upstream answer
n – →	A_NBA	A_NPA	A_NSA	Answer (OK, /OK) to upstream
o – →	A_NBA	A_NPA	A_NSA	Answer (OK, /OK) to downstream

An example of treatment of a new command follows the next step (see Figure 7.5 – Swimlane). Note that we then consider VEN 2.1 with client VEN 1.1 and the two providers VEN 3.1 and 3.2 (see Figure 7.1).

1 – Message R_NBA. The Negotiator Buyer Agent of VEN 1.1 sends a demand for product to VEN 2.1. This message wakes up the Negotiator Seller Agent of VEN 2.1 and the NBA of VEN 1.1 start waiting. The demand concerns one or more products with an indication of quantities, due dates, cost, etc.

2 – Message R_NSA. The NSA cannot find a solution by itself (i.e. insufficient stock, lack of information, etc.) and sends a request to its Negotiator Planner Agent. This message wakes up the NPA and NSA start waiting.

3 and 3'– Messages R_NPA 1 and 2. Again, the NPA cannot conclude by itself. It needs to know if raw materials could be available. In this example, two are necessary. These two messages wake up one NBA each, and the NPA start waiting.

4 and 4' – Messages R_NBA 1 and 2. The two awoken NBAs cannot construct a solution and contact the corresponding provider to ask them for raw materials with the NPA specifications. They then start waiting.

5 – Message A_NSA1. The NSA of VEN 3.1 answers NBA. Provider 3.1 cannot deliver its material following the NBA specification. Then it makes a proposal (prop1). The NBA quits the wait state and analyzes the proposal.

5,1 – Message A_NBA1. The NBA cannot conclude and transfers the prop1 to NPA. NPA quits the wait state and analyzes the proposal. NBA starts waiting again.

5,2 – Message A_NPA1. The NPA does not accept the prop1 and constructs another solution (prop2) which is sent to NBA. It quits the wait state and analyzes the proposal.

5,3 – Message A_NBA1. The NBA1 send the proposal to VEN 3.1 NSA. Then it starts waiting again.

5,4 – Message A_NSA1. The VEN 3.1 agrees proposal 2 and answers by an acceptation. Then the NSA dies.

5' – Message A_NSA2. The VEN 3.2 can answer positively to NBA2 demand. It answers by an acceptation and dies.

6 – Message A_NBA1. The NBA1 sends the acceptation of VEN 3.1 NSA to NPA and dies.

6' – Message A_NBA2. The NBA2 sends the acceptation of VEN 3.2 NSA to NPA and dies.

7 – Message A_NPA. The NPA aggregates the responses of the two NBA, transfers its acceptation to NSA, pre-schedule the command and dies.

8 – Message A_NSA. The NSA send the VEN acceptation to Client NBA and dies.

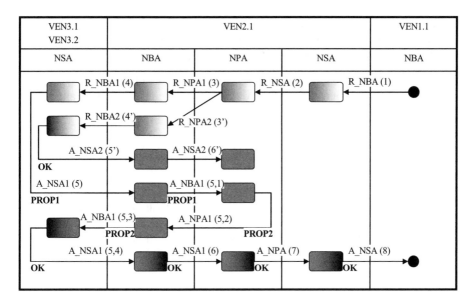

Figure 7.5. *Swimlane illustrating a global view of cooperative planning*

7.2.2. *Confirmed order management in a stochastic environment*

The studied orders are linked to firm orders; more specifically those which differ from previously stated plans established by a middle-term decision process. This difference could be caused by two factors. Firstly, the firm order could not respect the planned one in terms of quantities or delays. Secondly, an urgent non-planned order occurs. Even if those situations are singular, they are the principal cause of supply chain performance deterioration. The bullwhip effect is one of the most known consequences of this situation [MOY 03] and [MOY 07].

7.2.2.1. *Decision problem*

In the case of each new order arrival, i.e., a customer sends a planned (or unplanned) product order to the company. The company must perform some operations before introducing this new order into the production planning. First it must be verified if the order can be satisfied with existing inventories of finished products. If production must be added, then the planning must be modified and the company must consider two aspects. The first one is to verify the availability of inside capacities, such as product, reception and loading capacities, and outside capacities, such as component and transportation capacities (Figure 7.6).

In order to manage all capacities' constraints, we use the VEN modeled in Figure 7.2. This VEN, which represents the company, is divided into three structures (software agent), each of which collaborate to achieve the company goals:

– the Negotiator Seller Agent (NSA): the aim of this agent is to manage and negotiate sales. It contacts the NPA and several external buyer agents (its customers) directly;

– the Negotiator Planner Agent (NPA): its role is to manage production planning. It also provides forecasted planning and finished product availability. It contacts the other two agents directly;

– the Negotiator Buyer Agent (NBA): it manages and negotiates purchase operation. It contacts the NPA and several external NSA (its suppliers) directly.

The proposed management agents can use decision-making tools existing in the company.

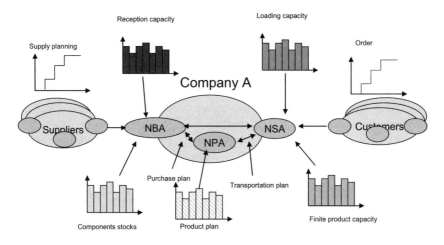

Figure 7.6. *Decision problem*

7.2.2.2. *Decision process for new order integration*

The problem could be analyzed with only internal processes or, if it is necessary, with external propagation requests (Figure 7.7).

We consider two categories of external problems. The first one is the component supply problem and the second one is finding and organizing their transportation (transport problem). The component problem occurs in the case of new order arrival inducing new production and an insufficient quantity of components in stock.

The transport problem occurs every time the company must deliver or transport products to its customers.

7.2.2.2.1. Example of a resolution mechanism

In this example, the company needs missing components in order to totally or partially produce the products corresponding to the order. Thus, the ordered quantity is insufficient in product stocks. The production capacity is available but the quantity of components existing in the stocks is insufficient (component problem). The internal transportation capacities are insufficient (transport problem). The company contacts its suppliers and transportation capacity suppliers (carriers) for providing the missing component quantity and transporting, totally or partially, the ordered quantity to the customer (Figure 7.7).

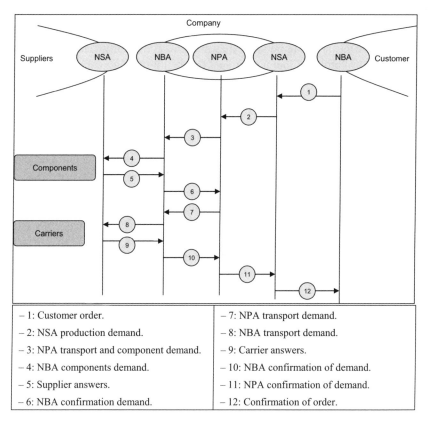

– 1: Customer order.	– 7: NPA transport demand.
– 2: NSA production demand.	– 8: NBA transport demand.
– 3: NPA transport and component demand.	– 9: Carrier answers.
– 4: NBA components demand.	– 10: NBA confirmation of demand.
– 5: Supplier answers.	– 11: NPA confirmation of demand.
– 6: NBA confirmation demand.	– 12: Confirmation of order.

Figure 7.7. *Example of a resolution mechanism*

7.2.3. *Experimental agent-based platform for tactical planning in the softwood lumber industry*

The softwood sawmilling industry provides an interesting context for agent-based planning and simulation technologies. The supply chains in this industry are typically composed of many business units responsible for forest operations, log transportation, sawing, drying and planing, lumber distribution and sales. The business units of the softwood lumber supply chain are distributed geographically and span a large territory as the forest is generally far away from the market. The business units of the supply chain can be owned by different parties or integrated within a large forest company. The production process is characterized by its one-to-many or many-to-many structures. A process consumes one or many products, which are always transformed into a basket of products (e.g. trees into logs, logs into boards).

The lumber business can be viewed as a hybrid commodity market where some customers act as "brokers" looking for spot availability at a good price while others sign procurement contracts and are looking for stable replenishment.

The experimental planning platform is based on the concept of distributed planning using multi-agent systems. Software agents are then developed for each functional unit of the value creation network. This allows companies to put specific planning methods in place that are both adapted to the particular unit and ensure synchronization of interactions with other units of the value creation network.

The architecture of the planning platform allows us to combine agent-based technology and operations research-based tools in order to take advantage, on the one hand, of the ability of agent technology to integrate distributed decision domains, and, on the other hand, of the ability of operations research to develop and exploit specific normative decision models.

The experimentation planning platform presented in this chapter attempts to address these two issues. In particular, we propose an agent-based architecture to develop an experimentation environment to design and test various configurations of distributed advanced planning and scheduling systems.

The system is composed of a supply chain modeler and planning units. The supply chain modeler enables the configuration of the systems, defining the different software components in each planning units, their planning responsibility, the conversation protocols and the task flows linking the planning units. The planning units are composed of the software components dealing with the planning of the unit; they are source, make or deliver agent. These are thus specialized to deal with the specific issues of the planning process they need to assume. For example, in the platform, three "make" agents were developed: the sawing, the drying and the finishing agents, as shown in Figure 7.8.

The structural description of a planning unit addresses the internal structure model which refers to the description of the software components and its planning process model which refers to the decision variables, constraints and the coupling constraints linking the different software components (agents). The internal structure of a PU is composed of both generic and customized software components. These were inspired from the SCOR model (source, make, deliver).

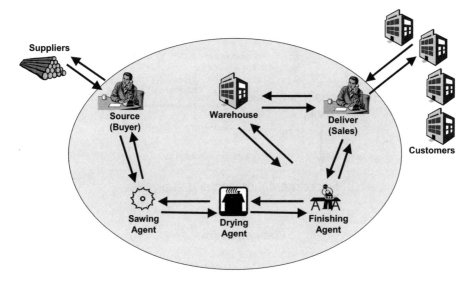

Figure 7.8. *Agent-based SC planning system*

The system is designed under the paradigm of collaborative planning which implies that the aim of all agents is to maximize expected total profit and achieve the best service level to the final customer. The planning sequence used in a planning unit to plan the internal supply chain upon the receipt of a new demand plan (from outside the planning unit) is divided into two distinct planning phases: the infinite supply plan and the finite supply plan.

Although the platform can be used to plan operations and synchronize them throughout the supply chain, it is also used to study and anticipate the behavior of the supply chain under different strategic and tactical configuration decisions, such as the location of the decoupling point or the allocation to different market segments (e.g. contract vs. spot market). In the experimental platform the agent-based SC planning system is used to test different scenarios which explicitly defines the system organizational configuration (e.g. business relations, decoupling point, etc.) and some environment specifications (e.g. log or lumber prices). The scenarios are then tested over a rolling horizon and decisions are optimized and synchronized as events occur (e.g. new demand, inventory status and execution information). The supply chain simulation tools enable the time synchronization of all agents as the simulation is carried out and captures the performance data, which serve for the final analysis. Figure 7.9 summarizes this explanation.

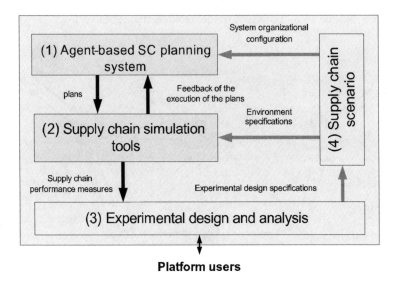

Platform users

Figure 7.9. *General overview of the experimentation platform [FRA 08]*

The first simulation function implemented is the development of a "customer" agent [FRA 08]. These simulate the behavior of different customers of the supply chain. In the context of the sawmilling industry, three customer types were modeled: the spot customer, the contract customer and the VMI customer. The information flow as well as the product needs (e.g. volume, quality, delay and price) between the customers and the supply chain is quite different for each of these models, raising the need for not only modeling the demand information but also the buying behavior of the different customer types.

The second simulation function tested relates to the development of a multi-behavior agent. The planning agent according to its ability to sense its environment may adopt different planning approaches. The design of this agent and the definition of the artificial intelligent planning model are conducted on the basis of a series of simulations [FOR 08]. These are intimately linked to the goal of the agent as well as its technical, behavioral and social competencies.

7.3. Simulation tools to design supply chain planning and coordination systems

In the last section, we presented an approach to synchronize decisions. The second part of the decision problem is the design of the decision system. This part presents an approach, based on the multi-agent paradigm, to fix this issue.

The first part deals with the order-promising evaluation problem. An evaluation of the management modes with decoupling point is performed in the second part. Finally, and after a presentation of the cooperation design problem, we present the Simulation Platform for Extended Enterprises (SPEE).

7.3.1. *Order management evaluation*

This section presents a methodology for representing and generating client behaviors, as well as on the demand and supply simulation approach to conduct different experiments on delivery time promising policies and delivery capacity. The proposed simulation approach allows businesses to estimate their capacity to make and honor promised delivery dates in a make-to-order context.

A set of client profiles, as well as a description of their design process, are proposed in [MON 07b]. Defining these profiles corresponds to specifying the parameters influencing the client's satisfaction level. When submitting an order to a supplier, the client states certain preferences. The delivery delay is one of these preferences. When the delivery delay proposed by the supplier corresponds to the client's expectations, the client has a maximum satisfaction level. Conversely, when the offered delay does not match the client's expectations, this results in a lower satisfaction level. When the satisfaction level is lower than the client's tolerance limit, the proposed delivery delay is refused and the sale is lost. Based on the relationship between delivery delay and satisfaction level, four client profiles are described in Figure 7.10 and used for demand simulations. When a client receives a product, at the moment when he wishes to receive it, he has a maximum satisfaction level for the delivery delay. This satisfaction level decreases as the delivery time diverges from the client's ideal delivery time, to finally reach a zero value. Each client has a particular satisfaction curve, stating his satisfaction level as a function of delivery time. In order to personalize these satisfaction curves for each client, a non-linearity factor is defined and called Degree of Non-Linearity (DNL), which varies in the interval $[-1,1]$. When modeling a client, his dissatisfaction tolerance index (DTI) is specified in the interval $[0,1]$. The delivery time corresponding to the DTI is called the rejection time (RT).

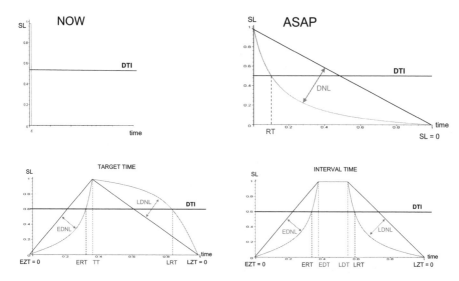

Figure 7.10. *Satisfaction curves for client types [MON 07b]*

A *NOW* client corresponds to a client with a satisfaction level equal to one for an immediate delivery and equal to zero otherwise. The *As Soon As Possible* (ASAP) client ideally has an immediate delivery, yet he is willing to accept some delay: when the offered delivery time (OT) is sooner than the rejection time (RT), i.e. OT < RT, the offer is accepted. The *Target Time* client would like the product to be delivered at a target time (TT). The structure of this satisfaction curve is defined by the following parameters: the target time TT, the early delivery time EZT corresponding to zero satisfaction or the positive satisfaction ZS at time zero, and the late delivery time LZT corresponding to zero satisfaction, the early degree of non-linearity (EDNL) and the late degree of non-linearity (LDNL). Given the curve structure, we can assess the early rejection time (ERT) before the target time and the late rejection time (LRT) after the target time. In fact, the intersection between the DTI and the satisfaction curve determines the two rejection times ERT and LRT on the time axis. For a TT client, the acceptance rule for an offered delivery delay is as follows: when the offered time OT is between the early and late rejection times, corresponding to ERT < OT < LRT, the offer is accepted. The *Interval Time* (IT) client prefers the delivery time to be within the interval between his earliest desired time (EDT) and his latest desired time (LDT). Specifically, the interval is set as [EDT, LDT] with EDT < LDT.

Once the various client profiles and their associated behaviors are defined, the supplier's behavior when facing a client's demand is considered. The interactions between the clients and the suppliers require the definition of delivery times. These policies can extend from the simple systematic proposition of a fixed delay to taking into consideration the satisfaction level of clients. In each case a client can accept the offered delivery time but cancel a delivery if the promised time is not respected and the delivery time becomes greater than his rejection time threshold (LRT). In order to determine a production plan, a scheduling policy must be defined. The determination of feasible delivery times is therefore dependent on scheduling policies. There are a variety of such policies, from the simplest myopic policies to complex policies involving the solution of mathematical optimization models, scheduling algorithms or elaborate sets of rules.

To allow the exact comparison of the impact of the supplier behavioral policies and capacity on client satisfaction and business performance, demand simulations are decoupled from supply simulations. A demand scenario sets all demand characteristics including a combination of the following distributions and their parameters: the overall demand distribution, the daily demand distribution, the product mix distribution, the order size distribution and the client profile distribution. Respecting a demand scenario, a demand simulation creates clients, specifies their request time and the product they want, defines a profile for each and generates their individual satisfaction curve. The overall output of a demand simulation is called a simulated demand. A supply scenario sets all characteristics of the supplier including its specific capacity as well as its behavioral policies and their specifying parameters: its delivery time promising policy, its scheduling policy, its stocking policy and its operating time policy.

A simulated demand can be fed as input to a variety of supply simulations which will then share the exact same set of clients with the same request time and products. Respecting a supply scenario, each supply simulation enacts the negotiation between the supplier and the client, the resulting offer made by the supplier, the offer acceptance decision by the client, the setting and adjustment of the supplier schedule, the actual production of the products by the supplier, the order cancellation decision by the client faced with lateness, as well as the actual delivery to clients or the storage of the cancelled product by the supplier. Given the probabilistic nature of a supply simulation, multiple supply simulations need to be run for each simulated demand to produce statistically significant performance results. Figure 7.11 provides performance results for an experiment testing 42 supply scenarios (sessions) for the demand scenario underlying 20 demand simulations each with the same demand scenario and a 100-day horizon.

The main purpose of the simulation environment is to facilitate the description of client/supplier relations, in a context where the behavioral representation implies multiple parameters to model and simulate each actor of the real system. The level of satisfaction of the client is influenced by the capacity of the supplier to offer and respect the required delivery dates. The supplier's capacity to answer the client's delivery needs depends on the policies used to determine promised dates. The provided simulation results help demonstrate how decision makers can assess the impact of their delivery time promising policies and supply capacity on business competitiveness through improved client satisfaction, order and delivery throughput, and resource use.

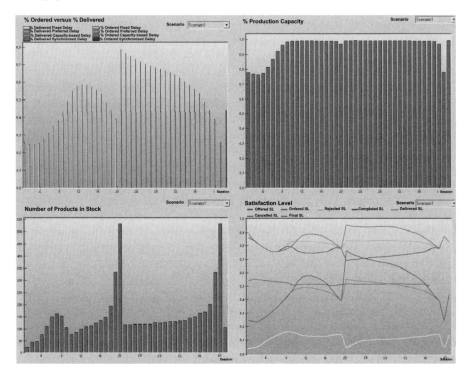

Figure 7.11. *Results of an illustrative experiment with 42 alternative supply scenarios [MON 07a]*

7.3.2. *Performance evaluation of various coordination policies according to the location of the decoupling point*

This section presents a methodology and associated tools for representing and evaluating supply chain performances particularly in a mass customizing context. It proposes to explore the behaviors from various coordination policies according to the position of the decoupling point. It allows us to estimate future performances according to management modes and information sharing.

Offer individualization, resulting from market evolutions, needs the definition of managing modes providing company coordination able to deal with the ever-growing product variety. Delivery time limits and customer demand lead-time constraints are becoming more and more important. In order to satisfy these time constraints, the operated management abilities represent the customer-supplier relationship [MAR 95], of which the main types are: *Make-to-Order, Make-to-Stock, Assemble-to-Order, Assemble-to-Stock, Deliver/Ship to Order, Deliver/Ship to Stock*, etc. Each processing or distribution activity on the products is disposed of two control modes of the material flow: *in stock* or *on order*. The limit between *push* and *pull* modes is concretized by a strategic product stock of which localization is called the *decoupling point* [CHR 00]. The position of the *decoupling point* governs the relationships established between companies in the supply chain according to whether they are upstream or downstream of this point. Upstream of the decoupling point, products are processed and delivered based on forecasts or lots, the size of which is determined by the calculation of an economic quantity (in managing systems such as MRP, APS, etc.). Downstream of the decoupling point, products are processed and delivered following the receipt of firm orders. This decoupling point allows us to determine a framework with the aim to study coordination modes in different management policies inside a supply chain [LAB 05].

In [LAB 06a] three scenarios are proposed, allowing us to study and analyze different organizational configurations of a specific supply chain, based on the position of the *decoupling point*. Each scenario relies on a management and control strategy involving material and informational flows associated with specific decision processes. According to the agent-oriented modeling approach, the models obtained for simulation are composed of a set of dynamic entities, or agents, of which behaviors depend on their interactions and on the environment in which they evolve [LAB 06b]. The decisions from the agents load to a permanent adjustment process for the organization in which they evolve (scheduling, planning, inventory management, etc.).

The supply chain considered, presented in Figure 7.12, is based on three manufacturers belonging to the golf club industry [MON 05a]. This SC organization takes into account five different personalization levels (popularizing, varying, accessorizing, parametrizing and tailoring) of products. Three suppliers stand upstream: (i) a head producer, (ii) a shaft producer and (iii) a grip producer. These suppliers are responsible for the routing of the components or raw materials they produce, to the golf club manufacturer. The golf club manufacturer is responsible for the personalization activities (finished product or components). This manufacturer has a relationship with: (i) a manufacturer for assembly subcontracting activities and (ii) a main distributor. The main distributor provides finished products to each market distributor. Distributors are in charge of stocking and supplying finished products for retailers in order to answer the demand. Retailers represent a physical interface by the final consumers. Consumers can procure or order golf clubs from the retailers according to five personalization levels [POU 06].

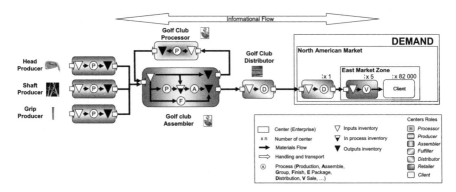

Figure 7.12. *Domain model of the industrial case*

We apply the agent methodological framework illustrated in Figure 7.13 [LAB 05]. This framework is composed of three stages: Conceptual Modeling, Operational Modeling and Experimentation. The *Conceptual Modeling* stage consists of modeling the structural and dynamic aspects of the supply chain and is realized in two steps: firstly an adapted domain model is generated, and then an agent-oriented conceptual modeling is derived and crystallized in the Conceptual Agent Model (CAM). The agent paradigm is then used to enrich this domain model by the description of its component decisional processes, from a social and local point of view. The agent-oriented modeling allows us to specify the dynamic characteristics of the system through the actions and behaviors of its interacting entities. The *Operational Modeling* stage is derived from the previous CAM, and leads to a multi-agent model to simulate the physical activities, the decisional processes and the informational and material flows of the supply chain in a mass customization context. The resulting model is the Operational Agent Model (OAM). In the *Experimentation* stage a MAS is derived from the previous OAM, and an experimental framework. This MAS is then integrated inside a simulation environment enabling simulated experiments on the supply chain.

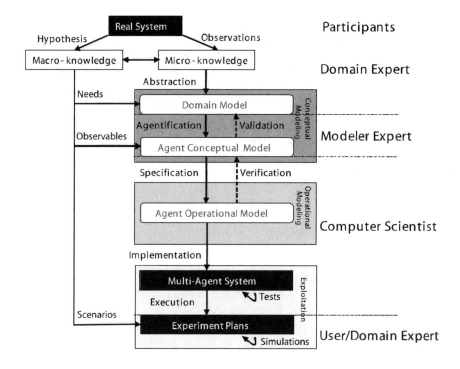

Figure 7.13. *Methodological agent framework for supply chain modeling and simulation [LAB 06b]*

In the AOM model, operational processes from decisional processes for agent representation, and agent behavior representation are distinguished [LAB 07]. The resulting MAS is composed of two heterogenous agent societies: a *cognitive agent society* and a *reactive agent society*. The agents of the cognitive society implement complex behaviors for decisional activities (for example, definition of the delivery planning, etc.). The agents of the reactive society perform operational activities as simple behaviors (for example, receiving or delivering finished products, etc.). Each center is represented by a cognitive agent, and each process is represented by a cognitive agent and by n reactive agents; n depends on the number of operational activities to be realized (ranging from 0 to n). Figure 7.14 shows part of this architecture restricted to the operational agent from the conceptual "agent shaft producer" and shows the accuracy simulation modeling can achieve.

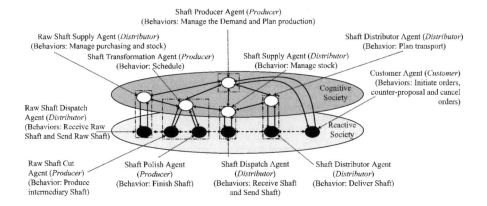

Figure 7.14. *Operational agent model of the producer shaft agent*

The supply chain modeled in Figure 7.12 is considered for the simulation of three scenarios focusing on the control of material and informational flows, as well as on the associated decisional processes. All these scenarios consider all the different personalization levels of products defined previously. The simulation multi-agent system is obtained according the design process and is issued on the platform presented in [LAB 07].

In the first scenario, for popular products (popularizing level), a decoupling stock (decoupling point) is set at the retailer level (Figure 7.2). The products of the other customizing levels are provided, assembled and delivered according to the orders. This level allows us to simulate a real time sharing of orders, for products of a customizing level other than popular products. The aim is to observe the supply chain reactivity and flexibility, in mass customization context. The inventory initialization depends on initial inventory, threshold and high value order. Distributor agents are responsible for the supply to all the retailers for the popular product type.

The second scenario is very similar to the first one (Figure 7.15). The difference is a higher coordination level obtained by a demand model sharing. The agent knowledge is fed by information relating to the demand evolution. We observe the issued decisions and their consequences on the inventory levels and on the size of the orders, involving a coordination level higher than in the first scenario. For the demand model sharing, the aim is to test a coordination level in which the agents exchange their beliefs facing the demand evolution. The retailer agents broadcast their decisions to their suppliers. This transmission mode is ensured as far as the assembly agent. The assembly agent integrates the data relating to the retailer forecasts. Inside the supply chain, a real modification of the agent performances at the level of the distributor-type agents can be observed. The strategy of demand model sharing allows us to reduce the uncertainty concerning the number of popular type products to be maintained in stock. This agent has available information on the forward-looking demand evolution, but does not have knowledge on the demand distribution during the forecast period considered.

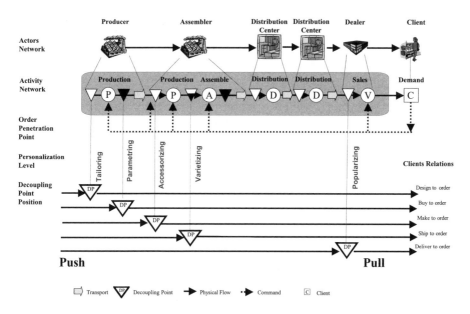

Figure 7.15. *Decoupling point locations in scenarios 1 and 2*

The third scenario differs from the previous scenarios with a new *decoupling point* location for the *variety personalization level*, as presented in Figure 7.16. There are 576 available references for variety-type products. The delivery delays caused at retailer level are the consequences of the difficulties encountered by the distributor agent, related to the retailers for inventory management. Given the fact that demand model sharing is used, the inventory level evolution follows the trend observed in the second scenario. However, this effect does not fit over the variety-type products.

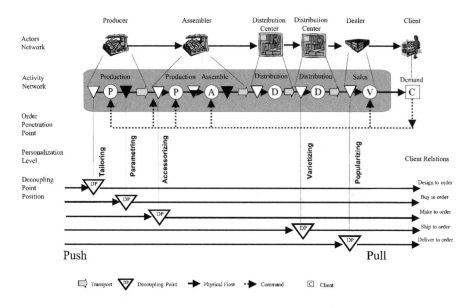

Figure 7.16. *Decoupling point locations in scenario*

7.3.3. *Design of cooperation mechanism [KHO 07]*

Many approaches exist to deal with supply chain management. These approaches aim to ensure decision coherence among the network and enable an efficient collaboration to guarantee the supply chain survival and stability. In order to analyze the negotiation performance in such a system, we propose using a simulation tool.

Some specific parameters must be defined to be able to evaluate supply chain performance. These parameters could be classified in two different fields: the network architecture and the negotiation process. From the point of view of architecture, its nature (number and size of tiers) or the supply strategy (mono- or multi-sourcing) are relevant. The maximum number of exchange flows conditions the negotiation or the number of proposition and scenario simultaneously treated.

The expected measures are linked to generated information flows and to cooperation and coordination success. Finally, the allocated time to achieve a decision is also taken into account (Figure 7.17). In fact, this is an important decisional parameter for an agile supply chain.

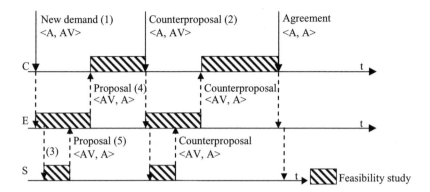

Figure 7.17. *An example of order generation based*

7.3.3.1. *Example of simulation for multi-negotiation parameter*

In order to illustrate the cooperation design based on simulation, we will look at the negotiation setting. Faced with its clients' requests, a company could act in two distinct ways.

First, it could process each order sequentially and separately. This way makes it possible to avoid resource reservation conflicts. Thus, this strategy guarantees analysis authenticity. In fact, in case of rejection due to incompatibility of a production plan, raw material or component supply, we are sure that this analysis is well founded. However, this analysis could cause the loss of some orders. In fact, the sequencing of order analysis could generate negotiation over delays.

The second strategy is the parallel processing of some orders. It allows us to take into account N orders simultaneously. When a negotiation is finished, another one starts to be analyzed. Sending an acceptation or refusal defines the end of a negotiation. This strategy allows parallel analysis and thus reduces waiting time. With this strategy, response time is not a cause of lost orders. However, here, the risk is of refusing an order which could be accepted with a valid analysis as in the first strategy. In fact, the parallel processing causes some temporary overload in the production plan. In this strategy, it is important to analyze the relationship between the maximum number (N) of simultaneous orders treated, the response time and the decision pertinence.

From the point of view of response time, as shown in Figure 7.2, there is a direct relationship between negotiation parallelization and processing speed. Thus, negotiation parallelization is a crucial parameter of negotiation agility. Nevertheless, we can note that a limit on this parallelization impact on the response time reduction is found.

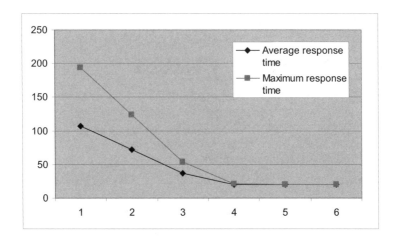

Figure 7.18. *Time to reply analysis*

From the point of view of lost orders, as shown in Figure 7.19, there is also a relation between negotiation parallelization and loss of orders. This loss is due to two reasons. Firstly, it could be caused by a delay response that is too long (response time in Figure 7.19). The impact of this factor decreases with parallelization growing. Secondly, a lost order could be caused by mistakes in the analysis (error of judgment in Figure 7.19). Now, the impact of this factor increases with the growth of parallelization. Thus, we are able to find equilibrium between these two impacts to define an optimal solution.

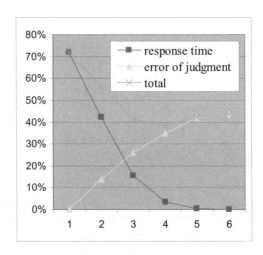

Figure 7.19. *Loss of orders analysis*

7.3.4. *SPEE*

Businesses seeking to meet growing demand usually face this opportunity by evaluating different strategic, tactical and operational transformation projects in order to choose the most profitable option with a high expectation of success. However, economic and technological conjectures have pushed businesses to not only consider their own business but their entire demand and supply chain as well, when aiming for current trends such as customer-centricity, collaboration, innovation, agility and personalization. These chains now include suppliers, assemblers, manufacturers, wholesalers, distributors, dealers, logistics providers, etc. Therefore, the transformation projects proposed often affect the core processes of more than one actor in the demand and supply chain and present great risk. Furthermore, substantial investments are required and the profitability for the entire chain is difficult to assess. The Simulation Platform for Extended Enterprises (SPEE) was developed to help decision makers facing this reality. This tool helps to visualize the dynamic performance of a demand and supply chain and can be used to contrast actual versus alternative business processes.

The SPEE relies on an agent-based modeling approach that closely mimics each decision-making actor in the demand and supply chain. The high level of modeling detail provides a realistic holistic representation that can investigate the impact of individual behaviors and interactions on the entire chain. One of the most important actors in a demand and supply chain is the end-user, here referred to as the client. Instead of using a stochastic distribution to represent the demand, each client is modeled individually with a personality, demand profile and behavioral capabilities. Their decision-making process when interacting with other actors in the chain is also explicitly modeled. The behavioral capabilities and the decision-making processes of all the other key actors in the demand and supply chain (i.e. purchasers, finance managers, marketing agents, production planners, dispatchers, sales personnel, etc.) are also modeled as faithfully as possible.

The case study currently used to develop and test the platform models the demand and supply chain of a recreational vehicle business which designs, manufactures and sells snowmobiles on the North American market [MON 05]. In order to meet the demand from clients in the market zone, dealers order snowmobiles from the assembler. The assembler orders the necessary parts from the suppliers, assembles the products and delivers them to the dealers through a logistics provider. Figure 7.20 illustrates the agents and their interactions for this case.

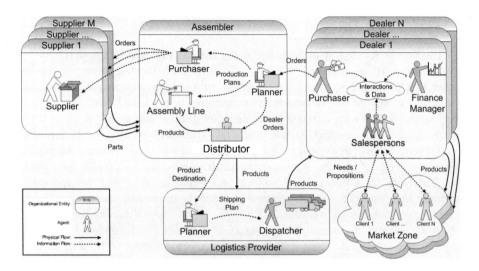

Figure 7.20. *Case study model – agents and their interactions [MON 07b]*

SPEE's architecture and communication protocols are specially designed to allow the agents, the simulation viewers and the synchronization server to run on different processors in order to achieve the computing performance necessary to sustain this holistic simulation. The synchronization server allows users to set the simulation speed so that decision makers can analyze the dynamics of the chain as the simulation runs or simply analyze the final results.

SPEE therefore supports holistic visualization capabilities to provide decision makers with a comprehensive view of the simulated demand and supply chain. It exploits multiple concurrent interfaces each dedicated to specific facets and actors of the chain in order to observe various perspectives such as sales, finance, production, inventory, transportation and supply. These viewers display performance and status indicators, traceability of products, messages, decisions and events. The viewers are designed so that decision makers can observe the demand and supply chain globally or analyze specific facets with focused data mining.

The viewers developed for the case study's recreational vehicle business that relate to demand chain visualization are shown in Figure 7.21. The first image shown is the client event map where the color of the star indicates the outcome of client visits to a dealership (purchased what he wanted, purchased a substitute product, did not purchase, etc.). The second image is the active client state graph which summarizes the information graphically. Next, the substitution matrix compares the snowmobile that the client wanted with the one that was purchased. Ideally, there would only be sales on the diagonal to show that all clients purchased what they wanted. The fourth image is the financial dealer map where the color of the star represents the dealer's financial health. Each dealer also has a financial cockpit, shown last, detailing inventory, sales, costs and gross margins.

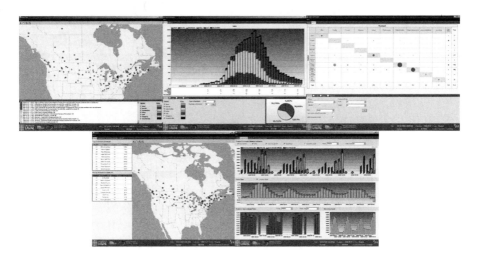

Figure 7.21. *Holistic demand chain visualization (adapted from [MON 07b])*

Other images are also dedicated to the supply chain as shown in the Figure 7.22. First, the product deployment graph shows how many products are on the assembly line, ready for distribution, at the dealers and sold to clients. Next, the stock tracking map displays the details of the stock status for the assembler, a dealer or a client. The transportation cockpit then summarizes the logistics provider's shipping activities. Shown last are the dynamic assembly line and bill of suppliers.

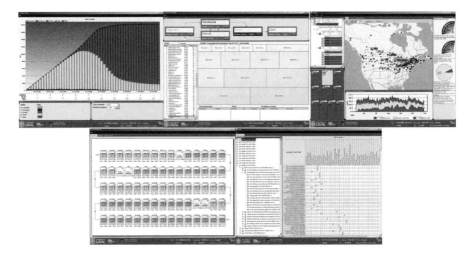

Figure 7.22. *Holistic supply chain visualization (adapted from [MON 07b])*

This simulation platform is designed to help decision makers understand the complex dynamics involved in their demand and supply chain. Once their actual chain is modeled, SPEE can be used as a virtual bench test for multiple applications at strategic, tactical and operational levels. For example, it can recreate past activities to illustrate past performance, validate the expected performance and robustness of the supply chain when faced with alternate future demand and event scenarios, and compare the performance of actual versus proposed supply chains facing the same demand.

7.4. Bibliography

[CAC 01] CACHON G.P., LARIVIERE M.A., "Contracting to assure supply: how to share demand forecasts in a supply chain", *Management Science*, vol. 47, no. 5, p. 629-647, 2001.

[CHR 00] CHRISTOPHER M., TOWILL D.R., "Supply chain migration from lean and functional to agile and customised", *Int. J. of Supply Chain Management*, vol. 5, no. 4, p. 206-213, 2000.

[FOR 08] FORGET P., D'AMOURS S., FRAYRET J.-M., "Multi-Behavior Agent Model for Planning in Supply Chains: An Application to the Lumber Industry", in *Supply Chain Theory and Application*, ARS Publishing, 2008.

[FRA 08] FRAYRET J.-M., D'AMOURS S., ROUSSEAU A., HARVEY S., GAUDREAULT J. "Agent-based supply-chain planning in the forest products industry", *Int. J. of Flexible Manufacturing Systems*, accepted, 2008.

[GAV 99] GAVIRNENI S., KAPUSCINSKI S.R., TAYUR S., "Value of information in capacitated supply chains", *Management Science*, vol. 45, no. 11, p. 16-24, 1999.

[KHO 07] KHOUIDER S., MONTEIRO T., PORTMANN M.-C., "Outil de simulation pour l'évaluation des performances de coordination dans un réseau d'entreprises distribué", 7th *Int. Industrial Engineering Conf.*, 2007.

[LAB 05] LABARTHE O., ESPINASSE B., FERRARINI A., MONTREUIL B., "A Methodological Approach for Agent Based Simulation of Mass Customizing Supply Chains", *Journal of Decision Systems*, vol. 14, no. 4, p. 397-425, 2005.

[LAB 06a] LABARTHE O., Modélisation et Simulation Orientées Agents de Chaînes Logistiques dans un Contexte de Personnalisation de Masse : Modèles et Cadre Méthodologique, PhD Thesis, Université P. Cézanne et Université Laval, 2006.

[LAB 06b] LABARTHE O., FERRARINI A., ESPINASSE B., MONTREUIL B., "Multi-agents Modelling for Simulation of Customer-Centric Supply Chain", *Int. J. of Simulation & Process Modelling*, vol. 2, no. 3/4, p. 150-163, 2006.

[LAB 07] LABARTHE O., ESPINASSE B., FERRARINI A., MONTREUIL B., "Toward a Methodological Framework for Agent-Based Modelling and Simulation of Supply Chains in a Mass Customization Context", *Simulation Modelling Practice and Theory*, vol. 15, no. 2, p. 113-136, 2007.

[LUC 04] LUCK M., MCBURNEY P., PREIST C., "A Manifesto for Agent Technology: Towards Next Generation Computing", *Autonomous Agents and Multi-Agent Systems*, vol. 9, p. 203–252, 2004.

[MAR 95] MARTEL A., ORAL M., Les défis de la compétitivité : visions et stratégies, vol. 2, Publi-Relais, 1995.

[MON 05a] MONTREUIL B., POULIN M., "Demand and supply network design scope for personalised manufacturing", *Int. J. of Production Planning & Control*, vol. 16, no. 5, p. 454-469, 2005.

[MON 05b] MONTREUIL B., "Production planning optimization modeling in demand and supply chains of high-value consumer products", in A. LANGEVIN et al. (Eds), *Logistics Systems: Design and Optimization*, Springer, 2005.

[MON 07] MONTEIRO T., ROY D., ANCIAUX D., "Multi site resources planning using multi-agent system", *Computers in Industry*, vol. 58, no. 4, p. 367-377, 2007.

[MON 07a] MONTREUIL B., LABARTHE O., CLOUTIER C., CHARTEL M., ZHENG X., Modeling Client Profiles for Delivery Time Simulation, CIRRELT research report, 2007.

[MON 07b] MONTREUIL B., CLOUTIER C., LABARTHE O., LOUBIER J., Holistic Modeling, Simulation and Visualization of Demand and Supply Chains, CIRRELT research report, 2007.

[MOY 03] MOYAUX T., CHAIB-DRAA B., D'AMOURS S., "Multi-Agent Coordination Based on Tokens: Reduction of the Bullwhip Effect in a Forest Supply Chain", *Proc. of the 2nd Int. Joint Conf. on Autonomous Agents and Multiagent Systems*, 2003.

[MOY 07] MOYAUX T., CHAIB-DRAA B., D'AMOURS S., "Information Sharing as a Coordination Mechanism for Reducing the Bullwhip Effect in a Supply Chain", *IEEE Transactions on Systems, Man, and Cybernetics*, vol. 37, no. 3, p. 396-409, 2007.

[OUZ 03] OUZIZI L., ANCIAUX D., PORTMANN M.-C., VERNADAT F., "A model for co-operative planning using a virtual enterprise", *Proc. of the 6th Int. Conf. on Industrial Engineering and Production Management*, 2003.

[POU 06] POULIN M., MONTREUIL B., MARTEL A., "Implications of personalization offers on demand and supply network design: a case from the golf club industry", *European J. of Operational Research*, vol. 169, p. 996-1009, 2006.

[ROY 04] ROY D., ANCIAUX D., MONTEIRO T., OUZIZI L., "Multi-agent architecture for supply chain management", *J. of Manufacturing Technology Management*, vol. 15, no. 8, p. 745-755, 2004.

Chapter 8

Simulation for Product-driven Systems

8.1. Introduction

Due to globalization, companies have to become more and more agile in order to face demand fluctuations and growing customization needs. In fact, the mass production market is a mass customization market, which could be defined as the production of a wide variety of end products at a low unit cost. This market typology evolution implies becoming a quick response to customer needs. The main problem for an efficient response seems to come from the global system inertia. During recent years, much effort has been expended to improve operating system reactivity (with the flexible manufacturing initiative for example), but the manufacturing decision process did not really change, and thus we are not able to fully make the most of these new operating system skills.

On the other hand, several new technologies and software developments appeared, offering new skills potentially useful for increasing flexibility and reactivity. Facing these new trends, a lot of new research works are focusing on identification technologies, such as Auto-ID, biometry or vision technologies. Radio frequency identification technology (RFID) represents a quick and safe way to track products, opening a method of linking informational and physical flows, and providing an accurate, real time vision of the shop floor. These new technologies appear like a catalyst to change the way production has been controlled for the last 50 years using traditional MRP² systems.

Chapter written by André THOMAS, Pierre CASTAGNA, Rémi PANNEQUIN, Thomas KLEIN, Hind EL HAOUZI, Pascal BLANC and Olivier CARDIN.

There is a general consensus in the IMS community between holonic control, production management and virtual enterprises [BAB 06] that the combination of both agent and infotronics technologies (such as RFID) may enable us to meet flexibility and adaptability issues as required by the increasing customization of goods and services.

As addressed by Marik [MAR 07], there is still a long way to go to make these heterarchical architectures efficient in a real industrial environment. Among the many issues to be solved, embedded devices as well as agent technologies are not yet sufficiently reliable and powerful to handle the scalability problems for fully distributing decision-making.

Another issue is thus to demonstrate the correct balance between centralized and distributed control capabilities of decision-making agents able to digitally interact one with the other from the operators throughout the processes down to the products and vice versa. That means analyzing hierarchical versus heterarchical control system architectures. Simulation seems the only recourse to analyze and compare alternative decision-making scenarios with regard to traditional ones.

8.2. Control architectures of manufacturing systems

8.2.1. *Hierarchical control architectures*

The traditional company organization seems to be hierarchical. This structure enables high level components to take decisions with a global vision of the whole system. Most of the business functions of a company are structured according to a hierarchical manner. Our main interest concerns flow management, so the core function studied in this chapter is the planning function. The well used model of the planning function is based on the five step Manufacturing Planning and Control System (MPCS) structure [VOL 97]. The aim of MPCS is to say what, when and how many to produce, according to sales forecasts, customer demand and production capacities. The decision frame at the highest level is macroscopic and long-term orientated, and becomes more and more detailed through successive steps to finally give the shop floor schedule.

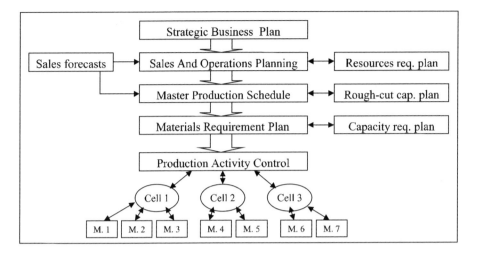

Figure 8.1. *Manufacturing Planning and Control System*

This hierarchical method ensures optimal and coordinated plans are achieved, by enabling the decision makers to take relevant decisions, according to synthetic and pertinent information (Figure 8.1). This top-down process ensures coherence between load and capacity (load/capacity balancing problem) at each decision level, by splitting the complex problem into several easier problems. On the other hand, when a special event occurs at the workshop level, the information has to go back to the upper level, to fix a new decision frame, and this information transmission process could take a lot of time, cutting down the system reactivity. To reduce this lack of flexibility, architectures have evolved to less rigidly linked nodes through heterarchical auto-organizing structures.

8.2.2. Heterarchical control architectures

Heterarchical production control systems rely on the distribution of every decision capacity, without any centralized view of the shop floor status. One of the most studied heterarchical architectures is based on multi-agent systems (MAS), which are a radical change from the usual hierarchical architecture. Research in this domain began in the 1980s, in particular with suggestions such as YAMS – Yet Another Manufacturing System [PAR 87] at the factory level. Multi-agent architecture relies on the overall system intelligence emerging from interactions between agents. Enabling such interactions assumes that agents are able to perceive their environment and to act on it. A heterarchical manufacturing system is usually composed of workstations and order agents, using an inter-agent negotiation protocol, such as the Contract Net protocol [SMI 80], to plan the workload on different resources.

The main problem in multi-agent systems is that every decision is taken locally, by one or more agents, each one having a partial vision of the global system. Consequently, it is impossible to ensure that the solution developed is the optimal one. As [VAL 97] pointed out, "the independence of agents prohibits the use of global information" in heterarchical control architectures, making "central scheduling or resource planning impossible". Moreover, problems like deadlocks could appear when the system size increases (a deadlock is a situation wherein two or more competing actions are waiting for the other to finish, so neither ever does).

8.2.3. *Product-driven architectures*

As mentioned in sections 8.2.1 and 8.2.2, both hierarchical and heterarchical approaches share benefits and drawbacks. As a consequence, the idea of coupling both systems emerged, with the aim of ensuring a global optimum while keeping the heterarchical system reactivity. One of the major issues of this is holonic manufacturing systems (HMS) [MCF 03], [VAL 06], [MOR 03]. The term holon is a combination of the Greek word *holos*, meaning *whole*, and the suffix *–on*, meaning *particle*. The holon concept was suggested by [KOE 67] to describe a basic unit of an organization in biological or social systems. Koestler observed that there are no non-interacting entities in living organisms or social organizations. Every identifiable unit of organization consists of more basic units while at the same time forming a part of a larger unit of organization. The HMS paradigm lies on the transposition of this concept in a production system, integrating hierarchy into distributed systems to combine reactivity to disturbances with high quality predictable performances. One of the existing holonic architectures is PROSA (Product Resource Order Staff Agents) [VAL 98], based on four agent types, three representing manufacturing entities (Figure 8.2), which are orders, products and resources, and one staff entity that coordinates the others.

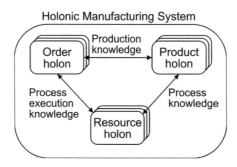

Figure 8.2. *Basic building blocks of a HMS and their relationships*

The order, product and resource holons are in charge of logistical concerns, product and process technological aspects, and resource control optimization, such as driving the machine at optimal speed and maximizing its capacity, respectively. The fourth type of agents, the staff holon, advises the basic holons about some features of the production system, such as scheduling priorities.

The emergence of Auto-ID technologies, such as Radio Frequency Identification (RFID) during the last decade, has made it possible to consider real implementation of these architectures, by authorizing products to hold a unique identifier, and sometimes to calculate treatments.

Auto-ID systems are usually made up of two types of components: readers and transponders. The physical principle of RFID technology is beyond the scope of this chapter, so we could summarize it as a tag (also called a transponder), held by a product and able to share data about it. These data are at least an identifier, and could represent several kilobytes. On the other hand, readers are in charge of establishing a contactless link between tag holders and the information system. As a new technology, many types of physical materials co-exist at this time: for example, several frequencies are used, some of which are usable all around the world while others are restricted in some areas.

At the current time, some ISO standards define air interfaces between reader and transponders, in particular ISO 18000 [ISO 04]. However, the standardization of information systems is still in progress. The EPC Global[1] proposition seems to be the most important one but is not yet admitted as a standard.

Potentially, unique item identification dramatically increases the supply chain visibility [MCF 03]. Neglecting reading errors, RFID technology enables us to thoroughly synchronize information system with the physical world, by always monitoring the position of each item, detecting changes in real-time. Considering this, unique item identification makes it possible to ensure every decision-making process is performed with data which actually reflects the real world, which avoids selling to clients products that are not in stock, or to produce again something already produced. Most of the work done in this domain deals with static analytical studies, which show that using RFID improves shelf availability [KAN 04], [SAH 05]. [LEE 04] note that static studies do not consider the dynamic effects of information accuracy and availability. They shown, using simulation, that the increasing precision raised by RFID technologies enables us to reduce by half the average finished good inventory, putting an end to products being out of stock. [JOS 00] also used a simulation approach to evaluate information visibility all along the supply chain.

---

1 "The EPC Global Network", 2004. http://www.epcglobalinc.org/.

We could note that major issues dealing with RFID technologies concern the impact of current information system accuracy improvement, but do not consider any option to radically change the usual control architectures. Few works deal with the evaluation of different system architectures working with the same controlled system. [BRE 01] proposed a performance comparison tool, based on simulation, but the represented system was adapted to fully meet requirements. For example, a RFID-enabled postulate is that embedding intelligence into the product could lead to some types of product-driven systems [WON 02], [MOR 03]. Firstly, it will enable collaboration mechanisms by associating any product entity with a computing agent. Furthermore, the product role could be enhanced from a basic manufactured entity to the synchronization tool between information and physical flows. In fact, information about a product cannot be de-synchronized when it is held by the product itself. Moreover, the "intelligent product" could take some shop floor control decisions, according to shop floor events. These types of decisions could be, through this product, synchronized with those coming from the business functions (the centralized ERP).

Some research works have shown that the solution to Business to Manufacturing (B2M) integration problems could be in the product [GOU 04], changing the usual pyramid vision of a company structure (Figure 8.3).

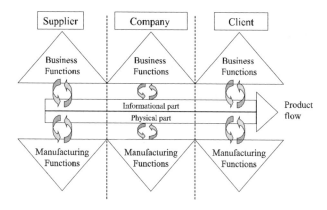

Figure 8.3. *Product-driven enhanced supply chain*

The simulation tools can meet two different aims:

– to *validate the holonic concept*, and then to study its true adaptation to a real system. The simulation will allow us to highlight that holonic systems could have better performances than hierarchical systems. In heterarchical manufacturing, the global behavior emerges starting from the local behaviors. Apart from simulation, we do not have any means of envisaging this global behavior;

– to *create computer aided decision systems for holonic manufacturing systems*. A significant problem of holonic manufacturing systems, concerning the decision-making, is the local vision of the context. Consequently, it is impossible to ensure that the solution developed is the optimal one. Simulation can be an invaluable tool to help the decision maker while enabling him to see the future consequences of his decision. This is the concept of proactive simulation.

8.3. Validation with simulation in HMS or product-driven systems

Using a holonic manufacturing system to control its shop floor is quite different from using a traditional hierarchical system. In fact, using an emergent system, with which the solution is generated at run time is something new compared to traditional predictive structures, where the solution is calculated offline using powerful algorithms.

There is a need to validate such a concept, and then to study its true adaptation to a real system, so as to show its better performances compared to hierarchical concepts. Valckenaers *et al.* [VAL 97] identified three types of approach in order to validate the relevance of a control system before its industrial use:

– implementation on a lab test bed;

– implementation of a pilot project on the shop floor;

– use of a simulation model.

Debugging and setting a control system needs stable and reproducible experimental conditions. However, physical systems are hard to bring under control and repeatability of experiments is not guaranteed. Adding the cost of hardware to build a pilot implementation and the implementation of a pilot on the shop floor seems to be a bad solution at this time. However, only using simulation could lead us to subdue some problems the modeler does not know.

The use of a lab test bed could underline some interesting problems, coming from hardware and environmental disturbances, but building an industrially sized test bed is quite expensive. In fact, it is really important to apply the technology in order to understand physical phenomena and to take them into account, for example, using RFID technology and the unperfected read rate.

Using a simulation model enables us to study the scalability of a control system when the model is reflecting a complex industrial case study. If properly developed, a simulation model could be used as an emulator, in order to set-up the control system before "plugging" it into the shop floor.

8.3.1. *Concept of emulation*

The emulation model does not integrate any decision rules, i.e. each point where decisions have to be made is converted to a synchronization point: a message, called a synchronization event, is sent to the control model, and the execution is paused until a resume order is received. On receipt of the synchronization event, the control model could calculate and send some information or parameters to the emulation model, in order to control it. For example, when parts are in front of a (numerically controlled) machine, the control system sends the machining program, or at the exit point of a stock area it sends localization information about where the pieces have to be sent.

The proposed methodology for building an emulation model is based on a systemic vision of the shop-floor system [MOI 84]. As we focus on products, we aim at representing their physical evolution. According to systemics, these evolutions can be modeled as shape, space and time transformations [PAN 07], [KLE 07].

Thus, the first step of the modeling methodology is a shop floor analysis, in order to determine every physically possible product life-cycle. A state-transition approach is used: states correspond to stable product positions and shapes while transitions model physically possible spatial and morphological transformations.

In the second step, we aim at modeling actuation on products. Transitions between product states are implemented by shop floor equipment. Therefore, we introduce two modeling constructs, *shape* and *space transformations*. These constructs must take into account physical constraints such as cycle and setup time, capacity, etc. Furthermore, a third construct is defined, *time transformation*, dedicated to model products waiting between transformations.

Each shape and space transformation block offers an interface, which enables an external system to interactively control it. Control messages make it possible to request the transformation to setup, or to begin operating. On the other hand, report messages enable us to know the transformation current state.

Using these three types of modeling construct, we are able to describe the shop floor structure in a generic way.

Finally, the emulation model would not be complete without a way of observing products. Thus, the third step of the methodology is concerned with product sensing. These modeling constructs include physical laws such as limited scope and sensing accuracy. A RFID transponder is a concrete example of shop floor equipment modeled as a product sensor.

In conclusion, these modeling constructs enable us to build an emulation model from the point of view of logistics. They aim to model the physical laws constraining product actuation, transformations and sensing, while offering interfaces to actuators and sensors.

8.3.2. *Simulation modeling with emulator and control system*

8.3.2.1. *Emulation model*

As previously mentioned, every type of element is represented by a basic element, that could be tuned according to the physical system it represents (batch size, transfer time, etc.). A basic element is constituted of five components (Figure 8.4):

– an entrance label;

– a first synchronization point, called pre-synchronization, in charge of correctly setting up the corresponding resource;

– a macro block representing the process performed by the resource, like in standard simulation model;

– a second synchronization point, called post-synchronization, managing the part route (the part moves away) and launching the next job to perform on the machine;

– an exit point, where the entity is routed to the next step of the process.

The synchronization procedure is quite simple: when a moving entity arrives at a synchronization block, a message holding entity and localization identifier is sent to the control system, then the entity is held until an order is sent back by the control system. This procedure is shown in Figure 8.5. The number of types of event is finite: we could define one for the pre-synchronization and one for the post-synchronization for each type of resource.

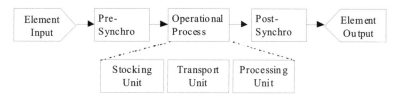

Figure 8.4. *Components of a basic element*

As opposed to usual simulation models, moving entities only hold a unique identifier, which refers to corresponding data in the control model. As a consequence, the emulation model cannot run without a control model, because entity-related data are not stored like attributes of an entity but in a database integrated into the control model.

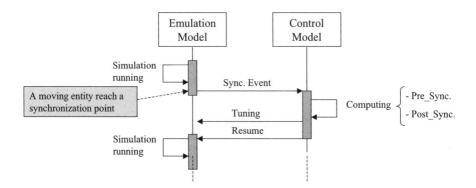

Figure 8.5. *Synchronization procedure*

8.3.2.2. *Control model*

The control model is a discrete-event system, which reacts to external events coming from the emulation module, from the user or from any other source. In order to control decision-making, the control model needs a physical world representation and a decision-making process. These components can be separated or not.

To ensure the ability to exchange control models, we define the communication interface between emulation and control model, i.e. to standardize messages between emulation and control models. Such a message contains the following information:

– synchronization point identifier, which makes it possible to identify the resource, its type and the synchronization type (pre- or post-synchronization);

– entity identifier, which is like a pointer on the entity description in the database.

This information enables the control model to update the information system and then calculate the attempted decision. This decision would lead to a parameterization of the emulation model (route or process tuning), and then a "resume signal" would enable the simulation to resume.

The first control model we designed represents the current industrial control system. We chose an object-oriented modeling method, where system components and moving entities are modeled like class objects (Figure 8.6). Data about objects are stored like attributes when decision processes are included in methods.

Products are represented like "Piece" and "Pieces_Batch" classes. They only hold attributes and methods to initialize or update these attributes. On the other hand, resources support attributes and decision methods, corresponding to pre- and post-synchronization.

Generally, the pre-synchronization procedure relies on an update of product status and a tuning of the resource (operation time, capacity, lot size, breakdown laws). Decision rules are integrated in a post-synchronization procedure, the aim of which is to control the part lot and to affect a new task to the resource.

Piece objects are dynamically linked with the location object corresponding to where they are, via the operation class. The set of operation objects enables us to implement a traceability concept relative to the resources (tracking) REF as well as that relative to the products (tracing) REF + Definitions. This information could of course be enriched by a description of the operation and other relevant information.

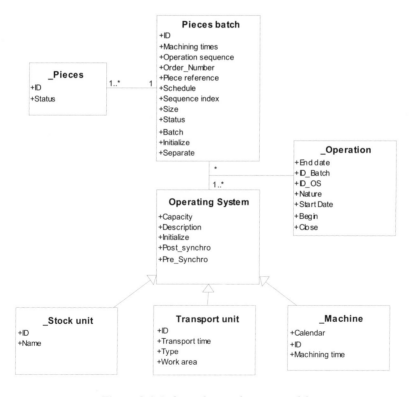

Figure 8.6. *Industrial control system model*

8.4. Simulation: a computer-aided tool for product-driven systems

Due to its distributed intelligence, product-driven control replaces predictive decisions by reactive and local ones. We could think that global decisions have disappeared. This is not true. In fact, at the root of the supply chain concept, there is a necessary global vision of the industrial system. A major goal of the supply chain is to "improve the flow of material between suppliers and customers at the highest speed" [PRO 06]. This goal suggests making global management decisions, which are not removed by product-driven control. In addition, the local decisions sometimes require the knowledge of the global behavior of the system.

In a product-driven control system, the product uses decision rules. To make its decision, the product applies these rules to its parameters to know what has to be chosen. However, in the majority of situations, the product is not the only actor in the decision-making. The decision is made by both the product and the production line decision center. Let us present the example of a ranking criterion in a queue. A product arriving in a queue has to decide its rank in this queue. From its parameters (due date, priority, etc.), it applies a ranking criterion (SPT, EDD, CR/SPT, etc.) in order to discover its position in the queue. However, it is the decision-making center of the production system that chooses the ranking criterion which has to be used by the product. Thus, the decision is made on two hierarchical levels.

In the problem-solving procedure, a decision center has a set of given alternatives and is aware of the consequences of each. In a general way, a decision requires two conditions. First, it is necessary to know all of the parameters influencing the decision-making. Then, the decision maker must have a forecasting tool allowing him to foresee, in the future, the consequences of his decision.

To make these global decisions, the managers need to have a global vision of the production system behavior.

The problem, in product-driven systems, is that the global behavior results from all of the local decisions which will be made in real time. It is thus very difficult for the manager to know the current state of his production system (Vision) and foresee its future evolution (Forecasts).

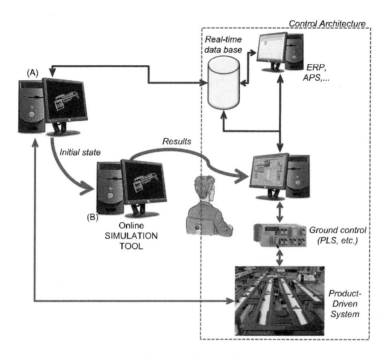

Figure 8.7. *Architecture for aid-decision by simulation in a product-driven system*

A new perspective is to consider simulation as a decision-aid tool in the context of a product-driven system. At the end of the 1990s, several studies were carried out about the future of discrete event simulation. Their main idea was to switch from a design-aimed simulation to a decision support simulation. This concept was named in [DAV 98] as "online simulation".

The major problem of this proposition is the initialization of the simulation. The majority of simulation tools begin their execution with an empty and inactive system. However, the state of the system when the pilot wants to launch a simulation is not empty. There are works in process. Thus, it is necessary to initialize simulations with a non-empty state.

In [CAR 07], Olivier Cardin proposes using two simulations to produce a decision-aid tool based on simulation. The first simulation (A) is an observer of the system. It reproduces the behavior of the real system. Its connection with the manufacturing execution system (MES) makes it possible to correct a possible drift during time. When the pilot wants to foresee the system behavior, he launches an online simulation (B). Then, the observer (A) gives to simulator (B) the actual state of the system to initialize the simulation. At the end of simulation (B), results are sent to the MES to allow the pilot to make his decision.

8.5. Industrial applications

8.5.1. *Furniture company case study*

8.5.1.1. *Context*

This case study is based upon the workshop of a ready-to-assemble furniture manufacturer (Figure 7.8). This workshop is composed of 8 machines, organized in production cells. The first machine is a disjunctive process: big particle panels arrive and are cut to the final piece sizes. This process is beyond the scope of this paper. What particularly interests us are the following drilling and grooving machines. Each one has particular features, and is able to complete several operations. Consequently, there are many possible operation sequences, and the diversity of the pieces (more than 1,800 furniture references, thus more than 10,000 piece references) makes physical flows and their control very complex. Moreover, about 70 batches are released every day, the average size of which is about 400 units, which involves several different and sizeable batches at the same time in the workshop. The end of the process is the packaging line, where pieces have to be grouped by furniture reference. Of course, all the parts belonging to the bill of material (BOM) of furniture have to be completed before starting to pack. Three intermediary stocks, composed of several FIFO stacks, enable us to buffer physical flow between machines.

We could summarize considering that the goal of the whole workshop is to deliver ready-to-assemble furniture on time to the client. The factory throughput is hardly linked with the packaging line throughput: any rate losses on the packaging line decrease the global throughput. On the other hand, pieces are moved into the workshop by the cutting tool. Logistic service considers as a rule that the aim of machining machines is to keep the edging stock before the packaging line between a low boundary and an upper boundary. Thus, decisions taken about the schedule of machining machines are quite important regarding the level and the nature of this WIP. This led us to focus, at first, on the inventory located between the cutting tool and the first machining cell, and then the feeding of following machines. The machining cell we studied is composed of three drilling machines (1, 2 and 3). Most of the pieces have to be drilled in this cell, after which they could be finished or need another machining in the second cell. Consequently, a scheduling decision taken with regard to drilling machines has an impact on other machines as well as on the packaging line efficiency. We could classify the objectives of scheduling decision about the feeding of drilling machines into two groups: local impact and global impact.

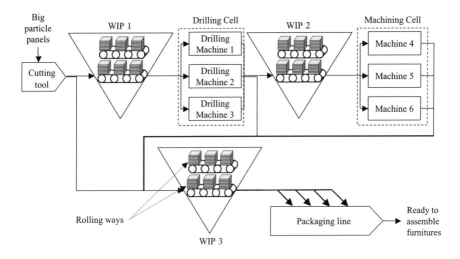

Figure 8.8. *Synthetic view of the workshop*

On the one hand, local impact is about drilling machine productivity:

– the schedule could be modified in order to reduce set-up times, which are not taken into account when calculating the detailed schedule. Grouping is carried out considering available orders and pieces plans;

– the choice could be made to use an alternative route, in order to face a breakdown or to balance the load between drilling machines. In fact, predictive scheduling is statically calculated without any visibility on the WIP evolution across time, which could lead to a physical inventory congestion;

– due to physical infrastructures, some lots are more easily accessible than others, so the feeding operator could decide to change the schedule function of piece location in order to reduce handling.

On the other hand, we could identify a global impact, which is about other machines and the packaging line:

– if the piece lot is finished after the drilling operation, it would be placed in the edging stock in front of the packaging line straight away, having an impact on its level;

– if the piece lots have to be machined in the second cell, it could be urgent, for example in order not to starve a machine. On the other hand, it could be better to wait in order not to congest the flow in front of a slowest machine.

If feeding operators could easily evaluate the local impact of their decision (if they have the knowledge), it seems difficult to evaluate the global impact, because they do not have the visibility on the global WIP of the workshop.

8.5.1.2. *Proposed architecture*

The pilot implementation aims at improving decision relevance with regard to the drilling cell (WIP 1), move about their local impact than about their global impact, giving to the feeding operator much important information, without necessarily swamping it with a mass of information.

The global physical architecture of the pilot project is (Figure 8.9a):

– pallets are tagged and associated with the lot they hold on output of machines;

– carts are equipped with reading points and detect every pallet movement;

– a middleware concentrates outputs from every reader, and transmits them to the location application,

The location application updates the area map, displays it to operators and supports the gap with the company information system. This piece of software is developed using a three-tier architecture.

In a first time, we propose to maintain the Sales and Operations Planning (SOP) and the Master Production Schedule (MPS) development processes following the MPCS. In fact, these are long-term plans, whose aims are, for the SOP, to size the production system according to the demand forecast, and for the MPS, to spread the load through time in order to smooth it. These processes, about the whole shop floor, need to be performed with a global view, and thus it seems to be logical to establish them following a centralized process.

At the detailed scheduling level, both solutions are possible. Having a global view on the system will enable us to calculate an optimized schedule which will be impossible to follow if a problem occurs. On the other hand, building a schedule in a distributed way at runtime does not ensure its optimality. We propose centrally generating a detailed schedule which becomes a framework, and distributed agents try to follow it. However, their intelligence will enable them to dynamically adapt it according to events occurring on the shop floor. This solution presents the advantage of following, as far as possible, the globally optimized schedule, and minimizing performance losses when differing from it.

We could distinguish two elements useful to obtain an efficient control on product flows (Figure 8.9b):

– a globally optimized framework, centrally calculated, using a lot of data from different company departments;

– dynamic information, coming from products and resources, which give a view on the global situation, in real time. Resources transmit information about their status and current performances, when products give technical information about their manufacturing sequence, their options or the position they are in, which enables us to have a view on the global WIP.

The control system relies on an unchanged MPCS system (SOP, MPS and detailed schedule), so current information system is always suitable. The question is about what information and procedure, particularly those held by the product, will enable an efficient shop floor control of manufacturing flows. This control system is not yet implemented, and to validate the future autonomous decision-making process, operators still have to take decisions according to information from tagged products.

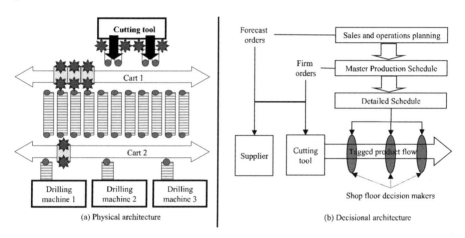

(a) Physical architecture   (b) Decisional architecture

Figure 8.9. *Proposed architecture*

The main benefits concern the automation of data sensing. Firstly, this would lead to any capture time being canceled, and ensure the event capture time coincided with the event occurrence time. This architecture provides a real time sensing of shop floor events. Secondly, pallet tagging reduces the data aggregation level. Previously, only the beginning and ending of an operation were tracked. Consequently, an operation had a binary status: begun or over. Now, the ability to know the number of processed pallets for a lot enables us to more precisely evaluate the task progress, for example in order to apply overlapping tasks. Also, identifying any lots makes it possible to have a view on the WIP level, but also on the nature of this WIP. For example, you could have a high WIP level but be unable to package any lot. Thirdly, data reliability improvement is strongly linked with RFID system performances. A good set-up will enable us to reach an almost 100% reading rate, and consolidation procedures will lead to a relevant view of the WIP. The only remaining weakness is about quantity: as the tags are on pallets, the quantity has to be inputted into a keyboard by an operator, with all the risks of errors this implies.

Operators previously did not have any decision support systems at their disposal. Previous attempts to give them a simulation tool failed due to two reasons: the model maintenance and its feeding. The new availability of accurate data about the shop floor evolution will enable us to continuously track the gap between reality and model evolution, making it possible to finely and continuously refine model parameters, improving its relevance. Moreover, another reason for errors in results given by previous simulations was due to a bad initialization. Data captured by an RFID system will represent a relevant information source to initialize the model. An indirect effect of RFID implementation concerns the computerization of the shop floor, enabling the operators to access technical data (such as alternative routes) and decision support systems.

The decision implementation will be improved by speeding up the appliance process and giving a detailed following of a decision impact. Firstly, the instantaneous location of piece lots will reduce decision appliance time, removing lot research time, and avoiding the machining of an incomplete lot. Secondly, the feeding operator will now be able to quantitatively evaluate the impact of the decision he took a few hours before, instead of the previous perception, which was a quite qualitative appreciation coming from the packaging line. This will provide him with the ability to learn about the system dynamics, and thus influence its reaction next time a similar situation occurs. The tracking could also lead to feeding the technical database, for example by noting a new possible alternative route.

Finally, the first and obvious benefit of using Auto-ID is to give information to shop floor decision makers in order to improve its efficiency. However, this could lead to achieving a local optimal, with quite a good efficiency for drilling machines, but leading to load shortage on the packaging line for example. A need emerged to enrich the static information (technical data) with dynamic information about flows, deadlines or resource status, in order to the drive drilling cell function of other cells, which are seen as clients. Firstly, we identified useful information, by listing every impact a decision on this decoupling point could have, and giving them to local decision makers. The analysis of the design and selection rules needed, in order to model them, to improve them when possible and then to develop an adapted distributed decision support system, which had to be done using the simulator presented previously. In practical terms, the intended benefits of such an implementation are:

– shortest time for machine feeding, due to the instantaneous location of piece lots, which remove the searching time. We note that, when the WIP1 level is quite high, dead time between two lots were often close to about 150% of set-up time, due to the lot search time;

– real time accurate visibility on WIP, which will lead to a reduction in shortages on packaging line. Simulation studies show that controlling drilling machines according to the WIP3 level and its nature (which references are in stock?) led to a reduction by half of the amount of idle time for the packaging line, which represents 10 operators;

– reducing paper and data associated with the product, improving data reliability and synchronism;

– improved control of resources, according to the packaging line needs and situation, seeing it as a client, and with an evaluation tool making it possible to evaluate effects of different solutions;

– improved quality, due to the automated checking of references on packaging line feeders. In fact, the RFID system immediately generates an alarm if feeders are incorrectly fed. Such confusion does not occur frequently, but each occurrence was very expensive, leading to residual inventories and consequently manual operation management.

8.5.2. *Multi-line synchronization*

8.5.2.1. *Industrial context*

The company Trane provides indoor comfort systems and comprehensive facility solutions for residential, commercial and industrial building needs. The 29 production sites are designed according to DFT concepts. This Just-in-Time methodology leads to a strictly similar assembly line organization (Figure 8.10).

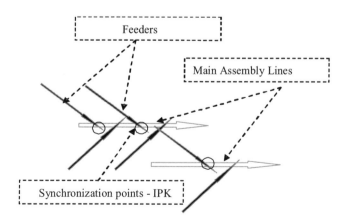

Figure 8.10. *DFT structure*

The objective is to optimize production using standardization processes. The production context is as follows: the shop floor is organized in pull production, and each finished product is assembled on a main assembly line.

To be sure that any component needed (semi-finished) arrives at the right time and thus avoids shortage there is the same inventory between the assembly line and each feeder (called - IPK in the Kanban process).

The other components are managed by the basic Kanban process. In addition, the control management must respect the objectives defined monthly by the tactical planning suggested by the ERP (enterprise resource planning). These objectives are detailed weekly at MPS (master production system).

To summarize this presentation, although this organization allows a good flexibility and reactivity on the level of material flow, it has many challenges: the first challenge is how to better synchronize assembly lines and its feeder, the second is how to give more visibility on the informational systems, for example what will the actual consumption of the component be, because today 80% of components are managed by Kanban and the consumption of inventories is realized in the backflushing phase. The third question is how to improve reactivity in case of disturbance? Consequently, this leads to synchronizing the simulation/emulation used in models to assure physical system control.

8.5.2.2. *System architecture at Trane*

8.5.2.2.1. Pilot presentation

To answer the questions presented in the introduction, a pilot was chosen to evaluate the pertinence of the product-driven system hypothesis. The pilot, called PilotAB, is composed of an assembly line with 4 workstations and a feeder also with 4 workstations. This feeder must feed the main assembly line on site A and satisfy the need for another production site called B (managed by a basic Kanban process) (Figure 8.11).

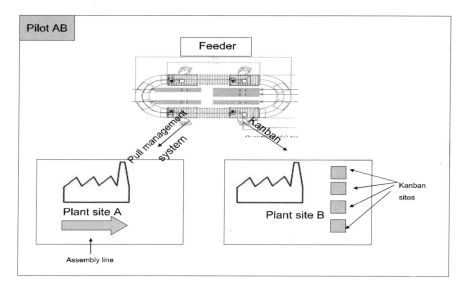

Figure 8.11. *Pilot AB view*

To summarize this part, site A needs are managed by a pull management system, and a Kanban process for site B. We must satisfy site A needs as a priority and be able to produce all the Kanban requirements per day for site B.

Discrete event simulation was chosen as the key question required for assessment of process cycle time and queueing time. Arena was selected due to its ease of use and the ability to deploy the model for future operational use at no additional cost. In fact, the Arena software makes it possible to simulate the behavior of an assembly line and the statistics generated give to the engineers good indicators to integrate an effective system of traceability and control.

8.5.2.2.2. Proposed architecture

In this case, we use the same architecture as presented previously. The control system is composed of a communication system connected with Oracle and the ERP (manufacturing orders and information traceability) and a user interface to help the human operator in his work by displaying the method sheet and the bill of materials (Figure 8.12).

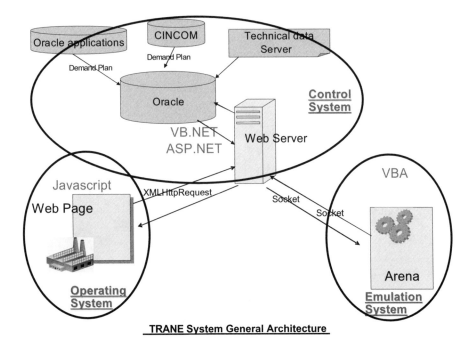

Figure 8.12. *The general architecture of the developed emulation testbed*

8.5.2.2.3. Control system description

The control system is developed as a web application with ASP.Net and VB.Net due to the multi-site context.

Concerning the pilot, the industrial aim is to produce ventilators according to component routings on different work stations. To assure product traceability and control material flow between the two sites, the web application is connected to an Oracle database.

The operator screen displays the following information:

– information specifying the demand (Work Order Number, item part number, quantity, etc.);

– bill of materials (these data come from the ERP);

– OMS (Operation Manufacturing Sheet): this is the description of the operations;

– information zones useful in case of breakdown in barcode or RFID tag scanning.

Figure 8.13 presents the Oracle database model where items and components are described and where control process information specifies how traceability and demand follow up are carried out. In particular, we follow-up the component life-cycle as the time spent in each workstation and the human operator working at this workstation.

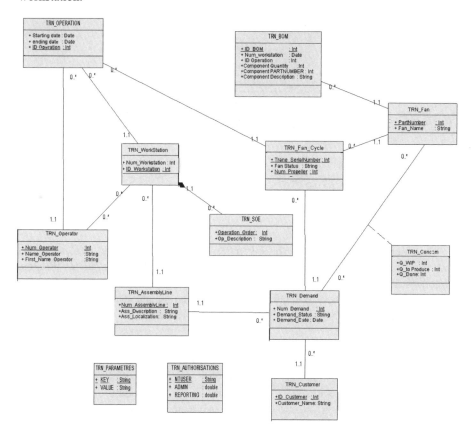

Figure 8.13. *Oracle database model*

8.5.2.2.4. Communication interface

We now describe the communication interface protocol (Figure 8.14) useful to assure communication between the two sites (the two emulation models), the Web application and the human interface.

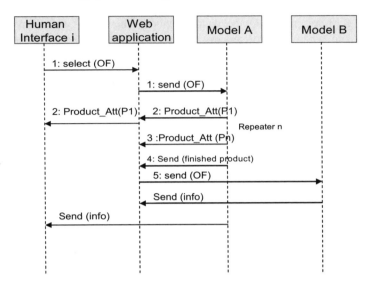

Figure 8.14. *A UML diagram for communication protocol*

The Web application sends the OF parameter to Arena which creates entities with the received attributes. Then, the emulation system (Arena) emulates the item barcode scan and sends the scanned information, via socket scanned information (Trane reference number, WO number, etc.). When Arena data are received the control system stores them in the database and at the same time a request is sent to the operator work center.

As soon as the Web application is launched, it sets up a server socket thanks to SocketClient DLL written in VB.Net. The socket is the only means of communication between the Arena models and control system and XMLHttpRequest objects are the only ones between work centers and the control system.

This system made it possible to obtain efficient communication between the architecture components but it does not make it possible to validate the correct operation of the Web application.

8.5.2.3. *Limits and perspectives*

In terms of synthesis, we were able to propose an effective way to synchronize several simulation models. We proposed a special architecture to manage the material flow between two sites and to assure traceability. This architecture is composed of a real control application connected with the physical manufacturing system on the one hand, and with an emulation system on the other. Thanks to this last system, it is possible to evaluate the decision-making process effect before actually implementing it in the operating (real) system.

The main weakness of this proposition lies in the time management. Effectively, time schedule periods are different in the emulation model (Arena) and the Web application and in certain circumstances it could be a problem. HLA is a good way of solving this problem and the following chapter is dedicated to this subject.

8.5.3. *AGP case study*

This work was carried out by Pascal Blanc at the time of his thesis [BLA 06]. In this industrial case, a make-to-order management policy is used to manufacture a highly customizable product. This product is very sensitive to quality problems. The process is mainly manual and is subject to numerous random events. Moreover, the firm has a high activity in prototype design. As a result, numerous normal and corrupted flows, due to rejection or reworking, intermix. In addition, the use of raw material and the maximization of the productivity are also a main objective. As a consequence, dynamic cooperative and/or competitive lot-sizing and scheduling mechanisms have to be developed. Controlling such a complex system at such a level requires the coordination of various complex models as well as the integration of this control in an existing control structure. A simulation model of this industrial application was made which uses both ARENA to model the physical system and a MAS platform to model the control system.

8.5.3.1. *Context*

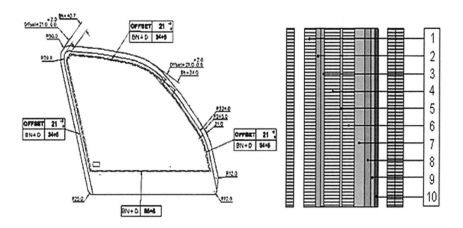

Figure 8.15. *The AGP product*

American Glass Product (AGP), in Curitiba, Brazil, produces laminated security glass for automotive application. The product is defined by its geometry (dimensions, curve), printed characteristics (logo of the client, black outline frame, antenna, demisting grid) and its composition (Figure 8.15). AGP mostly manages a design-to-order and a make-to-order policy.

The process is decomposed to three main parts (Figure 8.16): glass pre-process, plastic cutting and final assembly. The glass pre-process aims at preparing the glass strips: glass cutting, edge grinding and polishing, silkscreen printing and glass bending are the operations performed during this step. The plastic strips are then cut, according to a design, and the whole thing is finally assembled. For additional information, an extensive description of the process is available in [BLA 04].

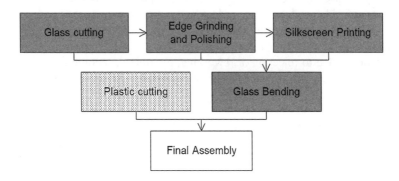

Figure 8.16. *Synoptic diagram of the process*

8.5.3.2. *Proposed architecture*

In order to build the HMS, various MAS development generic methodologies have been considered. The Vowel (AEIO) approach developed by [DEM 95] aims at defining a conceptual frame for the multi-agent system specification. AEIO stands for: Agent (structure, functions and behaviors), Environment (set of existing objects in the SMA), Interaction (languages and protocols) and Organization (relationships, dependencies, authorities). Cassiopeia, developed by [DRO 98], is based on role definition: individual, relational and organizational, and proposes five steps (or layers) to perform the design of the MAS: individual roles, dependencies, relational roles, groups and organizational roles. Gaia, from [WOO 00], proposes six models structured in a three level hierarchy: requirement statements, then roles and interactions, and finally agents, services and acquaintance. These methodologies are, generic as they may be, applied to almost any type of system. Furthermore, they allow us to describe the structure of the MAS, without imposing a specific platform. They have in common two levels of specification: the micro-level (definition of the agents) and the macro-level (definition of the interactions between agents).

The use of the holonic architecture PROSA greatly simplifies the design of the corresponding MAS, as the analysis step is almost completed since the roles of the agents and their interactions are already described. The conceptual architecture and the implementation step are also usefully completed using the holonic component-based approach, such as the one described by [CHI 00].

It is now necessary to describe a detailed and realistic mechanism for each agent to perform his role, at the micro- and macro-level.

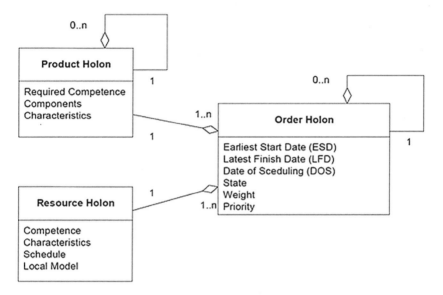

Figure 8.17. *UML class diagram of the basic holons*

At the micro-level, individual roles are defined for the basic holons. The class diagram (Figure 8.17) shows the relationships between the different classes of basic holons as well as their attributes. Product holons are information servers for other holons, they answer queries concerning the product model or product characteristics formulated by resource holons or order holons. To that end, they share the database access with the ERP [BAI 05].

Each order holon is linked to a product holon and controls the task required to manufacture this product, in accordance with the defined routing. Each task is defined by a standard duration, an earliest start date (ESD), a latest finish date (LFD) and a date of scheduling (DOS), if the task has been scheduled. This time-window approach gives an assessable margin of autonomy for the responsible resource holon to schedule this task. Order holons are also linked between them in accordance with the product model (BOM). Thus, if the product has components, the order holon is linked to order holon sons, and if the product is a component, the order holon is linked to an order holon father. A coordination mechanism is described in the next section to control the time parameter of each task in accordance with this structure. Finally, each order holon has a status (initialization, not scheduled, scheduled, scheduled out of bounds, manufactured), a priority (to classify the orders) and a weight (to indicate the importance of time limits).

Resource holons have to solve a lot-sizing and scheduling problem in accordance with their own model. They receive a task subscription from order holons as they own the specific competence to perform this task. They attempt to schedule this task according to their capacity and the requirements for this task to be performed (such as tool availability). In addition to the schedule produced, resource holons may produce other results, such as using raw material plans.

The interactions between holons are described at the macro-level. These interactions define the behaviors of the holons for various scenarios. To illustrate these interactions a simple example is presented (Figure 8.18).

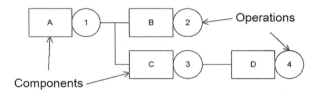

Figure 8.18. *Example of product model (BOM and routing)*

Creation of an order holon. An order holon is initiated with a product holon reference and a latest finish date (due date). It may be initiated by a user (commercial order for finished goods, internal order for stock in process), or by another order holon (father). The order holon first queries the correspondent product holon to retrieve the components it may require. If needed, the order holon will create order holon sons for each component initializing them with its latest finish date (Figure 8.19).

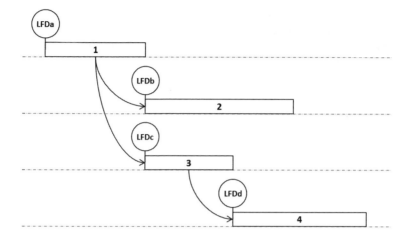

Figure 8.19. *Order holons establish latest finish date (LFD)*

The order holon then evaluates his earliest start date (Figure 8.20), using the earliest finish date of his order holon sons or the current time of the system. Inconsistencies may be detected at this point as the time-limit may not allow the task to be scheduled. In this case, a new latest finish date is calculated and the inconsistency is propagated to the order holon father, which will alter its own bounds of time.

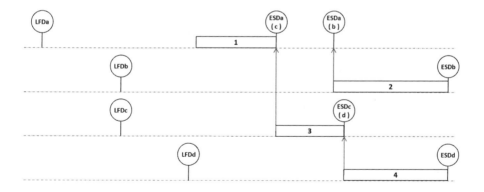

Figure 8.20. *Order holons establish earliest start date (ESD)*

The scheduling mechanism considers the earliest task first: a task may not be scheduled if the previous tasks are not scheduled. Once the time window is established for the earliest task, the corresponding order holon subscribes to a competent resource holon which attempts to schedule the task. Once again, inconsistencies may be detected at this point, resource holons are then able to negotiate the rescheduling of some tasks as the time window may absorb this type of disturbance (Figure 8.21), or to negotiate a bound of time for the least priority tasks if the workload is too high.

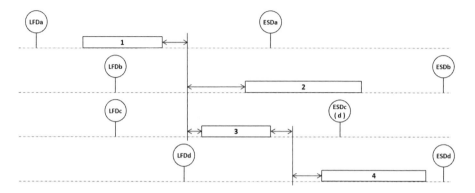

Figure 8.21. *Margin for disturbance absorption*

Once scheduled, the order holon informs its order holon father as it has to take the date of scheduling of his order holon sons into account to avoid inconsistencies (overlap of tasks).

Deletion of an order holon. The deletion of an order holon does not cause major disturbance, it just has to be propagated to order holon sons. It may be interesting to then reschedule the other order holon, for optimization purposes. This mechanism is described in the next section.

Reschedule for optimization purposes. The resource holon may attempt to reschedule in order to optimize its operation locally. The disturbances generated may be absorbed by the autonomy margin of each task. On the other hand, the tasks for which an inconsistency is detected may attempt to propagate the disturbance as it may bring an improvement of other schedule. Finally, the resource holon may dispose of its reschedule if no agreement is found.

Synchronizing with the physical system. The events registered from the physical system are not negotiable; they just may or may not lead to modifying the schedules and/or the time windows. Various scenarios are conceivable when synchronizing the physical system. Three main events are considered: the achievement of an operation, the loss of a product, and a resource breakdown. In case of loss of product, the creation of a new order holon may be necessary, thus the mechanism previously described is still valid.

8.5.3.3. *Evaluation of the control by simulation*

On the one hand, most manufacturing systems are too complex to allow the use of a realistic model evaluated analytically. On the other hand, the use of discrete-event simulation is costly because of the modeling effort required to design and run the simulation model. Furthermore, once modeled in a satisfactory way, the control model has to be implemented to be used.

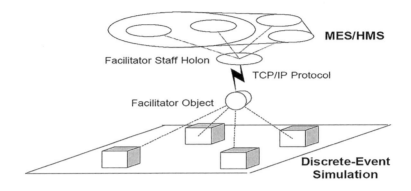

Figure 8.22. *Connection between MES/HMS and discrete-event simulation model for evaluation purposes*

To solve these problems, a staff holon able to interface the HMS with a discrete-event simulator is introduced (Figure 8.22). The simulation model only emulates the physical system, using a specific library of objects using Arena software. This mechanism is valid as the manufacturing system is composed of a product-driven control and a discrete-event-driven process.

This staff holon acts as routers and guarantees that the messages received from the environment reach the holon they are addressed to [GAL 01]. This mechanism emulates the flow of information coming from the physical system. The staff holon, called the facilitator, acts as a network server as incoming messages are transmitted via the TCP/IP protocol.

A specific object corresponds to the facilitator holon in the discrete-event simulation model. This object acts as a network client and relays the messages coming from the emulated physical part of the holons to the facilitator holon. It may also act on the physical simulated system, according to the messages received from the HMS. Communications between the HMS and the simulation model may be performed in a synchronous mode or in an asynchronous mode. In addition to this facilitator object, a generic resource holon object, which corresponds to the physical part of a resource holon has been developed. Order holons are linked to the entities of the simulation model. The facilitator staff holon is responsible for the correspondence between order holons and entities.

8.6. Conclusion

In this chapter firstly we presented the different control architectures of manufacturing systems. The new concept of the "product-driven system" (PDS) was explained. We showed that we are gradually moving from a predictive control to a reactive one. Product-driven control in manufacturing systems and holonic production systems fall under this evolution. In that context, simulation tools seem to be a good way to achieve the two different aims:

– to *validate holonic and PDS concepts*, and thus study their true adaptation to real systems. Effectively, apart from simulation, we do not have any means of envisaging this global behavior;

– to *create computer-aided decision systems for holonic manufacturing systems*. Simulation can be an invaluable tool to implement the concept of online simulation.

Firstly, we showed where simulation could be useful for validation of a HMS or PDS. For such an objective, generic simulation constructs and architectures were proposed for the emulation and for the control systems.

Then, we presented a new concept of online simulation. This type of simulation will allow us to foresee the future behavior of a PDS. In that sense, simulation will become a decision-aid tool.

Three industrial applications were then presented. The first one presented the application of generic simulation architecture to emulate a real production system. In the second one we highlighted the synchronization model problem and in that sense, we introduced the following chapter. Finally, the third application described the scheduling mechanisms used in a holonic production system and how that mechanism was simulated.

In this chapter we discussed the new piloting architectures proposed by the research community, over recent years. The validation of these new architectures is very important and it can only be realized with a lot of difficulties *in situ*. Thus, simulation is a very significant tool because it allows us to verify the aptitude of these new structures to answer the new challenges of the supply chain.

8.7. Bibliography

[BAB 06] BABICEANU R., CHEN F. "Development and Applications of Holonic Manufacturing Systems: A Survey" *Journal of Intelligent Manufacturing*, Springer, 17, pp. 111-131, 2006.

[BAI 05] BAÏNA S., PANETTO H., BENAL K., MOREL G., "Adapting HPM to B2M interoperability issues: Towards Interoperability between Business Management Level and Shop Floor Level", *INTEROP-ESA '05*, Geneva, Switzerland, 2005.

[BLA 06] BLANC P., Pilotage par approche holonique d'un système de production de vitres de sécurité feuilletées, Doctoral thesis, Ecole Centrale de Nantes and Nantes University, 2006.

[BLA 04] BLANC P., CASTAGNA P., DEMONGODIN I., MEBARKI N., "Multi-modelling and multi-agent approaches for the control evaluation: an industrial case", in *13th International Working Seminar on Production Economics (WSPE)*, IGLS Innsbrück, Austria, 4, pp. 33-43, 2004.

[BRE 01] BRENNAN R.W., NORRIE D.H., Evaluating the performance of reactive control architectures for manufacturing production control Computers in Industry, 46, 235-245, 2001.

[CAR 07] CARDIN O., Apport de la simulation en ligne dans l'aide à la décision pour le pilotage des systèmes de production, Doctoral thesis, Ecole Centrale de Nantes and Nantes University, 2007.

[CHI 00] CHIRN J-L., MCFARLANE D.C., "Application of the Holonic Component-based Approach to the Control of a Robot Assembly Cell", in *IEEE Conference on Robotics and Automation*, San Francisco, 2000.

[DAV 98] DAVIS W.J. "Online simulation: Need and evolving research requirements", in J. Banks (ed.), *Handbook of Simulation*, pp. 465-516, John Wiley and Sons Inc., 1998.

[DEM 95] DEMAZEAU Y., "From interactions to collective behaviour in agent-based systems", in *European Conference on Cognitive Science*, St. Malo, France, 1995.

[DRO 98] DROGOUL A., ZUCKER J.-D., Methodological Issues for Designing Multi-Agent Systems with Machine Learning Techniques: Capitalizing Experiences from the RoboCup Challenge, LIP6 1998/041, LIP6 research reports, 1998.

[GAL 01] GALLAND S., GRIMAUD F., BEAUNE P., CAMPAGNE J-P., "Méthodologie pour la simulation de systèmes industriels complexes et distribués au traves d'une étude de cas", in *4th Conférence Internationale de Génie Industriel*, Aix-Marseille-Ajaccio (Bertrand and Kieffer), 2, pp. 673-684, 2001.

[GOU 04] GOUYON D., SIMÃO J. M., ALKASSEM K., MOREL G., Product-driven automation issues for B2M-control systems integration in *Proceedings of the 11th IFAC Symposium on Information Control Problems in Manufacturing, INCOM'2004*, Salvador – BA: Brazil, 2004.

[JOS 00] JOSHI Y. "Information Visibility and its Effect on Supply Chain Dynamics", Master's Thesis, MIT, 2000.

[KAN 04] KANG Y., GERSHWIN S., "Information Inaccuracy in Inventory Systems Stock Loss and Stockout", *Joint MIT/INFORMS Symposium*, 2004.

[KLE 07] KLEIN T., THOMAS A., "Méthodologie de modélisation pour l'évaluation de systèmes de pilotage centralisés et distribués", *CPI'07*, Rabat, Maroc, 16 pp., 2007.

[KOE 67] KOESTLER A., *The Ghost in the Machine*, Hutchinson & Co Ltd, 1967.

[LEE 04] LEE Y.M., CHENG F., LEUNG Y.T., "Exploring the impact of rfid on supply chain dynamics" in *Proceedings of the 2004 Winter Simulation Conference*, pp. 1145-1152, 2004.

[MOI 84] LE MOIGNE J.L., *La théorie du système général. Théorie de la modélisation*, Presses Universitaires de France, 1984.

[ISO 04] ISO/IEC 18000, "Information technology – Radio frequency identification for item management", *JTC 1/SC* 31, 2004.

[MAR 07] MARIK V., LAZANSKY J., "Industrial applications of agent technologies", *Control Engineering Practice*, 15, pp. 1364-1380, 2007.

[MCF 03] MCFARLANE D., SARMA S., CHIRN J.L., WONG C.Y., ASHTON K., "Auto id systems and intelligent manufacturing control", *Engineering Applications of Artificial Intelligence*, 16/4: 365-376, 2003.

[MOR 03] MOREL G., PANETTO H., ZAREMBA M., MAYER F., "Manufacturing Enterprise control and management system engineering: paradigms and open issues", *Annual Reviews in Control*, 27:199-209, 2003.

[PAN 07] PANNEQUIN R., THOMAS A., MOREL G., "Benchmarking issues for product-driven decision-making", in *9th International Conference on the Modern Information Technology in the Innovation Processes of the Industrial Enterprise, MITIP'2007*, Florence, Italy, 2007.

[PAR 87] PARUNAK H. v. D. "Manufacturing Experience with the Contract Net" *Distributed Artificial Intelligence*, Pitman Publishing: London and Morgan Kaufmann: San Mateo, CA, pp. 285-310, 1987.

[PRO 06] PROTH J.-M., "Scheduling: New Trends in Industrial Environment", *INCOM'2006*, St. Etienne, pp. 41-47, 2006.

[SAH 04] SAHIN E., "A qualitative and quantitative analysis of the impact of the Auto ID technology on the performance of supply chains", Doctoral thesis, Ecole centrale de Paris, France, 2004.

[SMI 80] SMITH R.G., "The contract net protocol: high-level communication and control in a distributed problem solver", *IEEE Transactions on Computers* 29, pp. 1104-1113, 1980.

[VAL 97] VALCKENAERS P, VAN BRUSSEL H, BONGAERTS L, WYNS J., "Holonic manufacturing systems", *Integrated Computers Aided Engineering* 4, pp. 191-201, 1997.

[VAL 06]VALCKENAERS P., CAVALIERI S., SAINT GERMAIN B., VERSTRAEDE P., HADELI BANDINELLI R., TERZI S., VAN BRUSSEL H., "A benchmarking service for the manufacturing control research community", *Journal of Intelligent Manufacturing* 17: 667-679, 2006.

[VAN 98] VAN BRUSSEL H., WYNS J., VALCKENAERS P., BONGAERTS L., PEETERS P., "Reference architecture for holonic manufacturing systems: PROSA". *Computers in Industry*, 37 pp. 255-274, 1998.

[VOL 97] VOLLMANN T.E., BERRY W.L., WHYBARK D.C., *Manufacturing Planning And Control Systems*, 4th ed., McGraw-Hill: New York, 1997.

[WON 02] WONG C., McFARLANE D., AHMAD ZAHARUDIN A., AGARWAL V., "The Intelligent Product Driven Supply Chain", *IEEE Int. Conference on System Man and Cybernetic SMC'02*, 2002.

[WOO 00] WOOLDRIDGE M., JENNINGS N., KINNY D., "The Gaia Methodology for Agent-Oriented Analysis and Design", *Autonomous Agents and Multi-agent Systems*, 3, pp. 285-312, 2000.

Chapter 9

HLA Distributed Simulation Approaches for Supply Chains

9.1. Introduction

Supply chains and more particularly supply chain networks are increasingly subjected to large or extreme dynamic operations, where more flexibility and reactivity is asked of each actor on the one hand and a specialization bringing more productivity on the other hand. This results in an externalization of the non-competing activities and an increase in the number of actors interacting. In order to face the increasingly complex industrial engineering, several research tasks aim to develop and set up methodologies and tools for effective control of supply chain networks. The first validation phase of these research works consists of developing adapted simulation environments, allowing the analysis and evaluation before considering an operational deployment.

Let us note that building a monolithic model to represent the whole supply chain is a very hard task: analysis could be compelled to assume many simplifying hypotheses, at least producing invalid results. Furthermore, running such a monolithic model requires full data sharing, even if the company's data are partially or completely confidential. As a result, there is a real need for Distributed Simulation (DS) in SCM, because large amounts of data (i.e., production plans, inventories, etc.) are both confidential and remotely located in the data storage of different facilities. As defined by Fujimoto, distributed simulation refers to technologies enabling a simulation program to be executed on multiple and

Chapter written by Fouzia OUNNAR, Bernard ARCHIMEDE, Philippe CHARBONNAUD and Patrick PUJO.

geographically distributed computing systems, interconnected by a communication network, such as a computer network [FUJ 00]. Distributed Supply Chain Simulation (DSCS) is a specific application. In fact, certain applications (for performance, confidentiality, etc. reasons) require that the various components of a model are located on several computers with, possibly, heterogenous operating systems. The implementation of a distributed simulation of these models is then necessary. This implementation needs a communication protocol allowing the exchange of information between the various components. The appearance of standards of distributed simulation specification makes it possible to facilitate the implementation of such simulations. A treatment in distributed simulation must be ensured in order to respect the existing causality relations. In addition to the management of the events, it is important to have good time management. In fact, the problem of message coordination between the partners of the supply chains and of synchronization of these partners must be managed. In the following section, various techniques of existing distributed modeling and simulation are introduced: DEVS (Discrete-EVent system Specification), SIMBA (SIMulation-Based Applications), and HLA (high level architectures).

The following sections present research experiments in supply chains using distributed simulation for validation: self-organized control of a supply chain network and reactive control by evaluation of multi-site plans of enterprise networks.

Section 9.3 relates to the study and development of a self-organized control system for supply chain networks based on a holonic and decentralized architecture. Each supplier organizes and controls his own activities, obtained by proposing his best conditions for the execution of Calls For Proposals (CFPs) launched by customers. The decision-making mechanism is produced without hierarchy, thanks to the properties of a decision-making center, called Autonomous Control Entity (ACE), associated with each actor of the logistic network which makes it possible to quantify a multicriterion, according to the AHP (Analytic Hierarchy Process) method. This mechanism of collective and decentralized assignment of CFP is modeled using DEVS formalism. The models are integrated in a global simulation thanks to a distributed implementation via HLA representing a complex logistic network. This enables the analysis and validation by simulation of the negotiation mechanisms between the partner actors of the network.

Section 9.4 proposes a method and a tool based on distributed simulation to carry out the evaluation of the feasibility of the multi-site plans for the enterprise networks. The purpose of the method is to determine the feasibility of the production and to find a better logistic configuration within the framework of each evaluated scheduling strategy. The tool, based on distributed simulation architecture via HLA, allows the simulation and follow-up of the system state at any point of the enterprise network. The performance evaluation allows the accommodation of control in order to determine the best configuration allowing the absorption of a forecasted scheduling.

9.2. Modeling and discrete-event simulation

9.2.1. *Specification using DEVS and SIMBA*

A model is an understandable form of a system built to make it possible to find a response to a precise problem. There are two classes of resolution problem methods: analytical methods and methods based on simulation. The first enables us to seek a general solution but runs up against the problem of model complexity. The second are able to treat more complex models, but are limited to particular solutions. While acting on the models from a data and time basis, we thus define a simulation [ZAC 06b]. Modeling and discrete-event simulation makes it possible to deal with problems concerning systems whose temporal behavior is too complex to be treated analytically. Discrete-event modeling requires two principles [NUT 03]. The first is the unambiguous description of the system. The second is the definition of discrete-event simulation algorithms whose validity is founded and verifiable. The formal specification of these models can be established thanks to DEVS and SIMBA formalisms.

A behavior model of autonomous control is described by using DEVS (Discrete-event system Specification) formalism [ZEI 73]. A DEVS specification is independent of the simulation technology as well as the underlying host computer. Thus, we obtain models having only one interpretation and independent from any computer technology or from any commercial simulation software. The bases of a formal description in DEVS and the graphic composition rules of DEVS models are described in [CHA 04]. Furthermore, the hierarchical and modular description of the systems recommended by DEVS facilitates obtaining reusable models but also carrying out distributed simulations [HAM 06]. DEVS allows the description of the system behavior at two levels: the lowest level (DEVS atomic) describes the discrete-event system behavior as a succession of sequences of transitions between states of this system, carried out at the reception of an external event, or at the end of the state lifespan. The higher level describes the system as a network of components, which can be either of atomic DEVS models or of coupled DEVS models. A concept for formalization of modular and hierarchical models can be introduced by this means.

The modeling of a corporate network requires a simulation model for each company like for the transportation system between companies. These models can be managed by SIMBA, which is an ActiveX, enabling the modeling of virtual workshops by integrating the functionalities of simulation in applications thanks to COM OBJECT technology. This makes it possible to use programming models created with WITNESS. In order to facilitate the modeling of the corporate networks three types of generic and skeletal modules are necessary. The Station module enables modeling using WITNESS components (machine, stock and track) according to the level of aggregation, a machine in a site or a site in a corporate network. The Transportation module makes it possible to use a network of WITNESS tracks to model the physical framework of transportation between the machines in a site or between the sites in a corporate network. It collects all information relating to the tracks (journey times, number of vehicles able to circulate at the same time on the same track, etc.) and the routing of trucks and carriages. The physical framework of transportation must be defined in a specific function including, for every Station module, which track must be used to load and unload trucks or carriages in entrance and exit. Finally, the Configuration module describes the modeled system by defining WITNESS vehicles representing the carriages or the trucks as well as the name and the number of stations. The Configuration module makes it possible to establish connection between Transportation module and the Station modules using two specific WITNESS tracks for the entrance and exit representation.

9.2.2. *Model interoperability*

The concept of interoperability is increasingly used in engineering companies and its related standardization activities [CHE 02]. Nowadays, companies evolve in a worldwide heterogenous environment and work in a network. In this context of collaboration, interoperability is becoming a key factor of success. The main goal of interoperability is to improve the competitiveness of companies in a networked environment by facilitating their communication and interaction and thus, to reach their objectives [DAC 06]. Today, interoperability is developed in several domains, i.e., transport, military, medicine, etc. For each of them, interoperability is specifically defined and interpreted according to its own perspectives. At the beginning of the 1990s, in computer sciences, interoperability was defined as the ability of two or more systems or components to exchange information and to use the information that had been exchanged [IEE 90]. [EIC 04] specifies that interoperability is a key to increasing user confidence and value. Consequently, it seems that an interoperable system must be able to communicate. If a system is not interoperable, some risks can emerge inducing lack of performance, stability and coherence [ALO 06]. The interoperability is achieved when the systems interoperate their data, resources and business processes with semantics defined in a business context regardless of different languages, data formats, interfaces, execution platforms, communication protocols or message formats [TSA 05]. Interoperability is not only about transferring information but also performing an operation on behalf of another system [WHI 06].

9.2.3. *Model interaction protocols*

Several technologies appeared to facilitate the electronic data interchange between companies (EDI, XML, EDI/XML) and to improve the distributed coordination of the decision-making (Contract-Net). EDI (Electronic Dated Interchange) is characterized by the speed and reliability which include the safety of transmitted information. Nevertheless, EDI presents a major drawback linked to its difficulty of implementation. XML (eXtensible Markup Language) associated with EDI enables full engagement of companies in electronic processes. XML is a description language of data derived from SGML (Standard Generalized Markup Language) [ECO 03]. To go further in the interaction and the exchange of information and decision making, it is necessary to introduce coordination and negotiation capacities between companies. Contract-Net is the most known basic protocol. The Contract-Net interaction protocol is one of the communication protocols which better responds to the negotiation requirements [SMI 80]. In fact, Contract-Net specifies the interactions among several partners for an entirely automated and competitive negotiation thanks to the use of contracts. It enables the identification of each partner, and the forwarding of structured data according to the predefined messages. This protocol checks that no transmission error exists.

Distributed simulation can be advantageously introduced to solve the problem of sharing confidential data during the simulation of supply chains. Each partner company of the chain can establish their own model. Thus, the obtained models must have the capacity to communicate. Simulation modeling and analysis can be an extremely effective tool for supply chain performance analysis [BAN 06]. Many developments apply distributed simulation to this context. In fact, there is a real need for distributed simulation in SCM, because large amounts of data (i.e., production plans, inventories, etc.) are both confidential and remotely located in the data storage of different facilities. Advantages in using a DSCS approach in SCM are multiple:

– computational efforts are shared, improving the overall execution run-time drastically;

– once DSCS frameworks and IPC (Inter-Process Communication) formalisms have been established, simulation models can be developed by different development teams, using different simulation environments;

– in a DSCS framework each model runs separately, sharing only the pertinent data so that companies are not compelled to share sensitive information [REV 01]. In such a framework, the overall simulation can be broken down into component models, each one performing independent runs. Component models can execute a simulation run without knowing in detail the state of any other models, thus communicating through messages sent according to the adopted IPC schemas;

– as in DS, in DSCS component models can be coded by any simulation environment;

– the model of each organizational unit is somehow usable in multiple DSCS framework (modularity) and reusable in the same DSCS when the supply chain configuration changes over time (reusability).

In order to develop and run a DSCS framework, the proper information flows must be correct, adopting IPC formalisms and infrastructures. The most important framework for distributed simulation is HLA-RTI. HLA was developed by the American Department of Defense via its DMSO (Defense Modeling and Simulation Office) in order to carry out a total simulation made up of distributed and heterogenous simulations. In HLA, each participating simulation, called a federate, communicates with the other federates in an HLA federation. HLA is entirely standardized. For example, the standard IEEE P1516.2-2000 describes how the communications between models and the application via a "central coordinator" are carried out: the RTI (Run Time Infrastructure). The HLA protocol allows the reduction of the modeling and simulation costs and responses to the requirements of large simulations using geographically distributed components [MCL 00] [ZEI 99]. For this, HLA implements algorithms for the synchronization and respect of the chronology of the simulated events and in particular the algorithm defined in [CHA 78]. It facilitates the reusability and interoperability of simulations. The reusability means that the models of the simulation components can be reused in various simulation applications without the need to recode. The interoperability implies the capacity to combine simulation components on distributed platforms of various types. Thus, the interconnection of simulation platforms and higher level aspects such as the exchange of events and synchronization are considered in HLA. Run-Time Infrastructure (RTI) software implements specifications for distributed simulation (i.e. simulation-time advancing, state variable updating).

Other standards used for distributed simulation are presented below [BAN 06] [ENJ 06] [MEK 07]:

– another important middleware standard used for distributed simulation is CORBA® (Common Object Request Broker Architecture). CORBA connects distributed software components and defines a common architecture for distributed applications. CORBA has become a standard for communication among objects in a client-server environment. It is completely object-oriented and allows the applications to use local and remote objects, independently of component software or hardware. With a high degree of interoperability, CORBA ensures that distributed objects will be able to communicate. It is the most important alternative to the RTI environment, even if it is a general IPC infrastructure without any provision for synchronization of the events during the execution of a simulation;

– RMI (Java Remote Method Invocation®) enables the programmer to create distributed Java technology-based applications, in which the methods of remote Java objects from other Java virtual machines are applied, possibly on different hosts. An important aspect of RMI is the possibility of making safe the applied methods in order to avoid intrusions in the system. RMI does not guarantee execution simulation synchronization;

– DIS (Distributed Interactive Simulation) is a protocol which supports simulations made up of several simulators. This protocol is not used owing to the fact that interoperability was led by the data.

Contrary to all the other architectures (DIS, ALSP (Aggregate Level Simulation Protocol), CORBA, etc.), HLA ensures synchronization between the simulations. A considerable advantage of HLA is to give the possibility of integrating the real operation of one (several) company(ies) undertaken with the simulated operation of the other companies of the network. Global simulation can thus be carried out by combining one (several) real system(s) with simulation models.

HLA *federation* indicates a distributed simulation system using a set of basic simulations exchanging so-called federate information. HLA is formally defined by three components:

– HLA rules recapitulate the principles of HLA. They are summarized in 10 rules defining the operation of the federate (5 rules) and the federations (5 rules) [IEE P1516];

– OMT (Object Model Template) is the description of the elements (objects and interactions) which are shared through a federation [IEE P1516.2]. HLA requires that each federate and federation has to document its object model by using the OMT. In order to do this, HLA specifies two types of object models. The first is the Federation Object Model (FOM) which describes the set of the objects, attributes and interactions which are shared through the federation. The second is the Simulation Object Model (SOM) which provides information about the faculty of simulation for exchange of information when it takes part in a federation;

– HLA interface specifications describe the execution services provided to a federate by the RTI [SIR 98]. They indicate how federates interact during the federation execution [IEE P1516.1]. The RTI is software that conforms to the HLA interface specifications.

All the interactions between federates used the RTI. The interface between the RTI and federates is standardized, which ensures the interoperability of simulations and their capacity to evolve from one HLA federation to another. It is also thanks to the RTI (amongst other things) that synchronization is assured.

Each federate controls its advance in logical time, with respect to that of the clocks of other federates. HLA has management time mechanisms ensuring a time advance satisfying the causality laws of the events. In this case, the RTI guarantees that federates cannot receive events (updated of attribute or sending of interaction) to process in its past. The first base of HLA is that there is not any reference to a total clock of the federation. On the other hand, each federate must have its own temporal reference.

At the implementation phase of HLA concepts in each federate, the federate program inherits the FederateAmbassador class. This addition permits the federate to use the RTI services, to implement the callback services and to use the service related to the request for authorization of treatment of the next event. This request NextEventRequest() to the RTI obtains the authorization to process the next local event envisaged in the case of a simulation directed by the events. The RTI determines, according to the LBTS (Lower Bound one Time Stamp) and to the messages intended to this federate, if it can grant to it the authorization to process its next event. If it authorizes the federate to process the requested message, it sends the TimeAdvanceGrant() service.

HLA uses the Lookahead concept (L). L is the duration beyond its current date during which the federate attests that it will not transmit a message. Federates can dynamically modify the value of their Lookahead (during execution).

Various research experiments in supply chains are presented herein using distributed simulation.

9.3. Self-organized control of supply chain networks

9.3.1. *Problematics*

The supply chain control results in the management of its various flows, physical, informational, financial and decisional flows in an optimal way. The control of the relationship among partner companies involves all the actions they develop together to achieve their common objectives and to react at the right time to any failure on the part of any one of the partners. A negotiation among partners is thus required involving the management and organization of each partner's production [OUN 01]. Thus, the control of the relationship requires actions developed by all of the partners to achieve common goals at the operational level as well as at the organizational level. This control requires coordination and cooperation between the various partners; the coordination of the decisions is obtained by the cooperation of the various actors, cooperation which rests on a negotiation between all of the potential partners to achieve their common goal. Coordination aims to ensure a temporal agreement between the entities for a same action requiring their collective participation and having to be registered over the entire duration of the action [PUJ 02]. The cooperation is focused on the organization of the tasks in term of distribution, allowance and assignment of the actions to resources entities in order to search for a solution enabling us to reach this goal [PUJ 02]. The negotiation corresponds to the initial phase of the cooperation. It consists of the joint definition of the methods of the action assignment to these resource entities. Thus, the negotiation phase is very important for the success of the cooperation.

In a context of several companies linked through customer supplier relationships, product flows are generally static after a commercial negotiation. This can make flow management difficult, in particular when work overloads occur for one supplier. In a self-organized control system of a logistic network each supply flow is considered with respect to all potential suppliers. Each supplier participates in a common goal achievement (insure supply in good conditions) by organizing its own control [OUN 01]. The objective is to bring a support to the control of a logistic network at a tactical/operational level (medium/short term) by the dynamics of the customer-supplier relationships in this network.

After a description of the holonic approach for the self-organized control of a logistic network, the modeling of this same network is presented. Before approaching the distributed simulation of the global operation via HLA, the choice and the evaluation of the supplier process is presented.

9.3.2. *Choice of a decision structure*

Several possible control structures exist which are positioned compared to the decentralization of the decision capacity [PUJ 02] [TRE 02]. After a study of the various control structures and taking into consideration the operation of the organizations and supply chains, the heterarchic/completely decentralized structure (see Figure 9.1) called the isoarchic control structure was chosen [PUJ 07]. The heterarchic structure was proposed by [TRE 02] and the decentralized structure was proposed by [PUJ 99]. Heterarchy is related to the absence of relation master/slave, i.e., all the decision-making centers will be on the same level of decision. The decentralized approach of the decision-making mechanisms is based on the increasing autonomy of the actors of a production system and on their capacity to communicate with the other actors for a better reactivity. The decision system managing the operation of a set of components is called decentralized when these components organize their own operation without the direction of any higher hierarchical level decision-making center [OUN 01].

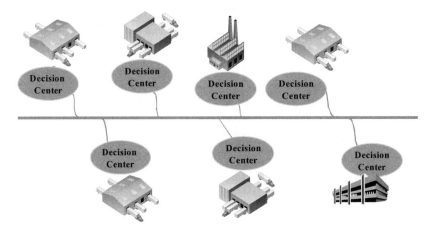

Figure 9.1. *Heterarchic/decentralized architecture for company networks*

9.3.3. *Holonic approach for self-organized control of logistic network*

The approach is founded on a self-organized and decentralized decision-making where each entity takes part in the completion of the common goal by assuming the organization and management of its own control [OUN 05]. Decentralized decision structure implies that in the absence of any hierarchy, each entity contributes to the proposal of solutions as well as to the evaluation of the solutions. This is possible thanks to the properties of a decision-making center associated with each entity. This is based on a holonic approach [OUN 07]. The holonic manufacturing system approach was studied in the context of the intelligent manufacturing systems project in the 1990s [MAT 95] [DEE 03]. The concept of holons features the strong characteristic of being able to represent a coherent and autonomous system while being at the same time part of a higher level system. This functional duality enables us to implement in a holon a behavior with high decisional value providing large autonomy. A holon is a conceptual entity based on the association of a material structure identified with an information system, equipping all of an intelligence enabling it to ensure its own operation in interaction with other holons [PUJ 07].

The self-organized control is characterized by an organizational architecture of the *flat holonic form* type [BON 00]. The description of the flat holonic form [OUN 06] is based on the three types of basic holons (Product Holon (PH), Resource

Holon (RH), Order Holon (OH)) defined in the reference architecture PROSA (PRoduct, Order, Staff, Architecture) [VAN 98].

Each company involved in a logistic chain becomes an RH when it is associated with a decision-making entity providing the capability to interact with other companies. All the resource holons make a logistic partnership network encompassing the concerned companies. The decision-making entity is called ACE, standing for autonomous control entity. It is composed of three modules (interaction, optimization, and planning). Each ACE communicates with the other ACEs via a communication network. They ensure an allocation of the tasks (OH), on the basis of a local evaluation of the potential performance of the associated RH and a collective negotiation for the optimal assignment of these tasks. Each RH has the capability with its ACE to self-evaluate its performance for executing a proposed task, with the aim to participate in the negotiations for allocating this task. In this architecture, the basic role of the ACEs is to manage all information exchanges in the network linking the different entities and to organize information processing leading to decision making. Interactions between the basic holons and an ACE are shown in Figure 9.2:

– the RH corresponding to the companies of the logistic network partnership and which, in addition to the ACE capability to ensure their own control, carries production capacity characteristics;

– the OH representing the organizational aspect of the product manufacturing tasks to be performed by the resources.

– the PH providing a technical description of the manufactured products (models, sequences, etc.) and thus completing production task specification.

All the information needed for performance evaluation by the ACEs is collected in these holons. This ACE contributes locally, at the level of the associated partner, to the assignment of the orders relating to the customer-supplier relationship.

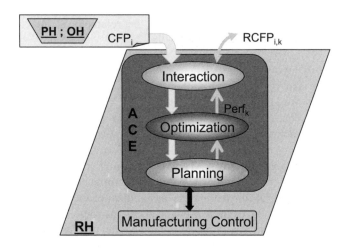

Figure 9.2. *Autonomous Control Entity (ACE)*

Each ACE is composed of three modules:

– interaction module: this module provides the assignment of orders to the various entities in the network. This assignment is based on decision-making linked to the competition between these entities (suppliers). The decision-making mechanism is based on impartial and common rules and criteria applied to all entities. This module manages, on the one hand, the publication of information about the calls for proposals and the response to the calls for proposals coming from outside towards the optimization module or vice versa. On the other hand, it manages the sorting of entities according to the received responses to a CFP (updating the CFP): for each new response to a CFP which is received, the corresponding call for proposals is updated if the received response is the first one or if it is better than the best response already received. The interaction module compares the performance of a CFP with the best response proposed on the network for this CFP, then sends the response if it is the best one [OUN 04];

– optimization module: this module allows the self-evaluation of each ACE regarding a received CFP in order to estimate its own capacity to respond to the CFP [OUN 04]. The performance evaluation is based on the Analytic Hierarchy Process (AHP) multicriteria method [SAA 80]. This method is used to classify CFPs at the level of each supplier (HR) [MEK 05a];

– planning module: the Analytic Hierarchy Process (AHP) multicriteria method is based on multiple criteria. Some of these criteria are defined by the customer according to the launched CFP, other criteria are parameterized by the supplier's own characteristics, among which is the operating time given by the production system planning. The planning module calculates the operating time of a call for proposals. Calculations are performed using an analytical method based on various planning states of the production system [MEK 05b]. The planning module sends the operating time which has been calculated to be used by the optimization module.

The global operation was modelized and simulated, the objective was to verify, by simulation, the equilibrium between load and capacity for a supplier and a load smoothing between the various suppliers of the network. In this perspective, we present below the modeling of an ACE using the DEVS formalism, then the integration of the DEVS models in the distributed simulation environment HLA.

9.3.4. DEVS-EPA modeling and distributed simulation in HLA environment

The behavior of the different ACEs simultaneously in interaction is comprehensible from the formal model of an ACE. Each ACE is modeled with the DEVS formalism (coupled DEVS models) (see Figure 9.3). The universal formalism was extended in order to allow the association of coupled and atomic models in a hierarchical and modular manner. The concept of the DEVS coupled model described the system as a network of components, which can be either DEVS atomic models or DEVS coupled models.

Figure 9.3 allows the identification of the input events[2], the output events[3], the set of components, the External Input Coupling relation (EIC = A), the External Output Coupling relation (EOC = B) and the internal coupling relation.

---

2 CFP: Call For Proposals launched by the ACE of another RH and received by the ACE.
  RCFP: Response received by the ACE to the previous Call For Proposals.
  LCFP: Local Call For Proposals launched by the entity.
  RLCFP: Response to a Local Call For Proposals, response proposed by one partner of the network and received by the ACE.
3 ERCFP: Entity Response to a Call For Proposals launched by a partner.

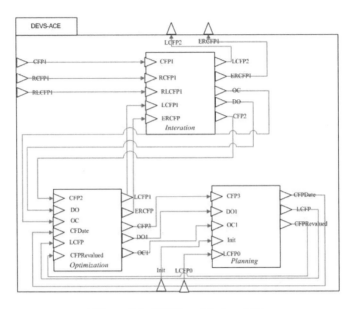

Figure 9.3. *DEVS model of an ACE*

The DEVS interaction, optimization and planning models are coupled DEVS models [MEK 07]. In order to integrate the DEVS-ACE models in HLA environment, we have split up the ACE federate into (see Figure 9.4) [OUN 06]:

– *simulators of the DEVS-ACE models*: a simulator is associated with each atomic model defined in the coupled DEVS model of an ACE;

– *local coordinator*: the local coordinator used a scheduler containing the **X**messages (input events) and the messages deduced from lifespans of its successors (atomic simulators of the different atomic models). It ensures the routing of the messages among the various simulators of atomic DEVS models according to the coupling relations, i.e. all the coupling relations that exist among the DEVS-ACE models. It handles a scheduler containing the input and output events. It also preserves the coupling relations among its simulators;

– *FOM*: the common data of the different federates' SOM enable us to produce the FOM of the DEVS/HLA federation. The objects are persistent shared information, contrary to the interactions which are temporary data (only emitted and received) [ZAC 06a];

– *interface between the simulators and the RTI*: the RTI is in relation with the model simulators by the simulation kernel. In fact, the goal of the simulation kernel is to manage the simulation. In other words, it allows the selection of the next chronological event of its scheduler, in order to process it. To do this, it calls the various methods of the local coordinator, in order to select the destination (next model to be activated according to the event). However, in the case of distributed simulation (in this case simulators of DEVS-ACE models which interact between them via the RTI), the couple, Local Coordinator–Simulation Kernel, will also have to ensure the management of the messages coming from the other federates. Lastly, it listens to all the events produced by the user interface part. The couple, Local Coordinator–Simulation Kernel, can thus simulate a coupled model in an autonomous way locally. For this, each coupled model DEVS and its associated Local Coordinator–Simulation Kernel must have a SOM defining information which they are able to provide in a distributed simulation respecting HLA.

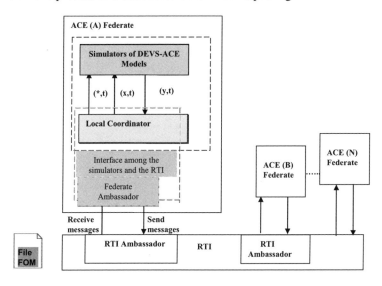

Figure 9.4. *Relations among the simulation components*

The described work was implemented under the simulation HLA environment. Simulating the approach allows us to illustrate the internal behavior of an ACE and the behavior of an ACE with other ACEs (i.e. the self-organization) in their attempt to seek the best response to a call for proposals. Starting from the interface depicted in Figure 9.5 the RTI can be launched (1), a partner can become a member of an enterprise network (2) or resign from a network (3). The interface offers to each ACE the possibility to launch local calls for proposals (4). The interface enables us to visualize the scheduler's events (5) and the federation's members (8). Each ACE can receive answers to local calls for proposals in order to determine the best supplier who will answer as well as possible (6). It can also receive answers to calls for proposals launched by other members of the enterprise network in order to compare its response with the one circulated on the network. Furthermore, the behavior of an ACE can be followed, starting from (7).

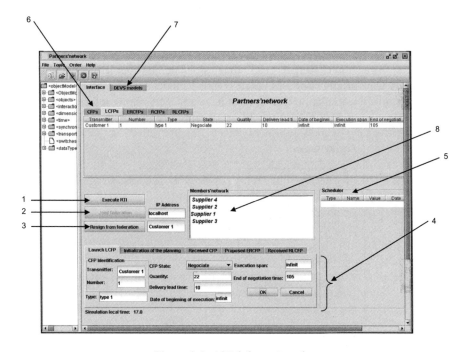

Figure 9.5. *ACE federate interface*

Before presenting the simulation of the global operation, it is necessary to describe the ranking and evaluation of the supplier process.

9.3.5. *Ranking and evaluation of the supplier process*

Self-evaluation is based on a set of qualitative and quantitative criteria (cost, lead-time, quality, etc.). Consequently, the use of a multicriteria method is essential. The proposed self-evaluation process is based on two phases: in the first phase, each supplier partner ranks the received CFPs according to several criteria. This enables the supplier to highlight the CFP on which it is most performant. Thereafter in the second phase, and in order to position itself regarding the other partners of the network, the supplier must calculate its performance with respect to the CFP classified first. The justification of the choice of the multicriteria methods used in these two phases is based mainly on the work in [OUN 99], [HAM 03], [ARN 04] and [MEK 07].

The multicriteria decision-making support methods allows us to help the decision maker during the refinement of his decision-making process which relates to the choice of an action among a set of potential actions, or on the ranking of a set of actions or scenarios, by examining the logic and the coherence of its preferences. These methods are based on four phases: drawing up the list of potential actions to study, drawing up the list of criteria to be taken into account, drawing up the table of performances and aggregating the performances. The AHP method was selected. This method enables the measurement of the coherence of the decision maker's preferences and the taking into account at the same time of the independence and the interdependence of the considered evaluation criteria. The interdependence results from the construction of a hierarchical structure reflecting the various levels according to the interdependence between the criteria. Consequently, this method allows the use of a complete list of evaluation criteria without excluding any. Note that the AHP method also allows the taking into account of qualitative and quantitative criteria. Developed by Thomas Saaty in 1980, the AHP method breaks up a complex decision problem into one or more levels of detail where the evaluation of the values is provided by pair comparisons. With an aim of providing a structuring approach, vectors of priorities are established using coherence measurements. The AHP method is thus a process of measurement inside structures or hierarchical networks, allowing individuals to express their preference among several criteria and alternatives with regard to each criterion and then, obtaining an overall ranking of the alternatives using the weights of the criteria. AHP is thus a decision-making process which directly interprets the data and information by forming judgments on which a scale of measurement is carried out inside a hierarchical structure. The AHP multicriteria method makes it possible for each supplier to sort amongst the calls for proposals which they can carry out [OUN 04] and select a convenient one. The first step for the implementation of the multicriteria algorithm based on the AHP method is to derive an adequate system of indicators providing each supplier with the ability to evaluate their performance as shown in Table 9.1. Eventually the performance of the call for proposals ranked first by each supplier can be evaluated.

The ranking of CFP is thus based on an adequate system of indicators. In order to develop this system, we have used an existing and reliable method. In their book, [CER 92] suggest a multi-step method of indicator construction. More particularly, this method addresses the construction of indicators for production management, but the principles and the steps followed remain perfectly suited to the indicators defined and formalized for the supplier evaluation problem. The identified indicators are distributed on five criteria: cost, lead-time, quality, reliability and strategy:

– cost criterion "C1": this quantitative criterion can be reduced to two indicators: cost of order "I_{21}" and cost of order delivery "I_{22}";

– lead-time criterion "C2": the lead-time is the time between the expression of a need by the customer and the actual satisfaction of this need. This quantitative criterion can be reduced to two indicators: production time "I_{11}" and delivery time "I_{12}";

– quality criterion "C3": the indicators for this criterion can be quantitative or qualitative, and aim at describing continuity of service, compliance with the rules and compliance with expectations concerning the product. This criterion can be reduced to three indicators: rate of conformity "I_{31}", respect of a referential "I_{32}" and rate of customer satisfaction "I_{33}";

– reliability criterion "C4": The objective of this criterion is to guarantee that the delivered products are reliable. This criterion can also be used to evaluate the capacity of the company to meet deadlines. This criterion can be reduced to two indicators: conformity in quantity of the orders "I_{41}" and respect for delivery times "I_{42}";

– strategy criterion "C5": this qualitative criterion can be reduced to two indicators: allowance of differed payment "I_{51}" and degree of privilege "I_{52}".

The evaluation of the supplier is carried out on the CFP classified first by the AHP method. The method of performance calculation must enable the taking into account of qualitative and quantitative criteria, it must be based on the set of criteria used in the study without excluding any and finally it must return as a result only one action and not several. The method of linear weighing is well adapted to these requirements [MEK 07]. From the indicator system described previously, it was possible to implement the adopted multicriteria method to evaluate and quantify the local performance of the suppliers. The local evaluation is calculated by taking into account the following parameters: the values of the indicators identified previously, the weights associated with the criteria (weights identified by the customer), Ki coefficients enabling us to penalize the supplier if the latter does not respond to the customer requirement.

This section defined a system of indicators for the application of the multi-criteria decision method (AHP) to the evaluation of each potential supplier. The application of the proposed multi-criteria method provides the alternative (the Call For Proposal) for which the supplier is the best.

9.3.6. *Analysis of the simulation results: manufacturing of cosmetic products by an enterprise network*

The case study corresponds to the manufacturing of cosmetic products. It makes it possible to analyze by simulation the negotiation mechanisms between the partner actors of the network. The studied network is composed of 17 companies, distributed on six principal activities related to the cosmetic product design and production: paper and cardboard production and transformation, plastic product fabrication and plastic conditioning for products, glass container manufacturing and product conditioning in glass containers, flexible tube manufacturing and flexible tube conditioning, printing and serigraphy.

Each company is characterized by its maximum capacity per activity and by a number of resources per activity. 16 types of products, coming from 5 base products (PF1, PF2, PF3, PF4, PF5), are manufactured by these different companies at different levels. Thus, each company can be a customer or a supplier according to the manufactured product. 16 logistic chains were obtained corresponding to the flows of the 16 different product types.

In a first step, enterprise networks operating in the conventional context of static customer-supplier relationships (constant flows and quantities) were studied by modeling and simulating a set of relationships between companies. In a second step, the same network (same production capacity, same processed products) was studied in a self-organized context of dynamic customer-supplier relationships. A comparison between the two contexts was analyzed.

The tests have been designed so that small disturbances with respect to nominal operations (such as increase of ordered product quantities) generate strong organizational perturbations in flow progress (blockage, saturation). The tests were performed in a nominal operation configuration and then in a disturbed operation configuration. The study was focused on two types of disturbances:

– test of saturation limit: this type of test concerns the introduction of a disturbance into the companies carrying the highest amount of activities. The disturbance consists of launching orders for additional batches by the customers of these companies during the same period (one week);

– test of load accumulation conjunction: in this type of disturbance, the considered companies are those making several products. In the same context with the first type of disturbance, it is assumed that during the same week suppliers receive orders for additional batches from their customers.

By means of the charts made for each type of disturbance and each approach at the level of the companies concerned with the disturbance, and by means of the superposition of capacity and load for each company, balance and load smoothing for all the companies of the network in the self-organized control context could be observed. The results related to the conventional control context show an overshooting capacity for the majority of the companies considered in the study. Generated capacity overshoots have a direct impact on the delivery of some products. Through the analysis of these results we could point out that some products were delivered with delay. In the conventional control context, the disturbance yields an overload for 11 companies. In the self-organized control context, it was noted that there is at worst systematically the same load and at best a load reduction for the same service delivered by the logistic network.

The opposite can be concluded in comparison with the conventional control model in which the chains are fixed and the customers launch orders only to their own suppliers, in the self-organized control model, customers launch CFPs on the network, then the potential suppliers negotiate to answer as well as possible to customer needs. Thus, the product chains are built by taking into account the real situation of the supplier companies. The building of these new chains is progressively carried out by allocating a launched CFP to the supplier having the best performance for this CFP. Best performance makes it possible to allocate the related order to the better suited supplier for the CFP, which guarantees a better customer satisfaction. In addition, a company cannot take a CFP if its maximum capacity is not compliant with it. This generates a load smoothing for each company and removes the delay problem due to the overshooting capacity caused in the control approach of static chains.

The presented self-organized control model cannot be applied to any type of network. It can be applied within a logistic network in which there is mutual trust among the partners or in a multi-site company. It is well adapted to two cases of sub-contracting: capacity subcontracting or co-contracting.

9.4. Reactive control by evaluation of multi-site plans

9.4.1. *Problem statement*

A company can participate in several supply chains while continuing to have a local and independent production. To produce a plan for a partner company is a very delicate operation because it is necessary to coordinate the realization of all their tasks of production by taking into account those planned by the other partners while making sure of their feasibility in the workshop. Various methods were proposed to validate multi-site plans. In [LEE 02], the presented analytical resolution is based on a set of mathematical equations representing the model of the considered supply chain. However, the incomplete modeling of the dynamic characteristics of the analyzed systems does not supply acceptable solutions. The simulation allows the evaluation of the supply chain by considering it as a single centralized company [LUD 04], [GUP 02], [KUB 99]. Nevertheless, difficulties linked to the significant number of entities to be modeled and to the level of detail required during a modeling form the first limits of this approach. Others concern the quantity of events to be simulated, the calculational power of computers, the re-use of the simulation models and the protection of intellectual property. The modeling of all the sites of a supply chain remains possible but simulation on a single processor is not always practical. It is also difficult to obtain a fine evaluation of the feasibility by basing itself on an aggregated model.

The evaluation of the feasibility of a multi-site plan does not come down either to the sum of the evaluations of the feasibility of the plans of every site. To manage the multi-site production and to coordinate the activity of a company with the partners of a SC, APS (Advanced Planning Systems) software is used. However, to better manage the possible conflicts between the various SC in which they are participating and/or to protect their local production, the partners can want to keep a certain confidentiality of their data and their configuration, to remain in control of their information system and to manage their own planning tool. Plans can then be more sensitive to disturbances. At the operational level, it is possible to set up a form of cooperation between the partner sites to ease the effects of this strategy. The plan of every partner is no longer a frame imposed by a planning tool but the result of a negotiation process between several planning tools.

The approaches distributed by development of the organization and evaluation of the feasibility of multi-site plans bring an answer to the limits quoted previously. They preserve the character decentralized by the decision-making and supply an interesting alternative in the approaches centralized for the control of the SC.

9.4.2. Development method and tools of multi-site plans

Even if the problems of organization are not strictly speaking distributed problems [GOT 93], the know-how on their resolution is split up. Every fragment is held by an individual actor but nobody holds everything [LOR 91]. The problems that must be resolved in the company are thus handled by isolated actors, each occurring in its domain of skill. The control of systems requires the use and cooperation of distributed scheduling systems able to manage the distributed aspect of the knowledge and of the data, and also, for the rather short delays, capable of proposing the most robust plans possible or of updating those when unforeseen events arise.

As an alternative to the centralized approaches, several organizational approaches based on the technology agent were developed [SHE 99], [MAT 99], [TRA 96]. The multi-agent systems offer a simple frame to model the various constituents of a production system [FER 89, 95, 99], [WOO 95]. The classes of agents represent the entities of the system (machines, manufacturing orders, operators, etc.) with their behavior (objectives, reaction to the events, etc.). The modeling by agents allows a "natural" distribution of the decision, the obtaining of the organization from the local behavior of the agents and facilitates the ability to react. The majority of these approaches are based on the communication protocol Contract-Net [SMI 80, 90], [SAA 96]. According to this protocol, an announcement concerning a task to be achieved is sent in the SMA by an agent product. Offers are carried out by the resource agents able to achieve the task. The offers are collected and compared by the agent product and a contract is signed with the agent with the best quote. In most of the approaches using this protocol, the agents modeling the products are responsible for the respect of the objectives of "external" production, i.e. those relative to the satisfaction of the customers, whereas the agents modeling the resources are responsible for the respect of the "internal" objectives, expressing the necessity of producing at the best cost and/or with the best quality.

Contract-Net offers a flexible frame for the management of the degrees of freedom which can exist in the choice of the resource to allocate to an operation. Thus, the scheduling methods based on this protocol are employed in real time for the adjustment of an existing scheduling or over a very short term, to integrate a new product without perturbing the existing scheduling [PAR 87]. When they are used in order to establish a projected scheduling, it amounts to applying the approach by placement in a distributed environment. In that case, it is necessary to define at first a priority to every customer. Certain customers can be penalized in practice, because of the difficulty allocating a good level of priority to them.

9.4.3. Conceptual multi-agent SCEP model

Although the approaches based on agent technology are considered as improvements of the approach by simulation, the problem of near-sightedness remains. The control of the systems is not effective enough when it advances without a good vision of the trajectory to be followed and when it rests only on repair or scheduling techniques over a very short term. The multi-agent SCEP (Supervision, Customer, Environment and Producer) model-directed planning proposes a useful method both for the development of projected plans and for their adjustment [ARC 97, 98, 01a]. Whatever the domain of application to which it applies, the organization can be returned to a problem of location in the time and in the space of a set of tasks by satisfying a certain number of temporal, technological, capacity or sequential constraints.

The SCEP model detailed in Figure 9.6 carries out the scheduling by indirect cooperation between a set of agent customers and a set of producer agents. This cooperation is performed in a synchronous way via an environment, under the control of the agent supervisor. The environment is a spatiotemporal blackboard describing the current state of the negotiation at various abstract levels. It consists of a set of "task" objects which evolve in the time and in the space according to the influence of the customers and producer agents. The "task" object is influenced by a single customer agent and by at least one producer agent. At first associated with an activity and with a project, the "task" object is at the end of the process also associated with a precise resource. The environment can be collected according to three views. The "activity" view describes the distribution of "task" objects in an activity space. The "resource" view describes it in a resource space and finally, the "project" view describes it in a project space. The considered resources are multi-activities. All the activities ensured by these resources constitute all the possible activities of the system. These activities as well as their number depend on the domain of application and on the problem of the considered organization.

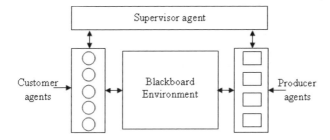

Figure 9.6. *SCEP model*

The producer agent is the intelligent entity responsible for the management of the temporal space available on a resource. It encapsulates the behavior (objectives, reaction to the events, constraints, planning strategies, etc.) of the resource and its administrator. Its skills are defined by the activities ensured by the resource, the coefficients of productivity indicating the efficiency with which the resource processes "task" objects associated with these activities, and the hourly rates allowing the estimation of the cost of this treatment. In the environment, the domain of influence of the producer agent is constituted by all the "task" objects positioned in the activity space partner in the activities ensured by the resource. The customer agent is the intelligent entity responsible for the management of all the operations necessary for the realization of a project. Encapsulating the behavior (objectives, reaction to the events, constraints, planning strategies, control of coherence, etc.) of the manager of a project, the customer agent's role consists of placing the operations in the time on resources of the system by best satisfying its objectives while respecting its constraints. In the environment, its domain of influence is constituted by all the "task" objects associated with the project.

At the beginning of the scheduling process, the supervision agent creates the customer and producer agents. In its demand, the customer agent creates in the environment and in the initialization step a "task" object for every operation by associating with it the identity of the operation, the identity of project and the required activity. The customer agent takes care of the control of the negotiation process between the agents. Every customer agent influences "task" objects which are associated with it by an offer defined with minimum operating time and a date as soon as possible. This offer, which represents the requirement of the customer agent, is in fact a plan operating as soon as possible in infinite capacity which is introduced on the blackboard. Further to the perception of the offers stemming from customer agents, the product agents alternately influence certain "task" objects by their bids. These bids consist of proposing for every "task" object an operating time (taking into account the productivity coefficient of the resource), a date of the beginning in which the "task" object can be positioned (taking into account the activity of the resource) and a cost of processing (based on the time rate of the resource). For every "task object", two different bids are made by every concerned producer agent: one proposes a location for the "task" object by taking into account all the bids made by the producer agent (actual position) whereas the other proposes a location by disregarding all other bids (potential position). After the perception of the propositions stemming from producer agents, the customer agent compares the various bids for every "task" object of its domain of influence, by taking into account its constraints and its objectives and the general coherence of the project. It can accept for a "task" object the actual position suggested by a producer agent. In that case, the negotiation process stops for the "task" object. The actual position is accepted when it gives complete satisfaction or, in the opposite case, when it is not worse than the best potential position. If the actual position does not give satisfaction and if the potential position is much better, the customer agent can take the risk of waiting, by hoping that this best potential position will become the actual position. In this purpose, the customer agent repeats its offer on the basis of the best potential position.

Although using the same basic principles as the Contract-Net, the protocol defined for the SCEP model presents numerous differences. While Contract-Net places the projects individually, operation by operation, without competition between them, SCEP puts the projects for every operation in competition, making the order of treatment of the projects in the result of little importance. However, this competition requires an intensification of the decision-making power of the customer agents. In SCEP, the customer agents can reject all the bids made by the producer agents. This was possible thanks to the concept of potential position and actual position which gives to the customer agents the possibility to improve a first solution during the resolution process. This property allows the use of the model SCEP both in estimation and in dynamics where Contract-Net was more or less quartered. Finally, a process of global validation can be used to validate in one pass all the operations of a project, on the basis of the actual positions suggested by the producing agents for every "task" object. A multi-graph is built, describing the possible choices to carry out the operations, and the most favorable road according to the held objectives (mainly time of completion and cost) can be adopted in a single stage [ARC 01a]. This possibility allows a more global view of the realization of a project, partially correcting the nearsightedness often inherent in the Contract-Net approach.

The scheduling ends when all the "task" objects are associated with a precise resource. It is performed in a finite number of cycles. Every cycle corresponds to an activation of the customer agents followed by an activation of the producer agents. The convergence of the model studied in [ARC 01b] shows that in every cycle at least one "task" object is associated with a precise resource. The number of "task" objects not associated in a precise resource decreases by at least a unit with every cycle. The organization process converges in the worst cases after a number of cycles equal to the number of "task" objects which are present in the environment.

9.4.4. *Principle of deployment in the SCEP network*

The integration in the SCEP model of a module of communication and ambassador agents enables us to establish connections of the customer-server type between a SCEP customer and SCEP servers. The ambassador agent is the representative of a SCEP server at the level of the SCEP customer. The SCEP server publishes, in the environment of the SCEP customer, the skills which it can give to the community and which it can and must ensure at any time. This publication is carried out through its ambassador agent by means of a contract defined by a list of activities with, for every activity, the capacities of the site modeled in terms of cost, time, and even of quality.

This organization allows every partner site to remain in control of its configuration. It can be adapted as we please according to the tasks to be carried out without preventing the other partner sites. It is to be noted that every partner site can ensure unpublishable local activities and that a published activity can be decomposed into several local activities. The ambassador agent has no information about the means which will be operated by the remote site to insure one of the published activities.

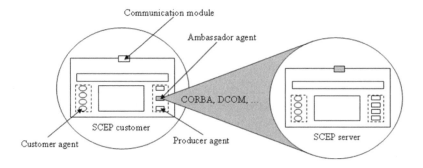

Figure 9.7. *Mechanism of inter-SCEP connection*

The SCEP customer in fact establishes cooperation between customer agents responsible for the management of multi-site or community projects and producer agents which are distant sites. The partner sites can simultaneously realize local and community projects. The first local projects are described at the level of the SCEP servers by means of local or published activities. The community projects, requiring the cooperation of the sites of the network, must be described at the level of the SCEP customer by means of published activities. The multi-site character is, however, completely transparent to them.

In the field of the production, the SCEP server can model indifferently a workshop with intra-site transport or an inter-site transport system. Figure 9.8 illustrates the connection between a SCEP customer and three SCEP servers necessary to establish cooperation between two production sites connected by a system of transport.

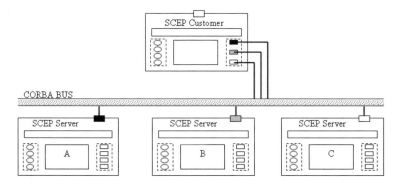

Figure 9.8. *Example of environment of multi-site scheduling by means of three SCEP servers and a SCEP customer implemented in R@MSES on a CORBA bus*

9.4.5. Development process of multi-site plans

The development process of the multi-site organization consists of resolving the scheduling at the level of the SCEP customer following the same process as that described previously. In every cycle, the ambassador agents perceive the environment of the SCEP customer, extract the information on the tasks (to plan, to cancel or to confirm) which concern the represented SCEP server, send them to the latter, wait, then influence the environment of the SCEP customer with the results of the processing of the transferred information. These results, stemming from a complete scheduling process by the SCEP server, appear in the form of potential and actual propositions. In the reception of a set of tasks to be carried out, the superintendent of a SCEP server generates or updates community sub-projects. The scheduling process of a SCEP server takes place afterwards according to the strategy adopted by the site. The search, for example, for the best satisfaction for the partners imposes a stronger priority for the community projects. The supervisor will thus at first look for a plan negotiated with its partners without taking into account local projects, planned in the second phase. At the end of the process, the supervisor sends to the ambassador agent the potential and actual propositions for the scheduled tasks.

The process of multi-site scheduling takes place in time and in space of all the "task" objects of the SCEP customer. Associated at the start of the scheduling process with an activity, "tast" objects are at the end associated with a site. In the considered site, the "task" object is associated with one or several resources. It is to be noted that two different sites can suggest planning the same "task" object during the scheduling process. The choice of the site is resolved at the level of the SCEP customer by the project agent concerned.

The development method of multi-site plans for companies organized in a network is thus based on a particular deployment of SCEP models. Every site participates in the calculation of the organization by means of a SCEP server ensuring it the confidentiality of its knowledge and of its internal organization. The adopted approach allows us to easily choose the best site as a given activity or to readjust envisaged plans by taking into account delay criteria, cost or time of inter-site transport.

9.4.6. Evaluation method and tools of multi-site plans

The architecture of proposed distributed simulation facilitates the evaluation of the feasibility of a multi-site plan in the presence or not of disturbances, the stake in adequacy of the configuration of the production units of the partner companies by making it possible for example to increase the capacity of machines, to engage temporary staff, to adjust the intra-site and inter-site transport systems, etc. It is also a question of improving the models and the methods of multi-site scheduling, the methods of control as well as the methods for reacting.

This architecture also has to allow an easy identification of the badly configured sites, the improvement of every site independently from one another, a site to absorb the delays of another site without readjusting the manufacturing plans, and the consideration of the causality problems due to the load and at the speed of the various simulators. In fact, leaving from the same point of synchronization, a simulator that must deal at every moment in time with numerous events and running on a very fast machine can require a much more consequent calculation time to arrive at a point of meeting, than another simulator slightly loaded with events, running in parallel on a slower machine and that must go to the same meeting point. Events arising at the good date in the temporal repository of the most loaded simulator and that must start before other events also arising at the good date in the temporal repository of the least loaded simulator can be registered after these last ones in the repository of a human observer; thus in the past of the least loaded simulator. In Figure 9.9, during the execution of the simulation, we can observe in the temporal repository of a human observer, an overlapping of two successive operations of the same project executed on two different sites while every site respects the envisaged plan perfectly.

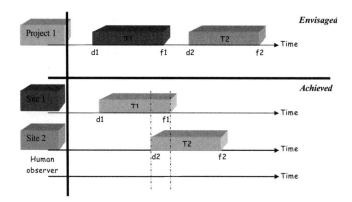

Figure 9.9. *Example of causality problem*

The consideration of the causality problem requires a real synchronization of the events arising during the execution of the virtual workshops [ENJ 04]. Thus, it is important that this new architecture is capable of guaranteeing the synchronization of simulators but also of freeing itself from software tools used for the generation of the multi-site scheduling as for the setting-up of the virtual workshops.

The conceptual F-R-PAC (Federation of Reactive Production Activity Control) model proposed associates an R-PAC federate in every site as shown in Figure 9.10.

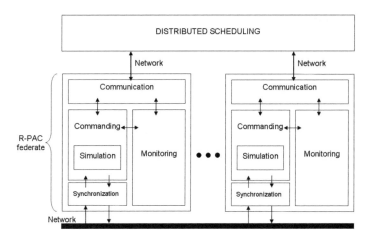

Figure 9.10. *F-R-PAC model*

Every R-PAC federate is organized around four functions: communication, monitoring, command and synchronization. The command function encapsulates a simulation function, the role of which is to manage the virtual workshop. It also controls the execution of the production and the launch of the tasks in the virtual workshop. The simulation function can integrate any discrete-event simulator, allowing any partner site to be modeled with the desired degree of precision. The partner sites can be indifferently production or transport sites. The monitoring function carries out the follow-up and the detection of the beginning and end events of tasks resulting from the virtual workshop. The communication function establishes the connection between the external scheduler and command and monitoring functions. The synchronization ensures the synchronization of the events arising in the virtual workshop with those arising in the other R-PAC federates.

F-R-PAC allows us to easily take into account all the new configurations of the network of companies which require, for every site, the adaptations of the corresponding virtual workshop. The F-R-PAC model was implemented (see Figure 9.11) by means of the R@MSES software with regards to the development of multi-site plans.

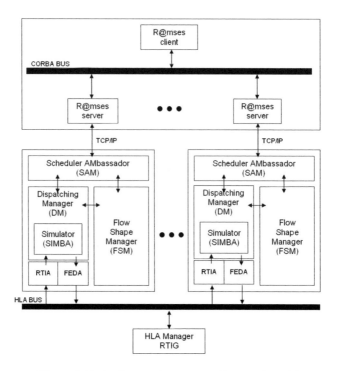

Figure 9.11. *Implemented structure of F-R-PAC model*

The virtual workshops are modeled by means of the activeX SIMBA (SIMULATION-BASED APPLICATIONS) of the company Lanner Group which, thanks to COM OBJECT technology, allows the integration of the features of WITNESS into applications requiring simulation techniques.

The synchronization function was realized thanks to the HLA protocol. The dispatching manager (DM) which realizes the command function reaches the features of HLA thanks to both RTI_A and FED_A ambassadors. The RTI_A defines the access services to the bus HLA. The FED_A defines the methods useful for the RTI, which the federate has to implant. The flow shape manager (FSM) follows the execution of the tasks launched by the DM and made by the virtual workshop. The Scheduler AMbassador (SAM) implements the communication function. It is in charge of the connection between the scheduling system and the federate. It receives the new plans to be executed on the virtual workshop and sends back the significant disturbances detected by the FSM.

The synchronization between the federate is based on the mechanism of publication/subscription of HLA. In the course of simulation, the R-PAC federate cooperates and reacts to the events which occur and which are conveyed over the network by means of dated messages. These messages ensure a regulated and forced functioning for all federates. The intra-federate synchronization concerns the connection between DM and the virtual workshop. It is based on the establishment of meeting points in which the simulator has to synchronize with the DM.

In reality, the difficulty lies in the cohabitation of these two levels of synchronization. In fact, the DM real controller of the federate has to pilot the encapsulated simulator, to advance it in time while satisfying the RTI which takes into account the speed of the other federates. In addition, it always has to make sure that the next meeting point is not too far away, to avoid desynchronization of the simulator. To synchronize the time advance of the encapsulated simulator with regard to the time advance of the other federates, the DM manages a local schedule containing envisaged dates of the beginning and the end of the launched tasks or that must be launched on the virtual workshop. This schedule is permanently updated according to the events arising in the virtual workshop and the messages resulting from the RTI.

In Figure 9.12, the example illustrates the cohabitation of both levels of synchronization of the federate. In order to guarantee the good execution of the plan, the DM has to determine the date of the closest event in the time according to the information collected in the simulator and the information pulled by its own schedule. This CDE (Current Date Event) can be a beginning or an end of planned operation, a beginning or an end of transport or a date corresponding to an awaited but delayed event. Then the federate asks for the authorization for the RTI to advance the simulator in this date (NER: Next Event Request). If the RTI considers that until this date no event resulting from the other federates will come to perturb the federate, then it authorizes the time advance of the simulator (TAG: Time Advance Grant). On the other hand, if the RTI refuses the advance in the date desired for the meeting, it proposes a new meeting point in a lower date corresponding to the next outside event concerning the federate. The authorization to advance to this date is granted (TAG) having invited the federate to become acquainted with messages on the state of objects concerning it, simulated by the other federates (RAV: Reflect Attribute Value). The DM can authorize the simulator to advance until the date of meeting imposed by the RTI. It should be noted that, until this date of meeting, several relaunchings of the simulator are possible after some stops of the latter because of dysfunctions or for the properties of the DM. Once the meeting point has been reached, the DM updates its schedule, passes to dated messages (UAV: Update Attribute Value) in its RTI states and begins the cycle again by proposing a new desired meeting date. The mechanism is seen out until the complete simulation of all the envisaged events.

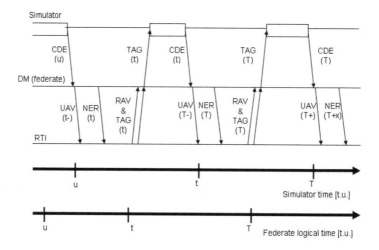

Figure 9.12. *Synchronized functioning of the federate*

9.4.7. *Evaluation by distributed simulation, interest and limits*

The F-R-PAC model was applied to the simple case of a network of companies established by three production sites geographically distributed (T, B, P) for which the feasibility of three different multi-site schedulings generated for an identical manufacturing of four tables have to be estimated. Tables are constituted of 4 feet, an upper tray and a lower tray. The upper tray is wooden on the outside, glass in the center. The central piece of wood of the upper tray forms the lower tray. For the manufacturing of a table, 7 manufacturing orders are necessary. Site T supplies the wood for the preparation of the feet as well as the trays. Site P prepares the glass trays. Site B takes charge of wood drillings for the assembly and of the conception of the feet and fastenings kit. The assembly of the upper tray and the final assembly of the piece of furniture in kit (four feet and fastenings, complete superior tray and lower tray) are also performed on site B.

Three multi-site schedulings result from the following three strategies:

– strategy A: manufacturing of 4 lots of 1 part. In this strategy 28 manufacturing orders are used;

– strategy B: manufacturing of 2 lots of 2 parts. In this strategy 14 manufacturing orders are used;

– strategy C: manufacturing of 1 lot of 4 parts. In this strategy 7 manufacturing orders are used.

The transport logistics between sites are ensured by a set of trucks each transporting a lot at the same moment which implies a number of different inter-site movements according to the strategy used. This number is more significant for strategy A. It is assumed that the inter-site and intra-site transport strategies are fixed and cannot evolve. Only the number of transport resources can vary. The generated schedules satisfy all the delay objectives imposed by the customers.

The evaluation of the feasibility of three schedules showed that it was impossible to respect the proposed plan and the objectives of delay in the case of strategy A whatever the number of means of transportation used in inter-site and intra-site. F-R-PAC thus allows us to judge the adequacy of the model used during the development of the scheduling and to correct the consequences of the aggregation, either by improving the model for the scheduling, or by making available the means required for carrying out the plan. By applying the same disturbances to the configurations held for strategies B and C, the simulations show that the most robust plan is the one generated for strategy C. The F-R-PAC model makes it possible to easily estimate the impact on the possible schedulings of the most frequent disturbances. A more complete description of the results profits of this case of study is given in [ENJ 06].

9.5. Conclusion

Today's global market is such a hypercompetitive environment, where shortened product lives and increased costumer expectations have forced companies to invest in, and focus their attention on, supply chain management. Simulation modeling and analysis can be an extremely effective tool for supply chain performance analysis. Many development proposals apply distributed simulation to this context. The introduction of distributed simulation makes it possible to solve the sharing confidential data problem during the simulation of supply chains.

In this chapter, various techniques of existing distributed modeling and SC simulation have been approached. The advantages of HLA were detailed by comparing some of the most well-known IPC standards in DSCS framework. Finally, research experiments in supply chains using distributed simulation were presented: self-organized control of a supply chains network and reactive control by evaluation of multi-site plans of enterprise networks.

The HLA standard allows the reusability and the interoperability of simulation components without the need for re-coding. Moreover, the implementation of the interface specification (RTI) proposes services (such as taking into account the Lookahead) which can considerably accelerate the execution of distributed simulation, while ensuring the respect of the existing causality relations as well as the coordination of the messages between the models. Lastly, HLA enables us to consider the implementation of simulation-reality couplings.

9.6. Bibliography

[ALO 06] ALOUI S., CHAPURLAT V., PENALVA J-M., "Linking Interoperability and Risk Assessment: a Methodological Approach for Socio-Technical Systems", track: "Networked Enterprise Control System Integration And Interoperability", in *12th IFAC Symposium Information Control: on Information Control Problems a Complex Challenge in Manufacturing for the 21st Century (INCOM 06)*, St. Etienne, France, May 17-19, 2006.

[ARC 97] ARCHIMÈDE B., *Ordonnancement d'ateliers: une approche coopérative par simulation*, MOSIM'97, Rouen, France, 5-6 June 1997.

[ARC 98] ARCHIMEDE B., COUDERT T., "A multi-agent scheduling approach for the flexible manufacturing systems", *IFAC Workshop on Distributed Computer Control Systems: DCCS'98*, Come, Italy, 1998.

[ARC 01a] ARCHIMÈDE B., COUDERT T., "Reactive scheduling using a multi-agent system: the SCEP framework", *International Journal Engineering Applications of Artificial Intelligence*, vol. 14, pp. 667-683, 2001.

[ARC 01b] ARCHIMÈDE B., COUDERT T., "Ordonnancement des systèmes flexibles de production. Une approche coopérative basée sur le modèle d'agents SCEP", *Journal Européen des Systèmes Automatisés*, vol. 35(9), pp. 1029-1054, 2001.

[ARN 04] ARNALDI F, Evaluation de la performance d'un système de production: application au choix des fournisseurs au sein d'un réseau logistique auto-organisé, Master's Research MCAO (LSIS), June 2004.

[BAN 06] BANDINELLI R., RAPACCINI M., TUCCI M., VISINTIN F., "Using Simulation for Supply Chain Analysis: Reviewing and Proposing Distributed Simulation Frameworks", *Production Planning and Control*, vol. 17(2), pp. 167-175, March 2006.

[BON 00] BONGAERTS L., MONOSTORI. L., MCFARLANE. D., KADAR B., "Hierarchy in distributed shop floor control", *Computer in Industry*, 43, pp. 123-137, 2000.

[CER 92] CERRUTI O, GATTINO B, *Les indicateurs et tableaux de bor*, Edition AFNOR, 1992.

[CHA 78] CHANDY K.M., MISRA J., "A Non-trivial Example of Concurrent Processing: Distributed Simulation", *Proceedings of IEEE COMPSAC'78*, pp. 822-826, 1978.

[CHA 04] CHÂNE F., GIAMBIASI N., PAILLET J.L., "Formal specification of reactive systems: DEVS or timed automata?", *Actes de CMS'2004*, I3M, Bergeggi, Italy, 2004.

[CHE 02] CHEN D., VERNADAT F.B., "Enterprise Interoperability: A Standardization View", *Proceedings of the IFIP International Conference on Enterprise Integration and Modelling Technology (ICEIMT'02)*, Kluwer Academic Publishers, Valencia, Spain, ISBN 1-4020-7277-5, 24-26 April 2002.

[DAC 06] DACLIN N., CHEN D., VALLESPIR B.A., "Methodology to Develop Interoperability of Enterprise Applications", track: Networked Enterprise Control System Integration And Interoperability, in *12th IFAC Symposium Information Control: on Information Control Problems a Complex Challenge in Manufacturing for the 21st Century (INCOM 06)*, Saint-Etienne, France, May 17-19, 2006.

[DEE 03] DEEN S.M., *Agent-based Manufacturing – Advances in the Holonic Approach*, Springer-Verlag Ed, ISBN 3-540-44069-0, 2003.

[ECO 03] ECOM, *Internet EDI (XML/EDI) Introduction Guidebook*, Electronic Comerce Promotion Council of Japan, March 8, 2003.

[EIC 04] EICTA, *Interoperability White Paper*, European Industry Association, (www.athena.ip.org), 2004.

[ENJ 04] ENJALBERT S., ARCHIMÈDE B., CHARBONNAUD P., "A HLA federation of reactive production activity control for extended enterprise performance evaluation", *5th EUROSIM Congress on Modelling and Simulation*, Paris, France, ISBN 3-901608-28-1 Publisher: EUROSIM-FRANCOSIM-ARGESIM, 06-10 September, 2004.

[ENJ 06] ENJALBERT S., Accommodation d'une planification multi-site vis-à-vis des perturbations, Doctoral thesis, Institut National Polytechnique de Toulouse (INPT), spécialité : Systèmes industriels, October 2006.

[FER 89] FERBER J., "Eco problem solving: how to solve problem by interactions", *Proceeding of the Ninth Workshop on Distributed Artificial Intelligence*, Rosario Resort, Eastsound, Washington, pp. 113-128, 1989.

[FER 95] FERBER J., *Les systèmes multi-agents: vers une intelligence collective*, InterEditions, 1995.

[FER 99] FERBER J., *Multi-agent Systems: An Introduction to Distributed Artificial Intelligence*, Addison Wesley Editions, 1999.

[FUJ 00] FUJIMOTO R.M., *Parallel and Distributed Simulation System*, John Wiley & Sons, Inc., New York, 2000.

[GOT 93] GOTHA, "Les problèmes d'ordonnancement. Recherche opérationnelle", *Operations Research*, vol. 27(1), 1993.

[GUP 02] GUPTA M., Ko H.J., Min H., "TOC-based performance measures and five focusing steps in job-shop manufacturing environment", *International Journal of Production Research*, vol. 40(4), pp. 907-930, 2002.

[HAM 03] HAMMAMI A., Modélisation technico-economique d'une chaîne logistique dans une entreprise réseau, Thesis, Ecole Nationale Supérieure des Mines de St. Etienne, September 2003.

[HAM 06] HAMRI M.E, Spécification, opérationnalisation et simulation des systèmes de connaissances réactifs : utilisation de Common KADS et DEVS, Thesis, Paul Cézanne University, Aix-Marseille, November 2006.

[IEEE 90] IEEE, *Standard Computer Dictionary: A Compilation of IEEE Standard Computer Glossaries*, Institute of Electrical and Electronics Engineers, New York, 1990.

[IEE P1516] IEEE P1516, *Draft Standard for Modeling and Simulation (M&S) High Level Architecture (HLA)*, Framework and Rules.

[IEE P1516.1] IEEE P1516.1, *Draft Standard for Modeling and Simulation (M&S) High Level Architecture (HLA)*, Federate Interface Specification.

[IEE P1516.2] IEEE P1516.2, *Draft Standard for Modeling and Simulation (M&S) High Level Architecture (HLA)*, Object Model Template (OMT) Specification.

[KUB 99] KUBOTA F., SATO S., NAKANO M., "Enterprise modelling and simulation platform integrating manufacturing system design and supply chain", *Proceedings IEEE International Conference on Systems, Man, and Cybernetics*, 4, pp. 511-515, 1999.

[LEE 02] LEE Y.H., KIM S.H., MOON C., "Production-distribution planning in supply chain using a hybrid approach", *Production Planning and Control*, vol. 13(1), pp. 35-46, 2002.

[LOR 91] LORINO P., *Le contrôle de gestion stratégique: la gestion par activité*, Editions Dunod, Paris, 1991.

[LUD 04] LUDER A., PESCHKE J., SAUTER T., DETER S., DIEP D., "Distributed Intelligence for Plant Automation Based on Multi-Agent Systems: The {PABADIS} Approach", *Production Planning and Control*, vol. 15(2), pp. 201-212, 2004.

[MAT 95] MATHEWS J., "Organizational foundations of intelligent manufacturing systems - the holonic viewpoint", *Computer Integrated Manufacturing Systems*, (8) 4, pp. 237-243, 1995.

[MAT 99] MATURANA F., SHEN W., NORRIE D.H., "Metamorph: an adaptive agent-based architecture for intelligent manufacturing", *International Journal of Production Research*, vol. 37(10), pp. 2159-2173, 1999.

[MCL 00] MCLEAN C., RIDDICK F., "Integration of Manufacturing Simulations Using HLA", in *Proceedings of the Advanced Simulation Technologies Conference*, 2000.

[MEK 05a] MEKAOUCHE L., OUNNAR F., PUJO P., GIAMBIASI N., "Management of calls for proposals within self organized enterprises network", *IMP'05, 21st Annual Industrial Marketing and Purchasing Conference, Rotterdam*, The Netherlands, 1-3 September 2005.

[MEK 05b] MEKAOUCHE L., OUNNAR F., PUJO P., GIAMBIASI N., "Self Evaluation of Company's Performance in Partnership Network", *IEEE International Engineering Management Conference (IEEE – IEMC)*, St. John's, Newfoundland, Canada, 2005b.

[MEK 07] MEKAOUCHE L., Pilotage holonique auto-organisé de réseaux logistiques : Validation par modélisation et simulation distribuée, PhD Thesis, Paul Cezanne University, Aix-Marseille III, 2007.

[NUT 03] NUTARO J.J., Parallel Discrete-event Simulation with Application to Continuous Systems, PhD Dissertation, Electrical and Computer Engineering Dept, University Of Arizona, Fall 2003.

[OUN 99] OUNNAR F., Prise en compte des aspects décision dans la modélisation par réseaux de Petri des systèmes flexibles de production, PhD Thesis, Institut National Polytechnique de Grenoble, 1999.

[OUN 01] OUNNAR F., PUJO P., "Décentralisation des mécanismes de pilotage de la relation donneurs d'ordres/fournisseurs", *Actes du 4e Congrès International de Génie Industriel*, vol. 2, pp. 1175-1185, France, 2001.

[OUN 04] OUNNAR F., PUJO P., MEKAOUCHE L., GIAMBIASI N., "Decentralized Self Organized Control of a Partnership Network in an Intelligent Supply Chain", *IMS International Forum: Global Challenges in Manufacturing*, Italy, 2004.

[OUN 05] OUNNAR F., PUJO P., "Supplier evaluation process within a self-organized logistical network", *International Journal of Logistics Management*, vol. 16:1, pp. 159-172, 2005.

[OUN 06] OUNNAR F, PUJO P., ZAHAF A., GIAMBIASI N., "Interoperability of Enterprises Network Holonic Control via HLA", *INCOM'06 Conference*, St Etienne, France, 17-19 May 2006.

[OUN 07] OUNNAR F., PUJO P., MEKAOUCHE L., GIAMBIASI N., "Customers-Suppliers Relationship Management in an Intelligent Supply Chain", *Production, Planning and Control*, vol. 18(5), pp. 377-387, July 2007.

[PAR 87] PARUNAK H.V.D., "Manufacturing experience with the Contract Net", *Distributed Artificial Intelligence*, M.N. Hunds (Ed.), pp. 285-310, 1987.

[PUJ 99] PUJO P., BROISSIN N., MEYER S., BERTRAND J.C., "Pilotage décentralisé des Systèmes de Production", in *3e Congrès International de Génie Industriel*, pp. 1975-1984, Montreal, 1999.

[PUJ 02] PUJO P., KIEFFER J.P., "Fondement du pilotage des systèmes de production", in *Collection IC2 – Productique: Fondements du Pilotage des Systèmes de Production*, Hermes Science Ltd., 2002.

[PUJ 07] PUJO P., OUNNAR F., "Vers une approche holonique des Systèmes Mécatroniques Complexes : Proposition d'un système de pilotage auto-organisé et isoarchique", *Journal Européen des Systèmes Automatisés*, vol. 41(6), pp. 673-706, 2007.

[REV 01] Revetria R., Tucci M., "Different approaches in making simulation languages compliant with HLA specification", in *Proceedings of SCSC 2001*, pp. 622–628, Orlando, FL, July 15-19, 2001.

[SAA 80] SAATY T.L., *The Analytic Hierarchy Process*, McGraw-Hill, New York, 1980.

[SAA 96] SAAD A., KAWAMURA K., BISWAS G., "Performance evaluation of Contract Net-based heterarchical scheduling for flexible manufacturing systems", *International Journal of Automation and Soft Computing, Special issue on Intelligent Manufacturing Planning and Shopfloor Control*, 1996.

[SHE 99] SHEN W., NORRIE D.H., "Agent-based systems for intelligent manufacturing: a state of the art survey", *Knowledge and Informaiton Systems*, vol. 1(2), pp. 129-156, 1999.

[SIR 98] SIRON P., "Design and Implementation of a HLA RTI Prototype at ONERA", in *Proceedings of the Fall Simulation Interoperability Workshop*, 1998.

[SMI 80] SMITH R.G., "The Contract Net Protocol: High level communication and control in a distributed problem solver", *IEEE Transactions on Computer*, 29(12), pp. 1104-1113, 1980.

[SMI 90] SMITH R.G., "The Contract Net Protocol", *The International Journal of Flexible Manufacturing Systems*, no. 2, 1990.

[TRA 96] TRANVOUEZ G., ESPINASSE B., CHIRAC J.P., "A multi-agent based scheduling system: a co-operative and reactive approach", *9th Symposium on Information Control in Manufacturing*, Enterprise Modelling and Integration: Principles and Applications; Chapman and Hall, ISBN 0 412 60550 3, Nancy-Metz, France, 24-26 June, 1996.

[TRE 02] TRENTESAUX D., Pilotage hétérarchique des systèmes de production, Mémoire d'habilitation à diriger des recherches, Valenciennes de Hainaut-Cambrésis University (UVHC) au LAMIH, September 2002.

[TSA 05] TSAGKANI C., "Inter-Organizational Collaboration on the Process Layer", *Proceedings of the IFIP/ACM SIGAPP INTEROP-ESA Conference*, Geneva, Switzerland, Springer Science, ISBN: 1-84628-151-2, February 23-25, 2005.

[VAN 98] VAN BRUSSEL H., Wyns J., Valckenears P., Bongaerts L., Peeters P., "Reference architecture for holonic manufacturing systems: PROSA", *Computers in Industry*, 37(3), pp. 255-276, 1998.

[WHI 06] WHITMAN L.E., SANTANU D., PANETTO H., "An Enterprise Mode of Interoperability", Track: Networked Enterprise Control System Integration And Interoperability, in *12th IFAC Symposium Information Control: on Information Control Problems a Complex Challenge in Manufacturing for the 21st Century (INCOM 06)*, St. Etienne, France, May 17-19, 2006.

[WOO 95] Wooldridge M., JENNINGS N.R., "Intelligent agents: theory and practice", *The Knowledge Engineering Review*, 10(2), pp. 115-152, 1995.

[ZAC 06a] ZACHAREWICZ G., GIAMBIASI N., FRYDMAN C., "Lookahead Computation in G-DEVS/HLA Environment", in *Simulation News Europe Journal (SNE), Special Issue 1, Parallel and Distributed Simulation Methods and Environments*, vol. 16(2), pp. 15-24, ISSN, 0929-2268, September 2006.

[ZAC 06b] ZACHAREWICZ G., Un environnement G-DEVS/HLA: application à la modélisation et simulation distribuée de workflow, PhD Thesis, Paul Cezanne University, Aix-Marseille III, 2006.

[ZEI 73] ZEIGLER B.P., *Theory of Modelling and Simulation*, New York, Ed. John Wiley, 1973.

[ZEI 99] ZEIGLER B.P., KIM D., BUCKLEY S.J., "Distributed Supply Chain Simulation in a DEVS/CORBA Execution Environment", *Proceedings of the 1999 Winter Simulation Conference*, pp. 1333-1340, 1999.

Chapter 10

Software Tools for Simulation

10.1. Short history of the tools for simulation in industrial engineering

The first tools for computer simulation intended for industrial engineering appeared in the 1950s. One of the pioneers is Jay W. Forrester, who was behind *System Dynamics* in 1956 and many computer applications.

It was in the 1960s that the first data-processing languages intended for discrete-event simulation appeared: GPSS (General Purpose System Simulation), CSL (Continuous Simulation Language), SimScript, Simula, etc.

The 1970s saw a period of expansion for simulation thanks to the progress of computer science. Whereas before, modeling was carried out by programming and simulation itself only obtained by calculations, *Visual Interactive Simulation* presented by [HUR 76] was the basis of the first "modern" tool, *See-Why*. These tools generally made it possible to free ourselves from the knowledge of a modeling language and brought additional help to the analysis of flows thanks to graphical animations of the process. It was in this decade that *DEVS* (discrete-event system specification) language and the first distributed simulation applications appeared.

In the 1980s, industrial production underwent a profound change to adapt to the market trends. New concepts appeared such as *Just-In-Time* (JIT), OPT, flexible manufacturing systems (FMS), logistics, etc., which led to the progressive disappearance of the Taylor methods. In parallel, computer science also underwent a profound development with the appearance of the *Personal Computer*, which

---

Chapter written by Franck FONTANILI, Pierre CASTAGNA and Bernard YANNOU.

allowed a considerable rise of simulation tools in engineering. Many software tools were born, and the majority still exist today, under more advanced releases: *Witness, Hocus, Genetik, Siman, Promodel,* etc.

From the 1990s and up to today, software tools for simulation did not bring great innovations but notable improvements appeared concerning the modeling facility (*Visual Interactive Modeling Systems – VIMS*), the possibilities of animation and 3D representation, the opening or compatibility with other data-processing applications (worksheets, databases, CAM, ERP, MES, etc.), distribution over the Internet, the coupling with optimization algorithms, etc. With the arrival of the concept of *Supply Chain Management* (SCM), new needs appeared in flow simulation, not only limited to a workshop but rather to networks of workshops and warehouses, and sometimes requiring a strong interaction with simulators of production plans (SOP, MPS, scheduling). The design and the control of a supply chain involve many questions:

– If a new factory and two new warehouses are added, what is the effect on the stocks?

– Do the peaks of request affect the chain?

– What are the effects of a modification of the inventory control parameters on the level of stocks?

– How can stocks be reduced without having an impact on the customer service ratio?

– etc.

To answer these questions, the various simulation tools constitute an invaluable help which seems impossible to circumvent to be guaranteed of any error.

10.2. Typology of the simulation tools for the supply chain

It is very difficult to establish a general typology of the simulation tools because the criteria are numerous and often dependent or crossed. The simulation models used in applications of production or operations management are usually classified starting from traditional criteria in the dynamic, discrete and stochastic type. To be more precise, we propose a downward typology, from general to specific in the field of simulation for SCM while going through discrete-event simulation.

10.2.1. *General classification*

[LAW 91] suggests a classification of the simulation models which distinguishes the physical models from the logical-mathematical models:

– *the physical models* are those in which the real system is represented by a counterpart or a model, on a different scale and possibly using different materials. They are used at the end of training: flight simulators, control, model of vehicles for aerodynamic tests, etc.;

– *the logical-mathematics* or *symbolic models* are defined by logical and quantitative relations which are handled and changed to see how the model of the real system reacts. They are carried out on computers. It is exclusively this type of model which will be presented in this chapter.

Another distinction relates to taking into account the risks or random variations in the model:

– if the system is independent of the influence of random or unforeseeable variables, *a deterministic model* is used;

– if the risks play a significant part in the behavior of the system (typical example: breakdowns), *a stochastic model* is used.

A third category distinguishes:

– *the static models*, for which time does not intervene. Example: a countable model allowing us to calculate the benefit at the end of the year using a spreadsheet;

– *the dynamic models*, for which the behavior is a function of time. Example: handling system in a factory.

Lastly, inside the dynamic models, we distinguish:

– *models with discrete-events* (or discontinuous models) in which changes of state occur only at the time of events such as the beginning or the end of an operation, the setting on standby of a part in a stock, release of a resource, etc.;

– *continuous models*, more adapted to continuous flows, which use mathematical equations to take into account the changes of state which are carried out continuously in the course of time. The values of the state variables are recalculated regularly according to these equations. Example: a chemical engine;

– *combined models* (or mixed models), which integrate the two aspects. Example: metallurgical or agro-alimentary industry.

In [CER 88], we find yet another classification of modeling for the simulation of flow according to the approach:

– Approach *by events*: this is the most general approach. It consists of gathering all the events which can occur and describing the logic of the changes of state. In the logic of the changes of states, we can distinguish:

- rules related to the procedures on the manufacturing process. For example: end of the machining of a part,

- rules related to control/management. For example: if batch A is ready before batch B, then start the manufacture of batch C on the heat treatment.

The difficulty of the control rules at the workstations is one of the problems of this approach. Once the work carried out for the modeling phase, writing the model consists of programming the logic of the changes of state. The software must be able to store the list of events created. The simulation run consists of the search of the next event envisaged in the list. The bill book is the module which manages the advance of time as the events appear.

– Approach *by activities*: this approach is based on natural reasoning: a process is described like the sequence of activities and delays. It can be seen through the activities by indicating the conditions necessary to their beginning and their end. Delays begin at the end of each activity. They finish when the conditions necessary to the following activity are met. Modeling consists of programming the conditions of release and end of the activities. With each increment of time, we examine whether the conditions of beginning and end of the activities are carried out.

– Approach *by process*: this approach is when modeling consists of gathering processes. The processes are formed of sequences of events and activities: duration of an activity, use of a machine, storage of parts, etc. These processes can be parameterized. In the software, they correspond to subroutines or primitives with which we can describe the operation of an installation. The power of a software will be related to the processes placed at the disposal of the user (handling by robot, by conveyor, etc.).

10.2.2. *Classification according to the versatility and the facility of use*

[PID 04] proposes a classification highlighting six categories of tools for simulation according to two criteria: the versatility and facility of use. Figure 10.1 illustrates this classification.

In the continuation of this chapter, we will focus on the *"Visual and Interactive Modeling and Simulation"* category whose position is dominant as far as industrial applications are concerned.

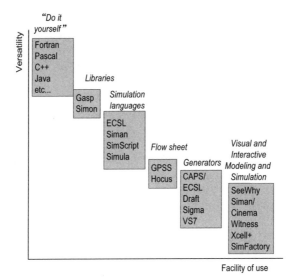

Figure 10.1. *Classification according to the versatility and the facility of use (according to [PID 04])*

10.2.3. *Classification of discrete-event simulation according to the life-cycle of the process*

Discrete-event simulation is the simulation mostly used in the field of logistic flows which cross the supply chain. In this chapter, we will thus focus on this category of simulation which can be classified according to the three phases of the life-cycle in which the process is simulated: design, improvement or execution. Figure 10.2 highlights this classification.

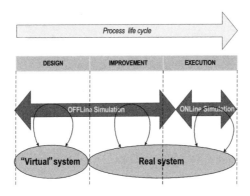

Figure 10.2. *Classification according to the three phases of the life-cycle of the process*

A large majority of applications are carried out in the design phase of a new process or improvement of an existing process. Simulation helps decide on the size of stocks and equipment, check management rules, measure random consequences of events (supply rupture, cancellation of order or rush order, etc.).

An emerging use of simulation is its use as an emulator. The idea is to use a simulator to reproduce the behavior of a real production system, this simulator being ordered by the future control system of the manufacturing unit. This provision allows the development of the control system whereas the real production system does not exist yet, the goal being to reduce the duration of the debugging run of the manufacturing unit. We can quote in that sense Arena RT™, planned for this type of use. Let us note in addition that the development of the possibility of coupling the majority of the tools facilitates this type of use.

In an operational production run of a process, simulation can be used like a control tool in order to determine or refine certain parameters before the execution of the production. It is an interesting complement to other planning tools such as the ERP, which aim to manage the medium or long term.

In this same production run, a not so widely held possibility of simulation consists of coupling it in real time with the real process (online simulation) in order to allow a reactive or corrective control. Simulations are started from events which occur on the real system and thus make it possible to measure the drifts compared to the target objectives: overrun lead-time in the event of a supply rupture, saturation of stocks in the event of cancellation of order, etc. If the drift is considered to be unacceptable and must be minimized, simulation can then be used to seek the correction to be applied to the control variables.

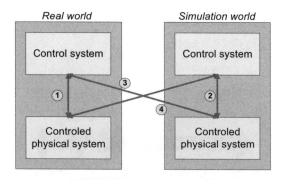

Figure 10.3. *Various uses of the flow simulation*

These different uses of flow simulation are summarized in Figure 10.3:

1. corresponds to the traditional control of the production system;

2. corresponds to "offline" simulation, corresponding to the majority of the applications;

3. corresponds to the concept of emulation;

4. corresponds to the concept of online simulation.

10.2.4. *Specific classification for SCM*

For all the applications in the field of supply chain management, various authors [KLE 03], [CAV 04], [BEL 05] emphasized:

– three main classes of approach:

  - continuous simulation,

  - discrete-event simulation,

  - business games;

– making it possible to solve four main types of problem:

  - checking and validation,

  - sensitivity analysis,

  - optimization,

  - robustness;

– starting from two types of modeling:

  - paradigm of local simulation,

  - paradigm of parallel and distributed simulation.

10.2.5. *The system dynamics software*

The pieces of software analyzed in this chapter are considered the most famous and the most used in industry as well as in education and research (see also [1, 2]). They are: *Ithink* [3], *Vensim* [4], *Powersim* [5], *Goldsim* [6], *Anylogic* [7], *Extend* [8] and *Modelmaker* [9].

The criteria used for comparing these pieces of software are: the application domains and claimed utility, the modeling language and the available facilities.

Concerning the targeted domains, a first category of system dynamics software is for the analysis of all-purpose dynamic phenomena. These pieces of software (Vensim and Modelmaker) may be *a priori* used within different scientific domains. A second class of DS software claim to mainly deal with issues of company management and social and economical phenomena in society. For example, Ithink tries to focus on strategic scenarios and process analysis. Powersim is supposed to analyze operational details as well as global strategies. Goldsim may be used to model physical, financial and organizational systems. Extend focuses on company processes. However, these pieces of software use very similar SD building blocks, i.e. stocks, flows and auxiliary variables and they share a number of similar generic facilities. We propose here to consider five categories of facilities:

– those allowing us to integrate or to be compatible with other modeling and simulation approaches than the sole SD. We mainly think of integrating the discrete-events approach;

– those of internal organization. They are of both types. The first type of facility aims to lower the apparent complexity of SD models by allowing a hierarchical structuring. In such a way, it becomes possible to benefit from a type of modularity in the model development, testing, storage and parameterization. It also allows us to design parsimonious models and to efficiently communicate and educate with these models. Finally, it makes it possible to tune the model grain size to observe what has to be observed at an adequate modeling level. The second aspect is about the ability to easily customize simulation interfaces so as to provide simple control boards with clever output graphics, both adapted to user needs and without requiring them to be experts in SD;

– those of facilities of use within the stage of model building. This concerns the presence of building block libraries, the ease of reusing some parts of previous models and the data exchange facilities with other software applications;

– those of causal analysis. Is it possible to identify causal chains and causal loops in which some given variables are involved?;

– those of mathematical analysis. Here, we think of sensitivity analysis and optimization facilities. Optimization generally aims at either calibrating certain parameters for matching at best some simulated behaviors to some data observed on the ground, or maximizing one or several given performance objectives. In order to carry out a sensitivity analysis, some uncertain parameters can be specified using probabilistic distributions. A Monte Carlo generation of crisp (or precise) values for these "uncertain" parameters within the allowable bounds of the distributions leads to a series of simulations, which leads in turn to a series of superimposed development curves for some dynamic variables. Consequently, the order of magnitude of the influence or sensitivity of a variable evolution may be understood according to the degree of uncertainty of some parameters. In fact, it makes it possible to figure out the robustness of simulation results.

Table 10.1 summarizes the facilities of the set of analyzed SD software applications.

	Mixed simulation approach		Organization		Facilities of use		Causal analysis		Mathematical analysis	
	Discrete-events	Others	Hierarchical modeling	Interfaces	Libraries	Data exchange	Feedback loops	Others	Sensitivity analysis	Optimization
Ithink	X		X	X		X	X		X	
Vensim	X			X		X	X	X	X	X
Powersim	X		X	X					X	
Goldsim	X		X	X		X			X	
Anylogic	X	X	X	X	X	X			X	X
Extend	X		X	X	X	X			X	X
Modelmaker	X		X						X	X

Table 10.1. *Facilities of system dynamics software applications*

To summarize, we can say that the utmost advantages of SD software are:

– the ease of generic and multi-domain modeling of dynamic systems and the ease of dealing with complex systems thanks to adequate organization facilities;

– the facilities of mathematical analysis.

We can only suggest some failings we consider important when the final objective is to be able to make decisions in the context of companies (see also [ELH 05b]):

– in the modeling language of these pieces of software, the ontology (i.e., the building elements of the SD model) is not particularly company-oriented, i.e. neither performance-oriented nor business-process-oriented. In fact, the classical ontology (stocks-flows-auxiliary variables) is not dedicated and therefore the generic models appear complex (see [LEF 02] for more compact formalisms) and not very meaningful for business players (see [ELH 05a] for a company-oriented ontology of an SD environment);

– concerning the post-processing facilities (after simulations and/or other mathematical analysis), there are still few facilities in terms of scenario editing and multicriteria assessments (and management of simulation results). Multicriteria assessments would be assumed to model the different stakeholders of an issue, the different expectations of these stakeholders, and the different preference aggregation models of these expectations. In addition, it would be useful to compare, considering the multicriteria, the different scenario performances from the different stakeholder viewpoints. Such facilities have been proposed in [ELH 05a, ELH 05b].

In the remainder of this chapter, we will focus on discrete-event simulation based on commercial tools of the VIS and VIMS type, knowing that they can be used to solve the four types of problems and the two types of modeling encountered in logistic chains.

10.3. Key points of the construction of a simulation model

In their majority, the commercial tools for flow simulation of the VIS or VIMS type allow a modeling starting from elements or objects making it possible to describe a process. These tools are directed towards the flow simulation, i.e. the simulation of the advance of products (physical flow) or data (informational flow) using one or more processes in the company. For the majority of the simulation tools, the products or the data which go through processes are called "parts", "items" or "entities".

Modeling for the flow simulation of a process can be broken up into two stages: a modeling stage of the various actions of the process and a description stage of the laws or rules of advance of the articles or entities through these actions. Apart from the actions of the process, modeling can comprise logic elements, names, variables and attributes. Lastly, the horizon of simulation is another important point for the simulation phase itself.

10.3.1. *Stage of modeling the actions of a process*

In a simulation tool, a process is modeled by successive or simultaneous actions enabling the items to evolve/move from an initial state to a final state: operations, transfers and delays:

– *operations* correspond to the actions which transform the items by contribution of added value or quality control: machining or measurement of a part, assembly of two components, filling or checking a form, examination or surgical operation on a patient, etc. These operations are modeled by machines or processors which are characterized mainly by the number of articles processed and the processing time;

– *transfers* move the articles, by unit or by batch, from one geographical place to another, without contribution of added value. Transfers can be modeled by specific elements such as conveyors, overhead traveling cranes, carriages, etc., which are characterized by a distance of displacement between two points and a time or rate of travel. For generic cases, another way of modeling transfers is to use machine or processor elements, but only the time of displacement is taken into account;

– *delays* are actions enabling us to retain or accumulate the articles without contribution of added value and displacement. They are generally modeled by stocks or queues, characterized by their capacity of accumulation in a number of items and by the management rule: FIFO, LIFO, etc.

10.3.2. *Stage of describing the laws and rules*

This stage describes the connection between the various elements of the model, either starting from a language and a syntax (Push, Pull, etc), or graphically by the realization of a flowchart while revealing, if necessary, the decision blocks (*decide* or *if*), when the flow is not single.

10.3.3. *Logic elements*

The items, stocks and machines constitute the main part of the physical elements of a discrete-event simulation model. To make the model work or to obtain information, we also need logic elements, which can be broken down into two categories:

– *variables*: in fact values characterize the elements of the system as a whole. We can reach variables from any physical element of the model. The analogy with a structured programming language is the concept of an aggregate variable;

– *attributes*: these are variables attached to a given item and that it carries with it during its lifespan in the model. To some extent it is the identity card of an item, in which we will be able to store for example his arrival time and his exit time, its cycle time on a machine, the number of holes to be bored on another machine, etc. Several different or identical items can thus have the same attribute, but this one will be able to have different values.

10.3.4. *Horizon of simulation*

Another characteristic of the models with discrete-events is the desired horizon of simulation. When a simulation is launched (with T = 0), the model does not contain an article and all the elements are in an available state. Two types of simulation can be programmed:

– *Simulation at finished or termination horizon*: in this case, simulation is carried out until an end condition is checked, for example, a workshop which works until all the articles have been processed. At the beginning of the simulation, the workshop is empty, just like at the end of the simulation.

– *Simulation at infinite horizon or stabilized rating*: in this type of simulation, we wish to study the behavior of the process only in a stabilized mode, without taking into account the warm-up period or the emptying of the process. There is thus no inevitable stop condition related to the absence of an item, but we define a sufficiently significant simulation duration to allow the system time to stabilize. The duration of the warm-up period is the subject of several research works [ZOB 99] but no general analytical method comes out of it. In practice, in order to determine it, simulation experts recommend to measure the total level of work-in-process in the model or outgoing flow. In fact, at the beginning of the simulation, the level of work-in-process will gradually go up then stabilize. In the same way, the outgoing flow will be initially zero, then will increase and be stabilized between two acceptable values. Another method consists of defining one warm-up period whose minimal duration is at least equal to 20 times the interval of time between the appearance of the event which has the weakest probability of appearance. For example, the event which has the weakest probability of appearance is a breakdown on a machine with an average interval of 5 days. In this example, we thus choose to have one warm-up period of 100 days corresponding to the appearance of 20 breakdowns, which corresponds to the size of a minimal statistical sample. With regard to the minimal duration of simulation in nominal rating, we can use the same method appreciably and observe the event which has the weakest probability of appearance. The ideal is to be able to draw the interval of time between two of these events on an histogram and to stop simulation when the form of the histogram tends towards the modeled mathematical distribution. For example, if the interval of time between two breakdowns is modeled with a negative exponential law, as long as the histogram of distribution in several classes of the various durations between two breakdowns does not fit this law, we can consider that the nominal rating is not reached. To refine this method, it is possible to use data analysis tools (see section 10.6.1).

10.4. Limits and objectives of simulation tools

10.4.1. *What they can do*

Before using this tool, it is important to know what we can expect, in particular compared to the mathematical modeling tools.

Here is a non-exhaustive list of the possibilities of flow simulation given to the user in the three phases of the life-cycle of a process:

– *in the field of design*: to justify and quantify the necessary investments, to specify and illustrate the statement of work, to define the global characteristics, to choose between different projects, to identify the bottlenecks, etc.;

– *in the field of improvement*: to identify existing problems, to evaluate various draft amendments, to choose between several improvement solutions, to guarantee the results of a modification, to choose the control rules and the management of the queues, to study the influence of the disturbances, to determine the capacities of the resources, etc.;

– *in the field of exploitation*: to anticipate deadlines (in addition to an ERP and a scheduler), to help make control decisions, etc.

This list shows the importance of this software tool, not only for industry, but also for researchers.

10.4.2. *What they cannot do*

They cannot optimize the performance of a system. They can only give answers to questions of the type: "What happens if...?". Once the model is programmed and validated, simulation works like a black box according to a scenario. It thus only reproduces the behavior of the modeled system. Figure 10.4 illustrates this principle (according to [BYR 06]).

They cannot give correct results if the data are inaccurate. A very important point relates to the data used by simulation. It is essential to check the validity of these data for fear of obtaining results without common measurement with those obtained on the real system. This is particularly critical when the simulated system is at a level of complexity which does not allow any analytical checking of the results provided by simulation. The simulation tools always make it possible to obtain a result, but do not bring anything for its validity compared to the real system which we simulate.

They cannot describe the characteristics of a system which has not been completely modeled. The modeling phase generally proceeds in several stages. We start by building a total model of the system, then it is gradually refined, by validating each stage before improving the model. The difficulty which arises at the time of modeling is to know the level of detail to choose so that the model is representative of reality. In that sense, it is thus preferable to refine the model, rather than to be satisfied with a too general and inaccurate model.

They cannot solve problems but only provide indications from which solutions can be deduced.

When the model is ready to be used for simulation, it is still necessary to know which information we want to observe during or at the end of simulation. This information, called "*Indicators*", is a variable of the system on which a statistical processing is carried out. The majority of the software packages propose standard results in the form of statistical reports/ratios which can be presented with graphs to facilitate the analysis. The "standard" indicators primarily relate to the quantities and durations relating to flows of items, as well as busy, broken down, blocked ratios of machines and resources. We can try to solve the problem arising thanks to the observation of the model and the indicators during and after simulation.

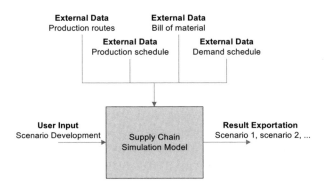

Figure 10.4. *Principle of the black box*

10.5. Methodology of a simulation project

In this chapter, the objective is to propose a general methodology for the realization of a project of flow simulation. The objective of this methodology is not only to provide a discussion thread to any simulation project, but also to be sure, before the beginning of the project, that we are in possession of all the useful data. A simulation study generally proceeds in four macro-stages (Figure 10.5): problem analysis, modeling and programming, experiments on the model (simulations), report/ratio and conclusions.

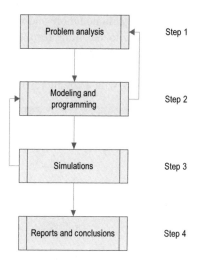

Figure 10.5. *Macro-stages of a simulation study*

As we can see in Figure 10.5, these macro-stages proceed in a sequential way, but loops are possible in order to correct or complete the development of the model according to the objectives.

Each of these macro-stages will now be detailed in several stages and the sequence of the project will be emphasized more precisely.

10.5.1. *Step 1: problem analysis*

The problem analysis is an essential preliminary of great importance, since it is this stage which must define precisely what to highlight with simulation, and what precision is expected. We also determine the performance indicators which will make it possible to check if we achieve the goals. Lastly, it is necessary to be able to provide numerical data to the model. These relate to all the elements used in simulation.

Lastly, in addition to the numerical and logical data, it can be useful to have graphical documents, at the same time as having a geometrical (or spatial) representation of the simulated system, but also to have a representation of flows. We will be able to use as a geometrical model a CAD drawing of the workshop to be simulated.

10.5.2. *Step 2: modeling and programming*

The construction of the model makes it possible to code the model with a suitable software tool. This stage is facilitated more and more by the evolution of the software packages whose tendency is to substitute for the primitives of a language a graphical, interactive and conversational interface. The designer of the model no longer needs to be a computer science specialist to use flow simulation. Figure 10.6 shows a graphic example of modeling with a commercial simulation tool (Arena).

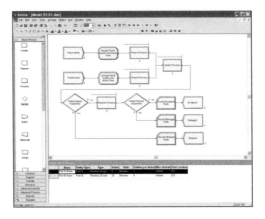

Figure 10.6. *Graphic modeling with Arena (VIMS)*

For the majority of tools, lines of code in a language containing orders are generated from the elements described in graphical modeling. It is then possible to intervene directly in this code to modify it, but this possibility is seldom used. On the other hand, such applications can automatically generate models in the specific language of the tool. Figure 10.7 illustrates an example of code obtained with the Siman language of the Arena tool.

```
14$    CREATE,      1,MinutesToBaseTime(0.0),Part A:MinutesToBaseTime(EXPO(5)):NEXT(15$);
15$    ASSIGN:      Part A Arrive.NumberOut=Part A Arrive.NumberOut + 1:NEXT(0$);
0$     ASSIGN:      Sealer Time=TRIA(1, 3, 4):
                    Arrive Time=TNOW:NEXT(2$);
2$     ASSIGN:      Prep A Process.NumberIn=Prep A Process.NumberIn + 1:
                    Prep A Process.WIP=Prep A Process.WIP+1;
47$    STACK,       1:Save:NEXT(21$);
21$    QUEUE,       Prep A Process.Queue;
20$    SEIZE,       2,VA:
                    Prep A,1:NEXT(19$);
19$    DELAY:       Triangular(1,4,8),,VA:NEXT(62$);
62$    ASSIGN:      Prep A Process.WaitTime=Prep A Process.WaitTime + Diff.WaitTime;
26$    TALLY:       Prep A Process.WaitTimePerEntity,Diff.WaitTime,1;
28$    TALLY:       Prep A Process.TotalTimePerEntity,Diff.StartTime,1;
52$    ASSIGN:      Prep A Process.VATime=Prep A Process.VATime + Diff.VATime;
53$    TALLY:       Prep A Process.VATimePerEntity,Diff.VATime,1;
18$    RELEASE:     Prep A,1;
67$    STACK,       1:Destroy:NEXT(66$);

66$    ASSIGN:      Prep A Process.NumberOut=Prep A Process.NumberOut + 1:
                    Prep A Process.WIP=Prep A Process.WIP-1:NEXT(4$);
```

Figure 10.7. *Example of code in Siman language*

Once the model is designed, we must check if the logical rules describing the flow are well programmed and correspond to the requirement. Simulations are carried out only to check the correct working of the model. If differences appear, it is necessary to be able "to trace" all the events of the model and to check their coherence compared to the data. The majority of software packages have a function enabling us to visualize the working of the model event by event.

This step must be closed by a validation which consists of making sure that the behavior of the model is in conformity with the schedule of conditions defined during the first stage. This validation is often delicate and will only be partial. A first technique consists of gauging the model on the real system. For example, we can compare the results provided by the model with the results of the real system, if this exists, starting from the same data input (see Figure 10.8).

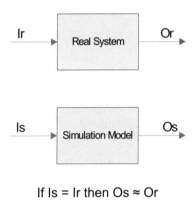

If Is = Ir then Os ≈ Or

Figure 10.8. *Calibration of the model (from [ROB 04])*

The statistical reports provided by the simulator can also help with this validation between simulated results and real results.

The graphical and dynamic visualization of the model is a considerable asset to facilitate its checking and its validation, since we can follow all the changes of state which intervene on the model; in addition the more general advantage of this functionality to communicate with non-specialists in simulation. The simple fact of having a representation and a realistic animation enables them to take an active part in this validation stage.

Lastly, a simulation study would not remove any analytical approach to the problem. The validation of a simulation model can be based on an analytical study. An interesting technique consists of simplifying the model to allow the analytical calculation of results and to compare them with the results provided by the simulator. For example, we can remove all the random generators from the simulation model to make its behavior deterministic. We can then plan in an exact way the indicators such as the busy ratios of resources, and check that these same ratios are obtained by simulation.

Although the model construction is increasingly facilitated by the evolution of software packages, the designer of a simulation model can hardly directly go from the real system (existing or to be designed), to the computer model. A certain number of intermediate stages are necessary to conclude the construction of the model. The methodology presented by [BRO 00] breaks up the process of modeling into four consecutive and possibly iterative phases (see Figure 10.9).

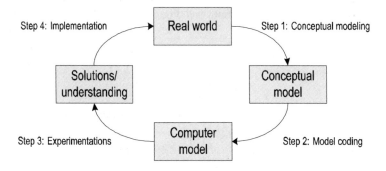

Figure 10.9. *Modeling process (according to [BRO 00])*

The most important stage is without doubt the production of the conceptual model. The objectives of such a model are multiple:

– structure and gather useful data for construction of the computer model;

– use it as communication tool between the various actors;

– represent physical flows as well as informational flows;

– identify and define the rules and laws useful for the control of the system;

– use it as support for the production of the computer model.

This conceptual model is theoretically completely independent of the computer model. There is no standardized formalism yet but certain recent works highlight the interest of using formalisms such as *BPMN* (Business Process Modeling Notation) or more generally the formalisms resulting from *enterprise modeling* with several views: functional, resource, decisional, etc. The description of the dynamics of the model can also be based on the modeling tools resulting from the world of automation, like *SART*, *Petri nets* or *SFC* (Sequential Function Chart). We think that the choice of the modeling formalism for the realization of the conceptual model initially depends on the actors of the study, the principal object of this conceptual model being the perfect comprehension between these actors.

10.5.3. *Step 3: simulations*

The use of simulation is the step where the model is used as experimental support to evaluate the dynamic behavior of the system. Of course, it is necessary to have defined the data on which we will be able to act to achieve the goals that we set in the first stage. A scenario or an experimentation is thus characterized by a data set which varies with each iteration of the experimental process. Methods such as the *design of experiments* can be used to organize the scenarios, to reduce their number and to interpret the results.

However, the use of design of experiments is not adapted to complex problems of optimization, where the number of solutions is very large. In this case, simulation is coupled with a solution generator and the results are then analyzed by an optimization algorithm. This coupling will be presented more in detail in section 10.6.

Lastly, it is necessary to be able to interpret the results provided by the simulation. This supposes, particularly in the case of stochastic models, a good knowledge of statistical concepts such as the confidence interval, the arithmetic or temporal mean, the standard deviation and possibly the spectral analysis.

10.5.4. *Step 4: report/ratio and conclusions*

This last macro-stage is important with respect to the customer of the simulation study. In fact, he may not be an expert in this field and it will be necessary to be able to present the results of the study so that they are comprehensible. Amongst other things, it is necessary to take into account the following notes:

– select the data tables relevant to the customer;

– explain the indicators used;

– justify the simplifying assumptions;

– use a graphics package to obtain the results;

– present the various solutions giving the same result and propose selection criteria;

– suggest new study tracks.

Figure 10.10 illustrates the details of these 4 macro-stages.

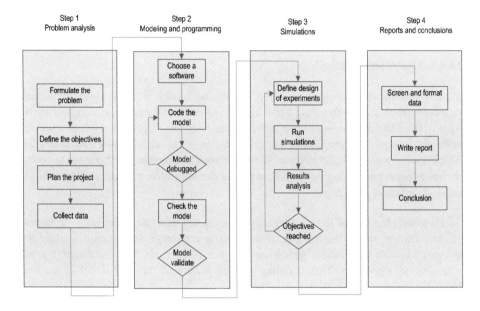

Figure 10.10. *Process of modeling and simulation*

10.6. Possibilities of coupling

One of the major tendencies in the development of simulation tools is their capacity to be coupled with other applications. In fact, once the model is built, the simulator behaves like a black box for the user: starting from input parameters, it carries out a simulation over a given duration and gives output results. Simulation alone is thus not easily exploitable without a minimum amount of expertise from the user. It is essential that simulation tools can be interfaced at the input or output with other applications. In the following chapters, we propose to present an outline of the possibilities of coupling for the majority of the tools currently on the market.

10.6.1. *Input/output data analysis*

One of the main difficulties in a simulation study is to have data representative of the real process. For example, the execution time of a task is seldom constant in reality. If we simulate with the average duration, we can not be sure that the results obtained will reveal what really occurs when this execution time varies from one cycle to another. The majority of the simulation tools are able to deal with random laws, the problem is knowing which law must be used to describe the variations of a continuous or discrete variable. For example, the table in Figure 10.11 gives a sample of the work durations between two breakdowns on a machine. To model these durations accurately and respect their real distribution, some tools for data analysis seek the best mathematical law automatically corresponding to a data set. StatFit ™ and ExpertFit ™ are the two major tools tackling this problem and are compatible with the majority of simulation tools on the market. Figure 10.11 (right) gives an outline of the result provided by StatFit on the basis of a sample of the given table. The work duration between two breakdowns could be modeled in the simulation tool with a normal law of 162 minutes average and 9.04 minutes standard deviation.

This kind of tool can be used for the analysis of the output results of the simulator in the same way used for data inputs (see for example its use to determine the duration of the warm-up period or the duration of a simulation run, section 10.3.4).

Breakdown no.	Duration of work (min.)
1	164.8474375
2	176.544791
3	168.2530951
4	154.3352807
5	149.2441004
6	158.0460376
7	150.1473122
8	158.3848624
9	177.4724099
10	176.7204766
11	159.6924927
12	151.0517682
13	159.7974596
14	156.0654012
15	157.8078059
16	148.2046718
17	158.3454342

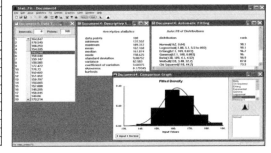

Figure 10.11. *Data analysis with StatFit™*

10.6.2. *Inputs/outputs via spreadsheet or database*

It can be very interesting to note that the simulation model exchanges data with a spreadsheet or a database. Instead of storing the data in the model, the access in reading or writing with cells of a spreadsheet or fields of a table enables us to develop user-definable models. The simulation model can thus be interfaced for example with an ERP database. A modification in the database is automatically taken into account in simulation without modifying anything in the model. It is a functionality which is now available on the majority of commercial tools. Figure 10.12 illustrates the use of functions to exchange data between Witness™ and Excel™.

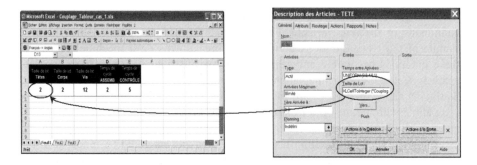

Figure 10.12. *Example of data exchange between Witness and Excel*

In the same way, Arena™ allows an easy interface with Excel files or databases. This is not the case for Quest™, which only allows exchanges with text files.

10.6.3. *Control simulator from an external client*

As shown in Figure 10.4, each scenario requires the modification of the input data of a simulation. When the number of scenarios is very significant, it can be useful to automate the execution of simulations by supplying the simulator either using various combinations of preset input data, or an optimization algorithm. In both cases, various simulations must be carried out automatically (in batches). Figure 10.13 illustrates this coupling between simulator and the design of experiments.

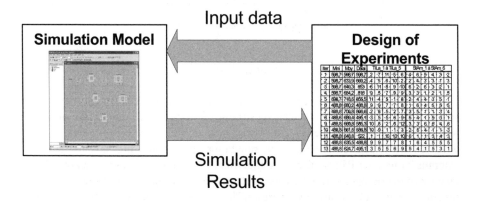

Figure 10.13. *Coupling between simulator and design of experiments*

The "client/server" principle is used. The simulator is regarded as a server and must answer a request coming from a client. The client can thus be either a simple design of experiment or an optimization algorithm which proposes a new solution to the simulator on each iteration, according to the results of the preceding iterations. According to the tool used, this coupling client/server can be carried out by OLE (Witness) or by sockets on IP ports (Arena, Quest). The simulator is thus controlled by the client, which compensates for one of the disadvantages of the simulation, which is not to allow the optimization of the modeled process. Many research works are interested in the development of algorithms containing metaheuristics (genetic algorithms, simulated annealing, Tabu search, etc.) and use these possibilities of coupling [PIE 03].

10.6.4. *Coupling with the real process (online simulation)*

This type of simulation being seldom used, the objective is to help control a real process. Figure 10.14 illustrates a coupling carried out by means of a programmable logic controller (PLC). The access to the basic data can be performed for example thanks to OPC standard (OLE for Process Control) or by the database of a manufacturing execution system (MES). The idea is to simulate the process on the short term and to measure the consequences of unexpected events (supply rupture, machine breakdown, rush order, etc.) compared to the objectives planned. Simulations started at the arrival of each critical event on the real process can thus make it possible to compare, when each event appears, the objective at the launching of a production with the objective reached if nothing has changed. In practice, the simulation tools are not designed to be interfaced with tools such as MES. The initialization of the simulation model in a state corresponding to the state of the real process and the response time of a simulation are the first technical difficulties. On the other hand, unlike the other tools of the information system such as the ERP, the MES tools allow us to follow the evolution of indicators associated with the physical process almost in real time, but thus do not facilitate a decision-making aid for the corrections to bring to the variable piloting. Several research works try to contribute to the integration of simulation with the use of MES for the decision-making aid in control [CAR 07a].

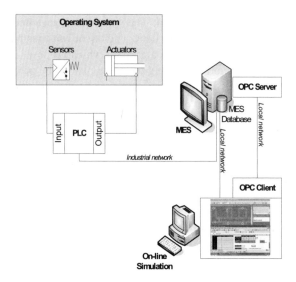

Figure 10.14. *Coupling with the real process*

10.7. Main functionalities and criteria of selection of a tool

The functionalities and criteria of selection of a simulation tool are very numerous.

[BAN 97] propose taking into account six criteria:

– *modes of entry (input considerations)*: keyboarding with computer mouse, importation of CAD drawings, importation of files, language syntax, presence of a debugger, interface with other languages, possibility of data analysis;

– *execution*: power of modeling, speed of execution, generation of achievable (run-time), random number generator, initialization of the statistics, replications with various random variable germs and attributes, portability on various platforms. We can note here the particular case of production systems called "*high rate systems*". They are characterized by a very significant number of products processed in a given time. We can quote for example bottle packing installations, processing thousands of products at a given time, with very short cycle times. The majority of the standard simulation tools do not really fit to this type of problem because they result in handling a significant number of entities which leads to a significant degradation of the simulation speed. Certain simulation tools are specialized in this type of problem. Thus, the Simpact company developed the Simas II® tool enabling the simulation of a high rate system. We can also in this field quote the "packaging" library of Arena allowing the modeling of a high rate system. The principle of these tools is to replace certain parts of the discrete model by a continuous model;

– *output consideration*: standard and personalized statistical reports/ratios, use of graphs, storage of the results in a database, design of personalized performances indicators, writing in files;

– *environment*: facility of use, facility of training, quality of documentation, possibility of animation, position of the distributor on the market, support;

– *cost*: the cost of the simulation software varies between €500 and €50,000.

[KLI 99] proposes slightly different criteria:

– material platform: PC, station, Mac, etc.;

– operating system: Windows, Linux, Unix, etc.;

– interface development: language, interactive, mixed;

– type of simulation: discrete, continues, both;

– data exchange: file, XL, ODBC, DDE, OLE, ActiveX, etc.;

– language: owner, general practitioner;

– animation: 2D, 3D, virtual reality;

– reports/ratios, results: tables, graphs, etc.;

[NIK 99] supplements these criteria by:

– the possibility of creating reusable modules (libraries);

– the possibility of an online use;

– the management of the replications.

10.8. Classification of the commercial tools

10.8.1. *Offer highlights*

The market of simulation tools is very competing. We present here an outline of the main tools classified according to 5 categories:

– *general practitioners:* Anylogic, Arena, EM-Seedling, Enterprise Dynamics, Extend, MicroSaint, Promodel, Quest, Simul8, Witness, etc.;

– *specialists*: Automod (conveyors, vehicles, gantries, carriers), Demo3D (handling operations), etc.;

– supply Chain Specialists: Eurobios SCS, SupplyChainSIM, scMod/scSIM, etc.;

– processes: Human (operators), Jack (operators), iGrip (robots), etc.;

– complementary: ExpertFit, StatFit (analyzes statistical), OptQuest (optimization), etc;

See websites of the distributors for more details.

10.8.2. *General presentation of three software tools*

Although the offer of tools for simulation is very important, in this chapter we propose to present three commercial simulation tools among the most known in companies and being used for the simulation of supply chains.

10.8.2.1. *Arena™*

Arena is a software environment basically using the Siman simulation language, which always constitutes the heart of it. Thanks to the power of its simulation language Arena is a very powerful tool and able to model in detail all the characteristics of a process. Unlike Quest and Witness, Arena uses very general concepts such as the concepts of resource queues. This conceptual positioning certainly makes modeling more difficult but it allows a broader spectrum of use. Thus, specialized libraries were created in varied fields like the definition of telephone exchanges, the simulation of maritime transport, or the simulation of road networks. By comparison with data processing languages, it could be assimilated to the C language or even to assembler language, especially as the execution of simulations is carried out from the compilation of the code, which gives it an advantage over its competitors in terms of speed. Arena comprises a graphical interface which makes it quite convivial and which handles building blocks: *Create, Dispose, Process, Decide, Batch,* etc.

10.8.2.2. *Witness™*

Witness is a tool that handles elements of a rather high level using a very convivial graphical interface. If the process to be modeled is composed of elements such as buffers, machines, conveyors, resources, etc, modeling is quite simple and fast. One of the strong points of Witness is its simplicity of implementation and modeling with a rather natural and intuitive approach. The construction of complex models is facilitated by the assembly of basic elements and the use of laws and very powerful actions to manage events. The execution of simulations is in the interpreted mode, which has the advantage of allowing modifications in the model and running the execution without compilation. The execution speed is on the other hand a little slower than with Arena.

10.8.2.3. *Quest™*

Quest is a simulation tool whose characteristic is to allow the construction and the animation of the model using the Catia geometrical modeler (Dassault system). This aspect very clearly distinguishes it from its competitors which only offer standard, very limited graphical possibilities, but still sufficient for needs only related to flow analysis. Quest thus brings an advantage when it is a question of communicating and representing the process in a very realistic way. The disadvantage of this advanced graphical design is its consumption of data-processing resources which necessarily involves less performance than its competitors in terms of execution speed. In the field of modeling, Quest uses, like Witness, high level elements (Machine, Buffer, Conveyors, etc.) allowing an easy modeling of a simple production system. The behavior of each element is defined by "*Logics*" which are data processing programs coded in *SCL* (Simulation Control Language). The access to these "logics" enables us to model a very large variety of behaviors. To the detriment of the simplicity of modeling, the SCL language requires a good competence in data processing.

10.9. Example of modeling with three tools

10.9.1. *Description of the process and knowledge model*

This example is relatively simple and makes it possible to compare the modeling step with the three selected tools. It is a process comprising the basic elements: items, stocks, machines, conveyors and resources. The "Head", "Body" and "Screw" components, which are supplied by suppliers, wait in three separate stocks. A machine carries out the assembly of one head with one body and two screws before the compound is inspected by batch of 4 on another machine. At the end of the inspection, the compounds are either shipped or scrapped. An operator, Jack, is charged to repair the INSPECT machine when it breaks down and to set up the ASSEMB machine every 15 operations. The assembly and inspection operations are carried out automatically, without an operator. This example thus comprises the main elements which we can find in all logistic chains. Figure 10.15 represents a conceptual knowledge model using the formalism of JIS Z 8206 standard. All the useful data are indicated in this model. It should be noted that the majority of these data follow laws of random distribution.

The objective of this example is only to quickly describe the construction of the model and the simulation results each with three tools. There is no objective of dimensioning or optimization. For each tool, only one replication is launched over a 100,000 minute duration.

A comparative study between several tools and for several cases is available online at http://www.argesim.org/comparisons/index.html.

A recent survey of the tools for simulation is accessible at http://www.lionhrtpub.com/orms/orms-12-05/frsurvey.html.

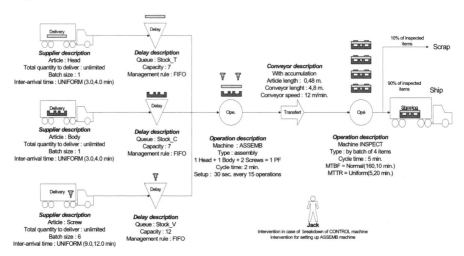

Figure 10.15. *Conceptual model*

10.9.2. *Modeling with Arena*

Modeling with Arena is carried out by building a network with blocks through which entities (or items) will circulate. Each block carries out an action on the entities. The blocks are selected in libraries, a model can use blocks from various libraries. Let us note that Arena allows the user building up his own libraries. In our example, the entities represent the various components of the products circulating in the production system.

The objects used to build the model use the "*BASIC Process*", "*Advanced Process*" and "*Advanced transfer*" libraries.

Figure 10.16 shows the model as it will be built.

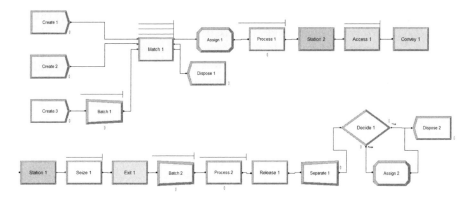

Figure 10.16. *Arena model with blocks*

The blocks *Create* 1, 2 and 3 enable us to define the arrival of entities corresponding to the bodies, heads and screws.

The parameters of each block are indicated through windows. Figure 10.17 shows the window corresponding to the arrival of item screw "Vis_e".

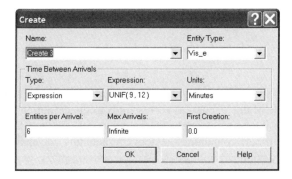

Figure 10.17. *Parameter setting of item arrivals with Arena*

The arrival is in batches of 6, the period of arrival being defined by a random number following a uniform law. The entity created is associated with a "Vis_e" type which will allow a statistical follow-up of the behavior of these entities and which makes it possible to associate a graphic icon for the animation of the model.

The *Batch 1* block sets up a group of two screws. The *Match 1* block ensures the synchronization between the arrival of a head, a body and a group of two screws. When the three arrive, screws and heads are removed (block Dispose 1) and the type of the body item is modified and becomes the item representing the assembly (block *Assign 1*). The *Process 1* block models the assembly operation. The resource *"Posts Assembly"* can be held. If this is already occupied, the entity will wait in the queue *"Process 1.Queue"*. Once the resource is reserved, the entity waits during the process (here 2 min) then it releases the resource which becomes available to process another entity.

	Name	Type	Capacity	Busy / Hour	Idle / Hour	Per Use	State Set Name	Failures	Report Statistics
1	Assemblage	Fixed Capacity	1	0.0	0.0	0.0		1 rows	☑

Resource - Basic Process

	Name	Type	Count	Down Time	Down Time Units
1	ArretAsmb	Count	15	0.5	Minutes

Failure - Advanced Process

Figure 10.18. *Parameter setting of a resource under Arena*

Figure 10.18 shows how the assembly resource is defined and the set-up stop which is associated with it. We will note the possibility of associating possession, and ownership costs for each use of the resource. This allows a very fine study of the production costs with the simulator.

| 5 | Process 1.Queue | First In First Out | ☐ | ☑ | (a) |

| 5 | Process 1.Queue | Lowest Attribute Value | Due Date | ☐ | ☑ | (b) |

Figure 10.19. *Definition of a queue under Arena*

Figure 10.19 shows the definition of the queue. We will note the definition of the management rule of this queue: (a) corresponds to the definition of a FIFO rule and (b) makes it possible to very simply program the EDD (Earliest Due Date) rule. Due Date being an attribute containing the delivery date, this rule enables us to choose in the file the entity minimizing this date. We can thus program very simply any rule of dynamic stock management.

The blocks *Station 1, Access 1* and *Convey 1* describe the access to a conveyor and the displacement on this last. Arena models in a very precise way the conveyors with accumulation, taking into account the dimension of the products in the phenomenon of accumulation. At the exit of the conveyor, we gather four entities (block *Batch 2*) before controlling them (Block *Process 2*). During this checking operation, if other products arrive at the front of the conveyor they must remain blocked on the conveyor. Thus, the *Sixteen 1* block reserves a resource of capacity equal to 4. If this resource is entirely consumed, the entities remain blocked before the *Sixteen 1* block and thus cannot leave the conveyor. The crossing of the *Release 1* block, at the output of *Process 2* makes it possible to release the four units of the resource and thus to let four other products leave the conveyor. The construction of the model allows a very precise description of the system operation. The *Separate 1* block allows the bursting of the group of the four entities which had been made up before the process of control. Lastly, the *Decide 1* block allows a random shunting of the entities. In 90% of the cases they go directly to the *Dispose 2* block. In the 10% of cases remaining, we modify the type of the entities which then represent bad products (block *Assign 2*)

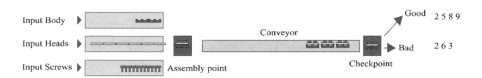

Figure 10.20. *Synoptics of animation with Arena*

Let us finally note the possibility of defining animated synoptics, allowing us to visualize the queues, the state of resources, the conveyors, as well as indicators, such as here the numbers of good and bad products. We also find the possibility of plotting dynamic curves during simulation, allowing for example the visualization of a number of products in a stock, during simulation time.

At the end of the simulation, a simulation report is generated, either in the form of a textual file, or in the form of an ACCESS database. By default, a statistical follow-up is carried out, concerning each queue and each resource. We also obtain results concerning the behaviors of the entities. These results are collected by type of entity (Work In Process, Mean Flow Time, etc.).

Particular blocks collect data during the simulation and restore a statistical follow-up on these data at the end of the simulation.

Before launching a simulation, the model is compiled, in a transparent way by the simulation environment. That allows a relatively fast operation of the simulator. As an indication, if graphical animation is removed, the duration of a simulation of this model for 100,000 minutes is approximately 1.2 seconds on a Windows PC with INTEL Pentium T2600, 2.16 GHz processor and 2 MB of memory.

10.9.3. *Modeling and simulation with Witness*

Modeling with Witness comprises 3 phases:

– *a declaration phase*: this is a phase of analysis which allows us to go from reality to the model by making a choice on the elements of the model which represent the real system best;

– *a representation phase*: this phase is not compulsory for running simulation, but it is essential to understand the dynamic of the system. It is thus highly advised not to neglect it and represent the system and its layout as real as possible;

– *a description phase*: each type of element has its own characteristics, for example: machine cycle time or conveyor speed. The logic of control to describe the routing of the articles circulating in the model is specified during that phase.

After the declaration, the representation and the description of the elements, the simulation can be launched immediately. The model can then be modified by adding, changing or removing elements and simulation can be started again without compilation and the impact of these changes can be evaluated. This facility to gradually build a model by testing each part is a powerful help to produce and realize valid models with confidence. It is thus advisable to follow a progressive step of construction and not simulate everything immediately.

In practice, the construction of the model can be performed using two methods:

– carry out all the 3 phases of declaration, description and representation;

– constitute and/or use a base of preset elements in order to simplify the realization of the 3 phases. This method enables us to gain much time for the construction of the model since all or part of these 3 phases is preset. The addition of a new element in the model is performed by a "drag and drop" between the preset element window and the model representation window. As an indication, the construction of the model of our example takes less than 15 minutes with the use of preset elements.

Figure 10.21 illustrates the multiwindow modeling environment of Witness in our example.

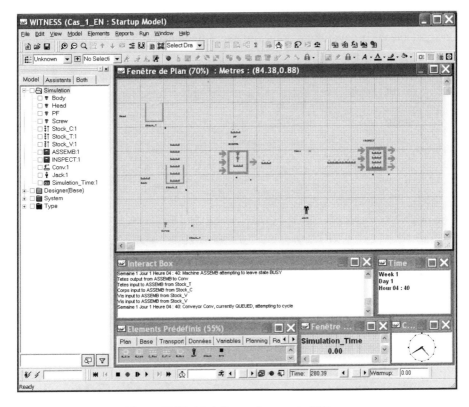

Figure 10.21. *Modeling environment of Witness*

The description of each element is carried out by informing fields in an interactive window. Each description window also makes it possible to reach actions or law editors which are executed when an event occurs on the element (input/output of an item, beginning or end of cycle, beginning or end of a breakdown, etc.). Figures 10.22 to 10.23 illustrate, for example, the description of the "Heads" items, "ASSEMB" machine and "Stock_T" stock.

For the description of an article, the law editor models the destination of the article when it arrives in the model. The "*PUSH to destination*" law is the most current law, but other more advanced laws are possible: *Wait, Least, Most, Percent, Sequence* and *Select*.

We can note that the description of a stock does not comprise a law editor. In fact, for Witness, a stock is regarded as passive, i.e. that it cannot pull or push items from or towards another element. On the other hand, it is necessary to specify the inventory control rule (FIFO, LIFO, bulk, etc.) by the entry and exit options. It is also possible to fix a minimum or maximum waiting time of the items in the stock.

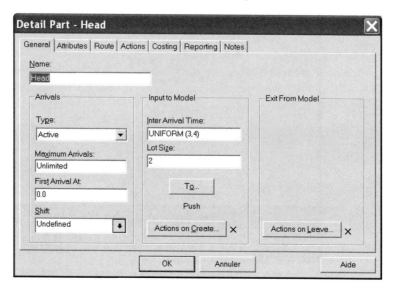

Figure 10.22. *Description of an article with Witness*

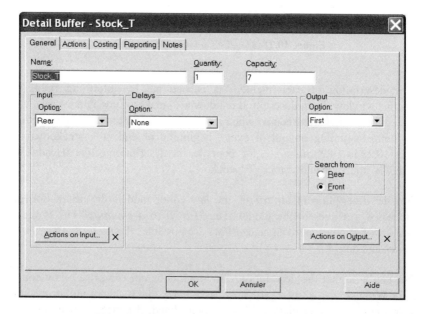

Figure 10.23. *Description of a stock with Witness*

The description window of a machine comprises an input law editor and an output law editor (see Figure 10.24). The most current laws are *PULL from destination* and *PUSH to destination*, but there are different more developed laws. For example, the input law of machine ASSEMB is *SEQUENCE /Wait Heads out of Stock_T#(1), Body out of Stock_C#(1), Screw out of Stock_V#(2), Stock_V#(2)*. This law describes the sequence of loading of the machine before beginning its cycle: first, take one head in Stock-T, then one body in Stock_C and finally two screws in Stock_V. It is also possible to describe conditional laws using variables, such as: *If Istate(CONTROL) = 2 then push to Stock_Waiting Else Push to Conv_1*.

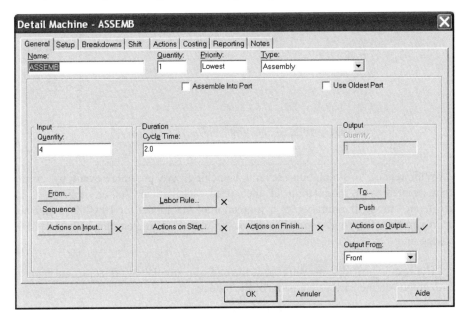

Figure 10.24. *Modeling of a machine with Witness*

Although the construction of a model with Witness is largely facilitated by a visual and interactive interface, it is however possible to visualize or modify the code of the model in WCL language (*Witness Command Language*). Figure 10.25 gives an outline of the code obtained to describe the ASSEMB machine.

```
TYPE: Assembly;
  Assembly quantity: 4;
  PRIORITY: Lowest;
  CYCLE TIME: 2.0;

INPUT RULE: SEQUENCE /Wait Head out of Stock_T#(1),
                   Body out of Stock_C#(1),
                   Stock_V#(2);

OUTPUT RULE: PUSH to Conv at Rear;
  SETUP_DETAIL
    Setup number: 1
    * Mode: Operations;
    * Ops to first: Undefined;
    * Ops between setup: 30;
    * Setup time: 30 / 60;
    * Description: Réglage 1
    * Station number: 1;

LABOR:
    Setup: Jack;

  ACTIONS, Out
    ICON = 254
```

Figure 10.25. *Example of code in WCL language*

With regard to simulation, several launchings are possible: event by event, uninterrupted with modulation of the speed, accelerated. As an indication, in accelerated mode, the duration of a simulation of this model for 100,000 minutes is approximately 5 seconds on a Windows PC with INTEL Pentium M760, 2 GHz processor.

The results provided by Witness at the end of a simulation are statistical reports with graphs on the various elements of the model:

– for articles: entered quantity, dispatched quantity, scrapped quantity, assembled quantity, rejected quantity, instantaneous work in process, average work in process, etc.;

– for stocks: total input, total output, currently inside, maximum loading, minimum loading, average charge, average waiting time;

– for machines: all rates in the various states over the duration of simulation: occupied, available, broken down, set up, etc; the number of operations carried out;

– for the conveyors: all rates in the various states over the duration of simulation: vacuum, in displacement, blocked, in accumulation, broken down, etc.; the number of articles on the conveyor, the total gone through, the average time of transfer of an article;

– for the resources: all rates in the various states over the duration of simulation: occupied, available; the number of tasks started, finished, pre-empted.

Apart from the standard statistics, it is possible to create specific indicators by using variables and functions. The value of the indicators can be updated over the course of simulation, and the coupling functions with Excel make it possible for example to file the various values in a worksheet and to visualize them on a graph.

A scenario management module (scenario manager) not only connects several replications automatically by modifying either the random series or the value of certain input variables, but also analyzes the results at the end of all the replications. Other optional modules are available: links with Visio, optimizer, virtual reality. For more details, see www.lanner.com.

10.9.4. *Modeling with Quest*

Quest (Queueing Event Simulation Tool) is the simulation tool of the Delmia suite™ of Dassault System, to model and design production equipment of a manufacturing company. This positioning places this tool in the field of the numerical factory.

A QUEST model consists of a set of ELEMENTS constituting a physical model, a set of PRODUCTS (PARTS), a set of CONNECTIONS connecting the objects and indicating how the "parts circulate", a set of PROCESS specifying the treatment of the products, and finally a set of LOGICS, which are programs defining the rules of behavior of each object.

QUEST uses an object-oriented methodology: each element belongs to a class. A class of elements is defined by a 3D model, a set of attributes and parameters defining the class, and a set of logics allowing decision-making during the simulation (Figure 10.26).

The construction of a model with QUEST is carried out while placing objects in the model. The 3D model associated with the objects can be selected in a library. It can also be built by means of a 3D modeler integrated to QUEST. It can also be imported after having been created with a CAD tool, in particular with CATIAV5. Figure 10.27 defines the layout of the elements for our example. The arrivals of components correspond to SOURCES elements, stocks to BUFFER elements, working stations to MACHINES elements, conveyor to CONVEYOR elements and the outputs of products to SINK elements.

Subsequently, we connect the elements to one another to express the possibilities of displacement of the products between the elements. The connections can be of the PUSH type. If the downstream element is available, the product is then sent towards it. They can be of PULL type. It is then the downstream element which takes the initiative to call the product. Figure 10.27 shows these connections in white arrows.

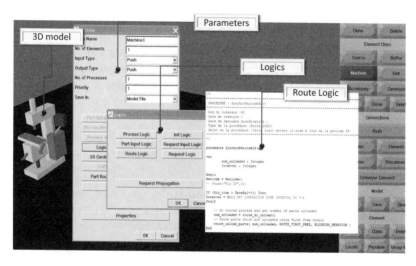

Figure 10.26. *Definition of a class of "Machine" objects with QUEST*

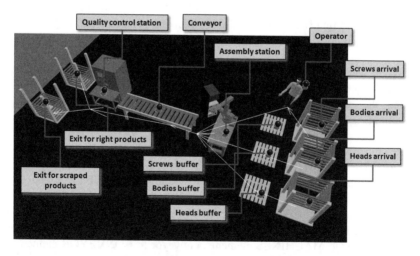

Figure 10.27. *Elements of the model*

The following stage consists of defining the products (PARTS) and the processes. A process is defined by the parts necessary to input, the cycle time and the parts generated at output. For example, the "Assembly" process requires one "body" part, one "head" and two "screw" parts. Its cycle time is 2 min and it generates the "assembly component" part at output. This process is then associated with the "assembly workstation" machine. After having defined the operator element, it can be associated with any process. We will define in our example a "repair controls" process of "repair" type. This type of process does not require parts at input. It will be noted that this process requires the presence of the operator. We will then be able to define a breakdown (FAILURE) with which we will associate the "repair controls" process and which will be itself associated with the "control" machine.

In this simple example, the construction of the model is very fast since in it we just have to place the elements, connect them and parameterize them. The standard logics correspond to our study case. If, on the other hand, it is necessary to intervene on the logics, modeling quickly becomes more complex. For example, Figure 10.28 presents a logic which models a rule of the "Clear a Fraction" type for the management of a stock.

```
/*
********************************************************************************************
   PROCEDURE :                          procedure ClearAFraction()
********************************************************************************************
   Nom du créateur :                    FC
   Date de création :                   08/10/2007 17:06
   Date de dernière modification :      08/10/2007 17:06
   Type de la procédure :               Route Logic
   Objet de la procédure :              Cette procedure permet la gestion d'un stock suivant la règle
                                        Clear A Fraction.
                                        Elle nécessite que le poste désservi par ce stock utilise la
                                        process Logique Prod_reglage()
********************************************************************************************
*/

Procedure ClearAFraction()
Var
        num_unloaded : Integer
        ii : Integer
        result : Integer
        the_part : Part
Begin
        Wait Until celem->out[1]->Num_in_parts == 0  -- On attend que le buffer d'entrée
        -- de l'élément suivant  soit vide
result = 0
-- Cette boucle permet de rechercher dans le stock si une part a un
-- attribut traitement correspondant au produit en cours sur la machine
For ii=1 to celem->Num_out_Parts Do
        If (celem->out_parts[ii]->Traitement==celem->out[1]->Produit_EC) Then
                result = ii
                Break
        Endif
Endfor
If (result<>0) Then      -- On a trouvé un produit correspondant au produit en cours. C'est lui qui est envoyé
                         -- vers la machine
        Route celem->out_parts[result] to celem->Out[1]
Else                     -- Il n'y a pas dans le buffer de produit correspondant au produit en cours. On envoie
                         -- vers la machine le produit qui s'y trouve depuis le plus longtemps.
        Route celem->out_parts[1] to celem->Out[1]
Endif
End
```

Figure 10.28. *An example of logic*

The model being built, simulation can be executed. 3D modeling allows a very realistic graphical animation (Figure 10.29). This animation is all the more realistic as we can define a kinematics program used with the element. We can thus visualize the movements of a robot or an operator. This kinematics program for each of them (machines, operator, etc.) can be directly generated by the robotics simulation tools of DELMIA suite.

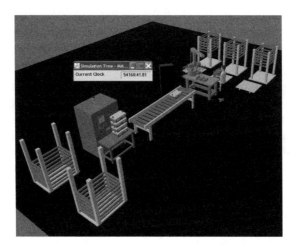

Figure 10.29. *The model during simulation*

At the end of the simulation, QUEST gives many standard results both relating to resources and products. Figure 10.30 indicates for example the operator reports carrying out repairs on the stations. We see that by the end of 100,000 min, he has walked 7.52 km in the workshop. We thus directly have the consequence of the layout on the distance covered by our operator.

Labor1_1 Statistics	
Labor Name	Labor1_1
Busy - Processing Time	8774.00 min
Busy - Empty Travel Time	205.652 min
Idle Time	91020.3 min
Avg. Utilization	8.97965%
Number of Parts Entered	0
Current Content	0
Avg. Contents	0.000000
Avg. Residence Time	0.000000 min
Distance Travelled	752192. cm

Figure 10.30. *Operator reports*

Contrary to Arena, there is no compilation of the model. This allows a greater flexibility to intervene during simulation, to the detriment of the speed of the simulation run. As an indication, by removing graphical animation, the duration of a simulation of this model for 100,000 minutes is approximately 12 seconds on a Windows PC with INTEL Pentium T2600, 2.16 GHz processor with 2 MB of memory.

10.9.5. *Example of modeling of a total logistic chain*

A comparative study between several simulation tools (AutoMod, EM-Seedling, Taylor, AnyLogic, Octave, Xpress) is presented in detail at http://www.argesim.org/comparisons/c14/definition/c14def.pdf. This comparison is based on a relatively simple case of a supply chain with 4 factories, 4 distributors and several customers.

10.10. Useful links

A collection of modeling and resources simulation on the Internet:

http://www.idsia.ch/~andrea/simtools.html

http://www.informs-cs.org/geninfo.html

Software suppliers:

[1] Institute D.M. of artificial intelligence, www.idsia.ch

[2] University of Karlsruhe (TH) – Institute of economical sciences and operational research, www.wior.uni-karlsruhe.de

[3] www.iseesystems.com

[4] www.vensim.com

[5] www.powersim.com

[6] www.goldsim.com

[7] www.xjtek.com

[8] www.imaginethat.com

[9] www.modelkinetix.com

10.11. Bibliography

[BAN 97] BANKS J., GIBSON R.R., "Selecting simulation software", *IIE Solutions*, 29(5), p. 30-32, 1997.

[BEL 05] BEL G., *Quelques spécificités de la simulation des chaînes logistiques*, présentation GDR Vendôme, 12/2005.

[CAR 07a] CARDIN O., CASTAGNA P., "Proactive production activity control by online simulation", *International Journal of Simulation and Process Modeling*, 2007.

[CAR 07b] CARDIN O., Apport de la simulation en ligne dans l'aide à la décision pour le pilotage des systèmes de production – Application à un système flexible de production, PhD Thesis, University of Nantes, 2007.

[CAV 04] CAVALIERI S., TERZI S., "Simulation in the supply chain context: a survey", *Computers in Industry* 53, p. 3-16, 2004.

[CER 88] CERNAUT, *La simulation des systèmes de production*, Cepadues editions, Toulouse, 1988.

[ELH 05a] ELHAMDI M., Modélisation et simulation de chaînes de valeurs en entreprise - Une approche dynamique des systèmes et aide à la décision: SimulValor, PhD Thesis, Ecole Centrale Paris, Laboratoire Génie Industriel, 2005.

[ELH 05b] ELHAMDI M., YANNOU B., "Évaluation des flux de valeurs d'une entreprise: une approche de dynamique des systèmes multicritère", *Proc. CIGI'05: 6ème Congrès International de Génie Industriel*, Besançon, 7-10 June, 2005.

[HUR 76] HURRION R.D., The design use and required facilities of an interactive visual computer simulation language to explore production planning problems, PhD Thesis, University of London.

[JIS 82] JIS Z 8206 Standard, Graphicals symbols for process chart, Japanese Industrial Standard, 1982.

[KLE 05] KLEIJNEN J.P.C., "Supply chain simulation tools and techniques: a survey", *International Journal of Simulation and Process Modelling*, vol. 1, no. 1/2, 2005.

[KLI 99] KLINGSTAM P, GULLANDER P., "Overview of simulation tools for computer-aided production engineering", *Computers in Industry*, 38, p. 173, 186, 1999.

[LAW 91] LAW A.M., KELTON W.D., *Simulation Modelling and Analysis*, 2nd ed., McGraw-Hill, New York, 1991.

[LEF 02] LEFÈVRE J., "Kinetic Process Graphs: Building Intuitive, Suggestive and Parsimonious Material Stock-Flow Diagrams with Modified Bond Graph Notations", *Proc. International Conference of the System Dynamics Society*, Palermo, Italy, July 28-August 1, 2002.

[NIK 99] NIKOUKARAN J., PAUL R.J., "Software selection for simulation in manufacturing: a review", *Simulation Practice and Theory*, 7, p. 1-14, 1999.

[PID 04] PIDD M, *Computer Simulation in Management Science,* John Wiley & Sons, 5th edition, 2004.

[PIE 03] PIERREVAL H., CAUX C., PARIS J.L., VIGUIER F., "Evolutionary approaches to the design and organization of manufacturing systems", *Computer and Industrial Engineering*, vol. 44, p. 339-364, 2003.

[ROB 04] ROBINSON S., *The Practice of Model Development and Use*, John Wiley & Sons, 2004.

[ZOB 99] ZOBEL C.W., "Determining a warm-up period for a telephone network routing simulation", *Proceedings of the 1999 Winter Simulation Conference*.

List of Authors

Didier ANCIAUX
LGIPM (Laboratoire de Génie Industriel et de Production Mécanique)
University of Metz
France

Bernard ARCHIMEDE
LGP (Laboratoire Génie de Production)
ENIT (Ecole Nationale d'Ingénieurs de Tarbes)
France

Éric BALLOT
Centre de Gestion Scientifique
Ecole des Mines de Paris
France

Gérard BEL
Toulouse
France

Lyes BENYOUCEF
COSTEAM Project
INRIA
Metz
France

Pascal BLANC
LSIS (Laboratoire des Sciences de l'Information et des Systèmes)
UMR CNRS 6168
Paul Cézanne University
Marseille
France

Valérie BOTTA-GENOULAZ
LIESP (Laboratoire d'Informatique pour les Entreprises et les Systèmes de Production)
INSA – Institut National des Sciences Appliquées de Lyon
France

Olivier CARDIN
Institut de Recherche en Communications et en Cybernétique de Nantes
University of Nantes-Ecole Centrale de Nantes
France

Pierre CASTAGNA
Institut de Recherche en Communications et en Cybernétique de Nantes
University of Nantes-Ecole Centrale de Nantes
France

Philippe CHARBONNAUD
LGP (Laboratoire Génie de Production)
ENIT (Ecole Nationale d'Ingénieurs de Tarbes)
France

Patrick CHARPENTIER
ENSTIB (Ecole Nationale Supérieure des Technologies et Industries du Bois)
CRAN (Centre de Recherche en Automatique de Nancy)
Epinal
France

Sophie D'AMOURS
Centre interuniversitaire CIRRELT, Consortium de recherche FORAC
Laval University
Quebec
Canada

Hind EL HAOUZI
ENSTIB (Ecole Nationale Supérieure des Technologies et Industries du Bois)
CRAN (Centre de Recherche en Automatique de Nancy)
Epinal
France

Bernard ESPINASSE
LSIS (Laboratoire des Sciences de l'Information et des Systèmes)
UMR CNRS 6168
Paul Cézanne University
Marseille
France

Alain FERRARINI
LSIS (Laboratoire des Sciences de l'Information et des Systèmes)
UMR CNRS 6168
Aix-Marseille University
EPUM – Ecole Polytechnique Universitaire de Marseille
France

Franck FONTANILI
Industrial Engineering Department
Ecole des Mines d'Albi-Carmaux
France

Michel GREIF
CIPE (Centre International de la Pédagogie d'Entreprise)
Paris
France

Vo Thi Le HOA
Laboratory of Economics and Management
University of Nantes-ENITIAA-Ecole des Mines de Nantes
France

Vipul JAIN
COSTEAM Project
INRIA
Metz
France

Thomas KLEIN
ENSTIB (Ecole Nationale Supérieure des Technologies et Industries du Bois)
CRAN (Centre de Recherche en Automatique de Nancy)
Epinal
France

Olivier LABARTHE
CIRRELT – Interuniversity Research Center on Enteprise Networks, Logistics and Transportation
Laval University – Faculty of Administrative Sciences
Quebec
Canada

Jacques LAMOTHE
Centre Génie Industriel
University of Toulouse – Mines Albi
Albi
France

Thibaud MONTEIRO
LGIPM (Laboratoire de Génie Industriel et de Production Mécanique)
University of Metz
France

Benoit MONTREUIL
CIRRELT Interuniversity Research Center on Enterprise Networks, Logistics and Transportation
Laval University – Faculty of Administrative Sciences
Quebec
Canada

Thierry MOYAUX
Department of Computer Science
University of Liverpool
UK

Fouzia OUNNAR
LSIS (Laboratoire des Sciences de l'Information et des Systèmes)
UMR CNRS 6168
Paul Cézanne University
Marseille
France

Rémi PANNEQUIN
ENSTIB (Ecole Nationale Supérieure des Technologies et Industries du Bois)
CRAN (Centre de Recherche en Automatique de Nancy)
Epinal
France

Florence PICARD
Laboratoire ETIS
CNRS, ENSEA, Cergy-Pontoise University
France

Patrick PUJO
LSIS (Laboratoire des Sciences de l'Information et des Systèmes)
UMR CNRS 6168
Paul Cézanne University
Marseille
France

Fouad RIANE
Centre de Recherches et d'Etudes en Gestion Industrielle,
Louvain School of Management, Facultés Universitaires Catholiques de Mons,
Belgium

Daniel ROY
Laboratory of Industrial Engineering and mechanical production
Costeam Team of INRIA
National engineering school of Metz – ENIM
Metz
France

Bertrand SIMON
CIPE (Centre International de la Pédagogie d'Entreprise)
Paris
France

Daniel THIEL
Laboratory of Economics and Management
University of Nantes-ENITIAA-Ecole des Mines de Nantes
France

Caroline THIERRY
Département de Mathématiques et Informatique
University of Toulouse 2 – Le Mirail
Toulouse
France

André THOMAS
ENSTIB (Ecole Nationale Supérieure des Technologies et Industries du Bois)
CRAN (Centre de Recherche en Automatique de Nancy)
University of Nancy
Epinal
France

Anthony VALLA
VALRHONA Company
Tain L'Hermitage
France

Bernard YANNOU
Laboratoire Genie Industriel
Ecole Centrale Paris
France

Index